Published for
OXFORD INTERNATIONAL
AQA EXAMINATIONS

T0337480

International AS Level
ECONOMICS

Stuart Luker
Wendy Davis

OXFORD
UNIVERSITY PRESS

OXFORD
UNIVERSITY PRESS

Great Clarendon Street, Oxford, OX2 6DP, United Kingdom

Oxford University Press is a department of the University of Oxford. It furthers the University's objective of excellence in research, scholarship, and education by publishing worldwide. Oxford is a registered trade mark of Oxford University Press in the UK and in certain other countries

British Library Cataloguing in Publication Data available

978-138-200685-9

10 9 8 7 6 5

Paper used in the production of this book is a natural, recyclable product made from wood grown in sustainable forests. The manufacturing process conforms to the environmental regulations of the country of origin.

Printed in Great Britain by CPI Group (UK) Ltd., Croydon CR0 4YY

Acknowledgements

The publisher and authors would like to thank the following for permission to use photographs and other copyright material:

Cover: J0hnTV/Shutterstock. **Photos: p1:** Elenabsl/Dreamstime; **p3:** Nickolai Repnitskii/Shutterstock; **p5:** wklzzz/123RF; **p8:** AJP/Shutterstock; **p10:** Surrphoto/Shutterstock; **p12:** Charlesimage/Shutterstock; **p14:** MihailDechev/iStock/Getty Images; **p17:** pio3/Shutterstock; **p19:** KamiGami/Shutterstock; **p21:** F8 studio/Shutterstock; **p25:** Rainer Plendl/Shutterstock; **p31:** Muzhik/Shutterstock; **p38:** Kittibowornphatnon/Shutterstock; **p42:** sergey0506/Shutterstock; **p44:** Egor Tetiushev/Shutterstock; **p51:** SeoLeo/Shutterstock; **p56:** nuclear_lily/Shutterstock; **p60:** Craig Yates/Alamy Stock Photo; **p63(tl):** Lighthunter/Shutterstock; **p63(tr):** mavo/Shutterstock; **p63(bl):** FrameStockFootages/Shutterstock; **p63(br):** Dmitry Kalinovsky/Shutterstock; **p65:** sydeen/Shutterstock; **p66:** smereka/Shutterstock; **p67:** Fonollosa/Iberfoto/Mary Evans; **p69:** Darren Brode/Shutterstock; **p73:** Stefan Holm/Shutterstock; **p74:** Jakrin Chaisuriyawat/Shutterstock; **p79:** zimmytws/Shutterstock; **p83:** Africa Studio/Shutterstock; **p85(tl):** TOM.RUETHAI/Shutterstock; **p85(tr):** Tyler Olson/Shutterstock; **p85(bl):** Suwin/Shutterstock; **p85(br):** David Woods/Shutterstock; **p88:** Andrey_Popov/Shutterstock; **p91:** Ru Bai Le/Shutterstock; **p93:** Roman Borodaev/Shutterstock; **p95:** Miroslav Hlavko/Shutterstock; **p97:** tristan tan/Shutterstock; **p101:** focal point/Shutterstock;

p103: Nickolay Vinokurov/Shutterstock; **p106:** Monkey Business Images/Shutterstock; **p108:** Kridsada Kamsombat/Shutterstock; **p110:** dpa picture alliance archive/Alamy Stock Photo; **p112:** primagefactory/123RF; **p116:** cinoby/E+/Getty Images; **p118:** Rawpixel.com/Shutterstock; **p121:** nitinut380/Shutterstock; **p122:** TORWAISTUDIO/Shutterstock; **p124:** N. F. Photography/Shutterstock; **p128:** GeorginaCaptures/Shutterstock; **p133:** icyimage/Shutterstock; **p137:** VanderWolf Images/Shutterstock; **p140:** Nick Fox/Shutterstock; **p144:** isak55/Shutterstock; **p147:** kogytuk/Shutterstock; **p148:** Homer Sykes/Alamy Stock Photo; **p150:** chuyuss/Shutterstock; **p153:** Patrick Foto/Shutterstock; **p159:** B.Zhou/Shutterstock; **p165:** Gualtiero Boffi/Shutterstock; **p166:** FernandoMadeira/Shutterstock; **p172:** MattiaATH/Shutterstock; **p181:** basel101658/Shutterstock; **p184:** xujun/Shutterstock; **p186:** Granger Historical Picture Archive/Alamy Stock Photo; **p189:** beboy/Shutterstock; **p192:** sorbetto/DigitalVision Vectors/Getty Images; **p197:** safakcakir/Shutterstock; **p201:** Joerg Boethling/Alamy Stock Photo; **p203:** apstockphoto/Shutterstock; **p208:** Alex Kolokythas Photography/Shutterstock; **p214:** Hyman P. Minsky. ©Levy Economics Institute of Bard College. Photo by Beringer-Dratch; **p215:** photomaster/Shutterstock; **p216(t):** Public Domain; **p216(b):** National Pictures/TopFoto; **p217:** Tom Mc Nemar/Shutterstock; **p220:** Djelen/Shutterstock; **p221:** Daisy Daisy/Shutterstock; **p226:** Iakov Filimonov/Shutterstock; **p228:** ivan_kislitsin/Shutterstock; **p231:** Chuck Nacke/Alamy Stock Photo; **p238:** Julien Hautcoeur/Shutterstock; **p242:** kakteen/Shutterstock; **p244:** Ortodox/Shutterstock; **p248:** Botond Horvath/Shutterstock; **p251(tl):** cristapper/Shutterstock; **p251(tr):** godrick/Shutterstock; **p251(bl):** Gang Liu/Shutterstock; **p251(br):** Orhan Cam/Shutterstock; **p252:** Mariano Gaspar/Shutterstock; **p255:** Ronnie Chua/Shutterstock; **p260:** Asia Images/Shutterstock; **p261:** Club4traveler/Shutterstock; **p270:** Vincent St. Thomas/Shutterstock; **p274:** Anastasios71/Shutterstock; **p276:** Historic Images/Alamy Stock Photo; **p283:** curraheeshutter/Shutterstock.

Artwork by Aptara

Every effort has been made to contact copyright holders of material reproduced in this book. Any omissions will be rectified in subsequent printings if notice is given to the publisher.

Contents

How to use this book

This book fully covers the syllabus for the Oxford AQA international AS Level Economics course (9640). Experienced examiners and teachers have been involved in all aspects of the book, including detailed planning to ensure that the content adheres to the syllabus.

Using this book will ensure you are well prepared for the assessment at this level and will give you a solid foundation for further study at university level and beyond. The features below are designed to make learning interesting and effective.

Activities

These are exercises that relate to the chapter content. They can be done in class or as part of individual study.

Get it right

These are helpful tips and hints to give you the best chance of success.

Case study

These are real-life examples to illustrate the subject matter in the chapters. These examples are accompanied by questions to test your understanding.

Progress questions

These questions appear throughout the book. They are designed to check that you understand the content as you learn. Answers for all progress questions are available in the back of the book.

Key terms

These are the most important vocabulary and definitions that you need to learn. They are also compiled at the end of the book in a glossary.

Exam-style questions

These questions appear at the end of each chapter section. They use the same command words, structure and mark assignment as the OxfordAQA exams. Answers for all exam-style questions are available in the back of the book.

Link

Links are provided to other parts of the book, and to the A2 course/book where appropriate, for you to find related information.

Quantitative skills

These are the skills required to calculate, illustrate, apply and interpret data and key economic concepts. The nine specific QS are listed in the syllabus.

The questions, example answers, marks awarded and/or comments that appear in this book were written by the authors. In examinations, the way marks would be awarded to answers such as these may be different.

At the end of the book, you will find a glossary of the key terms highlighted in orange in the text.

1 The economic problem and methodology

The operation of markets, market failure and the role of government

This section will develop your knowledge and understanding of:

→ how the central purpose of economic activity is the production of goods and services to satisfy needs and wants

→ how the key economic decisions are made: what to produce, how to produce and who is to benefit from the goods and services produced.

Activity

Food, clothing and shelter are traditionally thought to be what people need to survive. Do you think there is anything else necessary for people to survive in the modern world?

Key terms

Needs: goods and services required for people to survive.

Wants: goods and services that people would like but are not required for them to survive.

Economic activity: the production, distribution and consumption of goods and services.

Production: turning inputs, such as raw materials, capital and labour, into final output.

Welfare: the satisfaction or utility obtained from consuming goods and services, which contributes to the standard of living and happiness of an individual or group.

Link

Factors of production are covered in 1.2 "Economic resources" and the difference between production and productivity in 3.1 "Production and productivity".

The world's population is approximately 8 billion. People all need food, clothing and shelter to survive. They also want a range of other goods and services. Who decides what is produced? How do people obtain the goods and services they need and want? Why are some people better off than others? These are important questions. Economics can help to provide the answers.

The central purpose of economic activity

The central (or main) purpose of economic activity is the production of goods and services to satisfy people's needs and wants.

What is the difference between needs and wants?

Needs are goods and services required for people to survive. The main needs are food, clothing and shelter. Whatever people have they are likely to want more. **Wants** are goods and services that people would like but are not required for them to survive. Someone's wants might include a new mobile phone.

What is economic activity?

Economic activity is concerned with the production, distribution and consumption of goods and services. Wood from a tree is made into a table to be sold to someone able and willing to buy it.

Production of goods and services to satisfy needs and wants

Production involves turning inputs, such as raw materials, capital and labour, into final output. Production includes providing both goods and services, something of use that adds to people's welfare. **Welfare** is the satisfaction (called utility in Economics) obtained from consuming goods and services, which contributes to the standard of living and happiness of an individual or group.

For example, to make a book requires someone to write it, paper and other materials, somewhere for this to be done and someone to organise this. Education will usually require someone to teach, a variety of materials and equipment and somewhere to do this. People who buy these goods and services then obtain satisfaction or utility from their use.

Distribution and consumption

After the goods and services have been produced, they must be allocated to individuals for their use.

Progress questions

1 What is the central purpose of economic activity?

2 Give **two** examples of economic activity.

3 Which word means the satisfaction obtained from consuming a product?

4 Give **two** examples of inputs.

Quantitative skills

Two averages or typical values commonly used in Economics are the (arithmetic) mean and the median. The median is the middle value of a set of numbers when arranged in order. There are as many values above the median as below it. For example, the median is 5 for the numbers, 1, 3, 5, 8 and 12. There are two numbers below 5 and two above. If the set is changed to 1, 3, 5, 7, 8 and 12, the median is 6. There are three numbers below 6 and three above 6 and 6 is halfway between the two middle numbers of 5 and 7.

The mean is found by adding up the numbers and dividing by how many there are. For example, taking the first set of numbers used for the median, 1, 3, 5, 8 and 12, the total is 29. Dividing by 5 gives a mean of 5.8. Remember to include units in your answers where relevant.

Link

Utility and measures of economic welfare are covered in the A2 part of the course.

Case study: Time for tea?

People have been drinking tea for thousands of years. Apart from water, it is the most popular drink in the world. To grow tea requires high temperatures, lots of rain and a long growing season. Therefore, some countries are more suited to growing tea than others. Table 1.1.1 lists the top six tea-producing countries (in alphabetical order) and the amounts produced at a particular time.

▼ Table 1.1.1: Leading tea producers (figures relate to 2017)

Country	Output of tea (tonnes)
China	2,473,443
India	1,325,050
Kenya	439,857
Sri Lanka	349,699
Turkey	234,000
Vietnam	260,000

Source: www.worldatlas.com; accessed 15 October 2019

▲ Figure 1.1.1: A tea plantation

1 Calculate the median output of tea.

2 Calculate the mean output of tea, to **one** decimal place.

The key economic decisions

People have needs and wants that have to be satisfied. This leads to three important questions.

- Which goods and services should be produced and in what quantities?
- How should these goods and services be produced?
- Who should benefit from the goods and services produced?

How these decisions are made depends on the type of economy. This may be a free market, a mixed or a centrally planned economy.

Which goods and services should be produced and in what quantities?

To satisfy people's needs, food, clothing and shelter must be produced. However, many people will want, and be able to afford, much more than this. Some people only have enough money to pay for their basic needs. Others may have enough money to buy plenty of land and a large house, filled with expensive items.

Resources such as land have different uses, including for houses, factories and farmland.

A decision must be made about which goods and services to produce with the resources and in what quantities.

How should these goods and services be produced?

Some goods are produced using a lot of equipment. For example, modern car factories have robots doing most of the work, both in producing the parts and assembling the car. This is because it is usually cheaper and quicker to use machines when making a large number of items that are the same or similar. However, someone still needs to design the machine, switch it on and check the quality of the final products.

Some services need many workers because the people using the good or service have different requirements. For example, it would be difficult to programme a machine to cut someone's hair. However, hairdressers and barbers also need equipment such as scissors and hair dryers.

A decision must be made about how much should be used of the different inputs to provide a particular good or service. This will depend on the cost of alternative methods.

Who should benefit from the goods and services produced?

Economic activity is concerned with the distribution and consumption of goods and services as well as their production. How can what has been produced be allocated? This could be on the basis of ability to pay, tradition, need or by some other method. Welfare is affected by how goods and services are distributed as well as by what and how much is produced.

A decision must be made about who should benefit from the goods and services produced.

Primary, secondary and tertiary production

Production is often classified into one of three sectors.

- Primary
- Secondary
- Tertiary

Primary sector

Primary production involves extracting or acquiring raw materials from the land, sea or air. The primary sector industries are mining, quarrying, farming, forestry and fishing. The primary sector of an economy provides raw materials that are used to produce goods and services.

Secondary sector

The secondary sector involves any construction or manufacturing activities. The secondary sector uses the raw materials from the primary sector for construction or to make goods.

Tertiary sector

The tertiary sector involves providing services. These may be services directly involving the consumer, for example the services of a dentist. They also include services that enable the finished goods to reach consumers. For example, delivery drivers and people working in shops are employed in the tertiary sector.

Key terms

Primary sector: the part of the economy involved with extracting or acquiring raw materials.

Secondary sector: the part of the economy involved with construction or manufacturing.

Tertiary sector: the part of the economy that provides services.

Automation: using advanced technology to produce goods and services with little help from workers.

Progress questions

5   Classify each of the following jobs into primary, secondary or tertiary activities:
  i.   drilling for oil
  ii. driving a taxi
  iii. making tyres for a car
  iv. working in a car-assembly factory
  v.   growing coconuts
  vi. working as a market trader
  vii. fishing
  viii. building a hotel
  ix. working as a hotel cleaner.

Case study: Is automation taking over?

Automation involves using advanced technology to produce goods and services with little help from workers. It is found in the manufacture and assembly of almost every product. For example, robots can be found spray painting cars in many modern automotive factories.

Increasingly, artificial intelligence (AI) is being used to allow machines to react to, and learn from, their environment. Computer-controlled cars can drive themselves. Heating your home and switching on your lights can be done from your smartphone 100 miles away. Consequently, helped by the development of computers in recent years, an increasing number of jobs that used to be done by humans are now done by machines.

1   In a table, list **advantages** and **disadvantages** of automation.

2   Which jobs or types of job are **most** and **least** likely to be replaced by machines? Why?

▲ Figure 1.1.2: Robots are now used to produce a variety of goods and services

This section will develop your knowledge and understanding of:

→ the economists' classification of economic resources into land, labour, capital and enterprise, which are the factors of production

→ renewable and non-renewable resources

→ why the environment is a scarce resource.

Key terms

Economic resources (factors of production): inputs into the production process, needed to produce goods and services.

Land: natural resources.

Labour: human resources.

Capital: human-made resources.

Entrepreneur or enterprise: the person or group of people who takes risks, makes decisions and organises the production process.

Activity

Choose a good or service. In three columns – land, labour and capital – make a list of as many examples of factors of production as you can think of that are required to make this good, or to provide this service.

The classification of economic resources

Economic resources – also known as factors of production – are the inputs into the production process. They are what is needed to produce goods and services. There are four factors of production:

• Land

• Labour

• Capital

• Enterprise

Land

Land refers to natural resources. This includes anything found in nature, not created by humans. Land includes not just where production takes place but also what is below and above it. This could be in the ground or in the air. Examples of "land" include oil, gold, water, sunshine and air.

Labour

Labour refers to human resources. These are the workers who use the land and other resources to make goods and services. The input from labour could be physical or mental. Examples of labour include a farmer, factory worker, builder, teacher and doctor.

Capital

Capital refers to resources that have been made by people. These capital goods have been made to produce other goods and services. Examples include tools, machines, lorries and the buildings in which production takes place.

Enterprise

The **entrepreneur or enterprise** refers to the person or group of people who organise the production process. They make decisions about what and how goods and services should be produced. They also take risks, since the business may make a profit or loss.

In large firms, managers may be employed to organise the other factors of production. In this case, the shareholders who own the firm are taking the risk of losing their money. There is no one person or group who carries out all the roles of an entrepreneur.

Progress questions

1 What is another name for economic resources?

2 Classify each of the following into land, labour, capital or enterprise:

i. a car factory

ii. a field used to grow sorghum

iii. a bicycle-shop assistant

iv. a coal miner

v. an oilfield

vi. a person who owns a window-cleaning business

vii. fish in the sea

viii. a sweet-packing machine

ix. a parcel-delivery van

x. clean air.

Renewable and non-renewable resources

Another way of classifying economic resources is whether they are renewable or non-renewable resources.

Renewable resources

Renewable resources can be replaced naturally after a period of time. These include trees, fish, sunlight, wind and water for drinking. Some of them can be used to make energy, for example, solar power. Provided that the resource can be replaced at the same rate, or a faster rate, than it is being depleted (used up), it will not run out. Renewable resources often need to be managed carefully to make sure that they remain available.

Non-renewable resources

Non-renewable resources cannot be replaced naturally after use. They include coal, oil and diamonds. They are limited in supply and can run out.

Why the environment is a scarce resource

Resources are scarce if they are limited in supply. There are not enough to satisfy our wants. The natural environment is a scarce resource. It is limited in supply and has alternative uses. Production and consumption can both affect the environment. For example, global warming, as a result of production and consumption activities, is leading to rising sea levels.

As the world's population grows, more land is being used for housing and roads. Before this, the land may have been farmland, a park or a forest. Cars and factories add to pollution that can affect the quality of the air we breathe. Fewer trees can also have an impact on the air quality and other aspects of the environment.

Key terms

Renewable resources: resources that can be replaced naturally after a period of time.

Non-renewable resources: resources that cannot be replaced naturally after use.

Scarce resources: factors of production that are limited in supply; there are not enough to satisfy our wants.

Case study: Fish stocks

Although most of the world's land is owned by someone, most of the sea is not. Countries that border seas and oceans own part of these areas. Most countries used to claim between 3 and 12 (nautical) miles from land as part of their territorial waters. By the 1950s, valuable minerals were being found near the coasts of some countries. Coastal countries then tried to claim more of the seas and oceans.

In 1973, it was decided that all coastal countries had the right to own the waters within 12 miles of their land. Since 1982, they have also been responsible for a 200-mile Exclusive Economic Zone (EEZ). The country controls the exploitation and environmental quality of the area within 200 miles of its land. If two countries are closer than 400 miles apart, a median line separates the two areas.

This leaves two thirds of the world's seas and oceans with no ownership, as international waters. There have been several agreements between countries, many of which relate to fishing. For example, two international organisations covering the western, central and southern Pacific Ocean areas are particularly concerned about the depletion of mackerel and tuna.

Between 2006 and 2011, stocks of jack mackerel were estimated to have fallen by 63% in the area. The region's

▲ **Figure 1.2.1:** A renewable resource?

stock of large tuna able to breed was 12,000 tons in 2010, down from 168,000 tons in 1961. By 2016, it had risen to 21,000 tons.

1   Calculate the percentage fall in the stock of large tuna between 1961 and 2016.

2   Does this case study suggest that fish are a renewable resource?

3   What could be done to increase fish stocks for the future?

The fundamental economic problem of scarcity

The **fundamental (or basic) economic problem** is scarcity. Economic resources are limited. Apart from a few renewable resources, such as solar energy, the quantity of factors of production is limited or finite. For example, there is only so much land in the world or oil within it.

Wants are unlimited. Whatever they have, people will want more. This may be something they do not own, or a newer or better model of something they have. For example, someone who owns a bicycle may like a car. When the person owns a second-hand car, he or she may want a new car. When some wants are satisfied, new ones take their place.

Scarcity results from limited resources and unlimited wants.

Economics is sometimes defined as the study of how we use our scarce resources to satisfy our many wants. **Microeconomics** is the study of parts of the economy and this is the focus of the first five chapters of this book. Microeconomics involves studying the behaviour of individuals, firms and industries. Examples of microeconomic topics include what determines the price of rice and why one industry may have many firms and another industry may have only one.

Scarcity and choice

The scarce resources of land, labour, capital and enterprise have alternative uses. Land can be used for housing, farmland, roads and many other purposes. Labour may be used in different sectors of the economy and in many different jobs. Capital often has many uses. For example, computers are used in all industries, but a specialist piece of equipment may be designed for a particular purpose, such as a blast furnace used in the steel industry. An entrepreneur may be able to organise the factors of production in a variety of businesses.

Choices must be made about how scarce resources are allocated between different uses to satisfy our unlimited wants. How these decisions are made depends on the type of economy. The choices may be made by free markets, governments or a combination of the two.

Key terms

Fundamental (or basic) economic problem: that scarce resources are not enough to satisfy our many wants.

Economics: the study of how we use our scarce resources to satisfy our many wants.

Microeconomics: the study of parts of the economy, including the behaviour of individuals, firms and industries.

Key terms

Economic agents: a person, firm, organisation or government that has a role in the economy.

Self-interest: focusing on your own needs and wants.

Rational behaviour: that people will consider alternative choices and make decisions that will provide them with the most benefit, welfare or satisfaction.

Opportunity cost: the next best alternative forgone.

Activity

Think of something you bought recently.

1. To what extent did you consider alternatives?
2. Did you behave rationally?
3. What influenced your purchase?

Opportunity cost

Resources have alternative uses and people have many wants, so choices are necessary. What individuals or households buy is limited by the amount of money they have. In Economics, we usually assume that economic agents behave rationally. The main **economic agents** are individuals or households, firms and governments. Economic agents have a role in the economy and can influence it through producing, buying and selling.

Economic theories usually assume that individuals are motivated by **self-interest**, focusing on their own needs and wants. **Rational behaviour** assumes that people will consider alternative choices and make decisions that will provide them with the most benefit, welfare or satisfaction.

When individuals are considering how to spend their money, they may have a list of alternatives, in order of preference. For example, a person is considering spending $20. Their first choice may be to buy a T-shirt, their second choice is to see a movie, their third choice is to buy a book and their fourth choice is to save the money. Assuming that they are behaving rationally, they will buy a T-shirt, since this will give them the most satisfaction.

▲ **Figure 1.3.1**: One of many choices

The term **opportunity cost** is used for the next best alternative forgone. This is the person's second choice, the next item they were unable to have by using the money for their first choice. In the example above, the opportunity cost of the T-shirt was seeing the movie.

Progress questions

1. What is the basic economic problem?
2. Why is choice necessary?
3. A person has $10. They are considering whether to spend it on flowers, food or a visit to a museum. They would prefer to go to the museum than spend it on flowers but they believe that the food would give them the greatest satisfaction.
   i. What will the person spend the $10 on if they are behaving rationally?
   ii. What is the opportunity cost of this?

The allocation of resources in different types of economy

In order to allocate resources, decisions need to be made about what to produce, how to produce it and who should benefit. How these decisions are made depends on the type of economy. There are three types of economy:

- Free market
- Centrally planned
- Mixed

Free market economy

A market consists of all the buyers and sellers of a good or service. The market for holidays to Peru consists of all the people who buy and sell holidays to Peru. Buyers and sellers do not necessarily have to meet in a particular place since the sale may be made online, by telephone or by post.

In a completely free market economy, decisions about what to produce, how to produce it and who should benefit are taken by buyers and sellers, with no involvement by government. Those who are willing and able to buy and sell the goods and services are free to do so. The way in which the prices of goods and services are determined by the free market forces of demand and supply is known as the price mechanism.

In market economies, decisions are left to the private sector, the part of the economy not under government control. Free market economies are also known as capitalist or laissez-faire economies.

Key terms

Market: all the buyers and sellers of a good or service.

Free market economy: where decisions about what to produce, how to produce it and who should benefit are taken by buyers and sellers, with no involvement by government.

Price mechanism: the way in which the prices of goods and services are determined by the free market forces of demand and supply.

Private sector: the part of the economy not under government control.

Decisions are based on consumers' spending. Prices of goods and services are determined by buyers and sellers. The goods and services that are most in demand are likely to be the ones that are produced. People will be willing to pay more money for these goods and services and suppliers will want to sell these products to make more profit. How resources are allocated will be determined by people's preferences.

Since sales are on the basis of people being willing and able to pay, those with little or no money will not be able to buy as much, and may not even be able to buy the basic necessities. This can lead to inequality.

If looked at from the viewpoint of the benefit to society as a whole, there may be too many of some products available and not enough of others. These are examples of market failure.

Centrally planned economy

In a centrally planned economy, in its extreme form, all decisions about what to produce, how to produce it and who should benefit are taken by the government. Decisions are left to the public sector, the part of the economy under government control. The government owns the factors of production. It decides which combination of goods and services should be produced.

Link

Demand and supply and the determination of market prices are covered in Chapter 2 "How markets work".

Link

Market failure is covered in Chapter 5 "Market failure and government intervention in markets".

Key terms

Centrally planned economy: where decisions about what to produce, how to produce it and who should benefit are taken by the government.

Public sector: the part of the economy under government control.

The government decides how resources are allocated and how the goods and services produced are distributed to consumers. Centrally planned economies are sometimes known as command economies.

This system requires considerable planning. There will need to be long-term plans, maybe over five or ten years, with targets set for production.

A centrally planned economy can result in a fairer distribution of goods and services. For example, the government can make sure that education and healthcare are widely available, which some people in a free market economy may be unable to afford.

In a free market economy, allocation is based on ability to pay. Consumers' spending encourages firms to produce more of some goods and less of others. If the government decides what is produced, there may be shortages of some goods and surpluses of others. Allocation requires rationing and/or price controls and may not match people's preferences. Also, there may be a lack of incentive to work hard or to produce better products.

Key term

Mixed economy: where some decisions about what to produce, how to produce it and who should benefit are taken by buyers and sellers, and some decisions are taken by the government.

Mixed economy

In a **mixed economy**, some decisions about what to produce, how to produce it and who should benefit are taken by buyers and sellers and some decisions are taken by the government. In mixed economies, some decisions are left to the free market and some are made by the government.

Pure free market and pure centrally planned economies both have problems, so neither type exists in its extreme form. All economies in the world are mixed but with different amounts of government intervention. Both the private and the public sectors are involved, to some extent, in decision making.

Some countries choose to leave most of the decisions to buyers and sellers, with limited intervention by the government. For example, the government may provide goods and services such as education, which otherwise would not be provided in sufficient quantities for society to benefit fully. The government may also tax products it believes to be harmful, for example cigarettes. In other countries, the government or state controls most of the major industries, such as the supply of rail, electricity and water services.

▲ **Figure 1.3.2**: An important industry

Activities

1. Find out whether rail, electricity and water services are run by the government in your country.
2. If at least one of these industries is run by the government, find a country where this industry is in the private sector. If none of these industries is run by the government, find a country where at least one of these industries is run by the government.
3. Choose either free market economies or centrally planned economies and list **two** advantages and **two** disadvantages of this type of economy.

This section will develop your knowledge and understanding of:

→ how production possibility diagrams illustrate different features of the fundamental economic problem, including: resource allocation, opportunity cost and trade-offs, unemployment of economic resources, economic growth

→ why all points on the boundary are productively efficient but not all points on the boundary are allocatively efficient.

Production possibility diagrams

Resource allocation

Production possibility diagrams are a way of illustrating different features of the fundamental economic problem of how best to allocate our scarce resources.

Production possibility boundaries (PPBs) show the quantities that can be produced of two goods or services with the current state of technology, when resources are fully used. They show the different combinations of two products that can be made using the firm's or country's resources. A PPB is also known as a production possibility curve (PPC) or a production possibility frontier (PPF). This is shown on a production possibility diagram.

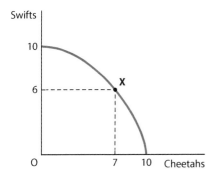

▲ **Figure 1.4.1**: A production possibility diagram

Resources are scarce and have alternative uses. Figure 1.4.1 shows different combinations of two types of bicycle, Swifts and Cheetahs, that can be produced by a firm in a month, if its resources are fully employed. If the firm only makes Swifts, it can make 10 in a month. If it only makes Cheetahs, it can make 10 in a month. The firm must decide how to allocate its limited resources. Last month, the firm operated at point X, producing six Swifts and seven Cheetahs, to match the orders they received.

Opportunity cost and trade-offs

PPBs can be used to illustrate opportunity cost and trade-offs. A trade-off is where two things cannot be achieved at the same time – one thing must be given up for another. An improvement in

> **Key term**
>
> **Production possibility boundary** (also known as production possibility curve or production possibility frontier): a curve showing the quantities that can be produced of two goods or services with the current state of technology, when resources are fully used.

> **Get it right**
>
> Unlike most diagrams in Economics, the axes for a production possibility diagram can be labelled either way round. Production possibility diagrams can be used in macroeconomics, the study of the economy as a whole, as well as in microeconomics.

> **Key term**
>
> **Trade-off**: where two things cannot be achieved at the same time, one must be sacrificed for another.

one situation will lead to the other becoming worse, so a decision must be made about which is more important and which should be sacrificed.

A bakery can make cakes and/or buns. Figure 1.4.2 shows the different combinations of cakes and buns that can be made when using all its resources. For example, if the bakery only makes cakes, it can produce 50 cakes a day. If it only makes buns, it can produce 100 buns a day. Buns and cakes are traded off. To make more cakes, resources need to be switched from making buns.

The bakery can produce at any point on the curve, which shows the different possible combinations of cakes and buns. For example, at point A, the bakery produces 20 cakes and 76 buns.

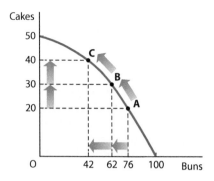

▲ **Figure 1.4.2**: The production possibility boundary of a bakery

The shape of the PPB

PPBs are normally drawn bulging out (concave) from the origin. This is because some resources may be better at producing one good than the other. For example, some of the workers at the bakery may be better at making buns than making cakes. Switching one of these workers from making buns to making cakes may involve giving up a large number of buns in exchange for making only a few more cakes.

Starting at point A on the curve, the bakery is making 20 cakes and 76 buns. If it wants to produce 30 cakes, it can only produce 62 buns. The opportunity cost of increasing the number of cakes by 10, from 20 to 30, is 14 buns. This is the fall in the number of buns the bakery can then produce.

▲ **Figure 1.4.3**: Cakes from the bakery

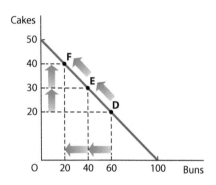

▲ **Figure 1.4.4**: A straight-line PPB

If the bakery increases cake production by another 10 cakes, from 30 to 40 cakes, production of buns falls from 62 to 42 buns. This might involve switching another worker to cake production, who is much better at making buns. The opportunity cost has increased to 20 buns.

With a concave PPB, there is an increasing opportunity cost when production of one of the goods is increased. If all the resources are equally good at producing both cakes and buns, the PPB is a straight line, as shown in Figure 1.4.4.

If the bakery operates at point D, it can make 20 cakes and 60 buns. When the number of cakes made increases by 10, from 20 to 30 cakes, the number of buns that can be produced falls from 60 to 40 buns. When the number of cakes increases by a further 10, from 30 to 40 cakes, the number of buns that can be produced falls from 40 to 20 buns. Each time an extra 10 cakes are produced, the opportunity cost (trade-off) is 20 buns. With a straight-line PPB, the opportunity cost is constant.

Activities

Draw a PPB bulging in (convex) to the origin.

1 Why is the curve this shape?
2 What happens to the opportunity cost as the production of one good is increased?

Progress questions

1 Using Figure 1.4.1, what is the opportunity cost, in terms of Swifts, when production of Cheetahs increases:
   i. from 0 to 7
   ii. from 7 to 10?
2 Using Figure 1.4.2, what is the trade-off when changing production of:
   i. buns from 62 to 76
   ii. cakes from 20 to 40
   iii. cakes from 50 to 20
   iv. buns from 0 to 42?
3 Using Figure 1.4.4, what is the opportunity cost when increasing production of:
   i. cakes from 20 to 50
   ii. cakes by one cake
   iii. buns from 20 to 60
   iv. buns by one bun?

Using production possibility diagrams

Unemployment of economic resources

Production possibility diagrams show the quantities that can be produced of two goods or types of good when resources are fully used. The PPB shows what can be produced at **full capacity**, when a firm, or an economy, is producing its maximum output from the available resources, given the current level of technology. If some resources are not fully employed, the firm will be operating inside the PPB. It will have **spare capacity**.

Figure 1.4.5 shows the bakery with spare capacity. At point Y, the bakery is making 20 cakes and 42 buns a day. The workers and/or equipment are not being used fully. This may be because production is based on the quantity of cakes and buns that people are willing to buy.

If orders for cakes and buns increase, the bakery could bring its unemployed resources into use. It can move to a point closer to, or on, the PPB. Increasing the output of cakes from 20 to 30 a day and the output of buns from 42 to 62 has no opportunity cost. This is shown as the movement from point Y to point B on Figure 1.4.5. The output of both cakes and buns can increase without any trade-offs.

Key terms

Full capacity: when a firm, or an economy, is producing its maximum output from the available resources, given the current level of technology.

Spare capacity: where a firm, or an economy, has some resources not fully employed.

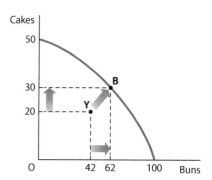

▲ Figure 1.4.5: Unemployed resources

Economic growth

In the long run, **economic growth** is an increase in productive potential. The firm or the economy as a whole is now able to produce more than before. For example, technical progress or more training for the workers may enable the bakery to produce both more cakes and more buns in a day. The PPB will shift to the right, as in Figure 1.4.6.

If the change affects only one of the products, then the new PPB will shift out for one product, as in Figure 1.4.7. For example, a new machine that makes cakes more quickly may increase the productive potential for cakes but have no effect on the output of buns.

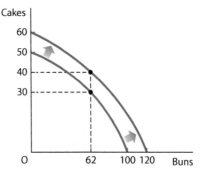
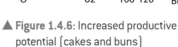
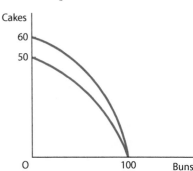

▲ **Figure 1.4.6:** Increased productive potential (cakes and buns)

▲ **Figure 1.4.7:** Increased productive potential (cakes only)

Figure 1.4.6 shows that if no cakes are made, the bakery can now make 120 buns in a day instead of 100. If it makes 62 buns in a day, it can now also make 40 cakes instead of 30 cakes.

Figure 1.4.7 shows that if no buns are made, the bakery can now make 60 cakes in a day instead of 50. If it makes no cakes, it can still only make 100 buns.

Figure 1.4.8 shows an increase in the productive potential of the economy as a whole. The country can produce both more goods and more services than it could before. The PPB will shift outwards (to the right).

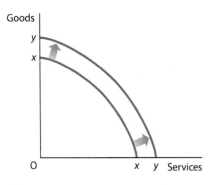

▲ **Figure 1.4.8:** Economic growth

If something happens to reduce the productive potential of a firm or the economy as a whole, the whole curve will shift inwards (to the left).

Productive and allocative efficiency

All points on a PPB are productively efficient. **Productive efficiency** is where it is not possible to produce more of one good or type of good without producing less of another. On Figure 1.4.2, points A, B and C are all productively efficient. On Figure 1.4.5, point B is productively efficient but point Y is productively inefficient, since more could be produced of one good without having to reduce production of the other.

Not all points on the PPB are allocatively efficient. **Allocative efficiency** is the combination of goods that best meets people's preferences. For example, Figure 1.4.1 showed that six Swifts and seven Cheetahs may be allocatively efficient if that combination of bicycles matches people's preferences. This will be the best use of the scarce resources.

Link

Productive efficiency will be looked at again in 3.4 "Economies and diseconomies of scale" and both productive and allocative efficiency will be explained further in the A2 part of the course.

Case study: Bravo Bicycles

Cycling is a popular sport and a means of transport. Over 100 million bicycles are produced in the world each year. China has the highest number of bicycles but the country with the highest number of bicycles per person is the Netherlands.

Bravo Bicycles is a small business selling two types of bicycle, Swifts and Cheetahs. Table 1.4.1 lists different combinations on the firm's PPB of how many of each type of bicycle the firm could produce in a three-month period.

▲ **Figure 1.4.9**: There are more than a billion bicycles in the world

▼ **Table 1.4.1**: Possible combinations of Cheetahs and Swifts

Cheetahs	Swifts
0	30
7	28
13	24
18	20
20	18
24	13
28	7
30	0

1 State a combination of Cheetahs and Swifts that is productively efficient.

2 Why may Bravo Bicycles produce 10 Cheetahs and 20 Swifts?

3 Does Bravo Bicycles have a straight-line PPB?

4 Give one reason why, a year later, the PPB for Bravo Bicycles may have shifted to the left.

Economics as a social science

A social science involves the study of society and the relationships between individuals in society. It considers human behaviour and can help to explain how society works. Social sciences provide information that helps governments and other policymakers. For example, it can help to explain why people are unemployed or why economic growth occurs. Economics is a social science and other social sciences include sociology and psychology.

Similarities and differences in methodology from other sciences

A natural science involves the study of the physical world. It helps to explain how the world around us works. Natural sciences look at what happens in nature. **Empirical evidence**, obtained through observation, experience and laboratory experiments, is used to develop and test theories. Biology, Chemistry and Physics are natural sciences.

Economics also uses empirical evidence to develop and test theories. However, economics usually relies on events to produce the evidence. Natural sciences often use laboratory experiments to produce evidence, but in Economics it is very difficult to design experiments that are valid. In spite of these difficulties, some economists have started to use experiments to test and develop theories.

Another difference between economics and natural sciences is that the behaviour of people is less predictable than what happens in the natural world. Also, people's behaviour can change over time and may depend on the circumstances in which they find themselves. However, like natural scientists, economists study evidence and look for relationships that may lead to the development of new theories.

Economists often make assumptions about the behaviour of economic agents and use logical analysis to make predictions developed from these assumptions. Predictions are tested against the evidence. If the evidence contradicts the theory, the theory is modified or discarded. However, because Economics studies human behaviour, the theories developed are less certain. It may take many years before sufficient evidence is available to reject a theory. Economic theories are also modified as new evidence becomes available.

Key terms

Social science: the study of society and the relationships between individuals in society.

Empirical evidence: evidence based on observation, experience and laboratory experiments.

Formal sciences do not use empirical evidence but they start with a set of definitions, or principles, from which theorems are logically developed. Mathematics and logic are formal sciences.

The difference between positive and normative statements

Positive statements can be tested against the facts or evidence. These statements may be true or false. Positive statements include: "the population of Malaysia in 2019 was over 30 million" and "the price of gold will rise in the next 12 months". Both these statements can be tested either now or in the future.

Normative statements are based on value judgements, people's views of what is good or bad, right or wrong. Normative statements include: "more money should be spent on education" and "the distribution of income is unfair". Other people may disagree with these statements. Normative statements often contain the words "should" or "ought" or consider **equity** (whether something is fair or just).

How value judgements influence economic decision making and policy

Value judgements are views about what is good or bad, right or wrong, in a moral sense. Value judgements reflect what we think is important, and should or should not be done. Normative statements are based on our value judgements. If we value education and think it is important, then we may believe that more money should be spent on education. Value judgements affect our decision making and also the decision making and policy of firms and governments.

What else influences people's views?

Resources are scarce and have alternative uses. Economic agents such as individuals, firms and governments have limited money and must make decisions about how best to use their money or resources.

What people, firms or governments view to be the best option will depend on the consequences of different decisions and on moral and political judgements. Individuals will consider what is the right thing to do or buy. For example, some people will be willing to pay a higher price for Fairtrade products so that farmers and other workers in developing countries can have a higher income and better working conditions.

Although firms are often assumed to try to make as much profit as possible, the decisions of owners and managers may be affected by what they think is right or wrong. For example, they may sacrifice some of their profits to improve the working conditions for their employees or to provide money for projects in the local community. It is usually assumed that governments consider what is best for the welfare of the country as a whole.

▲ Figure 1.5.1: Mathematics has a different methodology

Key terms

Positive statement: a statement that can be tested against the facts or evidence.

Normative statement: a statement based on a value judgement.

Equity: fairness.

Value judgement: a view about what is right or wrong, good or bad, in a moral sense.

Progress questions

State whether each of the following statements is positive or normative.

1 The distribution of wealth is unequal.

2 An unequal distribution of wealth is unfair.

3 People should be able to choose what they buy.

4 Average incomes will rise in the next year.

5 Firms selling electricity ought to lower prices.

Exam-style questions

1   The table below shows possible combinations of two types of chocolate bar that could be made by a firm. What is the opportunity cost of making the second milk chocolate bar in terms of plain chocolate bars?

Milk chocolate	Plain chocolate
0	13
1	9
2	5
3	2
4	0

A 1   C 3

B 2   D 4   [1 mark]

2   Which one of the following is an example of the factor of production capital?

A   A doctor   C   Diamonds in the ground

B   A factory   D   Money in a savings account   [1 mark]

3   Define "value judgement".   [3 marks]

4   The table below shows the share of national output of the agricultural sector for selected countries in a particular year.

Country	Agricultural sector as share of national output (%)
China	6.9
Colombia	8.9
India	17.4
Mexico	3.7
Nigeria	17.8
Norway	2.7

Source: https://en.wikipedia.org/wiki/List_of_countries_by_GDP_sector_composition; accessed 15 October 2019

You are advised to show your working for the calculations below.

(i) Calculate, to **the nearest whole number**, the median share of national output of the agricultural sector for the countries listed in the table.   [3 marks]

(ii) Calculate, to **one** decimal place, the mean share of national output of the agricultural sector for the countries listed in the table.   [3 marks]

5   A firm produces two goods.

With the help of a production possibility diagram, explain why there may be an increasing opportunity cost when production of one of the goods is increased.   [9 marks]

Get it right

In longer written answers in economics, it is often helpful to define key terms, particularly those that appear in the question.

2 How markets work

The operation of markets, market failure and the role of government

This section will develop your knowledge and understanding of:

→ factors which determine the demand for a good or service

→ how a demand curve shows the relationship between price and quantity demanded

→ causes of shifts in the demand curve.

Link

Free markets are explained in 1.3 "Scarcity, choice and the allocation of resources".

Key term

Demand: the quantity that consumers are willing and able to buy at a given price in a given period of time.

Quantitative skills

When drawing diagrams in Economics which involve quantity and price, the quantity is always put on the horizontal axis and the price on the vertical axis.

Activities

Identify a product that you buy often. Ask four friends or members of your family how much they would be willing to buy of this product at five different prices in a given time and put your answers in a table or spreadsheet.

1 Calculate the market demand at each price.

2 Draw a demand curve showing how much would be bought at each price.

3 What do you notice?

What determines the price of a good or service? Why is the price of gold higher than the price of bananas? In free markets, the price of a good is determined by demand and supply.

Demand

Demand is the quantity that consumers are willing and able to buy at a given price in a given period of time. It is not the same as a want. Whatever people have, they are likely to want more. In Economics, demand means effective demand. The want has to be supported by the ability and willingness to pay for the good.

In Economics, the market demand is the total amount that all the individual consumers of a product are willing and able to buy at a given price in a period of time.

Factors which determine the demand for a good or service

The price of the good or service

As a rule, the higher the price, the lower the quantity demanded and the lower the price, the higher the quantity demanded. As price increases, consumers cannot afford to buy as much and may also buy alternative products which are now relatively cheaper.

This inverse relationship between price and quantity demanded (where price and quantity demanded move in opposite directions) is shown in the diagrams below, Figures 2.1.1 and 2.1.2.

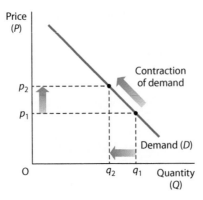

▲ **Figure 2.1.1**: A contraction of demand

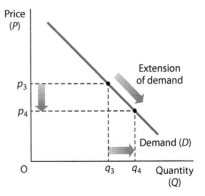

▲ **Figure 2.1.2**: An extension of demand

A demand curve shows the relationship between price and quantity demanded in a given time period. A point on the curve shows the quantity consumers are willing and able to buy at that particular price. If the price of the good or service changes, this is shown as a movement along the demand curve. In Figure 2.1.1, as price rises from p_1 to p_2, the quantity demanded falls from q_1 to q_2. This movement back along the demand curve, showing a lower quantity demanded, is called a contraction of demand.

In Figure 2.1.2, if price falls from p_3 to p_4, the quantity demanded rises from q_3 to q_4. This movement along the curve because of a fall in price is called an extension of demand.

Conditions of demand

Factors which determine the demand for a good, other than the price of the good, are known as the conditions of demand. These include:

- income
- wealth
- the price of related goods and services
- individual preferences
- population.

Income

Income is a flow of money, received by an economic agent (such as an individual, firm or the country as a whole), over a period of time. Generally, the higher the income, the higher the demand. These products are known as **normal goods**, for example new shoes. This is because more can be bought with a higher income. There may also be products where demand falls as income rises, known as **inferior goods**.

This does not mean that inferior goods are of low quality, but they are often cheaper alternatives which are more likely to be bought by people on low incomes. For example, a supermarket's own brand of tea may be cheaper than that of a well-known manufacturer. If their incomes rise, these consumers may then switch to what they believe to be better products.

Wealth

Wealth is a stock of assets owned by an economic agent at a point in time. If people own assets, such as money in the bank or property, they are able to buy more. This will increase demand. The opposite applies if wealth falls.

The price of related goods and services

The price of substitutes

Substitute goods are alternative products – if the price of one good increases, so will demand for the other. These are also known as **goods in competitive demand**. Similarly, if the price of one good falls, so will demand for the other. For example, in many countries, tea and coffee are alternative drinks. If the price of coffee rises, fewer people will buy coffee and this will increase the demand for tea.

> ## Key terms
>
> **Income:** a flow of money, received by an economic agent over a period of time.
>
> **Normal good:** a product where demand increases if income rises.
>
> **Inferior good:** a product where demand decreases if income rises.
>
> **Wealth:** a stock of assets owned by an economic agent at a point in time.
>
> **Substitute goods or goods in competitive demand:** alternative products – if the price of one good increases, so will demand for the other. They are in competitive demand.

The price of complementary goods

Complementary goods are products that are bought or used together – if the demand for one good increases, so will demand for the other. These are also known as **goods in joint demand**. Similarly, if the demand for one good falls, demand for the other will also fall. For example, if the price of cars rises, fewer people will be able to afford to buy cars and this will also reduce the demand for fuel.

Individual preferences

Everyone is different and so is the combination of goods and services they buy. This is sometimes called their pattern of demand. People's preferences may be influenced by a number of factors:

Advertising

Advertising aims to inform consumers and to persuade them to buy some products instead of others, perhaps to buy a different make of car. Successful advertising will therefore increase demand for one product and may reduce it for others. Products may also go in and out of fashion.

Social and emotional factors

We traditionally assume that consumers act rationally, considering the satisfaction they will gain from a product (sometimes called utility in Economics) in relation to its price. However, this is not always the case.

Behavioural economics suggests that we are influenced by a variety of social and emotional factors and do not always act rationally. Products may be bought on impulse or we may be influenced by what our friends do.

Population

The more people that live in a country, the greater the demand for a product is likely to be. For example, China and India would be expected to have a higher demand for a particular product, **other things being equal**, than smaller countries such as Malaysia and Singapore.

The expression "other things being equal" is a common assumption in Economics and is sometimes written in its Latin form, ceteris paribus.

Movements along a demand curve and shifts in the demand curve

Movements along the demand curve

As said previously, if the price of a product changes, this causes a movement along the demand curve because the demand curve shows how much will be demanded at different prices. If there is a change in any other factor that influences the demand for a product, except for its price, then there is a shift of the demand curve.

Shifts of the demand curve

If there is a change in income, wealth, the price of related goods and services, individual preferences, population or any other non-price factor that could affect the demand for a product, then the whole demand curve will shift.

A shift to the right shows an increase in demand, where at each and every price more is demanded than before. Similarly, a shift to the left shows a decrease in demand, where less is demanded at each and every price.

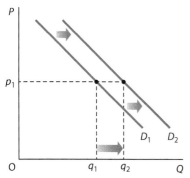

▲ **Figure 2.1.3:** An increase in demand

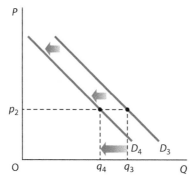

▲ **Figure 2.1.4:** A decrease in demand

For example, in Figure 2.1.3, after the demand curve for mobile phones has shifted from D_1 to D_2, at price p_1, demand has increased from q_1 to q_2. This may be because of a rise in incomes.

Similarly, in Figure 2.1.4, after the demand curve for bananas has shifted from D_3 to D_4, at price p_2, demand has fallen from q_3 to q_4. This may be because of a fall in the price of pineapples.

Progress questions

1. What causes a movement along the demand curve as opposed to a shift of the demand curve?

2. What is another term for complementary goods?

3. Will an increase in income shift the demand curve for an inferior good to the left or the right?

Case study: Changes in China's automotive market

China is the world's biggest automotive market. In 2015, there were around 21 million sales. It is also the largest carbon emitter in the world with 10% of its greenhouse gas emissions coming from transport. This is partly because of its large population.

There is growing concern in many countries about the amount of pollution caused by fossil fuels such as oil. Therefore, the Chinese government is encouraging the use of green energy, including for vehicles. Although only a small part of the market, sales are increasing for vehicles using these fuels. By 2025, one in every five cars sold in China must use alternative fuels, such as electricity.

1. What is the economic term used to describe the relationship between fossil fuels and electricity in this example?

▲ **Figure 2.1.5:** Inside a modern car factory

2. Draw a diagram to show the change in demand for oil if more consumers buy vehicles that use electricity.

This section will develop your knowledge and understanding of:

→ the meaning of price, income and cross elasticity of demand

→ the relationship between income elasticity of demand and normal and inferior goods

→ the relationship between cross elasticity of demand and substitute and complementary goods

→ the relationship between price elasticity of demand and firms' total revenue (total expenditure)

→ factors that influence these elasticities of demand.

Demand is affected by many factors. These include the price of the good, income and the price of other goods. Price, income and cross elasticities of demand measure the extent of changes in demand following changes in the price of that good, changes in income or changes in the price of another good.

Elasticities of demand

Elasticity is a measure of how much one variable changes in response to a change in another. There are three elasticities of demand.

- Price elasticity of demand
- Income elasticity of demand
- Cross elasticity of demand

Price elasticity of demand

As well as knowing that a change in price will cause a change in the quantity demanded, it is often useful to know how much the demand will change relative to the change in price. Will it change by a larger or smaller percentage? Price elasticity of demand (PED) provides a numerical value using these percentage changes:

$$PED = \frac{\text{percentage change in quantity demanded}}{\text{percentage change in price}}$$

Using the Greek letter delta (Δ) for change and accepted abbreviations, this can be shortened to:

$$PED = \frac{\% \, \Delta \text{ in QD}}{\% \, \Delta \text{ in P}}$$

Price elasticity of demand is a measure of the percentage change in quantity demanded as a result of a given percentage change in price, or simply, the responsiveness of quantity demanded to a change in price.

In most situations, a rise in price will reduce the quantity demanded and a fall in price will increase the quantity demanded.

Elastic and inelastic demand

Since price and quantity demanded change in opposite directions, this means that PED will be negative.

Key term

Price elasticity of demand: a measure of the percentage change in quantity demanded as a result of a given percentage change in price, or simply, the responsiveness of quantity demanded to a change in price.

If the percentage change in price is less than the percentage change in quantity demanded, demand is said to be elastic. If the percentage change in price is greater than the percentage change in quantity demanded, demand is inelastic.

The concept of elasticity is used ideally for small changes but in the real world, changes may be quite large.

Example

In the diagram to the right (Figure 2.2.1), price has risen from $8 to $10. As a result, the quantity demanded has fallen from 50 to 25 units.

1. What is the value of PED?

2. Is demand for the product elastic or inelastic?

Answers:

1. The percentage rise in price is 25% (+25) and the percentage fall in quantity demanded is 50% (−50).
$$PED = \frac{-50}{+25} = -2$$

2. The percentage change in quantity demanded is greater than the percentage change in price, so demand is elastic.

Ignoring the minus sign, if demand is elastic, PED will be a number greater than 1, since the number on the top of the equation will be bigger than the number on the bottom. Elasticity has no units.

The graph below (Figure 2.2.2) and the following calculation show inelastic demand:

If price falls from $10 to $2, quantity demanded rises from 40 to 44 units. Here the percentage change in quantity demanded (+10%) is less than the percentage change in price (−80%), so demand is inelastic.
$$PED = \frac{+10}{-80} = -0.125$$

Ignoring the minus sign, if demand is inelastic, PED will be a number less than 1, since the number on the top of the equation is smaller than the number on the bottom.

For a downward-sloping straight-line demand curve, PED becomes less elastic as price falls. However, in the real world, demand curves are unlikely to be straight lines.

Link

The changing PED of a downward-sloping straight-line demand curve will be discussed further in the A2 part of the course.

Activities

Draw a straight-line demand curve starting at $10 on the price axis and ending at 10 units on the quantity axis.

1 Calculate PED when price falls from $8 to $7.

2 Calculate PED when price falls from $2 to $1.

3 What happens to PED as price falls?

Get it right

You should not refer to a good as an elastic or inelastic good. The good is not elastic or inelastic. It is the demand (or supply) for the good that is elastic or inelastic.

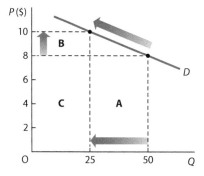

▲ **Figure 2.2.1:** Calculating PED

Quantitative skills

Percentage changes are commonly used in Economics. Make sure you have a method that works. The difference between the new and the old figures should be divided by the old/original figure before multiplying by 100. If there is a decrease, state this or use a minus sign. Do not forget to include the percentage sign. Use a calculator if helpful and check your calculations carefully.

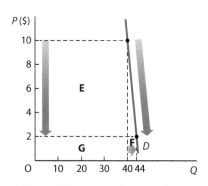

▲ **Figure 2.2.2:** Inelastic demand

Perfectly elastic, perfectly inelastic and unit elasticity

There are also three extreme categories of PED, shown below:

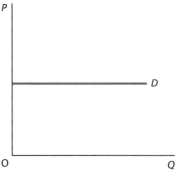

▲ **Figure 2.2.3**: Perfectly elastic

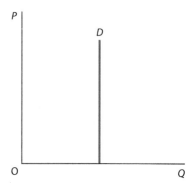

▲ **Figure 2.2.4**: Perfectly inelastic

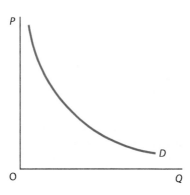

▲ **Figure 2.2.5**: Unit elasticity

If demand is perfectly elastic, there could be any demand at a particular price but none at a higher price. The percentage change in price is zero, giving a value for PED of infinity (∞).

If demand is perfectly inelastic, demand stays the same at all prices. The percentage change in demand is zero, giving a value for PED of zero. This could happen for an individual's demand for a product over a narrow range of prices.

If demand is of unit elasticity, the percentage change in demand is the same as the percentage change in price and since one of these will increase and the other will decrease, the value of PED will be –1. For example, a 10% rise in price causes a 10% fall in demand. This could happen on rare occasions.

Relationships between price elasticity of demand and firms' total revenue (expenditure)

Multiplying the price by the quantity sold gives the income from sales or **total revenue** of the firm. It is also the total expenditure (spending) of the consumers.

What will happen to total revenue if demand is elastic?

If PED is elastic, the percentage change in demand is greater than the percentage change in price.

For example, in Figure 2.2.1, when price rose by 25%, demand fell by 50%. The rise in price was more than offset by the fall in the quantity sold. At the original price of $8, the total revenue/expenditure was $400 ($8 × 50 units) but when price rose to $10, total revenue fell to $250 ($10 × 25 units).

Before the price rise, total revenue is A + C. After the price rise, total revenue falls to B + C. The revenue lost from area A is bigger than the revenue gained from area B.

Had the price fallen from $10 to $8, total revenue would have risen from $250 to $400.

Therefore, when demand is elastic, changes in price and total revenue move in opposite directions.

What will happen to total revenue if demand is inelastic?

If PED is inelastic, the percentage change in demand is less than the percentage change in price. For example, in Figure 2.2.2, when price fell by 80%, demand only rose by 10%. The rise in quantity sold was not enough to offset the fall in price.

At the original price of $10, the total revenue was $400 but when price fell to $2, total revenue fell to $88.

Before the price fall, total revenue is E + G. After the price fall, total revenue falls to F + G. The revenue gained from area F is smaller than the revenue lost from area E.

Had the price risen from $2 to $10, total revenue would have risen from $88 to $400.

Therefore, when demand is inelastic, changes in price and total revenue move in the same direction.

What if demand is perfectly elastic, perfectly inelastic or of unit elasticity?

If demand is perfectly elastic, there is no demand at a higher price. If price rises, total revenue falls to zero.

If demand is perfectly inelastic, demand stays the same at all prices. If price increases by 10%, total revenue will rise by 10%. If price falls by 20%, total revenue falls by 20%. Therefore, the percentage change in total revenue will be the same as the percentage change in price.

If demand is of unit elasticity, the percentage change in demand is the same as the percentage change in price. For any change in price, total revenue will stay the same.

▼ Table 2.2.1: Summary table for PED

Category	Relationship between % changes in P and QD	Value	What happens to total revenue when price rises
Perfectly elastic	QD falls to zero after any rise in P	PED = ∞	Falls to zero
Elastic	% change in QD > % change in P	PED < −1	Falls
Unit elasticity	% change in QD = % change in P	PED = −1	Stays the same
Inelastic	% change in QD < % change in P	−1 < PED < 0	Rises
Perfectly inelastic	No change in QD after any change in P	PED = 0	Rises by the same percentage as price

Factors that influence PED

Whether PED is elastic or inelastic depends on how much demand changes in response to a change in price. This depends on, for example:

- substitutes
- width of market
- time
- percentage of income spent on the product.

Substitutes

The most important factor influencing whether demand for a product is elastic or inelastic is the availability of substitutes in that price range. If there are similar products that could be bought, demand will usually be elastic. It will be responsive to changes in price.

For example, if the price of one brand of TV increases, there is likely to be a greater percentage fall in demand (than the percentage rise in price) as people buy other brands of TV instead.

There may be some people who buy a Sony TV because they believe them to be more reliable and of better quality than other TVs. This may be because they owned Sony TVs before. They may buy a particular brand of a product through habit. Their demand will be inelastic but overall, demand for one brand is likely to be elastic.

If the price of petrol rises, there is likely to be a smaller percentage fall in demand as those people with vehicles that use petrol have little alternative (at least in the short run) than to continue to buy petrol.

Width of market

The example of TVs can be used to explain another factor influencing PED. Generally, the wider the definition of the market, the less elastic the demand for the product.

The market for Sony TVs will be smaller than the market for TVs as a whole. If the price of Sony TVs changes, demand is likely to be more responsive than if the price of all TVs increases. This is also because there are more substitutes available for Sony TVs than for TVs as a whole.

Time
The example of petrol can be used to explain a further factor influencing PED. Usually, the longer the time period, the more elastic the demand for a product.

In the short run, people who have a car that uses petrol cannot easily reduce the amount of petrol they buy if the price of petrol increases. If the price of petrol remains high for a long time compared with other fuels, such as electricity, then in the long run they may buy a car that uses a different fuel. There are substitute fuels available but not for the vehicle they have and it is not worthwhile changing straight away.

Percentage of income spent on the product
When the price of a good or service changes, this may be a small or large percentage of a person's income. Even if the price increases by 50%, if this is a very small percentage of a person's income, they may not believe that it is worth looking for a substitute. Their demand for the product is likely to be inelastic.

If a large percentage of income is spent on the product, such as a car, demand may be more elastic. Changes in price will be more significant and have more effect on demand.

Necessities and luxuries?
Sometimes, it is said that the demand for necessities is inelastic and that the demand for luxuries is elastic. This is based on the fact that people cannot survive without necessities but do not need luxuries.

This cannot be treated as a general rule. For example, the demand for fruit is relatively inelastic but the demand for melons may be elastic. This is because there are substitutes for melons which people may buy instead if the price of melons rises.

Case study: The price of postcards

Birdwing is a small firm in Sri Lanka making postcards. The price it pays for raw materials has increased. The firm is considering raising the price of a postcard from 100 to 120 Sri Lankan Rupees (LKR). It estimates that this will reduce its demand for postcards per week from 1000 to 900.

1   Use the information above to calculate the PED for postcards if the price increases from 100 to 120 LKR.
2   Calculate the expected change in total revenue.
3   Is demand in this price range elastic or inelastic? Explain your answer.

▲ **Figure 2.2.6**: A beach in Sri Lanka

Income elasticity of demand

It is also useful to know how much demand for a product will change if people's incomes change.

Income elasticity of demand (YED) is a measure of the percentage change in quantity demanded as a result of a given percentage change in income, or simply, the responsiveness of quantity demanded to a change in income.

The following formula is used to calculate income elasticity of demand:

$$\text{Income elasticity of demand} = \frac{\text{percentage change in quantity demanded}}{\text{percentage change in income}}$$

Using accepted abbreviations, this can be shortened to:

$$\text{YED} = \frac{\% \ \Delta \ \text{in QD}}{\% \ \Delta \ \text{in Y}}$$

YED can be positive or negative, depending on whether it is a normal good or an inferior good.

Normal goods

With normal goods, as income rises so does demand. Income and demand are directly related. Similarly, if income falls, less will be bought.

This means that YED will be positive for normal goods.

For example, if a 10% increase in incomes results in a 6% increase in the demand for washing machines:

$$\text{YED} = \frac{+6}{+10} = +0.6$$

Some goods will have higher values of YED than others.

Luxury goods (sometimes called superior goods), such as holidays, will usually have higher values of YED than other normal goods such as food. If a person's income rises by 50%, the increase in their quantity demanded for holidays may be 60% but the increase in their quantity demanded for food may only be 20%. Therefore, as income rises, it is likely that a higher percentage of income will be spent on holidays and a lower percentage on food.

Inferior goods

Inferior goods have negative YED.

This is because income and demand are inversely related. For example, if income rises, demand falls. If a 5% increase in income results in a 2% decrease in demand for second-hand clothes:

$$\text{YED} = \frac{-2}{+5} = -0.4$$

Cross elasticity of demand

Another type of elasticity is concerned with how changes in the price of one good affect the demand for another good. There are three possibilities.

- Substitute goods
- Complementary goods
- No relationship

Cross elasticity of demand (XED or CED) is a measure of the percentage change in quantity demanded of one good as a result of a given percentage change in the price of another good, or simply, the responsiveness of quantity demanded of one good to a change in the price of another.

The following formula is used to calculate cross elasticity of demand:

$$\text{Cross elasticity of demand} = \frac{\text{percentage change in quantity demanded of good A}}{\text{percentage change in price of good B}}$$

Using accepted abbreviations, this can be shortened to:

$$\text{XED} = \frac{\%\ \Delta\ \text{in QD of A}}{\%\ \Delta\ \text{in P of B}}$$

XED can be positive or negative, depending on whether the goods are substitute goods or complementary goods.

Substitute goods

With substitute goods, a rise in the price of one good results in more being demanded of the other.

For example, if the price of Good A rises, fewer people will buy Good A and more will buy an alternative such as Good B instead. Similarly, if the price of a good falls, fewer people will buy substitute goods.

This means that XED will be positive for substitute goods.

For example, if an 8% increase in the price of one brand of mobile phone results in a 6% increase in the demand for another:

$$\text{XED} = \frac{+6}{+8} = +0.75$$

Two products which are good substitutes are likely to have a higher value for XED. This is because a change in the price of one good will have a large impact on the demand for the other good. This is shown in the numerical example for mobile phones. Some people may be loyal to a particular brand of mobile phone but otherwise, a change in price will encourage them to switch brands.

Complementary goods

With complementary goods, a rise in the price of one good results in less being demanded of the other.

For example, if the price of Good A rises, fewer people will buy Good A and also fewer people will buy Good B to use with it. Similarly, if the price of a good falls, more people will buy the complementary good.

Key term

Cross elasticity of demand: a measure of the percentage change in quantity demanded of one good as a result of a given percentage change in the price of another good, or simply, the responsiveness of quantity demanded of one good to a change in the price of another.

Link

Substitute and complementary goods were introduced in 2.1 "The demand for goods and services", when explaining how changes in the price of a related good or service could affect the demand for a product.

This means that XED will be negative for complementary goods.

For example, if a 6% increase in the price of mobile phones results in a 3% decrease in the demand for mobile-phone cases:

$$\text{XED} = \frac{-3}{+6} = -0.5$$

Two products which go together well are likely to have a higher (negative) value for XED. For example, the goods will be closer complementary goods if their XED is −0.7 than if XED is −0.2.

No relationship

If there is no relationship between the two products, XED will be zero. If there is little connection between the products, XED will be close to zero.

For example, a 5% change in the price of tables may have no effect on the demand for bus travel. This is because tables and bus travel are neither substitute goods nor complementary goods.

Progress questions

4   If YED is +0.3, what type of good is it?

5   If XED is −0.3, are the goods in competitive or joint demand?

6   You are a manufacturer in an emerging economy. Would you prefer your product to have a high or low value for YED? Explain your answer.

The supply of goods and services

Supply

Supply is the quantity that firms are able and willing to sell at a given price in a given period of time. It may not be the same as the amount produced. Wages and transport costs may be higher than the revenue a farmer will receive from harvesting and selling their grain crop. It may then be left in the fields for animals to eat. This is not part of supply unless the grain is available for sale.

The market supply is the total amount that all the individual firms of a product are able and willing to sell at a given price in a given period of time.

Factors which determine the supply of a good or service

The price of the good or service

As a rule, the higher the price, the higher the quantity supplied and the lower the price, the lower the quantity supplied. As price increases, firms are willing to offer more for sale. This is because if prices are higher, they are likely to make a higher profit. This provides the incentive to expand production. The higher price will also attract new firms into the market.

Profit is total revenue minus total cost. In Economics, it is often assumed that firms will aim to maximise profit.

In the example above, if the price of grain increases, the farmer may then be willing to harvest and sell their crop. The difference between their total revenue and their costs has increased.

This direct relationship between price and quantity supplied (where price and quantity supplied move in the same direction) can be shown in diagrams (see Figures 2.3.1 and 2.3.2).

A supply curve shows the relationship between price and quantity supplied in a given time period. If the price of the good or service changes, this is shown as a movement along the supply curve. In Figure 2.3.1, as price rises from p_1 to p_2, the quantity supplied rises from q_1 to q_2. This movement along the supply curve is called an extension of supply.

Key terms

Supply: the quantity that firms are able and willing to sell at a given price in a given period of time.

Profit: total revenue minus total cost.

Activity

Find out about a business in your local area. Have its sales increased or decreased in recent years and why? Alternatively, look up the accounts of a well-known company to find this information.

If the price falls from p_3 to p_4, as in Figure 2.3.2, the quantity supplied falls from q_3 to q_4. This movement along the curve, due to a fall in price, is called a contraction of supply.

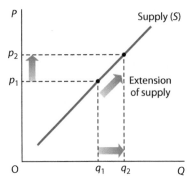

▲ **Figure 2.3.1:** An extension of supply

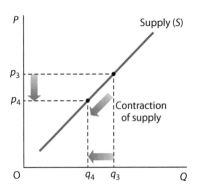

▲ **Figure 2.3.2:** A contraction of supply

Conditions of supply

Factors which determine the supply of a good, other than the price of the good, are known as the conditions of supply. These include:

- costs of production
- productivity
- technical progress
- number of firms in the market
- weather and other events
- indirect taxes and subsidies.

Costs of production

Costs of production include:

- wages
- raw materials
- energy
- transport
- interest on loans.

If costs of production rise, for example, higher oil prices increase the cost of transport, the firm will want to charge a higher price than before for a particular quantity of their product. Another way of looking at this is to say that, at any given price, firms will be willing to offer less for sale. Supply will decrease at each and every price. Higher costs may make it unprofitable for some firms to continue to supply the product at a given price. They may then leave the market, further reducing supply.

Similarly, if costs fall, for example if the price of raw materials falls, then supply is likely to increase.

Productivity

Productivity measures how much each factor of production produces in a given time. For example, labour productivity is how much a worker produces in a given time. Labour costs are affected by wages and the amount workers produce. If wages stay the same but productivity increases, for example because of increased training, labour costs per unit produced will fall. This will encourage an increase in supply.

Technical progress

Technical progress may lead to the development of better machines or methods of production. This may help the firm to produce goods more quickly and cheaply, increasing supply. Technical progress is another reason for higher labour productivity. However, this will often happen over a long period of time.

Number of firms in the market

Another factor that can affect the quantity supplied at a given price over a period of time is the number of firms in the market. Other things being equal, if firms leave the market, perhaps if the owner decides to retire, supply will decrease. If firms join or leave the market for reasons other than a change in the price of the product, the supply curve will shift. If more firms join, the curve shifts to the right.

Weather and other events

The output of many goods, particularly agricultural goods, depends on the weather. Good weather will increase supply and bad weather will reduce it.

There may be other factors that affect supply at different times, such as wars or strikes.

Indirect taxes and subsidies

Indirect taxes

An **indirect tax** is a tax on spending. In many countries, this is an important source of government income. The firms have to pay money to the government, which adds to their costs in the same way as higher wages for example. This will reduce supply.

Subsidies

A **subsidy** is a payment to producers to reduce costs. This will increase supply at any given price, shifting the supply curve to the right.

Movements along a supply curve and shifts in the supply curve

Movements along the supply curve

As happens with demand, if the price of a product changes, this causes a movement along the supply curve because the supply curve shows how much will be supplied at different prices. If there is a change in any other factor that influences the supply of a product except its price, then there is a shift of the supply curve.

Shifts of the supply curve

If there is a change in productivity, technical progress, the number of firms in the market, weather, indirect taxes, subsidies or any other

Key terms

Productivity: how much a factor of production produces in a given time.

Labour productivity: how much a worker produces in a given time.

Indirect tax: a tax on spending.

Subsidy: a payment to producers to reduce costs and increase supply.

Link

There is more information on productivity in 3.1 "Production and productivity".

Link

The use of indirect taxes and subsidies is explained in 5.7 "Government intervention in markets".

factor that could affect the costs of production, then the whole supply curve will shift.

A shift to the right shows an increase in supply, where at each and every price more is supplied than before. Similarly, a shift to the left shows a decrease in supply, where less is supplied at each and every price.

For example, in Figure 2.3.3 after the supply curve for shirts has shifted from S_1 to S_2, at price p_1, supply has increased from q_1 to q_2. This may be because of higher productivity.

Similarly, in Figure 2.3.4 after the supply curve for watermelons has shifted from S_3 to S_4, at price p_2, supply has fallen from q_3 to q_4. This may be because of cold weather.

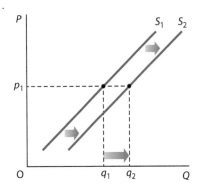

▲ **Figure 2.3.3**: An increase in supply

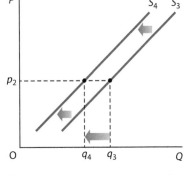

▲ **Figure 2.3.4**: A decrease in supply

Progress questions

1 Explain why a supply curve slopes upwards from left to right.

2 Will a subsidy increase or decrease supply?

Case study: Problems hit Madagascar's vanilla crop

Vanilla is used in cooking in many parts of the world. Madagascar, an island in the Indian Ocean, produces 80% of the world's supply of vanilla. In 2017, the island was hit by Cyclone Enawo. This was followed by a major drought. Many of the flowers which produce the vanilla seed pods were destroyed. In the next year, the price of vanilla rose from $400 to $600 per kilo.

1 On a diagram, should the problems in the vanilla market, caused by the weather, be shown as:
   * a contraction of supply
   * an extension of supply
   * a shift of the supply curve to the left
   * a shift of the supply curve to the right?
   Explain why.

2 Draw a diagram to show the effect of the higher price of vanilla on the supply of food products which contain vanilla.

▲ **Figure 2.3.5**: Vanilla

This section will develop your knowledge and understanding of:
→ the meaning of price elasticity of supply
→ factors that influence price elasticity of supply.

In the same way that PED measures how much demand changes in response to a change in price, **price elasticity of supply** (PES) is a measure of the percentage change in quantity supplied as a result of a given percentage change in price, or simply, the responsiveness of quantity supplied to a change in price. The formula is:

$$PES = \frac{\text{percentage change in quantity supplied}}{\text{percentage change in price}}$$

Using accepted abbreviations, this can be shortened to:

$$PES = \frac{\% \, \Delta \text{ in QS}}{\% \, \Delta \text{ in P}}$$

In most situations, a rise in price will increase the quantity supplied and a fall in price will reduce it.

Elastic and inelastic supply
Since price and quantity supplied move in the same direction, this means that PES will be positive.

In a similar way to PED, if the percentage change in price is less than the percentage change in quantity supplied, supply is said to be elastic. If the percentage change in price is greater than the percentage change in quantity supplied, supply is said to be inelastic.

Examples
In the diagram below (Figure 2.4.1), price has risen from $8 to $10. As a result, the quantity supplied has risen from 20 to 40 units.

1. What is the value of PES?

2. Is supply of the product elastic or inelastic?

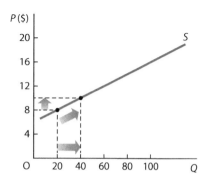

▲ **Figure 2.4.1:** Calculating PES

1. The percentage rise in price is 25% (+25) and the percentage rise in quantity supplied is 100% (+100).

$$PES = \frac{+100}{+25} = +4$$

2. The percentage change in quantity supplied is greater than the percentage change in price, so supply is elastic.

If supply is elastic, PES is greater than 1.

The following graph (Figure 2.4.2) and calculation show inelastic supply.

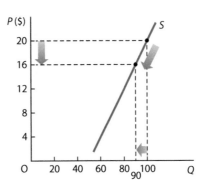

▲ **Figure 2.4.2:** Inelastic supply

If price falls from $20 to $16, quantity supplied falls from 100 to 90 units. Here the percentage change in price (−20%) is greater than the percentage change in quantity supplied (−10%), so supply is inelastic.

$$\text{PES} = \frac{-10}{-20} = 0.5$$

If supply is inelastic, PES is less than 1.

Perfectly elastic, perfectly inelastic and unit elasticity

There are three extreme categories of PES, shown below.

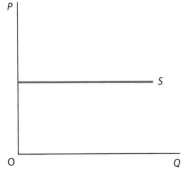

▲ **Figure 2.4.3:** Perfectly elastic

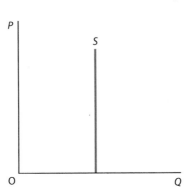

▲ **Figure 2.4.4:** Perfectly inelastic

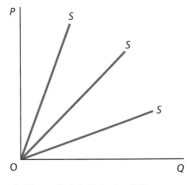

▲ **Figure 2.4.5:** Unit elasticity

If supply is perfectly elastic, there could be any supply at a particular price but none at any lower price. Firms will supply whatever is demanded at the given price or above.

Again, like demand, if supply is perfectly inelastic, it stays the same at all prices. The percentage change in supply is zero, giving a value for PES of zero. If a sports venue or theatre has a fixed number of seats, its supply will be perfectly inelastic.

If supply is of unit elasticity, the percentage change in supply is the same as the percentage change in price. For example, a 10% rise in price causes a 10% rise in supply. PES will be +1. This applies to any straight line from the origin.

▼ Table 2.4.1: Summary table for PES

Category	Relationship between % changes in P and QS	Value
Perfectly elastic	QS falls to zero after any fall in P	PES = ∞
Elastic	% change in QS > % change in P	PES > 1
Unit elasticity	% change in QS = % change in P	PES = 1
Inelastic	% change in QS < % change in P	1 > PES > 0
Perfectly inelastic	No change in QS after any change in P	PES = 0

Factors that influence PES

In a similar way to demand, whether PES is elastic or inelastic depends on how easy it is to change the supply of the good or service in response to a change in the price of the product. This depends on, for example:

- availability of stock
- spare capacity
- impact on costs
- nature of product
- time
- state of the economy.

Availability of stock

Many firms keep spare supplies of their product in case there is a need for more. They may also add to these stocks if they cannot sell everything they have produced. If firms have stock available, they will be able to increase their supply if the price rises, making supply elastic. If the product can be stored, if price decreases, firms may add to their stock, so it can be sold later.

If the product cannot be stored easily and cheaply, supply will be less elastic. For example, fresh milk only lasts for a few days. Tinned food will usually last much longer. The supply of fresh milk is likely to be inelastic but the supply of tinned food is likely to be elastic.

Spare capacity

If a firm has spare capacity, it is able to change the amount it produces more easily than if it is working at full capacity. For example, if price rises, it will be able to increase production, by bringing its spare factors of production into use, making supply elastic.

If the firm is working at full capacity, it will be more difficult to increase output. All the machines may be in use. This will make increasing output more difficult. It may take time to obtain more machines, or other factors of production, to increase capacity.

Impact on costs

If the cost of producing extra goods is more expensive than the current cost per item, firms may be unwilling to increase production. For example, workers may have to be paid a higher wage rate to work extra hours. This makes increased production less profitable and may make supply inelastic, at least in the short run.

Nature of product

For some products, particularly agricultural products or minerals, supply will be inelastic because it takes time to increase supply. For example, rice usually takes between four and five months to grow. It would take time to reduce or increase the amount of rice available in response to a decrease or increase in price. Similarly, if the price of copper rose, it will take time to find and mine new areas of copper.

Time

The longer the time period the more elastic the supply. This is because there will be more time for firms to change their supply by changing their factors of production. Also, firms can more easily enter or leave the market.

In Economics, there are two main time periods, the short run and the long run.

In the **short run**, at least one factor of production is fixed in supply. For example, it may only be possible to increase or decrease production by changing the amount of labour. Supply is likely to be inelastic.

In the **long run**, all factors of production are variable. It is possible to change all the factors of production in response to changes in price. Supply will be elastic.

The short run and long run are not set periods of time in terms of weeks or years. They will vary according to the product. For example, a window-cleaning service could be set up or closed down much more quickly than a power station producing electricity.

Sometimes, a third time period is included – the very short run or momentary period. This refers to the supply available at that time, which cannot be changed. For example, the fish delivered to a market in the morning is limited to that quantity. Supply is perfectly inelastic.

State of the economy

This is related to the spare capacity of the country as a whole. If the economy has spare capacity, for example unemployment is high, the supply of many goods and services will be elastic. This is because firms will find it easier to obtain extra resources to increase production if price increases.

If the economy is working at full capacity, it will be more difficult and maybe more expensive to obtain the scarce factors of production to increase supply.

Key terms

Short run: the time period when at least one factor of production is fixed in supply.

Long run: the time period when all factors of production are variable.

Case study: Gepetto's toys

Gepetto makes wooden toys for children. He employs one other worker for three days a week. Wooden toys are becoming more popular as some people are concerned about the impact of plastic on the environment. The price of wooden toys has increased by 5% in the last month and Gepetto believes that the price will increase even more in the next year.

1   What would you advise him to do and why?
2   Using your knowledge and understanding of the factors that influence price elasticity of supply, what does your advice depend on?

▲ Figure 2.4.6: A wooden toy

Progress questions

1   If PES is 1.5, is supply elastic or inelastic?
2   If supply is perfectly inelastic, what is the change in total revenue if demand increases causing price to rise by 4.5%?
3   If PES is 0.3 and the change in quantity supplied is a decrease of 6%, what is the percentage change in price?

This section will develop your knowledge and understanding of:

→ how the interaction of demand and supply determines equilibrium prices in a market economy

→ the difference between equilibrium and disequilibrium

→ why excess demand and excess supply lead to changes in price

→ causes of fluctuations in commodity prices, including speculation.

How the interaction of demand and supply determines equilibrium prices in a market economy

In a free market economy, where there is no intervention by the government, the price of a product is determined by the **market forces** of demand and supply.

As price rises, the quantity demanded falls and the quantity supplied rises. Therefore, there will usually be one price where demand and supply cross. This is the price where demand and supply are equal. This **equilibrium price** is also known as the market-clearing price because all the products available for sale at this price will be sold. The amount sold at the equilibrium price is the **equilibrium quantity**.

At equilibrium, there is no tendency to change, unless there is a shift in either demand or supply. The equilibrium price and quantity for a product can be seen in Figure 2.5.1 at p and q.

Difference between equilibrium and disequilibrium

Disequilibrium refers to a situation where two related variables, such as supply and demand, are not equal. There will be forces at work that will lead to a change in the price and quantity sold in this case.

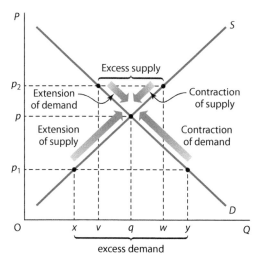

▲ Figure 2.5.2: Equilibrium and disequilibrium

> ### Link
>
> This section brings together the content of 2.1 "The demand for goods and services" and 2.3 "The supply of goods and services". It also draws on part of 2.2 "Price, income and cross elasticities of demand" and 2.4 "Price elasticity of supply".

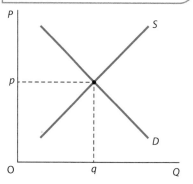

▲ Figure 2.5.1: Equilibrium

> ### Key terms
>
> **Market forces:** demand and supply, which determine the price and quantity sold of products in a market economy.
>
> **Equilibrium price:** the price where demand and supply for a product are equal.
>
> **Equilibrium quantity:** the quantity where demand and supply for a product are equal.
>
> **Disequilibrium:** where there are forces at work that will lead to a change in a variable.

Why excess demand and excess supply lead to changes in price

Figure 2.5.2 shows both equilibrium and disequilibrium in the market for pencils. If the market is in disequilibrium, it will usually move towards equilibrium.

- p is the equilibrium price, where S = D. q is the equilibrium quantity sold at this price.

- At prices below p, for example p_1, there is a **shortage/excess demand** of pencils of y − x, which can be written as xy. This is because at p_1, the quantity demanded of pencils at y is greater than the quantity supplied of x. In this case, price will tend to rise towards equilibrium. As price rises, this causes a contraction of demand and an extension of supply of pencils. This is because buyers will be less willing and able to buy pencils but suppliers will want to sell more, attracted by higher profits.

- At prices above p, for example p_2, there is a **surplus/excess supply** of pencils of w − v or vw. This is because at p_2, the quantity supplied of pencils at w is higher than the quantity demanded of v. As a result, price falls towards equilibrium. As price falls, this causes an extension of demand and a contraction of supply of pencils. In this case, buyers are able and willing to buy more but there is less incentive for suppliers to sell as many.

Case study: The market for strawberries

There are several small stallholders in a local market selling fruit and vegetables, including strawberries. At a higher price, they will offer more for sale, to make more profit. They have also noticed that the demand for strawberries changes with price.

Table 2.5.1 shows the demand and supply of strawberries per day at different prices.

▼ **Table 2.5.1:** Demand and supply of strawberries per day

Price per kg (€)	1	2	3	4	5	6
Demand (kg)	12	10	8	6	4	2
Supply (kg)	2	4	6	8	10	12

▲ **Figure 2.5.3:** Strawberries for sale

1 Use the information in the table to draw a diagram showing the demand and supply for strawberries.

2 What is the equilibrium price of strawberries and how many kg will be sold at this price?

3 If the stallholders charge €5 per kg, will there be excess supply or demand and by how much? Explain how the equilibrium price will be restored.

4 What will happen if the stallholders charge €2 per kg? What would you advise them to do and why?

Use of demand and supply diagrams to analyse causes of changes in market prices

Section 2.1, "The demand for goods and services", covered reasons why a demand curve may shift, either to the right, if there is an increase in demand, or to the left, if demand decreases. These reasons included changes in income, wealth, the price of related goods and services, individual preferences, population, or any other factor that could affect the demand for a product except the price of that good.

An increase in demand

Figure 2.5.4 shows what happens when there is an increase in demand. For example, a rise in population may have increased the demand for rice from D_1 to D_2. Demand is now higher at each and every price.

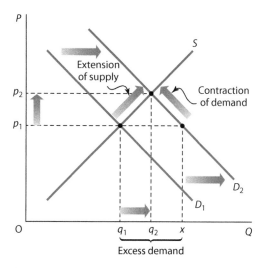

▲ **Figure 2.5.4**: An increase in demand

What happens next? How does the market reach a new equilibrium? At the old equilibrium price of p_1, there is excess demand of q_1x because demand is now higher than supply. Price will tend to rise because buyers who cannot obtain the product will bid up its price. This will cause an extension of supply, as sellers hope to make more profit but there will also be a contraction of demand, as some buyers are no longer able and willing to pay a higher price for rice. The market will reach a new equilibrium price of p_2 where q_2 is sold.

If demand increases, both the equilibrium price and the equilibrium quantity sold will increase.

Quantitative skills

When drawing diagrams in Economics, if there is more than one of a particular type of curve, number them in a logical order. For example, in Figure 2.5.4, the original demand curve is D_1 and the new demand curve is D_2. In the same way, the old equilibrium price and quantity, where D_1 and S cross, are labelled p_1 and q_1. The new equilibrium is at p_2 and q_2, where D_2 and S cross. Also, when including a diagram as part of your analysis, refer to it fully in your explanation.

Get it right

When explaining what happens after a shift in demand or supply, the excess demand or supply is at the old equilibrium price, not at the new price.

A decrease in demand

Figure 2.5.5 shows what happens when there is a decrease in demand. For example, a fall in income may have decreased the demand for new cars from D_1 to D_2. Demand is now lower at each and every price.

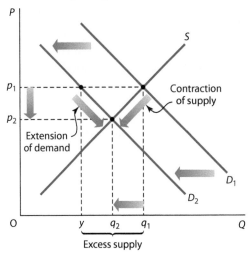

▲ **Figure 2.5.5**: A decrease in demand

At the old equilibrium price of p_1, there is excess supply of yq_1 because supply is now higher than demand. Price will tend to fall. This will cause a contraction of supply as sellers are likely to make less profit and there will be an extension of demand as more buyers are able and willing to buy new cars at a lower price. The market will reach a new equilibrium price of p_2 where q_2 is sold.

If demand decreases, both the equilibrium price and the equilibrium quantity sold decrease.

An increase in supply

Section 2.3, "The supply of goods and services", covered reasons why a supply curve may shift, either to the right if there is an increase in supply or to the left if supply decreases. These reasons included changes in productivity; technical progress; the number of firms in the market; weather; indirect taxes; subsidies; or any other factor that could affect the costs of production.

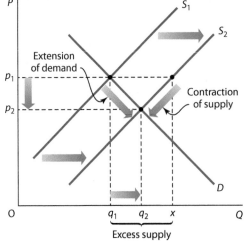

▲ **Figure 2.5.6**: An increase in supply

Figure 2.5.6 shows what happens when there is an increase in supply. For example, technical progress may make computers cheaper to produce, so they are more profitable to sell at each and every price. This increases the supply of computers from S_1 to S_2.

At the old equilibrium price of p_1, there is excess supply of q_1x because supply is now higher than demand. Stocks of unsold computers will start to build up and price will tend to fall. This will cause a contraction of supply as sellers are then likely to make less profit and there will be an extension of demand as more buyers are able and willing to buy computers at a lower price. The market will reach a new equilibrium price of p_2 where q_2 is sold.

If supply increases, the equilibrium price falls and the equilibrium quantity sold rises.

A decrease in supply

Figure 2.5.7 shows what happens when there is a decrease in supply. For example, a rise in wages of farm workers may have decreased the supply of potatoes from S_1 to S_2. Supply is now lower since it is less profitable at each and every price.

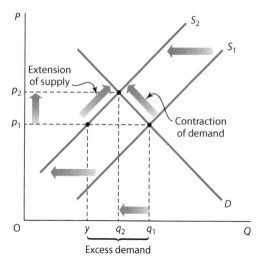

▲ **Figure 2.5.7**: A decrease in supply

At the old equilibrium price of p_1, there is excess demand of yq_1 because demand is now higher than supply. As some buyers who cannot obtain potatoes bid up the price, it will tend to rise. This will cause an extension of supply as sellers hope to make more profit but there will also be a contraction of demand as fewer buyers are then able and willing to pay a higher price for potatoes. The market will reach a new equilibrium price of p_2 where q_2 is sold.

If supply decreases, the equilibrium price rises and the equilibrium quantity sold falls.

Therefore, when there is a shift in one or both of the demand and supply curves, the market price and quantity will adjust to a new equilibrium.

Significance of different price elasticities of demand and supply

When a demand or supply curve shifts, there will be a change in the equilibrium price and quantity sold. However, how much the price and quantity change will depend on the price elasticities of demand and supply for the product.

Significance of PED

Figure 2.5.8 shows what happens to price and quantity sold after an increase in supply according to whether demand is elastic or inelastic.

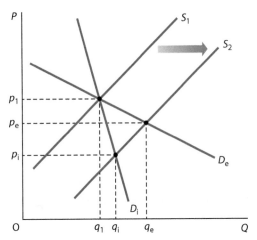

▲ **Figure 2.5.8:** Significance of PED when supply changes

The market for mangoes starts in equilibrium at p_1 and q_1. As a result of a subsidy, supply increases to S_2. This will reduce the equilibrium price and raise the quantity sold at that price.

If demand is elastic, as shown by the demand curve D_e, the percentage change in demand to q_e is greater than the percentage change in price to p_e. If there are substitutes for mangoes, people will buy many more mangoes, even when the price falls by a small amount.

If demand is inelastic, as shown by the demand curve D_i, the percentage change in demand to q_i is less than the percentage change in price to p_i. Even a large fall in the price of the product will lead to relatively little more being bought.

Significance of PES

Similarly, Figure 2.5.9 shows what happens to price and quantity sold after an increase in demand according to whether supply is elastic or inelastic.

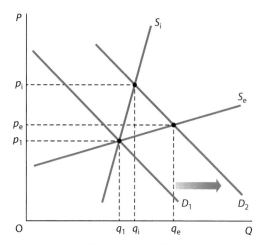

▲ **Figure 2.5.9**: Significance of PES when demand changes

The market for chicken starts in equilibrium at p_1 and q_1. As a result of a successful advertising campaign, demand increases to D_2. This will raise both the equilibrium price and the quantity sold at that price.

If supply is elastic, as shown by the supply curve S_e, the percentage change in supply to q_e is greater than the percentage change in price to p_e. If it is easy to increase the supply of chicken, farmers will want to sell much more chicken, even when the price rises by a small amount.

If supply is inelastic, as shown by the supply curve S_i, the percentage change in supply to q_i is less than the percentage change in price to p_i. Even a large rise in the price of the product will lead to relatively little more being available for sale.

If demand or supply is **elastic**, there will be a **greater percentage change in quantity** sold than price.

If demand or supply is **inelastic**, there will be a **greater percentage change in price** than quantity sold.

Progress questions

1 What happens to equilibrium price and quantity sold if demand increases and supply is:
   i. perfectly elastic
   ii. perfectly inelastic
   iii. of unit elasticity?

2 If there is a decrease in the supply of oil, is there likely to be a greater percentage change in price or quantity sold? Why?

3 If incomes rise, what will happen to the price of a normal good? Show this on a diagram.

4 If wages in the bicycle industry rise by 10% and productivity rises by 50%, is the equilibrium price likely to rise or fall? Why?

Causes of fluctuations in commodity prices, including speculation

Commodities are raw materials, agricultural or mining products, for example copper, oil or wheat. They are primary products.

Many commodities, especially mining products, are only produced in certain countries, where they occur naturally. For example, Russia and Botswana are the world's leading producers of diamonds.

The climate of a country will determine which agricultural products can be produced cheaply and in large quantities. For example, parts of Brazil have just the right temperature and amount of rain to grow coffee.

Commodities are not normally differentiated by brand names and their price is determined by world demand and supply for the commodity.

There are many factors that can affect the demand and supply of a commodity. For example, when **economies are growing rapidly**, incomes will be rising and people can afford to buy more. This will increase the demand for raw materials to make more products. For example, the increased demand for housing and roads in China has increased the demand for sand and other raw materials.

The supply of many commodities, especially agricultural products, can be greatly affected by the **weather**. It takes time to grow another crop or to find and set up another diamond mine. For these reasons, the supply of commodities is often inelastic, at least in the short run. If supply is inelastic and demand changes, there will be a more than proportionate change in price.

Demand may also be inelastic if the resource has no good substitutes. Any change in supply will have a large impact on price.

This can lead to large fluctuations in commodity prices. Figure 2.5.10 shows what happens to price and quantity sold after an increase in demand and a decrease in supply if both are inelastic.

With incomes rising, the demand for pasta in some emerging economies has increased considerably. This will raise the demand for durum wheat needed to make pasta. If there is poor weather in Canada, this will reduce the supply of this type of wheat.

In Figure 2.5.10, the old equilibrium price is p_1, where q_1 is sold. If demand increases and supply decreases, the price of wheat will rise. If both demand and supply are inelastic, this price rise to a new equilibrium of p_2 will be much greater than if demand and supply are elastic.

Whether the quantity sold decreases, increases or stays the same depends on how much demand and supply change. In Figure 2.5.10, the equilibrium quantity sold decreases because supply has fallen by more than demand has risen.

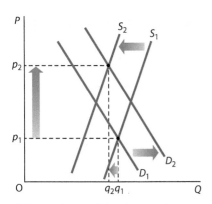

▲ **Figure 2.5.10**: Price change when demand and supply are inelastic

Speculation

Speculation is the buying or selling of an asset to make a profit, by predicting that the price will rise or fall in the future. An **asset** is something of value that is owned.

Commodities, such as oil or gold, are example of assets that often fluctuate in price. If a person or business expects the price of gold to rise, they may buy gold now in the hope of selling it at a higher price in future. They are not interested in using the gold in production but just to make money from the rise in price. This is a risk, since they would lose money if they are wrong and prices fall.

This demand for speculative reasons adds to the total demand for the commodity. If many people buy gold expecting its price to rise, even if nothing else changes, this extra demand may cause the price to rise. Some people may then choose to sell, making the profit they expected. This will increase the supply of gold, which will reduce its price. When a commodity is bought for speculative reasons, this will be another cause of fluctuations in price.

Sometimes, the price of a commodity or other asset can increase quickly over a short period of time, usually due to speculation. This is called an **asset bubble**. Speculators may buy, for example, houses expecting the price to rise even more.

As the price rises, people expect that it will rise even more. This increases demand and raises the price, encouraging others to buy the asset. If the price becomes much higher than the asset is really worth (for example, house prices rise much faster than incomes), the speculative bubble may then burst as many people sell the item and the price falls rapidly.

Key terms

Speculation: the buying or selling of an asset to make a profit, by predicting that the price will rise or fall in the future.

Asset: something of value that is owned.

Asset bubble: when the price of a commodity or other asset increases quickly over a short period of time, usually due to speculation.

Case study: Tulip mania

One of the first asset bubbles happened in the seventeenth century in the Netherlands. Tulips are the country's national flower and were first brought to the country in the late 1500s. At the time, the Netherlands was the richest country in Europe. Many people had money to spare and as new varieties of tulip were developed, people started to buy and sell the bulbs, more for profit than to grow the flowers.

Demand was higher than supply and by the 1620s, the price of tulip bulbs, particularly rare types, was rising steadily. This encouraged even more people to buy the bulbs, hoping that the price would rise even more. Some people mortgaged their homes to buy bulbs to sell at a profit.

At the beginning of 1637, the price of one popular bulb rose from 125 to 1500 florins. Soon after, people started to doubt whether the price could continue to rise. As people lost confidence and started to sell, the price collapsed. Many families lost all their money.

1   Calculate:
    i.   1500 divided by 125
    ii. the percentage increase from 125 to 1500 florins
    iii. what percentage 125 is of 1500, to **one** decimal place.

▲ Figure 2.5.11: Tulips

2   Find out about another asset bubble. When and why did it start? When and why it end? Possible examples include the Wall Street Crash, the dotcom bubble and housing market bubbles in various countries at different times.

This section will develop your knowledge and understanding of:

→ how changes in one market are likely to affect other markets

→ joint demand, competitive demand, composite demand, derived demand and joint supply.

Link

Joint demand and competitive demand were explained in 2.1 "The demand for goods and services".

How changes in one market are likely to affect other markets

Products can be related in a number of different ways. These include the goods being in joint demand; competitive demand; composite demand; derived demand; and joint supply.

If supply or demand changes in one market, this will affect the price and quantity sold of that good. This will then affect the demand or supply of related goods, changing their price and quantity sold in the same or a different way, depending on the relationship between the goods.

Joint demand

Goods in joint demand/complementary goods are products that are bought or used together. If the demand for one good increases, so will demand for the other. Similarly, if the demand for one good falls, demand for the other will also fall. Examples include electric cars and electricity, torches and batteries, and printers and ink cartridges.

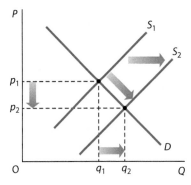

▲ **Figure 2.6.1:** The market for electric cars

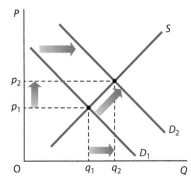

▲ **Figure 2.6.2:** The market for electricity

If supply changes for one of the products, due to a change in costs, this will change its price and quantity sold. This then affects demand for the other product.

In recent years, there have been increasing concerns about the effects on the environment of using petrol and diesel as fuel for cars. Technical progress has led to a fall in the cost of producing electric cars. This increases the supply of electric cars, as shown by the shift from S_1 to S_2 in Figure 2.6.1. This causes excess supply at the old equilibrium price of p_1 leading to the fall in the price and an extension of demand. More electric cars will be sold, other things being equal.

Electric cars run on electricity. With an increase in the use of electric cars, there will also be an increase in the demand for electricity. The demand curve for electricity will shift from D_1 to D_2 in Figure 2.6.2. This will cause excess demand at the old equilibrium price of p_1 and is likely to lead to an increase in the price and quantity sold of electricity.

If the products are in joint demand, if demand for one good changes, demand for the other will change in the same direction. The extent of the change in demand may be different for the two markets. For example, electricity is used for many other products as well as cars.

Competitive demand

Goods in competitive demand/substitute goods are alternative products. If the price of one good rises, so will demand for the other, as people switch to a cheaper alternative. Similarly, if the price of one good falls, so will demand for the other. Examples include travelling by car or bus, potatoes from two different shops and two brands of toothpaste.

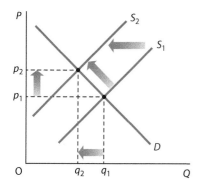

▲ Figure 2.6.3: The market for cars

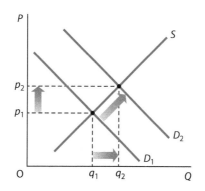

▲ Figure 2.6.4: The market for bus travel

Figure 2.6.3 shows the effects of a government increasing the tax on cars. This will increase firms' costs and shift supply to the left from S_1 to S_2. The excess demand at the old equilibrium price is likely to lead to an increase in price from p_1 to p_2. This causes a contraction in demand and fewer cars will be sold at the higher price.

The increased price of cars will encourage people to look for substitutes and it is likely that the demand for bus travel will rise. This is shown by the shift from D_1 to D_2 in Figure 2.6.4. This again causes excess demand at the old equilibrium price of p_1 and is likely to lead to an increase in the price and quantity of journeys by bus.

Progress questions

1 Draw a diagram to show the effects of a subsidy for bus travel.
2 How is this likely to affect the price and quantity sold of cars?

Activities

Draw two diagrams to show the effects of an increase in the cost of producing electricity on the markets for electricity and for electric cars.

1 What happens to the price and quantity sold of electricity?
2 How does this affect the market for electric cars?

Composite demand

Goods are in **composite demand** if they have more than one use. For example, the demand for wool is composed of the demand for wool for carpets, coats, hats and many other goods. Other products in composite demand are milk (including for cheese, cream and butter) and wood (for boats, furniture and musical instruments).

An increase in demand for one use will raise the price of the product in composite demand and increase the costs of production for the other goods it makes.

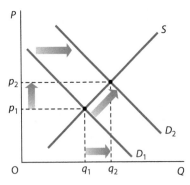

▲ **Figure 2.6.5:** The markets for boats and wood

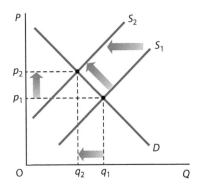

▲ **Figure 2.6.6:** The market for furniture

Figure 2.6.5 shows the effects of an increase in demand for wooden boats. This also increases the demand for wood to make the boats. In both cases, the demand curve shifts to the right from D_1 to D_2. The same diagram can be used for both wood and wooden boats, although the prices and quantities for the two goods will differ.

The excess demand at the old equilibrium price is likely to lead to an increase in price from p_1 to p_2. This causes an extension in supply and more wooden boats and wood will be sold at a higher price.

The higher price of wood will increase the costs of firms making other products that use wood, for example furniture. This is shown by the shift from S_1 to S_2 in Figure 2.6.6. This again causes excess demand at the old equilibrium price of p_1 and is likely to lead to an increase in the price of furniture and a fall in the quantity sold. This will also apply to other products that use wood.

Derived demand

Goods need resources to make them. **Derived demand** is where the demand for a factor of production results from the demand for the product it makes. For example, wood is in derived demand for making wooden boats and furniture and the demand for steel leads to a derived demand for steelworkers.

If the demand decreases for a good, there will be a decrease in demand for the factors of production that make it. For example, a decrease in the demand for steel will decrease the demand for steelworkers, and the raw materials and equipment needed to make steel.

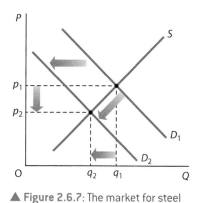

▲ **Figure 2.6.7**: The market for steel

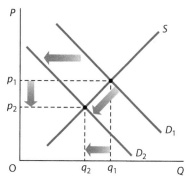

▲ **Figure 2.6.8**: The market for steelworkers

Figure 2.6.7 shows the decreased demand for steel and Figure 2.6.8 shows the decreased demand for steelworkers (and all the other factors of production used to make steel). In both markets, there will be excess supply at the old equilibrium price of p_1 after a decrease in demand from D_1 to D_2. If less steel is being produced, there will be less demand for steelworkers to make it. This will decrease the price and the quantity sold of both steel and the resources needed to make steel.

Joint supply

Goods are in **joint supply** when the output of one good results in the output of another good. The products are either produced/found together or one is a by-product of the other (produced when making something else). For example, lead and zinc ores are usually found together and when wheat is grown, after the grain has been removed, the stalks that remain of the crop (straw) can be used for fuel, to feed animals, or to make baskets.

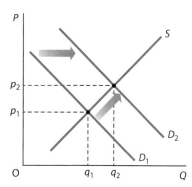

▲ **Figure 2.6.9**: The market for wheat

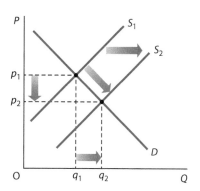

▲ **Figure 2.6.10**: The market for straw

Figure 2.6.9 shows the effects of an increase in demand for wheat from D_1 to D_2. This causes an increase in the price of wheat from p_1 to p_2, which leads to an extension of supply from q_1 to q_2. The extension in supply of wheat also results in more straw being supplied. Figure 2.6.10 shows the resulting increase in the supply of straw from S_1 to S_2 leading to a fall in its price and an increase in the quantity sold.

Key term

Joint supply: when the output of one good results in the output of another good.

Quantitative skills

A ratio gives one value in proportion to another. The second number shows how many times greater it is than the first. For example, if half as much lead as zinc is found in the same ore, then the ratio of lead to zinc is written as 1:2 or 1 to 2. If in a certain quantity of ore there is 60g of lead and 80g of zinc, this cancels down to 3:4 for the ratio of lead: zinc.

A question may give a specific instruction in terms of the final answer. For example, if asked to calculate the ratio of 60g of lead to 80g of zinc in relation to how much 1g of lead is equal to in terms of zinc, to **one** decimal place, then the answer would be 1:1.3.

Case study: The Kenyan flower industry

Flowers grown in Kenya are sold in over 60 countries and the country is the leading supplier of flowers to the European Union. The Kenyan climate allows flowers to be grown throughout the year. The industry has been growing steadily for many years both in terms of the number and value of flowers produced, although competition is increasing from countries such as Colombia and Ecuador. There are around 100 000 people working on flower farms as part of the total of 500 000 jobs in the flower industry in Kenya.

Mwangi and Kimani Flowers have a flower farm near Lake Naivasha. The business grows roses, lilies and carnations, which are mainly sold abroad. They employ 50 workers and have a packaging shed where the flowers are assembled into bouquets. They also produce gift cards which are included with some of the bouquets of flowers.

1 Use the information in the case study to identify:
   i. a pair of complementary goods
   ii. a pair of substitute goods
   iii. an example of derived demand.
2 What is the ratio of people working on flower farms to the total number working in the flower industry in Kenya?
3 For each 50 workers employed at the flower farm, how many more jobs in Kenya is this likely to support?

▲ **Figure 2.6.11:** The market for flowers

Factor markets and goods markets

In a market economy, there are two main markets – for the factors of production and the final goods and services. There are three economic agents involved in these markets – buyers of goods and services, sellers of goods and services and the owners of the factors of production.

The buyers in the factor market are the producers that want these resources to make goods and services. The sellers in factor market are the owners of the resources. In the goods/product market, the buyers are the consumers of the goods and services and the sellers are the firms. The firms/producers are therefore involved in both the factor and the goods market.

The rationing, incentive and signalling functions

There are three main functions of the price mechanism – rationing, incentive and signalling. These help to coordinate the decisions of buyers and sellers in a market economy. When the price changes, these functions affect the decisions of the buyers and sellers in that market and what happens to the allocation of the goods and services, and factors of production.

The rationing function refers to the allocation of scarce resources and finished goods to those able and willing to pay. For example, if demand increases, price rises causing some potential buyers to drop out of the market. If price falls, rationing is less severe and more people will be able and willing to buy the product.

The signalling function is the idea that changes in price provide information to buyers and sellers in a market. The changes by many consumers and producers resulting in a change in the price of a good, are brought together as a single piece of information.

The incentive function means that changes in price make producers or sellers of factors of production more or less likely to sell their goods or services. For example, an increase in price will encourage sellers to supply more because if prices are higher, they are likely to make a higher profit. Similarly, a fall in prices will provide less incentive to firms and owners of factors of production to supply more goods and services.

Key terms

Factor market: the market for buying and selling resources/factors of production.

Goods/product market: the market for buying and selling goods and services.

Rationing function: the allocation of scarce resources and finished goods to those able and willing to pay.

Signalling function: the idea that changes in price provide information to buyers and sellers in a market.

Incentive function: the idea that changes in price make producers or sellers of factors of production more or less likely to sell their goods or services.

Link

The price mechanism was introduced in 1.3 "Scarcity, choice and the allocation of resources", and the incentive function in 2.3 "The supply of goods and services".

Link

The economic problem was explained in 1.3 "Scarcity, choice and the allocation of resources".

How the price mechanism is the way in which the basic economic problem is resolved in a market economy

The basic economic problem is that resources are scarce but wants are many. Decisions have to be made about how best to allocate these scarce resources to alternative uses. In a market economy, this is done by supply and demand, through the workings of the price mechanism and its functions of rationing, signalling and incentives, with little, if any, involvement of governments.

Example

As biofuel has become a more popular fuel, there has been an increase in demand for crops such as sugar cane which can be used to make biofuel. Figure 2.7.1 shows what happens to the sugar cane and its related factor markets.

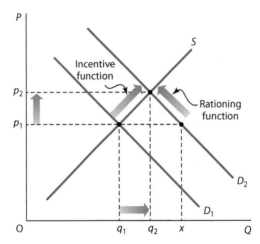

▲ **Figure 2.7.1:** The sugar cane market

As demand for sugar cane increases from D_1 to D_2, there will be excess demand of q_1x. This will force the price upwards. As price rises, this is signalling to buyers and sellers of sugar cane that something in the market has changed. The higher price acts as an incentive for suppliers to offer more sugar cane for sale, causing an extension in supply.

The higher price also acts as a rationing device, since some buyers will no longer be willing or able to buy the sugar cane at the higher price. There will be a contraction in demand. Through the functions of signalling, incentives and rationing, a new equilibrium price of p_2 will be reached where q_2 is sold.

These changes also affect the factor market. Figure 2.7.1 could also represent the demand for the factors of production needed to produce sugar cane. As demand rises for sugar cane, there will also be an increase in demand for the factors of production involved, since their demand is derived from the demand for sugar cane. This will include the land on which to grow the sugar cane, as well as labour and equipment.

For example, as demand for land to grow sugar cane increases, its price will rise. This will signal to farmers wishing to grow sugar cane and owners of land that something has changed in the market. As price rises the owners of the land will have more incentive to use or sell their land for sugar cane production. Also, as price rises, some potential buyers will be rationed out of the market.

Advantages and disadvantages of the price mechanism

The price mechanism works automatically to allocate scarce resources to those willing and able to pay. In this way, the choices of millions of buyers and sellers of millions of products are coordinated, without intervention from governments.

Adam Smith, the eighteenth-century Scottish economist, referred to the process as "the invisible hand of the market". Individuals act out of self-interest and the combination of goods and services produced as a result will benefit society as a whole. It is an impersonal way of allocating resources, goods and services which is simple and happens automatically. There is no need for a government or central authority to be involved, which would use up further resources.

If resource allocation is left to the price mechanism, there is **consumer sovereignty**. This means that consumers determine which goods and services are produced and in which quantities. Spending on a product is a "vote" for more of that good to be supplied.

There is freedom of choice. Consumers can buy what they want but only if they have enough money. Producers can supply what they want but, to make a profit, they will supply what is in demand. Competition will help to keep prices low and resources should be used efficiently. No regulation is needed.

However, the price mechanism also has disadvantages. If left to the market forces of supply and demand, some products will be overproduced when compared to what would benefit society. Others will be underproduced or not produced at all.

Inequality of income and wealth will mean that some people cannot afford to buy as much as others, or even basic necessities. This is because goods and services are allocated on the basis of ability to pay, and not need. This gives people with more income and wealth more influence in determining what goods and services are provided.

It is assumed that competition between firms will lower prices. In some markets, large firms may develop. As they try to increase profit, prices may rise. If there are many firms, resources may be wasted on advertising to persuade consumers to buy from a particular firm.

If the price mechanism is not used to allocate resources, the government or central authority will need to do this for all or some goods and services.

> ### Key term
>
> **Consumer sovereignty:** when consumers determine what is produced through their spending.

> ### Link
>
> Examples of why markets may fail to produce the "right" quantity for society are explained in 5.1 "The meaning of market failure".

▼ Table 2.7.1: Advantages and disadvantages of the price mechanism

Advantages	Disadvantages
• Automatic allocation of resources • Consumer sovereignty • Freedom of choice • Supply of goods/services matches people's preferences • Resources used efficiently • No regulation needed	• Some goods/services overproduced, underproduced or not produced at all • Some people unable to afford basic necessities • Rich people have more influence on what is produced • Potential for large firms to develop and exploit customers • Resources wasted on advertising

Case study: Magnificent Margaret

Margaret has a small business, Magnificent Margaret. She works from home making birthday cards to sell in a local shop.

Recently, Margaret introduced a new shape of birthday card. She wasn't sure whether to charge a higher price or not. She agreed with the shop owner to start selling these cards at the same price as her other cards for three months. The new shape of card proved to be popular and sold out in two months, even though the shop, with Margaret's agreement, increased the price of the cards after one month.

▲ Figure 2.7.2: Birthday cards

Using the example of the new shape of birthday card, explain how the price mechanism works. Include **at least two** functions of the price mechanism in your explanation.

Extending the use of the price mechanism into new areas of activity

In recent years, the use of the price mechanism has been extended to new areas of activity.

Example 1 – cleaning services provided by the NHS

In the UK, the National Health Service (NHS), funded by the government, used to provide its own catering and cleaning services. Since the 1980s, the NHS has employed other firms to do these jobs.

Firms bid for the contract, which creates a market in this service. A firm is then chosen to do the work for a set period of time. It was hoped that this would result in competition to obtain the work and then it would be done more cheaply and/or better.

In the 1990s, there was an increase in hospital infections, some of which, according to an international study, were linked to cleaning. This was an **unintended consequence**, an unexpected effect of introducing a market for cleaning for the NHS. Unintended consequences may be good, bad or even lead to the opposite effect.

Sometimes, the expected benefits of an action, such as introducing markets, may be offset or outweighed by unexpected disadvantages. It is important that there are regular reviews to check the quality of the service being provided.

Example 2 – fines for lateness
Many child-care centres charge or fine parents if children are collected late. A study of six child-care centres in Israel showed that when they started to charge people for lateness, it did not have the desired effect. It led to more people arriving late to pick up their children.

Some child-care centres in Canada started charging in the 1980s, to cover the overtime they had to pay staff. Charging $1 a minute was intended to encourage people not to be late. It could also pay for the worker's time. It was expected that the charge would encourage more parents to arrive on time.

Before the charges/fines were introduced, parents relied on the goodwill of the workers to stay late and would usually try to arrive on time, so they did not exploit this. Now they were able to buy this time, many viewed it as part of the total cost of the care and made less effort to arrive on time. They no longer had to feel guilty or apologise directly to the person who had spent extra time looking after their child.

Introducing the price mechanism for the additional time had unexpected/unintended consequences. To be effective, a high charge/fine must be used.

> ### Key term
> **Unintended consequence**: an unexpected effect of an action.

> ### Activity
> Investigate another area in your economy where the price mechanism has been extended in recent years. Have there been any unintended consequences?

> ### Progress questions
> 1   List the **three** functions of the price mechanism.
> 2   List at least **two** advantages and **two** disadvantages of using the price mechanism to allocate resources.

Exam-style questions

1 Which one of the following would cause an extension of supply of pineapples?

   A A fall in the price of pineapples   **C** A tax on pineapples

   B A subsidy on pineapples   **D** An increase in demand for pineapples   [1 mark]

2 Rice and pasta are substitute goods. If the price of rice increases, what is likely to happen to the price and quantity sold of pasta?   [1 mark]

	Price	Quantity sold
A	Fall	Fall
B	Fall	Rise
C	Rise	Fall
D	Rise	Rise

3 The price of a product rises by 5% and as a result, total revenue rises by 6%. What is the price elasticity of demand for the product?

   A Elastic   **C** Perfectly inelastic

   B Inelastic   **D** Unit elasticity   [1 mark]

4 Define "market forces".   [3 marks]

5 The quantity supplied of silver rises by 18% as a result of a price rise from $500/kg to $575/kg. Calculate the price elasticity of supply of silver.   [4 marks]

6 In a particular country, there are two main brands of washing powder. The table below shows the price of one brand, Washo, and the sales of another, Cleano, over a five-year period.

Year	Price of Washo ($ per kg)	Sales of Cleano (millions of kg)
2015	4	2
2016	4.50	2.3
2017	5	2.2
2018	4.75	2
2019	6	2.4

(i) Explain why changes in the price of Washo might affect the sales of Cleano.   [6 marks]

(ii) To what extent do the data suggest that changes in the price of Washo affect the sales of Cleano? Use the data in the table to support your answer.   [6 marks]

7 With the help of a diagram, explain how a fall in the price of copper will affect the market for copper pipes.   [9 marks]

8 Analyse the likely effects on the market for woollen carpets of an increase in popularity of woollen coats.   [12 marks]

3 An introduction to production, costs, revenue and profit

The operation of markets, market failure and the role of government

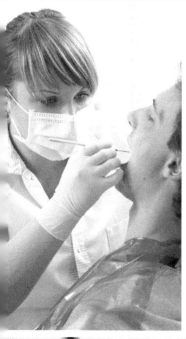

This section will develop your knowledge and understanding of:

→ how production converts inputs, such as raw materials, capital and labour, into final output
→ the importance of the natural environment in sustaining economic activity
→ the meaning of productivity, including labour productivity.

Link

Production was introduced in 1.1 "The nature and purpose of economic activity" and the factors of production were covered in 1.2 "Economic resources".

Production

Production involves turning inputs, such as raw materials, capital and labour, into final output.

The inputs or economic resources (factors of production) are: land (natural resources); capital (human-made resources); labour (human resources); and enterprise or the entrepreneur (the organiser or risk-taker). These inputs are combined to create goods and services.

For example, a person decides to open a business selling furniture. As an entrepreneur, they make the decisions about what to produce and how to produce it. They take the risks involved and the resulting profit or loss.

The entrepreneur may employ additional workers (labour). They will need raw materials such as wood and somewhere to carry out their business (land). The business will also need equipment, to cut and shape the wood (capital).

The importance of the natural environment

Provision of inputs

Economic activity is concerned with the production, distribution and consumption of goods and services. The furniture business is an example of economic activity. The natural environment plays an important part in sustaining economic activity. It provides inputs for the productive process.

Link

Economic activity was introduced in 1.1 "The nature and purpose of economic activity" and the environment as a scarce resource in 1.2 "Economic resources".

For example, the wood to make the furniture comes from the environment. It may have been growing naturally or land may have been set aside to plant trees, to provide wood to make furniture and other wooden products. Trees needs the right growing conditions to produce good-quality wood.

Other products of the environment include minerals, such as iron, copper and diamonds, and agricultural products. Iron can be used to make steel, which can be used in the building, medical and transport industries. We rely on agricultural products for our food.

Productive activity as a source of potential damage

As the world's population and incomes have grown, so has the demand for inputs. Although some resources are renewable, such as sunlight and wind for energy, others are not. This may be because once they are used, they cannot be replaced, such as coal and oil, or because renewable resources are being used up more quickly than they can be replaced. This applies to some fish in parts of the world.

Economic activity may damage the environment. Mining and quarrying can cause pollution, both when the minerals are extracted and also by leaving behind an unattractive landscape. However, in some areas, old quarries have been filled with water to become nature reserves, which can then be used for leisure.

Link

Renewable and non-renewable resources were covered in 1.2 "Economic resources".

Case study: Palm oil – good or bad?

▲ **Figure 3.1.1**: Oil palm trees

Palm oil has many uses including for cooking oil, washing powder, soap and biofuel. With growing populations and health concerns about substitute goods, the demand for palm oil for food has doubled over the last 15 years. It is also the most productive oil crop. The fruit from the oil palm tree produces 10 times as much oil as sunflowers and 11 times more oil than soybean plants. Oil palms also need less fertiliser.

To produce more palm oil, more of these trees have been planted. This has resulted in cutting down forests that are the homes of animals such as orangutans. Forests help to keep the air clean and reduce soil erosion. With forests being cleared, there is also a greater risk of fires in the dry season. This can cause clouds of ash in some areas, which then cause breathing problems. When the palm trees grow too high, they are cut down for more to be planted.

1 Around 0.25% of the world's farmland is used to grow palm trees to produce oil and 0.5% is used for sunflowers. Use the information in the case study to calculate how many times more oil is obtained in the world from palm trees than sunflowers.

2 Identify **two** advantages and **two** disadvantages of producing more palm oil.

3 Draw a supply and demand diagram to show the effects of an increase in the use of palm oil on the market for soybeans used to produce oil.

4 Assess whether more should be done to control the amount of land used for palm oil.

The meaning of productivity

Productivity measures how much a unit of a factor of production produces in a given time. Unlike production, productivity compares the inputs to the output. It can therefore be used as a measure of efficiency. Production is the total amount produced in a given time, regardless of the inputs that were used.

Labour productivity is how much a worker produces in a given time. For example, the production of a furniture business may be six tables in a week. If there are two full-time workers, the productivity of a worker/labour productivity is three tables a week. A year later, perhaps due to more training or experience, the production rises to eight tables a week. If the firm still has two workers, labour productivity is four tables per worker per week. The workers are now more productive than before.

Activities

Choose another agricultural product or raw material.

1 Find out which parts of the world it is grown in or mined.

2 What are its uses?

3 Has there been any damage to the environment as a result?

Get it right

Do not confuse production with productivity. They are linked but are not the same.

Productivity can also apply to other factors of production. For example, it can be used as a measure of how much an area of land or a piece of equipment can produce in a given time.

Link

Productivity, including labour productivity, was introduced in 2.3 "The supply of goods and services" and will be looked at again in 6.2 "Macroeconomic indicators", when considering data commonly used to measure the performance of an economy.

Progress questions

1 How are production and the natural environment linked?
2 Explain the difference between production and productivity.

Case study: The amazing growth of maize

▲ **Figure 3.1.2:** Maize

The United States is the world's largest maize producer, followed by China and Brazil. In 1940, the average amount of maize produced per hectare (yield) in the United States was 2 tonnes. In 1980, it was 5.7 tonnes per hectare and it is now 10 tonnes per hectare.

1 Give **two** reasons why the yield of maize may have increased in this time.
2 What was the percentage increase in the yield of maize between 1940 and 1980?
3 If 39,000,000 hectares are used to grow maize in the United States, use the current yield to calculate the production of maize.

3.2 Specialisation, division of labour and exchange

This section will develop your knowledge and understanding of:

→ the benefits and costs of specialisation and division of labour

→ why specialisation requires an efficient means of exchanging goods and services, including the use of money as a medium of exchange.

Specialisation and division of labour

Specialisation is where different firms, regions, countries or factors of production concentrate on the production of different goods or services. This happens because different firms, regions, countries or factors of production have different natural advantages or strengths.

For example, Chile produces approximately a third of the world's copper, and copper mining provides between 10% and 20% of the country's income. If minerals are not found in a country, it will need to buy them from other countries. The landscape of Chile varies from snow-topped mountains to dry deserts. Some regions, such as Patagonia in the south and the Atacama Desert in the north, have been very successful in promoting the natural beauty of their area and have attracted increasing numbers of foreign tourists in recent years. This has created more jobs and increased local incomes. Although Chile also produces other goods and services, some regions specialise in copper mining and tourism.

Firms and factors of production will also specialise. A firm may assemble cars or perhaps make a particular part for a car, such as car tyres. Machines may be designed for a specific purpose and they have replaced workers in many jobs in recent years, such as self-service tills in shops.

Division of labour is when a worker performs one task or a narrow range of tasks as part of the production process. Instead of making whole tables, a worker may specialise in making the legs for tables.

▲ **Figure 3.2.1**: Adam Smith

Activity

Adam Smith wrote about the impact of division of labour in a pin-making factory in his 1776 book *An Inquiry into the Nature and Causes of the Wealth of Nations*. Find out how division of labour in the factory increased productivity.

Get it right

Division of labour is the application of specialisation to workers in the production process. Specialisation is a general term and division of labour is an example of specialisation.

Key terms

Specialisation: where different firms, regions, countries or factors of production concentrate on the production of different goods or services.

Division of labour: when a worker performs one task or a narrow range of tasks as part of the production process.

Activities

1 Make a list of **at least six** different jobs in your school or college.

2 Choose another good or service and make a list of **at least six** different jobs involved in supplying that good or service.

Benefits and costs of specialisation and division of labour

Benefits

Countries can take full advantage of their resources and focus on what they do best. If specialisation occurs on a world basis, this increases the size of the market for each producer. Any surplus goods can be sold to other countries.

Firms and workers will "learn by doing" more quickly if they focus on one or a narrow range of tasks. Training will take less time. If workers are more skilled, this may lead to more pay, which may increase motivation. It may also enable the use of specialist machinery.

Production should be quicker, increasing productivity. If more is produced in a given time from a set amount of inputs, the cost of producing each unit (average cost or unit cost) will fall. Producing on a large scale may lead to even greater savings. This will enable firms to reduce prices for consumers. They may also benefit from a greater variety and quality of products.

If countries, regions, firms and factors of production concentrate on what they do best, then specialisation, including division of labour, will help to make the best use of the world's scarce resources.

> **Key term**
>
> **Average cost or unit cost**: the cost of producing each unit, total cost divided by the number of units produced.

> **Link**
>
> Average costs will be covered in 3.3 "Costs of production" and 3.4 "Economies and diseconomies of scale".

> **Activities**
>
> 1 Find out which products your country specialises in.
> 2 Why has your country focused on these products?

Costs

Overspecialisation may cause problems. A country or region that focuses on one or a few products for its income may have nothing else to rely on, for example, if a natural resource runs out or its price falls. Specialisation may lead to products being mass produced with less variety available.

Specialisation leads to interdependence, where individuals or firms depend on each other. For example, if there is only one firm producing a part needed in the next stage of the production process, and there is a hold-up in its production, the firms involved later in the process will be unable to carry out their work until more parts become available.

> **Key term**
>
> **Interdependence**: when two things, for example individuals or firms, depend on each other.

There is a human cost. Workers carrying out the same tasks all day every day may become bored and boredom can result in a loss of job satisfaction. This can also lead to mistakes and poorer-quality products. Workers may take more time off (higher absenteeism) and stay in jobs for shorter periods of time (higher labour turnover). Firms will then have to spend more money recruiting and training new workers.

If a machine can be developed that can carry out the same task as the workers, they may lose their job. They could have few skills to offer in a different job. Countries, regions, firms and workers will be vulnerable to changes in demand.

▼ **Table 3.2.1**: Summary of benefits and costs of division of labour

Benefits	Costs
• Production is quicker	• Workers may become bored
• Less training time is needed for workers	• They may lack job satisfaction
• Average cost is lower	• They have few skills to offer in other jobs
• Consumers benefit from firms' reduced prices	• They could be replaced by machines
• Firms are more able to use specialist machinery	• There is less variety of products
• Resources are used efficiently	• Interdependence can cause problems

Case study: Division of labour — how far to go?

▲ **Figure 3.2.2**: The result of teamwork

Economic theory suggests that division of labour will increase productivity and reduce average cost. However, repetitive work that requires little skill is boring and can lead to a lack of job satisfaction.

About 30 years ago, Volvo, the Swedish automotive company, was one of a few firms experimenting with organising their workers into teams, often in threes, instead of having people working individually.

The teams could organise themselves how they wished, in order to produce the target output for that session. Instead of working all day, for example, on fitting the back lights of the car, workers could work on all parts of the electrical system. Workers could take breaks when they liked and every team had its own workshop and sauna.

Now, teamwork is much more common. About 80% of the world's work is done by teams.

1   What are the advantages of an automotive company using teams instead of people working individually?

2   What are the disadvantages of a business allocating work to teams instead of to individuals?

3   Assess whether there should be more division of labour or whether more work should be allocated to teams.

The need for an efficient means of exchanging goods and services

In early history, families and communities had to be self-sufficient. They had to provide everything they needed. This meant that what they had was very limited.

If different firms, regions, countries or factors of production concentrate on the production of different goods and/or services, there needs to be some way of obtaining the other goods and services they need or want. This involves trading what has been produced.

Trading could involve barter, which is the exchange of goods and services for other goods and services. This requires a double coincidence of wants. You have to find someone who has what you want and will accept what you have to trade. This is difficult. There also needs to be a good transport and communication system, for you to find the other person or firm and to be able to exchange the products easily.

Over time, a medium of exchange developed. This is something not wanted for itself but to be used as a way of obtaining other goods and services. Money acts as a medium of exchange. We use it to buy what we need and want, and to receive payment for what we sell. Without an efficient means of exchanging goods and services, such as money, specialisation could only take place to a very limited extent.

> **Key terms**
>
> **Self-sufficient:** providing for your own needs.
>
> **Barter:** the exchange of goods and services for other goods and services.

> **Key terms**
>
> **Double coincidence of wants:** having to find someone who has what you want and will accept what you have to trade.
>
> **Medium of exchange:** something not wanted for itself but to be used as a way of obtaining other goods and services.

> **Progress questions**
>
> 1 What is the difference between specialisation and division of labour?
> 2 Explain **two** advantages and **two** disadvantages of specialisation for a country.
> 3 Explain **two** advantages and **two** disadvantages of division of labour.
> 4 What is necessary for specialisation to take place?

3.3 Costs of production

This section will develop your knowledge and understanding of:
→ the difference between the short run and the long run
→ the difference between fixed and variable costs
→ the difference between average and total costs.

The difference between the short run and the long run

In Economics, there are two main time periods. In the short run, at least one factor of production is fixed in supply. For example, a business may have a certain amount of equipment in a limited work area. In the short run, it may only be possible to increase or decrease production by changing the amount of labour.

In the long run, all factors of production are variable. It is possible to change all the factors of production in response to changes in demand. For example, another factory could be built and more equipment bought to increase the capacity of the business.

The short run and long run are not set periods of time in terms of weeks or years. They vary according to the product. For example, it takes about six years after a rubber tree is planted before any latex from it can be harvested. In this case, the short run is six years.

The difference between fixed and variable costs

Fixed costs

Fixed costs (FC) are (short-run) costs that do not change with output. They must be paid even when there is no output. For example, if the factory is closed for some reason, there will still be some costs to pay. Fixed costs are sometimes known as overheads.

Fixed costs are associated with the fixed factors of production. They include the rent of the factory or office, and interest on loans. Average fixed costs (AFC) are the fixed costs per unit of output. They are calculated by dividing the total fixed costs by the number of units produced (Q).

$$AFC = \frac{FC}{Q}$$

For example, if fixed costs are $6,000 a month and 20 items are produced in this time, the average fixed costs are $300.

Although fixed costs stay the same in the short run, average fixed costs do not. The greater the output, the lower the average fixed costs because the fixed costs are spread over a greater number of units. For example, if fixed costs are $6,000 a month and 50 items are produced, the average fixed costs fall to $120.

Figures 3.3.1 and 3.3.2 show the relationship between fixed costs and average fixed costs. Fixed costs stay the same. If the fixed costs are $6,000 a month, FC is a horizontal line at this amount. Average

Link

Time periods, including the short run and the long run, were introduced in 2.4 "Price elasticity of supply".

Key terms

Fixed costs: costs that do not change with output.

Average fixed costs: fixed costs per unit of output.

fixed costs fall as output increases, rapidly to start with and then more gradually, as the fixed costs are spread over an increasing number of units. Note the difference in scale on the vertical axes.

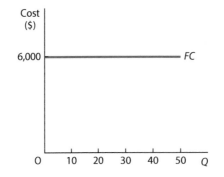

▲ **Figure 3.3.1**: Fixed costs (FC)

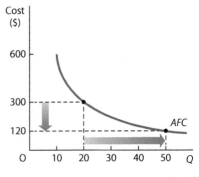

▲ **Figure 3.3.2**: Average fixed costs (AFC)

Variable costs

Variable costs (VC) are costs that change with output. As output rises, so do variable costs. If the factory is closed, there will be no variable costs to pay.

Variable costs are associated with the variable factors of production. They include wages, raw materials and packaging costs. **Average variable costs** (AVC) are the variable costs per unit of output. They are calculated by dividing the total variable costs by the number of units produced (Q).

$$AVC = \frac{VC}{Q}$$

For example, if variable costs are €4,000 a month and 200 items are produced in this time, the average variable costs are €20.

It is likely that average variable costs will fall as output increases but after a certain point, they are likely to rise. In the long run, all costs are variable because all factors of production are variable.

Progress questions

1 What is the difference between the short run and the long run?
2 Give an example of:
   i.   a fixed cost
   ii. a variable cost.
3 If the average fixed costs of producing 20 units are $500, what are the total costs when output is zero?

Quantitative skills

As with supply and demand diagrams, when drawing cost and revenue diagrams, the quantity is always put on the horizontal axis. The vertical axis should be labelled cost, revenue, or cost and revenue, whichever is appropriate for the curves drawn. Alternatively, a currency sign can be used, for example $.

Case study: Sven's TT bats (part one)

Table tennis is the most popular racquet sport. It is played throughout the world, particularly in Asia and Europe, and became an Olympic sport in Seoul, in 1988.

Sven owns a business making table tennis bats. Table 3.3.1 lists the fixed and variable costs for different levels of his firm's output per month but some of the figures are missing.

▼ **Table 3.3.1:** Fixed and variable costs of Sven's TT bats, per month

Output (units)	FC (€)	AFC (€)	VC (€)	AVC (€)
0				
100			2,500	
200	1,000	5	4,000	20
300			5,250	
400			6,000	
500	1,000	2	8,000	

1 Copy and complete the table (apart from the two shaded boxes).

2 Use the information to draw:
  i. a graph of AFC and AVC
  ii. a graph of FC and VC.

▲ **Figure 3.3.3:** An Olympic sport

The difference between total and average costs

Total costs

Short-run costs can be variable costs or fixed costs, depending on whether or not they increase with output. The **total costs** (TC) of a business relate to all costs and are therefore made up of the fixed costs plus the variable costs.

$$TC = FC + VC$$

For example, in Table 3.3.1, the total costs of producing 200 units of output per month are €5,000 (€1,000 + €4,000).

In the short run, as output increases, fixed costs stay the same but variable costs increase, so total costs will also increase with output. In the long run, when there are no fixed factors of production, all costs are variable. For example, in the long run, if the firm increases output it may need to rent a new factory, so rent increases.

Average costs

Average costs (AC) are the costs of producing each unit of output and are sometimes called unit costs. They are calculated by dividing the total costs by the number of units produced.

$$AC = \frac{TC}{Q}$$

For example, in Table 3.3.1, the average costs of producing 200 units are €25 (€5,000 ÷ 200).

Key term

Total costs: all the costs of a business, fixed costs plus variable costs.

Link

Average costs were introduced in 3.2 "Specialisation, division of labour and exchange".

Average costs include both fixed and variable costs, so can also be calculated as the average fixed costs plus the average variable costs.

$$AC = AFC + AVC$$

Again, using Table 3.3.1, the average costs of producing 200 units can be calculated as €5 + €20 = €25.

Case study: Sven's TT bats (part two)

Table 3.3.2 lists the total and average costs for different output levels of Sven's table tennis bat business. The figures relate to possible outputs of bats per month but again, some of the figures are missing.

▼ **Table 3.3.2:** Total and average costs of Sven's TT bats, per month

Output (units)	TC (€)	AC (€)
0		
100		
200	5,000	25
300		
400		
500		

▲ **Figure 3.3.4**: Table tennis bats

With the help of your completed table from the previous case study (Table 3.3.1), calculate the missing figures (apart from average costs for zero units).

Quantitative skills

You should be able to calculate average and total costs.

A note on the shape of the average cost curves

Both the short-run average cost (SRAC) curve and long-run average cost (LRAC) curve may be U-shaped but for different reasons.

Short run

In the short run, at least one factor of production is fixed in supply. Short-run average costs are made up of average fixed costs and average variable costs. In the short run, average fixed costs fall as output increases because the fixed costs are spread over a greater number of units.

Average variable costs are also likely to fall, as better use is made of the fixed factors of production. Also, if labour is the variable factor, more division of labour can take place, helping an extra worker to add more to output than the previous one. After an optimal point where there is the ideal combination of the variable factor and fixed factors, average variable cost will start to rise.

When there are fixed factors of production, extra workers will not be able to keep increasing output at the same rate. Eventually, an extra worker will add less to output than the existing average and average variable costs will rise. If this is not offset by the fall in average fixed costs, then average costs will also rise. The output where short-run average costs is minimised is shown as q on Figure 3.3.5. This means that the SRAC curve is likely to be U-shaped.

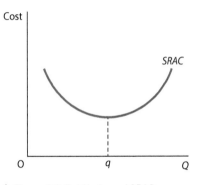

▲ **Figure 3.3.5**: A U-shaped SRAC curve

Link

The link between the law of diminishing returns and the shape of the SRAC curve is explained in the A2 part of the course.

Long run

In the long run, all the factors of production are variable. A firm may decide that a certain combination of land, labour and capital works best. The firm can then increase the number of these combinations it employs if demand increases. Again, it is likely, but not certain, that the long-run average cost will fall initially as output increases but after a certain point, average costs may rise. However, this depends on the good or service being produced and the extent of the economies or diseconomies of scale.

Link

There is more on the shape of the LRAC curve in 3.4 "Economies and diseconomies of scale" and the relationship between the SRAC and LRAC curves is covered in the A2 part of the course.

Progress questions

4   State **two** ways of calculating total costs.
5   If fixed costs are $10,000 and the average variable costs of producing 100 units are $120, calculate:
   i.   total costs
   ii. average costs.

The difference between internal and external economies of scale

Economies of scale are a fall in long-run average costs due to the growth of a firm or the industry in which it operates. This can be separated into internal and external economies of scale.

Internal economies of scale are a fall in long-run average costs due to the growth of the firm.

External economies of scale are a fall in long-run average costs due to the growth of the whole industry. All firms can benefit from the growth of the industry, in the form of lower long-run average costs.

Key terms

Economies of scale: a fall in long-run average costs due to the growth of a firm or industry.

Internal economies of scale: a fall in long-run average costs due to the growth of a firm.

External economies of scale: a fall in long-run average costs due to the growth of an industry.

▲ **Figure 3.4.1**: An increase in the scale of production

Internal economies of scale

There are many reasons why a firm producing on a larger scale could reduce its costs per unit. These relate to different aspects of the business and can be classified under the following headings.

- Technical
- Marketing
- Financial
- Risk-bearing
- Managerial

Technical economies

Technical economies are lower average costs due to the production process being carried out on a larger scale. Average costs fall because more units are being produced. For example, some pieces of equipment have a large capacity, the capital is indivisible (not available in smaller sizes). If the firm produces more units, more effective use is made of the equipment, spreading its cost over more units of output.

Some items of equipment and transport have a variety of sizes. Being able to use larger pieces of equipment or transport may reduce average costs. For example, an oil tanker that is twice the length, width and height of another tanker holds eight times as much oil. A lorry with twice the capacity of a smaller one does not need two drivers.

Producing larger quantities will enable the firm to take more advantage of division of labour. As workers become more specialised, their productivity should rise.

Marketing economies

Marketing economies are obtained by spreading the selling or buying costs over more units of output. For example, making more of the same product or a greater variety of products carrying the firm's name helps to reduce advertising costs per unit.

Larger firms buying raw materials or parts in large quantities may be able to obtain these at cheaper prices than smaller firms. A bulk-buying discount is even more likely if the firm buys a large proportion of another firm's output because this gives the buying firm a strong bargaining position.

Financial economies

Financial economies arise because larger firms find it cheaper and easier to finance growth. They may be able to negotiate a lower rate of interest on a loan. This is partly because they have more assets, so are more likely to be able to pay back the loan. Also, from the lender's point of view, it is cheaper to arrange a few large loans than many smaller loans, so some of these savings can be passed on to the borrower.

Larger firms may also have more sources of funds. For example, they may be able to obtain money by selling shares in the firm. They may also be able to borrow from a wider variety of institutions.

Risk-bearing economies

Larger firms will find it easier to spread the risks and uncertainties of trading. They may sell a wider variety of products than a smaller firm and/or sell in more countries or regions. Increases and decreases in demand are more likely to balance out, making total demand more stable.

If a firm sells only one product in one country and demand for this product falls, it is at more risk of going out of business. A fall in demand is likely to raise the firm's costs per unit as costs are now spread across fewer units. It may also be less risky for a large firm with many products to introduce a new one.

> ### Key term
>
> **Technical economies**: a fall in average costs due to the production process being carried out on a larger scale.

Activity

Choose a local business. If it doubles in size, how do you think its average costs will be affected and why?

Managerial economies

A large firm will be able to afford to employ specialist staff in different parts of the business. In smaller firms, the owner is likely to have a wide range of responsibilities, such as managing the firm's sales and accounts. Employing an expert in a narrow role may help the firm run more efficiently, reducing average costs. A large firm may have its own sales managers and accountants, for example.

External economies of scale

Most external economies of scale arise due to the localisation of a growing industry. This means it is concentrated in one or a few locations. Some of the ways that this could lead to lower average costs for firms in the industry involve:

- labour
- suppliers of local services
- disintegration
- research and promotion of the industry.

Labour

Local colleges may run courses training people who work in that industry, reducing the training costs of the firms.

Suppliers of related services

Firms that provide parts or services for the industry may locate nearby. This will reduce transport costs and improve communication between the different parts of the industry. For example, an area that specialises in horse racing is likely to attract vets who are specialists in treating horses.

Disintegration

Disintegration (or vertical disintegration) is where different parts of a production process are carried out by different firms. For example, to make woollen clothes, the wool has to go through a number of processes including cleaning, spinning, weaving and finishing. If a firm only carries out one process, it may operate on a larger scale and be more likely to be able to use the most up-to-date equipment and techniques, reducing the cost of that stage of the process.

Research and promotion of the industry

It is easier to organise cooperation between firms if they are in the same area. This may include operating joint research facilities, or promoting the industry to the public or government to improve its position.

Key terms

Localisation: when an industry is concentrated in one or a few locations.

Disintegration: where different parts of a production process are carried out by different firms.

Case study: Silicon Valley

Silicon Valley is an area in California, USA, which has become associated with innovation. Its name came from the silicon used to make computer chips. It is home to 3 million people, whose income per head is among the highest in the world.

There are about 2,000 technology companies located in Silicon Valley, including Google and Apple. Many of the firms are the leaders in their industries and as well as software and social media businesses, the area contains firms involved in lasers and robotics. It is also home to a number of business support companies such as Hewlett-Packard and Adobe.

There are many well-respected universities and colleges in the surrounding area. Many of the founders of the companies and their technical support staff were trained in local universities, including Stanford and the University of California at Berkeley. Since many of the founders trained together, there is much more cooperation and support than in alternative locations.

Professional networks help to share information, and by working together on projects they can all benefit. Being close to suppliers, customers and research facilities gives the firms several advantages.

However, one problem that has arisen from the rapid growth of the area and its attraction to so many firms

▲ **Figure 3.4.2**: Silicon Valley – centre of innovation

is a shortage of skilled workers. For example, the United States cannot provide enough software engineers. Many top engineers from other countries, especially from India and China, now work in the area and 38% of the people in Silicon Valley were not born in the United States. Not surprisingly, with high demand and limited supply, the price of land and housing is also high.

1 Is the case study mainly discussing economies and diseconomies of scale that are internal or external?

2 Identify **at least two** reasons why a high-tech firm may choose to locate in Silicon Valley.

3 Identify at least **two** reasons why average costs may be higher if a firm is located in Silicon Valley.

Diseconomies of scale

Diseconomies of scale are a rise in long-run average costs due to the growth of a firm or industry. Again, this could be due to the growth of the firm or the industry in which it operates.

Reasons for internal diseconomies of scale

On the **technical** side, operating with large-scale equipment can be a problem if the equipment breaks down and there is a hold-up in the production process.

The main reason for rising average costs as a firm grows is due to the more complex **management** structure. This could lead to a number of problems relating to:

- coordination
- communication
- workers' morale.

Key term

Diseconomies of scale: a rise in long-run average costs due to the growth of a firm or industry.

Get it right

Economies and diseconomies of scale are long-run concepts and apply when all factors of production are variable.

Coordination

Larger firms are likely to be split into a number of different departments, for example sales and accounts. These have to be coordinated and the managers will need to work together. Decision making in larger firms is likely to be slower and the firm may not be able to react as quickly if there is a change in the market.

Communication

As well as making decisions, managers must make sure that they are carried out. This can be difficult and costly in big businesses because there may be many layers of management. Communication is vital to make sure that everyone knows what they should be doing and that problems can be passed back. This can be time-consuming and involve many meetings in large firms.

Workers' morale

When a firm has hundreds or thousands of employees, it is difficult to make everyone feel that what they do is valued. It may also take more time to sort out problems. Consequently, workers may lack motivation and there could be other labour issues in large firms.

Reasons for external diseconomies of scale

If the industry is growing, this could lead to shortages of certain types of labour. Firms may have to offer higher pay to attract enough skilled workers. If the growing industry is localised, this will also push up the price of land in the area. Rises in the prices of factors of production will raise the average costs of a firm.

> **Progress questions**
>
> 1   What is the difference between internal and external economies of scale?
> 2   Give an example of:
>   i.   a technical economy of scale
>   ii. a marketing economy of scale.
> 3   Give an example of an external economy of scale.
> 4   Give **two** reasons why the growth of a firm may increase its average costs.

> **Link**
>
> The shape of the LRAC curve was introduced in 3.3 "Costs of production" where the U-shaped SRAC curve was also explained.

Economies of scale, diseconomies of scale and the LRAC curve

Economies and diseconomies of scale affect long-run average costs as the scale of production changes. The factors of production can change in the same or different proportions in the long run. A firm may believe that a certain combination of land, labour and capital works best to minimise average cost or it may decide to change the ratio between the different factors as it increases the scale of production.

Up to a point, increasing the scale of production may lead to lower long-run average costs, as the firm is able to take advantage of economies of scale. Bulk buying and employing specialists may lower its costs per unit of output.

At some point, diseconomies of scale, perhaps due to problems of coordinating a larger firm, may more than offset the economies of scale. Average costs start to rise. In this case, the LRAC curve will be U-shaped as in Figure 3.4.3.

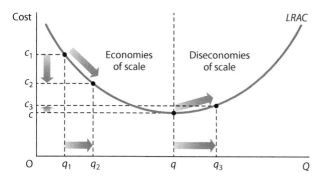

▲ **Figure 3.4.3**: A U-shaped LRAC curve

Up to output q, as output increases, average costs fall. For example, if the firm produces q_1 units, its LRAC is c_1. If output increases to q_2, LRAC falls to c_2. The firm is benefiting from economies of scale. At q, long-run average costs are minimised at c, the firm is **productively efficient**. At outputs greater than q, average costs rise. For example, if output increases to q_3, LRAC rises to c_3. The firm is experiencing diseconomies of scale.

The shape of the LRAC curve depends on the good or service being produced and the extent of the economies or diseconomies of scale. Some activities, particularly personal services such as hairdressing, may benefit less from economies of scale than, for example, car manufacturing, where there are considerable technical economies of scale. In some cases, the LRAC curve may not be U-shaped as economies of scale continue to offset any diseconomies, as output increases.

> **Key term**
>
> **Productive efficiency for a firm**: where average costs are minimised, the lowest point of the AC curve.

> **Link**
>
> Productive efficiency on a production possibility boundary was covered in 1.4 "Production possibility diagrams" and will be looked at again in the A2 part of the course. Alternative shapes of the LRAC curve are covered in the A2 part of the course.

> **Activity**
>
> Other than hairdressing and car manufacturing, choose two other examples of production, one that has few economies of scale and another that has many. Explain why this applies to each of your examples.

3.5 Average revenue, total revenue and profit

This section will develop your knowledge and understanding of:

→ the difference between average and total revenue
→ why the average revenue curve is the firm's demand curve
→ why profit is the difference between total revenue and total costs.

The difference between average and total revenue

Total revenue (TR) is income from sales. It is calculated by adding up all the money received from selling the firm's goods and services. If all the units are sold for the same price, then the total revenue is calculated by multiplying the price (P) by the number of units sold (Q).

$$TR = P \times Q$$

For example, if 50 units are sold per day at a price of \$15, the total revenue per day is \$15 × 50 = \$750.

Average revenue (AR) is the revenue per unit sold. It is calculated by dividing the total revenue by the number of units sold.

$$AR = \frac{TR}{Q}$$

For example, if the total revenue is \$750 and 50 units were sold, the average revenue is \$15. Average revenue is the same as price when all the units are sold for the same price.

Quantitative skills

Why is average revenue the same as price?

This is because AR = TR ÷ Q and since TR = P × Q, AR is also (P × Q) ÷ Q = P.

Key term

Average revenue: the revenue per unit sold, calculated by dividing the total revenue by the number of units.

Link

Total revenue was introduced in 2.2 "Price, income and cross elasticities of demand" and profit in 2.3 "The supply of goods and services".

Why the average revenue curve is the firm's demand curve

A demand curve shows the quantity consumers are able and willing to buy at a given price in a given time. Figure 3.5.1 shows how many of a firm's take-away meals are demanded per day at different prices.

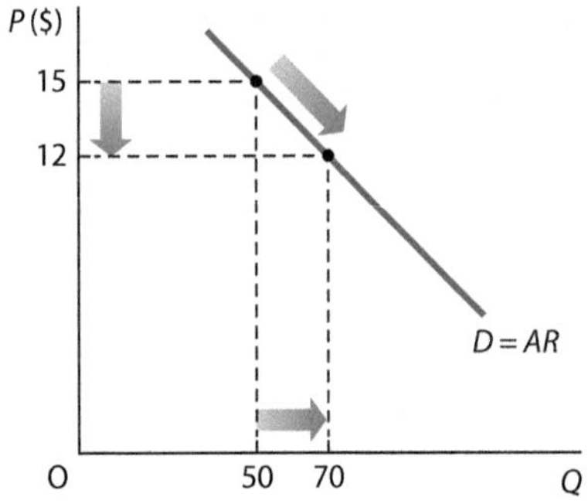

▲ **Figure 3.5.1**: Demand (D) as the AR curve

If the price of a take-away meal is \$15, 50 meals are sold in a day. The total revenue is \$750 and the average revenue is \$15. If the price is reduced to $12, 70 meals are sold in a day. Total revenue is now $840 and average revenue is $12. At each point on the demand curve, the price and average revenue are the same. The demand curve shows the average revenue for each quantity, so the demand curve is also the average revenue curve.

Why profit is the difference between total revenue and total costs

Total costs are everything the firm has to pay in connection with the provision of its goods or services and total revenue is all the money it receives for its goods or services. If the firm's total revenue is greater than its total costs, it has made a profit. This is what is left over from its income after paying all its costs. If the total costs are greater than the firm's total revenue, it has made a loss.

$$Profit = TR - TC$$

The profit per unit can be calculated by dividing the total profit by the number of units sold (Q). It may also be calculated as the difference between average revenue and average cost.

$$Profit\ per\ unit = \frac{TR - TC}{Q} = AR - AC$$

Quantitative skills

$(TR - TC) \div Q$ can also be written $(TR \div Q) - (TC \div Q)$, which is the same as $AR - AC$. You should be able to calculate average revenue, total revenue and profit.

Case study: Sven's TT bats (part three)

After making table tennis bats for many years, Sven decides to start making and selling table tennis balls. He researches the market, and Table 3.5.1 shows his estimates of costs and revenue per month for four possible outputs of boxes of balls at different prices. Some of the figures are missing.

1 Copy and complete the table.
2 What are the price and quantity where profit is estimated to be at its highest?

▼ **Table 3.5.1:** Costs, revenue and profit for boxes of table tennis balls, per month

Quantity	AC (€)	AR (€)	TC (€)	TR (€)	Profit (€)
100	5.50	6			
200			1,000	1,150	
300	4.80			1,650	
400			1,900		200

▲ **Figure 3.5.2:** Table tennis balls

Progress questions

1 What are **two** ways of calculating the profit per unit?
2 The AR curve is the same as which other curve?
3 If the average revenue for 20 units is $10 and TC is $250, will there be a profit or loss and of how much?

Exam-style questions

1 Which one of the following is a true statement about costs?

    A Average cost is fixed costs plus variable costs.

    B Average fixed costs do not change with output.

    C Average variable costs may fall or rise with output.

    D Total costs fall as output increases.   [1 mark]

2 Specialisation is most likely to require

    A a large number of firms.

    B a medium of exchange.

    C a system of barter.

    D higher productivity.   [1 mark]

3 Define "division of labour".   [3 marks]

4 The following table shows costs and revenue when 100 units are produced by a firm.

Quantity	Average fixed costs ($)	Average variable costs ($)	Total revenue ($)	Profit ($)
100	6	?	1300	200

You are advised to show your working for the calculations below.

(i) Calculate average fixed costs if output falls to 50 units.   [2 marks]

(ii) Calculate average variable costs when 100 units are produced.   [4 marks]

5 Analyse the likely effects on a firm's long-run average costs of an increase in production.   [12 marks]

6 Use the information in the case study on Silicon Valley (in 3.4 "Economies and diseconomies of scale") and your knowledge of economics to assess whether a government should intervene to help to establish an expanding industry in a particular area.   [20 marks]

Get it right

When provided with information about an industry, situation or recent experience, using it to support your points will strengthen your arguments.

4 Competitive and concentrated markets

The operation of markets, market failure and the role of government

4.1 Market structures

This section will develop your knowledge and understanding of:

→ why there is a range of market structures and how they affect the behaviour of firms

→ factors including the number of firms, the degree of product differentiation and ease of entry which are used to distinguish between different market structures.

Key terms

Market structure: the characteristics of an industry that affect the conduct of firms in that market.

Product differentiation: how firms make their goods and services appear different from other firms' products.

Barriers to entry: factors that make it difficult for new firms to come into a market.

Activities

Choose a local business that you think may be in monopolistic competition.

1 How many of this type of business are there in the local area?
2 How are the businesses similar?
3 How are the businesses different?

Market structures and how they affect the behaviour of firms

The number of firms in an industry could range from one to many thousand firms. The goods or services produced may be the same or similar, which may or may not make them good substitutes. It may be easy for new firms to start making the product or there may be factors that make it difficult for firms to come into the market. The characteristics that will determine the market structure are:

* the number of firms
* the degree of product differentiation
* the ease of (or barriers to) entry into the market.

Market structure refers to the characteristics of an industry that affect the behaviour (conduct) of firms in that market. **Product differentiation** relates to how firms make their goods and services appear different from other firms' products. This is done to try to attract and keep their customers. **Barriers to entry** are factors that make it difficult for new firms to come into a market.

Types of market structure

There are four main types of market structure.

* Perfect competition
* Monopolistic competition
* Oligopoly
* Monopoly

Perfect competition refers to a market with a large number of buyers and sellers, where products are identical, there is perfect information and there are no barriers to entry into or exit from the industry.

Monopolistic competition is where there is a large number of small firms, selling similar but not identical products, and there are

Key terms

Perfect competition: a market with a large number of buyers and sellers, where products are identical, there is perfect information and there are no barriers to entry into or exit from the industry.

Monopolistic competition: a market with a large number of small firms, selling similar but not identical products, and with few barriers to entry into and exit from the industry.

few barriers to entry and exit from the industry. Fast-food shops and hairdressers are good examples of monopolistic competition in many countries. Firms differentiate their products to attract new buyers and to keep their existing customers.

Oligopoly is where a small number of firms control the supply of a good or service. Examples include airlines and oil companies.

Monopoly is where one firm controls the supply of a good or service. In many countries, for example, there is only one firm providing rail services or electricity.

Significance of market structure for behaviour

An **industry** consists of all the firms involved in producing a particular good or service. Market structures therefore range from industries where many firms make identical products to where there is only one firm in the market. Most firms operate in markets between these two extremes.

The number of firms in the market, the extent of the differences between their products and how easy it is for firms to join or leave the market affect the behaviour of firms. The greater the number of firms, the fewer the differences in products and the fewer the barriers to entry and exit, the smaller the influence an individual firm has on the market.

For example, small firms with many competitors will have little or no power in the market. They will be price takers. A **price taker** is a firm that has to accept the price set by the market supply and demand. If there is only one or a few firms in the market, they are likely to have much more power over what happens in the market, including being able to set the price. They are likely to be **price makers**.

Factors used to distinguish between market structures

The main factors that are used to distinguish between different market structures have been identified as the number of firms, the degree of product differentiation and the ease of entry into the market.

The number of firms

If there are many firms in an industry, each is likely to have a small **market share**. This means that one firm is likely to account for a small percentage of the sales in that industry. This will give the firm little, if any, influence on the market.

If there are only a few firms in the market, they will have more power but it depends on their market shares and whether they work together or not. If there is only one firm in the industry, it has much more influence on the market. However, if it is a state-controlled firm, the government may, for example, set limits on the prices the firm charges.

Degree of product differentiation

Product differentiation relates to how firms try to make their goods and services appear different from other firms' products. Generally, the more

Link

There is more on barriers to entry and their significance in 4.3 "Competitive markets", 4.4 "Monopoly and monopoly power" and the A2 part of the course.

Progress questions

1 What are the **three** main characteristics of an industry that affect the influence a firm has in the market?

2 State the **four** types of market structure.

3 Will an increase in product differentiation increase or decrease the cross elasticity of demand for the product and why?

firms differentiate their products, the greater their ability to set price. This is because the products will not be such good substitutes for each other. So, if the price of one good increases, consumers may not switch to another. If firms can meet the preferences of buyers, they will keep existing consumers and attract new customers. This will increase their sales and profits and may enable the firms to charge higher prices.

Product differentiation includes differences in packaging, design or the image presented through advertising. If the products are the same or similar, it is likely that the price charged will also have to be the same or similar.

Ease of entry into the market

It may be easy for new firms to start supplying the products or there may be barriers to entry. The easier it is for new firms to come into the market, the less power existing firms have to set prices. If the firms set high prices and are making high profits, this will attract other firms into the market. Whether they enter the market or not depends partly on the barriers to entry.

Barriers to entry include the cost of setting up the business. For example, if expensive, specialist equipment is required, a new firm may be less willing and able to enter the market. Also, new firms may have to spend large amounts of money on advertising if the existing firms have well-known brands and good reputations.

Case study: The smartphone market

▲ Figure 4.1.1: Smartphones — a way of life?

In 2019, Samsung, Huawei and Apple were the leading producers of smartphones. 10 years earlier, Nokia had been the market leader. The mobile phone industry has experienced rapid technological change in the last 20 years and the product has come a long way from just being used to make phone calls.

The introduction of Apple's iPhone in 2007 revolutionised the product for both business and leisure use. A keyboard, connection to the internet, with access to emails, social media and much more, are now taken for granted. The smartphone has become a part of everyday life in many countries, as prices have fallen and additional features have been developed and added.

Although there are a few firms with a significant market share, there is considerable competition in the market. New models are regularly brought out, to encourage existing owners to upgrade their phone and to attract new users. Prices vary according to the number and quality of the features of the phone and the terms of the contract for its purchase and use.

1 What type of market structure best describes the smartphone market? Justify your answer.

2 Give **two** examples of how smartphone companies may differentiate their product.

3 Identify **two** barriers to entry to the smartphone market.

4.2 The objectives of firms

This section will develop your knowledge and understanding of:
→ profit as an important objective of most firms
→ why firms may also have other objectives including survival, growth and increasing their market share.

Profit as an important objective of most firms

Profit is what is left over from a firm's revenue after paying all its costs. Profit has a number of functions in a free market economy:

- reward for risk-taking
- incentive
- source of funds.

Reward for risk-taking

Profit is the reward for taking risks and is used to pay the owners and shareholders. There is no guarantee that a business will be successful and profit is the reward for bearing this uncertainty.

Incentive

Profit provides an incentive to set up and continue in business. It is a signal for entrepreneurs to enter a growing industry or to produce more of their existing products.

Source of funds

Profit is often used to finance **investment**. Investment is usually defined as an increase in the capital stock, although some investment expenditure may be on equipment to replace capital goods that are worn out or outdated. The investment may be in physical capital (buildings, machinery or other equipment) or in human capital (skills and experience of workers). Profit can help the business to expand, by improving existing products and developing new ones.

> **Key terms**
>
> **Investment**: an increase in the capital stock.
>
> **Profit maximisation**: producing where total revenue minus total cost is greatest.

Profit maximisation

Profit is therefore an important objective of most firms and it is often assumed that their main objective will be to **profit maximise**, producing an output where total revenue minus total cost is greatest.

Other objectives

The objectives of a firm will affect its behaviour. A firm may have other objectives apart from maximising profit, for example:

- survival
- growth
- increasing market share.

Survival

In most countries, there will be thousands of new businesses starting each year. However, many will fail in the first few years of trading. Rather than trying to make as much profit as possible, some firms will just be trying to survive in the market. They need to make enough money to cover their costs. If they cannot cover their costs, they must consider whether their situation will improve or whether they should leave the market.

Growth

Due to a lack of capital, most firms will start small. Some owners may be happy for their business to remain small but, for a variety of reasons, others will want their business to grow. This may involve making more of the same product or selling a wider range of products. A larger business may also be able to increase its profits.

Increasing market share

Rather than just increasing the size of the business, some firms will aim to increase their market share, the percentage of the market they control. To persuade customers to switch away from their rivals, they may have to lower their prices. This could reduce their profits in the short run but if they have a larger market share in the long run, they will have more power over the market.

They also hope to increase brand loyalty, where customers continue to buy products from a particular firm. This may be achieved through product differentiation. The firm may then be able to raise its prices, increasing profits in the long run.

Additional objectives

As well as survival, growth and increasing market share, business owners and managers may have a variety of other objectives, which will influence the firm's behaviour. For many small business owners, job satisfaction, through providing a quality product and having a good relationship with their customers, is important.

The aims of some owners may be influenced by their moral judgements. For example, the firm may have a policy of buying Fairtrade products even though they are more expensive. They may give some of their profits to charity. If the firm is under government control, it is generally assumed that its main objective is what is best for the welfare of the country as a whole.

It is likely that most firms have a range of objectives but they must make enough profit to stay in business. Therefore, profit is an important objective of most firms.

Key term

Brand loyalty: where customers continue to buy products from a particular firm.

Link

1.5 "Economic methodology" discussed how moral judgements influence economic decision making.

Progress questions

1 Why may a firm want to increase its market share?

2 List **three** other objectives of firms.

3 What is often assumed to be the main objective of firms?

Case study: Ecosia

▲ Figure 4.2.1: Over 90 million trees planted

Trees help to improve soils and provide a home for wildlife. Some people claim they are vital in our fight against climate change. Ecosia is a search engine, founded in 2009 and based in Germany. The founder, Christian Kroll, was travelling the world looking for an idea for a business that would have a positive impact on society. On visits to Nepal and Argentina, he came up with the idea of a search engine that would pay for the planting of trees.

When people use Ecosia to search the web and click on an advert, the firm receives income. It gives 80% of its profits to non-profit organisations to plant trees. On average, Ecosia earns €0.005 per click and it costs €0.22 to plant a tree. The firm also earns some income from selling T-shirts and other clothing from its online store.

Ecosia is involved with tree planting in 15 countries, including Peru, Ethiopia and Indonesia, helping the local communities in a number of ways. So far, it has paid for over 90 million trees to be planted. These are mainly the types of tree usually found in those places, which should help to keep the soil fertile, but in some places the firm has also planted non-native fruit or nut trees with native trees.

1   On average, how many clicks on adverts are needed to finance the planting of a tree?
2   How may the planting of trees help communities in countries such as Peru, Ethiopia and Indonesia?
3   To what extent do you think Ecosia's use of profits for tree planting will encourage people to use its search engine?
4   Apart from making profits to plant trees, what other objectives might Ecosia have?

Activity

Find out about four firms (other than Ecosia) that give some of their profits to charity. How much have they given and to which charities?

This section will develop your knowledge and understanding of:

→ the main characteristics of a perfectly competitive market

→ why in such markets the price is determined by the interaction of demand and supply

→ why profits are likely to be lower in a competitive market than in a market dominated by a few large firms.

Link

Perfect competition was introduced and defined in 4.1 "Market structures".

The main characteristics of a perfectly competitive market

A perfectly competitive market is one of the four market structures but it is a theoretical extreme. It has the following characteristics:

- large number of buyers and sellers
- homogeneous or identical products
- free entry and exit
- perfect information.

Large number of buyers and sellers

There are thousands, or even millions, of buyers and sellers in a perfectly competitive market. The amounts bought and sold by each buyer and seller make up a tiny percentage of the total amount of purchases and sales, so no buyer or seller has any influence on the price of the good or service.

Homogeneous goods

The products sold in a perfectly competitive market are homogeneous (identical). There is no branding of goods or services and there is no reason to prefer the products of one firm over another.

Key terms

Homogeneous goods: identical products.

Perfect information: where anything that may affect a buyer's or seller's decision making is known and understood.

Free entry and exit

There is nothing to stop new firms from coming into the market (no barriers to entry) or to stop existing firms from leaving the market.

Perfect information

Perfect information means that anything that may affect a buyer or seller's decision making is known and understood. Everyone knows at the same time what is happening in the market, including the price being charged by all the sellers. Also, with perfect information, there is no need for advertising.

Although perfect competition is a theoretical extreme, it provides a benchmark (standard) against which the behaviour and performance of real-world firms can be judged. However, examples of real-world markets that have many of the characteristics of perfect competition include the market for foreign currency, such as the dollar, and many agricultural products such as fruit and vegetables.

Case study: Central de Abasto – the largest market in the world

▲ Figure 4.3.1: A perfectly competitive market?

The Central de Abasto (supply centre) in Mexico City is the largest wholesale market in the world, although firms there sell to consumers as well as to other retailers. Opened in 1982, there are more than 2,000 businesses selling fruit, vegetables and meat. Next to it is the Nueva Viga market, the second largest seafood market in the world. This part of the market has about 25,000 visitors a day.

The market is laid out according to what is being sold. For example, there is a section just for potatoes. Plants, flowers and seasonal produce are sold in the outdoor section. The market acts as a meeting place between large numbers of buyers and sellers. The total amounts traded here have a significant effect on the prices of many goods and services.

To what extent does the Central de Abasto have the characteristics of a perfectly competitive market? Consider each of the four characteristics of perfectly competitive markets.

Why price in perfectly competitive markets is determined by demand and supply

In a perfectly competitive market, there is a large number of buyers and sellers, none of which has any power in the market. The price of the product is determined by the market demand and supply. Figure 4.3.2 shows the market for a product in a perfectly competitive market.

The market demand and supply curves show the total demand and supply at different prices, during a given time, of all the buyers and sellers in the market. The equilibrium price of the product is p where q will be sold.

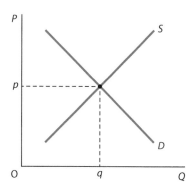

▲ Figure 4.3.2: How price is determined in a perfectly competitive market

Activities

Visit a fruit and vegetable market and choose a particular fruit or vegetable to research.

1   Count how many stalls are selling this product.
2   Do the products look similar?
3   Write down the prices being charged for this product by each seller.
4   To what extent does this have the characteristics of a perfect market?

Why profits are likely to be lower in a competitive market

A **competitive market** has many buyers and sellers, good market information and ease of entry. No single buyer or seller can influence market price and output. Perfect competition is an example of a competitive market but competitive markets do not necessarily have all the features of perfect competition. For example, products could be similar, perhaps with brand names, rather than being identical. In this case, firms will be trying to outdo their rivals.

Individual firms in competitive markets have little or no power to set price, even if some work together, because there are so many of them. Price is set by the market demand and supply and individual firms are mainly price takers. If a firm sets its price higher than other firms, it will find it difficult to sell its products because consumers know they can buy a similar product more cheaply from another firm. However, if they can differentiate their products and build brand loyalty, firms in competitive markets will have some market power.

If firms make high profits and there are few barriers to entry, this will attract other firms into the market. The higher supply will lower price and reduce profit margins. This will keep prices and profits lower in competitive markets.

If a market has one or a few large firms, these firms have some power to set price, they are price makers. If there is only one firm, consumers have no choice but to buy the products from the firm. What happens to demand when the firm increases its price will depend on the price elasticity of demand for the product.

If there are a few firms, their products are likely to be differentiated by advertising and there may be brand loyalty, with consumers willing to pay higher prices for what they believe to be better products. This will affect the product's cross elasticity of demand. Brand loyalty will make it less likely that consumers will switch to substitute goods if rivals reduce their prices, which will make the cross elasticity of demand for the product low.

With few firms in a market, there are likely to be barriers to entry that stop other firms coming into the market to take advantage of the higher prices and profits. The firms may also work together, agreeing to set a high price to increase their combined profits.

For these reasons, prices are likely to be lower in a more competitive market. If prices are lower, it is also likely that profits will be lower. However, the competitiveness of the market and its effects on price and profits will depend on the number of firms in the market, the extent of product differentiation and barriers to entry. If there are more firms, less product differentiation and few barriers to entry, the market is likely to be more competitive, keeping prices and profits lower. However, if large firms can take advantage of economies of scale, this could also lead to lower prices.

Key term

Competitive market: where there are many buyers and sellers, good market information and ease of entry.

Get it right

Competitive and perfectly competitive markets are not the same. A perfectly competitive market is an extreme example of a competitive market. Be clear which situation is being discussed.

Link

There is more about how firms compete in 4.5 "The competitive market process".

Activity

Copy Figure 4.3.2. and use this to show how higher supply will lower price.

Progress questions

1 Why would a firm in perfect competition not advertise?

2 Why do low barriers to entry and good market information keep down profits?

3 A firm is considering increasing price by 10%. If its price elasticity of demand is -0.5, what is likely to happen to profits and why?

This section will develop your knowledge and understanding of:

→ the difference between pure monopoly and monopoly power

→ how monopoly power is influenced by various factors including barriers to entry, the number of competitors, advertising and the degree of product differentiation

→ concentration ratios and how to calculate a concentration ratio

→ why the basic model of monopoly suggests that higher prices and profits and inefficiency may result in a misallocation of resources compared to the outcome in a competitive market

→ potential benefits from monopoly, including economies of scale and possibly more invention and innovation.

The difference between pure monopoly and monopoly power

A **pure monopoly** is when there is only one firm in the market. It is a market structure where one firm controls the supply of a good or service. There are few examples of pure monopoly unless the market is very narrowly defined. In practice, we often refer to firms that have a dominant share of a market as monopolies as well.

In many countries, there is only one firm providing utilities or public services such as water, rail services or electricity. In the world, there are many airlines. There are fewer that fly to an individual country and there may only be one that flies to a small island. In the last case, the firm has a monopoly of the market but the market is very narrowly defined.

A pure monopoly has considerable **monopoly power**. This refers to the ability of a firm to influence price and output. It is able to increase

Link

Monopoly was introduced and defined in 4.1 "Market structures".

Key terms

Pure monopoly: when there is only one firm in the market.

Monopoly power: the ability of a firm to influence price and output.

Case study: Flights to Shetland

▲ Figure 4.4.1: A local resident

The Shetland Islands (Shetland) are a small group of islands, 170 kilometres north of the Scottish mainland and 300 kilometres west of Norway. Home to about 20,000 people, the economy relies on agriculture, fishing, oil and tourism. Shetland can be reached by ferry or plane.

Currently, the only flights from the rest of the United Kingdom to Shetland are operated by Loganair. There are flights to Shetland every day from other Scottish airports, taking between an hour and an hour and a half. The alternative is an overnight ferry taking 12 hours. In the summer, there are also flights from Norway.

In a recent search, a return flight from Glasgow to Shetland typically cost between £400 and £500, for a total distance of about 970 kilometres. This is roughly the same distance as a return flight from Barcelona to Madrid in Spain. Even though there were only two airlines offering flights between these two cities on the dates investigated, prices started at just over £100 for a return flight.

1 Does Loganair have a pure monopoly?

2 Why is it more expensive to fly between Glasgow and Shetland than it is to fly from Barcelona to Madrid?

price without losing buyers to its competitors, although it will still lose sales, because its customers are less willing and able to buy the product at a higher price. However, a firm does not have to be a monopoly to have monopoly power. Many firms, particularly if they have a large market share, will have some monopoly power.

Factors that influence monopoly power

Monopoly power is influenced by:

- barriers to entry
- the number of competitors
- advertising
- the degree of product differentiation
- imperfect information.

Both individually and in combination, these factors have a large impact on the monopoly power of firms in a market.

Barriers to entry

If there are few or low barriers to entry, it is easy for new firms to start supplying the product. This will mean that the firms in the market have less monopoly power. If prices and profits increase, this will attract other firms to the market. This suggests that prices will be lower and output higher if a market has low barriers to entry.

The number of competitors

If a firm has few competitors, there are few alternative sellers. This is likely to mean that the firms in the market have some monopoly power. However, this also depends on their market shares. In a market with four firms, one with a market share of 60% is likely to have more monopoly power than if it only had a 15% market share. However, a firm with a market share of 15% is likely to have some monopoly power if it has hundreds of small competitors.

Advertising

Firms usually advertise in order to persuade customers to buy more of their products. It is a way of promoting their goods and making clear the differences between their products and those of other firms. It can act as a barrier to entry since, if a market has products with well-known brand names, it may be difficult and expensive for new firms to attract customers to their products. If firms in a market spend a lot of money on advertising, it is likely to give them some monopoly power. If they increase prices, many customers will continue to buy their products due to brand loyalty.

The degree of product differentiation

If the products in a market are identical or very similar, firms are unlikely to have monopoly power. If one firm charges a higher price, consumers will buy from another firm. The greater the differences in the products, the more control the firms are likely to have over the price and output they set.

Link

Barriers to entry, the number of competitors, advertising and the degree of product differentiation were introduced in 4.1 "Market structures" and perfect information in 4.3 "Competitive markets".

Progress questions

1 What is the difference between pure monopoly and monopoly power?

2 For each of the following, other things being equal, state whether it is likely to increase or decrease a firm's monopoly power:

   i. lower barriers to entry

   ii. an increase in its market share

   iii. successful advertising by the firm

   iv. less product differentiation

   v. improved access to information through the internet.

Imperfect information

Monopoly power can also be affected by the availability of information. If firms do not know about the profits being made in an industry, they may not enter the market, even if it is easy to do so. Advertising may make products appear different when they may be similar and it may cause consumers to know more about some brands than others. Also, many consumers may not know what prices other firms are charging. This imperfect information may increase the monopoly power of some firms.

Concentration ratios and how to calculate them

A concentration ratio is a measure of the combined share of the largest firms in an industry, usually as a percentage of the total. This is most likely to apply to the largest three, four, five or even eight firms. For example, if the three largest firms in an industry have market shares of 34%, 25% and 16%, the three-firm concentration ratio is 75%.

A concentration ratio usually measures sales but could be used to measure employment, for example. It is often used to show the extent of control of the largest firms and is an indicator of the market structure. In the above example, a three-firm concentration ratio of 75% suggests that the market is an oligopoly, where a small number of firms control the supply of a good or service. The firms may have 25% of the market each and be competing fiercely against each other. However, a concentration ratio of 75% would also occur if the three largest firms in the market had shares of 70%, 3% and 2%, suggesting a monopoly and a lack of competition.

Quantitative skills

When you are asked to calculate a concentration ratio, the information provided may include a category called, for example, "others" or "the rest", to indicate the combined share of all the other firms in the market not listed separately. This is not the share of a single firm and should not be counted when calculating a concentration ratio.

Concentration ratios are normally quoted as percentages but they may be written as a decimal. For example, 0.34 is the same as 34%. If you write the ratio as a percentage, do not forget to include the percentage sign.

Key term

Concentration ratio: a measure of the combined share of the largest firms in an industry, usually as a percentage of the total.

Case study: The market for gasoline in Japan

▼ Table 4.4.1: Market shares of the leading gasoline firms in the Japanese market

Firm	Market share (%)
Cosmo Oil	11.4
ExxonMobil	19.4
Idemitsu	14.2
Nippon Oil	23.9
Showa Shell	14.4
Others	16.7
Total	100

Source: http://allon.info/japan-market-share.html; accessed 28 October 2019

▲ Figure 4.4.2: A concentrated market

Table 4.4.1 shows the market shares of the leading gasoline firms in the Japanese market at a particular time.

1 Calculate:
   i. the three-firm concentration ratio
   ii. the five-firm concentration ratio.

2 Idemitsu and Showa Shell later announced plans to merge. Assuming they are now one firm, calculate:
   i. the three-firm concentration ratio
   ii. the four-firm concentration ratio.

3 Use these concentration ratios and any other knowledge you have of the gasoline market, to discuss to what extent the firms in this market are likely to have monopoly power.

A high concentration ratio indicates a concentrated market, where a few firms, or possibly only one, have a high market share. A low concentration ratio suggests that the market is more competitive but, depending on the shares of the firms involved, the market could also be competitive if there is a high concentration ratio.

Why monopoly suggests higher prices, profits and inefficiency, and a misallocation of resources

The basic model of monopoly suggests that higher prices, higher profits and inefficiency may result in a misallocation of resources compared to the outcome in a competitive market. However, the extent of this depends partly on factors such as barriers to entry and product differentiation.

A pure monopolist has the power to set either the price or the quantity it sells but cannot set both at the same time. This is because they are limited by the market demand. If the firm is the only one operating in the market, the demand curve for the product or industry will also be the demand curve of the firm. Figure 4.4.3 shows the demand curve for a product also being the demand curve for the monopoly.

As shown in Figure 4.4.3, if the firm wishes to sell 6,000 units, it can charge $5. if the firm chooses to set a price of $10, according to the demand curve, consumers will only be willing to buy 4,000 units. At a higher price, consumers will be less willing and able to buy the product. The firm cannot sell 6,000 units at $10, because this is not a point on the demand curve. A monopoly can choose the price or the quantity it sells but not both.

In a competitive market, there are many buyers and sellers, good market information and low barriers to entry. Individual firms in competitive markets have little or no power to set price or quantity. Price is set by the market demand and supply. If one firm increases its price, consumers are likely to switch to other firms selling the same or similar products.

If firms make high profits and there are few barriers to entry, other firms are likely to enter the market. This keeps prices and profits lower in competitive markets and output higher. For example, in Figure 4.4.4, the price in a competitive market may be p_c where q_c is sold. A monopoly is likely to charge a higher price but at p_m, it will only be able to sell q_m. The firm can limit the output to force up the price.

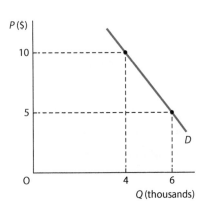

▲ Figure 4.4.3: Demand under monopoly

The outcome of a competitive market should match the wants and preferences of buyers. If a monopoly chooses a higher price where fewer items are sold, this can result in a misallocation of resources. This is an inefficient use of resources, where they are not put to their best or most effective use. Welfare is not maximised. Society would prefer more resources to be allocated to the production of these goods. Also, due to a lack of competitive pressure, the costs of a monopolist may not be as low as possible, which could result in a further waste of resources.

Overall, if there is a monopoly, it is likely that there will be higher prices and profits, compared to a competitive market and also that inefficiency may result in a misallocation of resources.

Potential benefits from monopoly

Economies of scale

In many industries, firms operating on a larger scale can take advantage of internal economies of scale, such as the use of large items of equipment or production lines and bulk buying. This reduces average costs. In this case, a monopoly may be more efficient than a competitive market.

For example, in Figure 4.4.5, if a monopoly produces q_m, it has a long-run average cost of c_m but a firm producing a quarter of this output at q_c, has a much higher long-run average cost of c_c. Even if the monopoly sets a high price to maximise its profits, this price may be lower than if there are many smaller competing firms having to cover higher average costs.

More invention and innovation

Another potential benefit from monopoly is more invention and innovation. A large firm, such as a monopoly, is likely to have more money available from its profits for **research and development (R&D)**. This involves using resources to design new or improved products. If successful, this may strengthen the firm's position in the market.

Invention is the creation of a new idea, product or process – for example, the invention of the telephone by Alexander Graham Bell. **Innovation** involves making changes to existing products by introducing new ideas that better meet existing needs or new requirements – for example, the introduction of the Apple iPhone. Phones existed before but Apple improved them to suit what people wanted. The iPhone is therefore an innovation, not an invention.

How much money the monopoly chooses to put into new developments may depend on barriers to entry and the nature of the product. If a market has high barriers to entry and it is not likely that another firm could develop a product that would replace the existing one, then invention and innovation may be more limited. However, if high profits are being made in an industry, this may encourage other firms to spend money on research and development to develop a better product as a replacement.

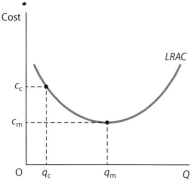

▲ Figure 4.4.5: The impact of economies of scale

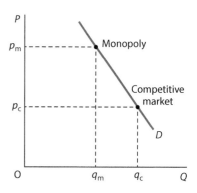

▲ Figure 4.4.4: Price and quantity in monopoly and competitive markets

Quantitative skills

When comparing price and quantity in different market structures, it may be helpful to use subscript letters such as "m" and "c" (as in Figure 4.4.4) rather than "1" and "2", but as long as the explanation is clear, it does not matter which labels are used.

Link

Internal economies of scale were explained in 3.4 "Economies and diseconomies of scale".

Key terms

Research and development (R&D): using resources to design new or improved products.

Invention: the creation of a new idea, product or process.

Innovation: making changes to existing products by introducing new ideas that better meet existing needs or new requirements.

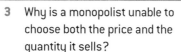

Progress questions

3   Why is a monopolist unable to choose both the price and the quantity it sells?

4   State **two** advantages and **two** disadvantages of monopoly.

5   Explain who may benefit if a firm spends money on research and development.

This section will develop your knowledge and understanding of:

→ how firms do not just compete on price but that competition will, for example, also lead firms to strive to improve products, reduce costs and improve the quality of the service provided.

Competition by price and other methods

The competitive process

Competition is a dynamic process, taking place over time. Firms will try to improve products, reduce costs and improve the quality of the service provided. Competition does not only take place between small firms. Many large firms compete strongly with each other.

Competition can benefit consumers through lower prices, more choice and improved quality. However, competition through more product differentiation can also lead to increased monopoly power. This may then result in consumers being exploited by less choice and higher prices, causing a misallocation of resources.

When there is competition, firms will try to outdo their rivals. They may be aiming to increase their sales, their market share or just trying to survive in the market. They may be trying to maximise their profit. Firms can compete in many ways. These can be divided into price and non-price competition.

Price competition

When a firm lowers its price, existing consumers may be willing and able to buy more and the firm may attract buyers from other firms. However, this depends on the cross elasticity of demand for the product.

The firm is more likely to be successful when competing on price if the products of the different firms are similar and there is little brand loyalty. How successful it is also depends on whether the rival firms lower their price. If other firms lower their price as well, the firms may all sell more but their market shares may stay the same. A firm may also lower its price to try to drive other firms out of the market, to increase its monopoly power.

Non-price competition

Non-price competition involves using methods other than lowering price to outdo rival firms and, for example, to increase their market share. These include:

- improving products
- reducing costs
- improving quality
- product differentiation.

> **Key term**
>
> **Non-price competition:** using methods other than changes in price to outdo rival firms.

Improving products

Innovation could result in better products, with more features, that offer increased value for money. This could encourage existing customers to buy the new product and attract more customers from other firms.

Reducing costs

If a firm can reduce its average costs, it may be more able to reduce its prices. This could be due to, for example, more specialisation or negotiating lower prices for its raw materials. If other firms are not able to lower their costs, this firm will either make more profit, to perhaps fund research and development, or be able to lower prices without reducing its previous profit per unit.

Improving quality

Products are not only chosen because of their price but also because of their quality. The importance of quality will depend on the product. If a firm can improve the quality of its product or make consumers believe that the quality is higher than the products of other firms, it may be able to sell more.

Product differentiation

There are many ways that a firm can make its products appear to be different from those of other firms and increase brand loyalty. Advertising helps to create an image for a product as well as telling potential buyers about its features. A firm selling cars may offer a longer warranty, free servicing or breakdown cover, or good after-sales service generally. This may encourage customers to choose the same firm when buying their next car.

Progress questions

1   State **three** reasons why firms may compete.
2   Explain the **two** main ways in which firms can compete.

Activity

Choose a product, other than cars and cola, and investigate how firms are competing through price and non-price competition. Are the firms emphasising differences in price or features of the product?

Case study: Cola wars

▲ Figure 4.5.1: Long term rivals

Coca-Cola and Pepsi (now part of PepsiCo) have been in competition in the soft drinks market for more than a century. The original recipe for Coca-Cola (Coke) was developed in 1886 and Pepsi-Cola (Pepsi) was created 12 years later. By 1904, Coke was selling over 1 million gallons a year and by 1907, the company was using well-known athletes to promote the product. In 1915, it developed the contour-shaped bottle still used today.

Despite going bankrupt twice in the early 20th century, Pepsi recovered and by 1945 had started to sell its drink in cans. In 1950, Coke was advertised on television for the first time. In 1961, Coke appeared in a film while Pepsi began its campaign, "Come Alive! You're in the Pepsi generation", then launched Diet Pepsi in 1964. In 1969, Coke switched to red and white with the slogan "It's the Real Thing".

Both firms also sell other products. Coke has 42% of the cola market to Pepsi's 31% but PepsiCo has a greater revenue overall. They each spend over $2 billion a year on advertising their products. Their logos have changed many times over the years and they have often been involved in price wars.

Use the information in the case study to illustrate at least **four** different ways in which Coca-Cola and PepsiCo have competed over the years.

Exam-style questions

1 Which one of the following changes is most likely to increase a firm's monopoly power?

    A A fall in the firm's market share

    B A higher cross elasticity of demand for its products

    C Greater product differentiation by the firm

    D Lower barriers to entry to the market   [1 mark]

2 Which one of these is a characteristic of a perfect market?

    A Advertising

    B Imperfect information

    C No barriers to entry

    D Similar products   [1 mark]

3 Define "pure monopoly".   [3 marks]

4 The pie chart shows the market shares of the main supermarkets in a country at a particular time.

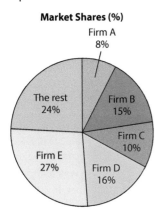

Market Shares (%)

Calculate the three-firm concentration ratio. You are advised to show your working.   [3 marks]

5 With the help of a diagram, explain how price and quantity sold are likely to differ in a competitive market compared with when a firm has monopoly power.   [9 marks]

6 Analyse the likely effects of a market becoming less competitive.   [12 marks]

5 Market failure and government intervention in markets

The operation of markets, market failure and the role of government

This section will develop your knowledge and understanding of:

→ how market failure occurs whenever a market leads to a misallocation of resources

→ the meaning of a misallocation of resources

→ how public goods, positive and negative externalities, merit and demerit goods, monopoly and other market imperfections, and inequalities in the distribution of income and wealth can lead to market failure.

Market failure as a result of misallocation of resources

In a free market economy, decisions about what to produce and who should benefit are taken by buyers and sellers. Goods and services are allocated to those able and willing to buy them. People with little or no money will not be able to afford to buy as much. This may be considered inequitable (unfair).

To make the most profit, firms will want to supply the products that are most in demand. As a result, too much or too little of some products may be produced for the benefit of society as a whole. This is an inefficient use of resources because the products are over or underproduced.

Market failure occurs when the market forces of supply and demand result in an inefficient and/or inequitable allocation of resources.

The meaning of a misallocation of resources

Market failure leads to a misallocation of resources when resources are not put to their best or most effective use. Welfare is not maximised. Society would benefit from a different allocation of resources. It may be that more or less of the product should be produced and/or it needs to be allocated to consumers in a different way. If left to the free market, price may be too high, too low or fluctuate too much.

Situations that can lead to market failure

Market failure covers a number of situations.

- Public goods
- Externalities
- Merit and demerit goods
- Monopoly
- Other market imperfections
- Inequalities in income and wealth

Public goods

If left to the free market, some goods, known as public goods, are unlikely to be provided since it would be impossible for firms to prevent people who had not paid from benefiting from the products.

Key term

Market failure: when if left to the market forces of supply and demand, there is an inefficient and/or inequitable allocation of resources.

Link

Some examples of market failure were mentioned in 1.3 "Scarcity, choice and the allocation of resources". A misallocation of resources was introduced in "4.4 Monopoly and monopoly power".

Activities

Use the example of street lighting as a public good.

1   Explain why it would be impossible for firms to prevent people who had not paid from benefiting from the product.

2   What other problem would there be in deciding a price?

An example of a public good is street lighting. The market is unlikely to provide the product.

Externalities

The consumption or production of some goods and services may lead to side-effects on other people or firms. These externalities can be good or bad. For example, pollution from a factory may damage the local air quality. The market either produces too much or too little output for the benefit of society as a whole.

Merit and demerit goods

Some goods may benefit or harm others as well as those consuming these products. There may be too few merit goods produced and too many demerit goods. Education is often considered to be a merit good.

Monopoly

To maximise profits, a monopoly may choose to raise its price above the level of a competitive market, causing less to be bought. Insufficient resources are therefore allocated to the product and those on low incomes cannot afford to buy as much. This is both inefficient and inequitable.

Other market imperfections

Imperfect information, the immobility of factors of production and unstable prices can all lead to situations where markets operate inefficiently.

Inequalities in income and wealth

Income and wealth are usually unequally distributed. Since the allocation of goods and services in a market economy is based on a person's ability to pay, those with more income and/or wealth can afford to buy more goods and services. This may be considered inequitable.

Link

Public goods; positive and negative externalities; merit and demerit goods; monopoly and other market imperfections; and inequalities of income and wealth will all be explained in more detail later in this chapter.

Progress questions

1   What is another word for unfair?
2   As well as being unfair, how else could resources be misallocated?
3   What term is used for side-effects on other people or firms?

Quantitative skills

To make comparisons easier, either over a period of time and/or for different data series, numbers may be quoted in index number form. The starting point of a data series is called the base year. The value at this time is given the figure of 100 and all the other values are related to this. For example, a value 20% higher than the base year would have an index number of 120. Index numbers are covered in more detail in 6.2 "Macroeconomic indicators".

Case study: The importance of education

Education provides benefits for the individual but other people in the country also benefit from a well-educated population. Table 5.1.1 shows the number of children completing secondary education in a small country over a number of years.

▼ Table 5.1.1: Number of children completing secondary education

Year	Total	Index (2003 = 100)
2003	67,295	100
2007	70,130	
2011	65,986	
2015	75,134	111.6
2019	80,263	

1   Calculate the missing index numbers to **one** decimal place, with 2003 as the base year.

2   Use these index numbers to calculate to **one** decimal place:

i. the percentage increase in the number of children completing secondary education between 2003 and 2019

ii. the percentage decrease in the number of children completing secondary education between 2003 and 2011.

3   How may a country benefit from a well-educated population?

▲ Figure 5.1.1: Education – a merit good?

Non-rivalry, non-excludability and their significance

Public goods, such as street lighting, are an example of market failure. They have two important characteristics. Pure **public goods** are products that are non-rival in consumption and non-excludable.

Non-rivalry in consumption

Non-rival in consumption (sometimes described as non-diminishable) means that consumption of a product by one person does not reduce the amount available to others. Using the example of street lighting, one person walking down a street does not reduce the quantity of light available to others. If two people walk down the street together, there is still the same amount of light available to both of them. So, how much light are they using? If a firm cannot determine how much of its product someone has consumed, how can it set an appropriate price?

Non-excludability

Non-excludable means that non-payers cannot be prevented from using the product. For example, if one person has paid for street lighting but the other person has not, how can the person who has not paid be stopped from benefiting from the light? In this case, why would the other person pay for it?

Significance of these characteristics and other examples

The firm cannot exclude those unwilling or unable to pay for the product and cannot determine how much has been consumed. For these reasons, firms are very unlikely to supply these goods since they have little chance of making a profit. The market for pure public goods is sometimes described as a **missing market**, since a market for the product does not exist. With public goods, there is demand for the product because there are benefits for consumers but firms are unwilling to supply the product.

However, if these goods are important, for example for public safety, they should be supplied. This requires the government to provide or pay for them to be provided, or they could make it possible for a firm

Link

Public goods, including the characteristic of non-excludability, were introduced in 5.1 "The meaning of market failure".

Key terms

Public goods: products that are non-rival in consumption and non-excludable.

Non-rival in consumption: where consumption of a product by one person does not reduce the amount available to others.

Non-excludable: where non-payers cannot be prevented from using the product.

Missing market: where a market for a product does not exist.

to collect revenue to pay for the public good. For example, in England and Wales, a charity called Trinity House looks after lighthouses and is allowed to charge ships a fee for using British and Irish ports. In China, the Maritime Safety Administration, a government agency, is responsible for lighthouses.

Other examples of public goods include national defence, the police service and flood defences.

Public goods and private goods

Public goods

As previously explained, public goods are non-excludable and non-rival in consumption. As a result of firms not being able to exclude non-payers and not being able to assess the quantity someone has consumed, markets generally fail to provide these products.

Private goods

Private goods are rival in consumption and excludable. **Rival in consumption** means that consumption of a product by one person reduces the amount available to others. If it is **excludable**, non-payers can be prevented from using the product.

Most products are both excludable and rival in consumption, making them private goods. For example, a chocolate bar is a private good. Only those able and willing to pay the price will be able to obtain the chocolate bar and if a person buys three chocolate bars, there are then three fewer available for other people to buy. The resources used to produce the chocolate bars could have been used to produce something else.

Case study: Flood defences in the Maldives

The Maldives, in the Indian Ocean, is the smallest nation in Asia, both by land area and population. Just under half a million people live on islands with an average height above sea level of 1.5 metres. Fishing and tourism are the main industries.

In the last 50 years, there have been about 30 floods, including the tsunami in 2004. Concerns are growing about global warming and rising sea levels. A report by the United Nations in 2007 claimed that if sea levels continue to rise at their current rate, the Maldives would be uninhabitable by 2100.

Sea walls, breakwaters and other flood defences have been built to reduce the risk of flooding but this may not be enough. The 3.5 metre sea wall built around the capital, Malé, home to a third of the population, cost $60 million with help from the Japanese government. A new flood-resistant island has also been built using sand from the ocean floor. This is higher than the rest of the Maldives.

When the tsunami hit the islands in 2004, it was estimated that half of Malé would have been destroyed without the sea wall. Although over 80 people on the islands were reported killed by the waves, all those in Malé survived.

1 How does the provision of a sea wall around Malé illustrate the characteristics of a public good?
2 Why does the risk of flooding in the Maldives suggest that the government should become involved?

▲ **Figure 5.2.1:** Under threat?

How a public good may become a quasi-public good

Pure public goods are non-rival in consumption and non-excludable. However, there are circumstances when a public good may take on characteristics of a private good. It is then known as a **quasi-public good**. This would require the product to be rival in consumption or excludable, at least to some extent.

For example, a public park or playing field that anyone can access could be classified as a public good. It is non-excludable. If it is a large area, it is effectively non-rival in consumption as well. However, if a large number of people choose to use it at the same time, it may start to become rival in consumption, as it becomes overcrowded, reducing its value to others. Alternatively, if the area is fenced off and an entrance fee is introduced, it then becomes excludable.

The significance of technological change

Technological change has also been responsible for some public goods taking on characteristics of private goods in recent years. The airwaves are used by mobile phone companies and to transmit radio and television programmes.

For many years, it was impossible to stop people accessing television programmes. In many countries, they also had to buy a licence each year from the government to legally access television and/or radio channels. This provided money for the service. Otherwise, the services were funded by advertising or by governments. About half of African and Asian countries still have television licences but there are few in the Americas.

Even without a licence, the service could still be accessed. This made television and radio services non-excludable. They were also non-rival in consumption, since consumption by one person did not affect their availability to others.

In recent years, it has become possible for companies providing television programmes and films to exclude non-payers by encryption of devices, so that only those who have the right equipment and have paid the subscription can access the programmes. Use of the airwaves has become excludable.

Use of the airwaves by extra people does not often limit their use by others but, at peak times, they can become overcrowded. The airwaves in most countries are controlled by the government. To reduce the likelihood of the airwaves becoming rival in consumption, some governments have sold licences to mobile phone companies for the right to use them. This also creates competition between the providers.

The free-rider problem

The problem of non-excludability leads to the **free-rider problem**. This is where people can consume as much as they like of a good without having to pay for it. They cannot be excluded and can consume unlimited quantities. As previously discussed, if individuals

> **Key term**
>
> **Quasi-public good:** when a public good has some characteristics of a private good.

> **Key term**
>
> **Free-rider problem:** where people can consume as much as they like of a good, without having to pay for it.

cannot be prevented from benefiting from street lighting, why would they pay for it? They can be free riders.

In many countries in recent years, people have been encouraged to recycle as much of their waste as possible, to reduce the amount going to landfill sites. We all benefit from increased recycling whether we recycle our own waste or not. We are free riding on what other people do. Similarly, we could all change our lifestyles to reduce air pollution but an individual will benefit from cleaner air whether he or she does something about it or not.

This may lead to the overuse of a product if people are not paying their fair share for its provision or perhaps paying nothing.

The tragedy of the commons

The free-rider problem can lead to the **tragedy of the commons**. This is where individuals act in their own self-interest and this results in the depletion (using up) or degradation (damage) of a shared resource. The idea was first recorded in the 19th century in the context of people grazing their animals on common land – "the commons"; that is, land not owned by anyone. In 1968, this idea became known as the tragedy of the commons after an article written by the American ecologist Garrett Hardin.

The commons can refer to any shared resource and is an example of an environmental market failure. It can, for example, also apply to the air or sea. If there are no limits on the amount of fish caught, individuals may catch as much as they can to increase their incomes but in time, some species will no longer exist. These individuals' actions can impact negatively on others, and themselves, in future. There is no incentive for an individual to limit consumption or use of a resource if other people then consume more rather than the resource being protected for the future.

Governments can help to regulate such situations but there are also examples of local communities cooperating to preserve common resources. Elinor Ostrom received the 2009 Nobel Prize in Economic Sciences for her work on this topic. For example, for over 500 years, an area of common land in the Swiss Alps has been run by a group of farmers, who each also has their own land. It is in their interests to preserve the common land for the future, so it can continue to benefit them all. Some common resources will be easier to manage in this way than others.

▲ Figure 5.2.2: Elinor Ostrom, first female Nobel Prize winner for Economic Sciences

Progress questions

1 Explain how public goods differ from private goods.
2 Give **two** examples of a public good.
3 Give **two** examples of a private good.
4 What is the free-rider problem?

Activities

Find out about an example where:

1 the tragedy of the commons is happening or has happened
2 a common resource is being managed by the local people
3 a common resource is being managed by a government or an international organisation.

This section will develop your knowledge and understanding of:

→ how externalities exist when there is a divergence between private and social costs and benefits

→ why negative externalities are likely to result in overproduction and positive externalities are likely to result in underproduction

→ why the absence of property rights may result in externalities and hence market failure.

Meaning and types of externalities

Externalities are side-effects or spillover effects, on other people or firms (known as third parties), due to the consumption or production of goods and services. These third parties are not involved in the production or consumption and the side-effects are not reflected in the price of the product. The side-effects can be good or bad.

Externalities may be the result of:

• consumption

• production.

Externalities can be:

• positive

• negative.

Consumption externalities are effects on third parties due to the consumption of goods and services. They are caused by the actions of individuals.

Production externalities are effects on third parties due to the production of goods and services. They are caused by the actions of firms.

Positive externalities are benefits to third parties, for which they do not have to pay. For example, if most people have been vaccinated against a particular disease, others are less likely to catch it. Positive externalities are also known as **external benefits**.

Negative externalities are costs to third parties, for which they do not receive compensation. For example, traffic noise may affect your sleep. If the traffic consists of people driving on holiday, it is a negative consumption externality but if the traffic consists of lorries transporting raw materials, it is a negative production externality. Negative externalities are also known as **external costs**.

Divergence between private and social costs and benefits

Externalities exist when there is a divergence (difference) between private and social costs and benefits. **Private costs** (also known as internal costs) are costs to those involved in a transaction. These are the costs to the consumers or firms involved. The cost of producing the good and the price paid by the consumer are private costs.

Link

Externalities were introduced in 5.1 "The meaning of market failure".

Key terms

Externalities: effects on other people or firms (third parties) due to the consumption or production of goods and services.

Consumption externalities: effects on third parties due to the consumption of goods and services.

Production externalities: effects on third parties due to the production of goods and services.

Positive externalities/external benefits: benefits of consumption or production to third parties, for which they do not have to pay.

Negative externalities/external costs: costs of consumption or production to third parties, for which they do not receive compensation.

Private costs: the costs to those involved in a transaction, the costs to the consumers and firms involved.

However, there may also be external costs – costs to other individuals or firms. For example, if a firm dumps waste in a river, the firm downstream may have to spend money on cleaning the water if it needs water for its production process. The **social costs** are the costs or harmful effects to those involved in the transaction and to any third parties affected. The social costs (SC) of an economic activity are the private costs (PC) plus the external costs (EC).

$$SC = PC + EC$$

If there are no external costs, the social costs will be the same as the private costs.

Similarly, **private benefits** (also known as internal benefits) are benefits to the firms and consumers involved in the transaction. These are the money received by the firms and the satisfaction or utility of the consumers. If third parties also benefit in some way, there will be external benefits as well. The **social benefits** are the benefits to those involved in the transaction and to any third parties affected. The social benefits (SB) of an economic activity are the private benefits (PB) plus the external benefits (EB).

$$SB = PB + EB$$

If there are no external benefits, the social benefits will be the same as the private benefits.

▲ **Figure 5.3.1:** Not just a private benefit

Progress questions

1 Classify each of the following into private costs, private benefits, external costs or external benefits:
   i.   the pleasure of eating an ice cream
   ii. the ice-cream wrapper dropped on the ground in a park
   iii. the price paid by the individual for the ice cream
   iv. the wages of the workers making the ice cream
   v.   the revenue of the ice-cream seller
   vi. the expansion of an ice-cream shop, reducing the welfare benefits the government has to pay to those who were unemployed.

2 If the private cost of an activity is $20,000 and the external cost is $5,000, what is the social cost?

3 If the private benefit of an activity is $20 and the social benefit is $22, what is the external benefit?

The effects of positive and negative externalities

If there are externalities, there is likely to be a misallocation of resources. The market either produces too much or too little for the benefit of society as a whole. If there are negative externalities, there is likely to be overproduction. Positive externalities are likely to result in underproduction.

When deciding how much to produce or consume, sellers and buyers only consider the private costs and benefits, the costs and benefits that affect them. They do not have to pay for the external costs or external benefits, so these are not part of their decision-making process.

There are four situations that could arise:

- negative externalities in production
- negative externalities in consumption
- positive externalities in consumption
- positive externalities in production.

Negative externalities in production

Negative externalities in production occur when the production process results in harmful effects on third parties – other firms or individuals, who are not involved in the production of the good or service. For example, dust from a cement factory may affect air quality, and land on cars, laundry and gardens. This external cost (negative externality) harms the quality of life of those living in the local area.

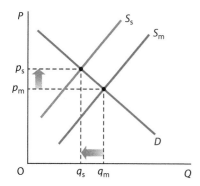

▲ **Figure 5.3.2**: Negative externalities in production

In Figure 5.3.2, S_m is the supply curve when firms only consider their private costs (and benefits). If there are negative externalities in production, the social costs are greater than the private costs. S_s shows the supply curve taking account of the full social costs. Left to the market, the equilibrium price is p_m and the quantity sold is q_m.

If the firms have to pay for the external costs as well as the private costs, they produce less and charge a higher price. If the firms pay for the social costs, the full cost to society, the equilibrium price will be p_s where q_s is sold. This is the **social optimum**, the quantity that reflects the social costs and benefits of the activity.

> **Key term**
>
> **Social optimum**: the quantity that maximises social welfare and reflects the social costs and benefits of an activity.

If left to the market, there is a misallocation of resources with too much being produced at too low a price. If there are negative externalities in production, there is likely to be overproduction.

Negative externalities in consumption

Negative externalities in consumption occur when the consumption process results in harmful effects on third parties, who are not involved in the individuals' decisions. For example, if people use their cars rather than walking or using public transport, they increase congestion on the roads. This adds to the journey times of others and may increase the risk of accidents.

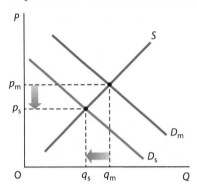

▲ **Figure 5.3.3**: Negative externalities in consumption

In Figure 5.3.3, D_m is the demand curve when individuals only consider their private benefits (and costs). D_s is the demand curve taking account of the social benefits. The market demand is higher than the demand that is best for society because there is no consideration of the negative effects on third parties. If there are negative externalities in consumption, the private benefits are greater than the social benefits. There is too much demand, which leads to a price and output that are both too high. If left to the market, the price will be p_m and the quantity consumed will be q_m.

If individuals considered the benefits for society as a whole rather than their own private benefit, they would drive less. If individuals take account of the social benefits, the full benefit to society, both the quantity consumed and the price will be lower, at q_s and p_s. This is the social optimum.

If left to the market, there will be a misallocation of resources with too much being consumed. If there are negative externalities in consumption, there is likely to be overconsumption and hence overproduction.

Positive externalities in consumption

Positive externalities in consumption occur when the consumption process results in beneficial effects on third parties, who are not involved in the individuals' decisions. For example, if some people are vaccinated against certain diseases, then others who are not vaccinated are also less likely to catch those diseases.

In Figure 5.3.4, D_m is the demand curve when individuals only consider their private benefits (and costs). D_s is the demand curve

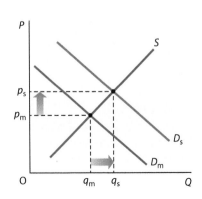

▲ **Figure 5.3.4**: Positive externalities in consumption

taking account of the social benefits. The market demand is lower than the demand that is best for society because there is no consideration of the positive effects on third parties. If there are positive externalities in consumption, the social benefits are greater than the private benefits. There is not enough demand, which leads to a price and output that are both too low. Left to the market, the price will be p_m and the quantity consumed will be q_m.

If individuals considered the benefits to society as a whole rather than just their own private benefit, more would be vaccinated. If individuals take account of the full social benefits both the quantity consumed and the price will be higher, at q_s and p_s – the social optimum.

Left to the market, there is a misallocation of resources with too little being consumed. If there are positive externalities in consumption, there is likely to be underconsumption and hence underproduction.

It is also possible that a product that results in positive externalities in consumption also generates negative externalities in production, for example. In this case, whether there is underproduction will depend on which of the externalities is greater.

Positive externalities in production

Positive externalities in production occur when the production process results in beneficial effects on third parties – other firms or individuals, who are not involved in the production. For example, new technology developed by one firm may benefit other firms by lowering their costs.

In Figure 5.3.5, S_m is the supply curve when firms only consider their private costs (and benefits). If there are positive externalities in production, the private costs are greater than the social costs. S_s shows the supply curve taking account of the social costs. Left to the market, the equilibrium price is p_m and the quantity sold is q_m, since the firm that developed the technology does not consider the lower costs of others.

If firms took account of the true costs to society of the external costs and not just the private costs, they would produce more and charge a lower price. If the firms consider the social costs, the equilibrium price will be p_s where q_s is sold. This is the social optimum.

There is a misallocation of resources with too little being produced at too high a price. If there are positive externalities in production, there is likely to be underproduction.

Quantitative skills

When drawing diagrams to illustrate externalities, if the externalities are in production, there should be two supply curves because firms' costs determine the position of the supply curve. If firms considered the external costs as well as the private costs, they would be willing to sell a different quantity.

If the externalities are in consumption there will be two demand curves. If consumers considered the external benefits as well as the private benefits, they would be willing to buy a different quantity.

Get it right

When externalities are involved or generated, it is important to consider their cause and whether they are good or bad. Are they caused by firms' production or by people's consumption? Are they beneficial or harmful to others? This will enable you to identify which of the diagrams (Figures 5.3.2, 5.3.3, 5.3.4 or 5.3.5) should be drawn to illustrate the situation.

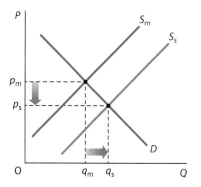

▲ Figure 5.3.5: Positive externalities in production

Activities

1   Draw a diagram showing the market and social optimum quantities for a product with negative externalities in consumption and positive externalities in production.

2   Is there overproduction or underproduction?

Case study: A new capital for Egypt

In 2015, it was announced that a new capital would be built for Egypt, 45 kilometres east of the current capital, Cairo. It is planned to house 6.5 million people, as well as becoming the new administrative and financial centre of the country. In the first phase of building, the project was expected to create 1.5 million jobs. It is intended that affordable housing will be available to those on low incomes but with more housing, house prices in Cairo may fall in future.

Cairo is one of the world's most crowded cities, with 20 million people living in or near the city. Pollution and traffic levels are high, with over a billion journeys on the subway system each year. There are also over 4.5 million cars on the streets of Cairo, the majority of them old and polluting. Every year, in the autumn, smog (a mixture of smoke and fog) hangs over the city, causing health problems. The city produces 10,000 tons of waste every day, much of which is not collected. Water pollution is another problem.

A new international airport has now been opened. This will service the new capital as well as reducing pressure on

Cairo's existing airport. A third airport, near the Giza pyramids, west of Cairo, also opened recently. This will provide better access to the pyramids. It is hoped that both new airports will attract tourists to the area, an important source of revenue.

Use the information in the case study regarding Cairo and the building of a new capital for Egypt to identify at least **two** of each of the following:

i.   private costs
ii. external costs
iii. private benefits
iv. external benefits.

▲ Figure 5.3.6: The pyramids, a major tourist attraction

Why the absence of property rights may result in externalities and market failure

Property rights refers to the authority to determine how a resource is used. It can apply to the ownership of land, sea, air or any resource on or within it. It can also apply to what people have created. For example, an inventor, or the writer of a book, may have **intellectual property rights (IPR)**. These rights refer to the ownership of a creation of someone's mind, such as a design or a piece of music. The absence of property rights may result in externalities and hence market failure.

If someone owns a piece of land, that person has the right to decide how it is used and is likely to look after it, to preserve its value in the future. If there is no clear owner and/or the land is commonly owned, it may be overused, as in the tragedy of the commons.

In the absence of property rights, people may act only considering their private benefits, for example overfishing in an area of ocean. This will cause negative externalities by reducing the stock of fish available to others in the future. If individuals also considered the external costs, they would fish less. Free riders have unlimited access to the resource if clear boundaries and legal limits are not in place, leading to overuse. There is no incentive for them to use less of the resource if it is simply used more by others.

If there were no intellectual property rights, it would be possible for another person or firm to copy or sell someone else's idea or product. This would lead to fewer new products and ideas being developed because there would be less incentive to do so if creators were unable to earn enough profit. This would cause market failure, since markets would be less efficient (and it is also inequitable).

Value judgements and the classification of merit and demerit goods

Some goods and services benefit or harm others as well as the individuals consuming them but not all goods and services that generate externalities are classified as merit or demerit goods. These merit goods and demerit goods may be produced in too little or too great a quantity, resulting in a misallocation of resources and market failure. Merit and demerit goods are examples of **partial market failure** – a market exists for the product but it does not result in the socially optimum quantity being produced and consumed, causing a misallocation of resources. The factors of production are not allocated in a way that maximises the economic welfare of society.

A **merit good** is a product that society or government judges desirable and too little is provided by the market for the benefit of society as a whole. In a free market economy, it would be underconsumed and hence underproduced. Health care and education are examples of merit goods. They may be considered to be important for the quality of people's lives but some people are unwilling or unable to buy enough education and health care for the well-being of themselves and others.

A **demerit good** is a product that society or government judges is undesirable and too much is provided by the market for the benefit of society as a whole. For example, smokers gain satisfaction from consuming cigarettes but if left to the free market, cigarettes would be overconsumed and hence overproduced. Cigarettes are an example of a demerit good. Some people may buy too many cigarettes for the well-being of themselves and others.

Whether a product is classified as a merit or demerit good depends on value judgements. These are views about what is good or bad, right or wrong. They reflect what is thought to be important, based on moral and political judgements. Governments consider what is best for the country as a whole and make decisions about which goods and services should be provided in greater or smaller quantities to achieve this. In some countries, a government may provide free or cheaper health care or entry to museums because it believes they are important.

In other countries, people may have to pay for health care or take out insurance. Museums may have to charge for entry to make a profit or to cover their costs. Resources have alternative uses and government

Link

Merit and demerit goods were introduced in 5.1 "The meaning of market failure" and value judgements were explained in 1.5 "Economic methodology".

Get it right

Merit and demerit goods are private goods. They are excludable and rival in consumption. The fact that some merit goods are provided free by the government does not make them public goods.

Key terms

Partial market failure: where a market exists for a product but it does not result in the socially optimum quantity being produced and consumed, causing a misallocation of resources.

Merit good: a product that society or government judges is desirable, too little is provided by the market for the benefit of society as a whole.

Demerit good: a product that society or government judges is undesirable, too much is provided by the market for the benefit of society as a whole.

finance is limited, so what the government considers to be a merit good, provided free or subsidised to increase consumption, depends on the government's value judgements.

However, it is generally believed that some products are so important that people should not be denied access to them if they are unable to pay. For example, most people believe that it is morally unacceptable not to treat someone who has been involved in an accident if they have no health insurance.

Similarly, value judgements also determine what is classified as a demerit good and may be taxed to increase its price, or what is restricted in terms of who can use it and where.

Case study: Education in Argentina and Chile

Argentina and Chile are neighbours in South America. Argentina has a population of about 45 million compared with about 19 million in Chile. Argentina's income per head in 2018 was $12,370 and Chile's was $14,670.

Education is provided free in Argentina, from primary to undergraduate university level. Private education is also available but the state provides subsidies for some of this. Education is funded by taxpayers. The literacy rate is 98.1%. This is the percentage of people aged 15 and over who can read and write. Public universities charge no tuition fees and are available to all. However, students have to pay for materials and transport, causing the majority to come from higher-income families.

In Chile, up to 90% of primary and secondary education is funded by the state giving vouchers to parents to spend at a school of their choice. Those with more money can pay extra for "better" schools. Schools in Chile may charge an annual fee plus another for monthly tuition. The literacy rate is 97.5%. All universities in Chile used to charge enrolment and tuition

fees but in 2016, 30 of the universities became free to those in the poorest 50% of the population. Otherwise, scholarships and low-interest loans are available to help students fund their university education.

1   Why may the funding arrangements for education in Argentina and Chile differ?

2   Why may less financial support be given to university education?

▲ Figure 5.4.1: Should university education be free?

Merit and demerit goods, and positive and negative externalities in consumption

Merit goods and positive externalities in consumption

Merit goods are likely to be subject to positive externalities in consumption. As well as the private benefits to the individual consumer, there are external benefits to third parties from their use. The social benefit is greater than the private benefit. However, since the consumers only consider the benefits (and costs) to themselves, these goods and services will be underconsumed and therefore underproduced. If the government considers the benefits, both private and external, to be important, it may intervene in the market to increase consumption and to try to prevent a misallocation of resources.

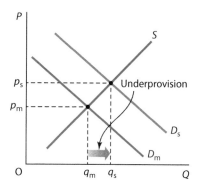

▲ **Figure 5.4.2:** Underprovision of merit goods

In Figure 5.4.2, D_m is the demand curve when individuals only consider their private benefits but demand is D_s if the benefits to society are taken into account. Left to the market, the price is p_m and the quantity consumed is q_m. There is underprovision of $q_m q_s$. There is not enough demand, or resources allocated to the activity, to achieve the social optimum.

For example, when deciding how much education or health care to demand, individuals only consider the benefits to themselves. However, we all benefit from a healthy, well-educated society since, for example, people in these societies are more productive and generate more income. We benefit from the education and good health of others as well as our own education and health.

If individuals considered the benefit to society as a whole rather than their own private benefit, demand would be higher. If individuals were to take account of the full social benefits, demand would be D_s and the socially optimum quantity of q_s would be consumed.

Not all products that result in positive externalities in consumption are merit goods. You may gain pleasure from sitting in your garden listening to your neighbour's music or looking at their attractive garden. There is underconsumption and a misallocation of resources due to the externalities but this does not make them merit goods. A government is unlikely to intervene to increase the quantity of either of these activities.

Demerit goods and negative externalities in consumption

Similarly, demerit goods are likely to be subject to negative externalities in consumption. As well as the private costs to the individual consumer, there are external costs to third parties from their use. Consumers overestimate the benefits to themselves and underestimate or ignore the negative effects. The private benefit is greater than the social benefit. However, since consumers only consider the benefits (and costs) to themselves, these products will be overconsumed and therefore overproduced. If the government considers the social benefits to be important, it may intervene in the market to reduce consumption, to try to prevent a misallocation of resources.

In Figure 5.4.3, D_m is the demand curve when individuals only consider their private benefits but demand is D_s if the benefits to

Link

The same diagram appears as Figure 5.3.4 to illustrate positive externalities in consumption.

Quantitative skills

When illustrating the misallocation of resources resulting from the consumption of merit and demerit goods using demand and supply diagrams, the externalities are in consumption with there being too little or too much demand if left to the market.

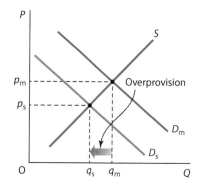

▲ **Figure 5.4.3:** Overprovision of demerit goods

Link

The same diagram was drawn as Figure 5.3.3 to illustrate negative externalities in consumption.

Get it right

Although merit and demerit goods may be subject to positive and negative externalities in consumption, this does not mean that all goods and services with positive or negative externalities in consumption must be merit or demerit goods.

Key terms

Information failure: where individuals or firms have incomplete or inaccurate information, resulting in wrong decisions.

Myopic/myopia: short-sighted/shortsightedness, focusing on the short-term effects rather than the longer-term consequences.

Link

There is more on imperfect information and the impact of biases on decision-making in the A2 part of the course.

Progress questions

1 Explain why the classification of merit and demerit goods depends on a value judgement.

2 Are demerit goods likely to have externalities in production or consumption?

3 Which is higher for a merit good – demand based on the private benefits or the social benefits?

4 Is the socially optimum quantity for a demerit good higher or lower than the free market quantity?

5 Explain why underprovision of health care may result from imperfect information.

society are taken into account. Left to the market, the price is p_m and the quantity consumed is q_m. There is overprovision of $q_s q_m$. There is too much demand, or resources allocated to the activity, to achieve the social optimum.

For example, when deciding how many cigarettes to consume, individuals only consider the benefits (and costs) to themselves, such as the pleasure gained from smoking. However, their consumption can also result in litter, the risk of fires and increased health care costs which may have to be paid by the state and taxpayers. Passive smoking can also cause other people to become ill. The consumption of cigarettes can have a negative impact on themselves and others.

If left to the market, there is a misallocation of resources with too much of the product being consumed. If there are negative externalities in consumption, there is likely to be overconsumption and hence overproduction.

If individuals considered the benefit and cost to society as a whole, not their own private benefit, demand would be lower. If individuals take account of the social benefits, demand is D_s and the socially optimum quantity of q_s is consumed.

Not all products that result in negative externalities in consumption are demerit goods. Going back to the earlier example, you may find your neighbour's music unpleasant and too loud, and they may not look after their garden. There is overconsumption and a misallocation of resources due to the externalities but this does not make them demerit goods. A government is unlikely to intervene to change the quantity of these activities.

How imperfect information can affect provision of merit goods and demerit goods

As well as underprovision of merit goods and overprovision of demerit goods resulting from consumers only considering the private benefits, there may also be resource misallocation resulting from imperfect information. **Information failure** is where individuals or firms have incomplete or inaccurate information (or have misunderstood it), resulting in wrong decisions.

People also tend to be **myopic** (short-sighted), focusing on their short-term satisfaction or utility, not taking account of the long-term costs and benefits.

For example, students do not always know or weigh up the longer-term benefits of obtaining further qualifications. They may focus more on how they wish to spend their time and money in the short term rather than working out what is best for their future income and job prospects. They may not know how much difference a good Economics degree could make to the rest of their life. Such merit goods are therefore underconsumed and underprovided partly due to imperfect information.

Similarly, users of cigarettes may focus on the satisfaction they receive from smoking now. They may not know the likelihood of developing smoking-related diseases later in life or they may choose to ignore this information. These demerit goods are therefore overconsumed and overprovided, partly because people are not perfectly informed.

This section will develop your knowledge and understanding of:

→ why imperfect and asymmetric information can lead to market failure

→ why the existence of monopoly and monopoly power can lead to market failure

→ why the immobility of factors of production can lead to market failure

→ why price instability may be a source of market failure.

Why imperfect and asymmetric information can lead to market failure

Imperfect information exists when buyers and/or sellers do not have all the necessary information to make the correct decision about a product. Sometimes consumers have too much choice and/or it may relate to a technical issue about which they know little. Both of these situations make it difficult to reach the right decision.

Asymmetric information is a form of imperfect information where one party (usually the seller) has more or better information than the other (usually the buyer). The party with better information has an advantage.

For example, when selling a second-hand car, the seller has far more knowledge of its quality than the buyer. Will the buyer get a good or a bad car for the money? With one party having more information, the wrong decision could be made. The buyer may miss out on a good car if he or she does not trust the seller, or may end up with a poor one. The seller may also lose out by not being able to make a sale at a reasonable price. The American economist, George Akerlof, wrote about "The market for lemons", with lemons being the term he used for a defective used car (as opposed to peaches for good cars).

Both imperfect information and asymmetric information are examples of information failure, where individuals or firms have inaccurate or incomplete information (or have misunderstood the data). This makes it difficult for economic agents to make rational decisions and is another possible cause of market failure. Consumers will be unable to weigh up all the costs and benefits to maximise their utility or satisfaction.

Imperfect information may lead to a misallocation of resources through the underconsumption of merit goods and overconsumption of demerit goods. If people are unaware of, or do not understand, the full effects both in the short term and the long term of consuming certain products, how can they decide which are best and what quantity they should buy?

Why monopoly and monopoly power can lead to market failure

Market failure occurs when there is an inefficient or inequitable allocation of resources. When there is a monopoly, or a firm has monopoly power, it is likely that there will be higher prices and

Link

Some examples of market imperfections have already been introduced. Information failure was mentioned in 5.4. "Merit and demerit goods"; aspects of market failure that could result when a firm has a dominant share of the market were covered in 4.4 "Monopoly and monopoly power"; and causes of fluctuations in commodity prices were explained in 2.5 "The determination of market prices".

▲ **Figure 5.5.1:** Does this look like a lemon or a peach?

Key terms

Imperfect information: when buyers and/or sellers do not have all the necessary information to make the correct decision about a product.

Asymmetric information: a form of imperfect information where one party has more or better information than the other.

Case study: The market for health insurance in Australia

Health care in Australia is provided by the state and also by the private sector through health insurance. There is a national health policy but state governments run the hospitals. The government's Medicare scheme provides free access to hospital treatment and subsidises other medical care. Many Australians take out private health insurance to avoid the extra charges or simply because their family has always had private health insurance.

Private health insurance has become increasingly expensive in recent years, forcing many people to reduce their level of cover, often to find that when they try to claim, their insurance does not cover what they need. There are 34 insurers in the market, so there is plenty of competition but a recent report claimed that there are 40,000 variations of what the policies cover. How can people understand and compare all the policies available?

Many experts claim that the private health insurance system is an example of market failure and should be replaced with a single provider.

1   Why may the Australian health insurance market be an example of market failure?

2   Explain how government subsidies may help to achieve the socially optimum amount of health care.

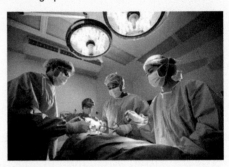

▲ Figure 5.5.2: A failing market?

Progress questions

1   Explain why there is asymmetric information when someone applies for a bank loan or a job.

2   How may monopoly power lead to market failure?

3   Explain **three** factors that may make it less likely for market failure to occur when a firm has monopoly power.

Key terms

Mobility of factors of production: the ability of resources to move from one place or type of work to another.

Immobility of factors of production: where resources find it difficult to move from one place or type of work to another.

profits, since the firm can limit the quantity it sells, to raise the price. How much they can do this depends on the price elasticity of demand, which is affected by product differentiation, brand loyalty and barriers to entry.

A higher price could be considered inequitable, since poorer people will be less able to buy the product. This would be more significant if the good or service is a necessity, with few substitutes.

The outcome compared to a competitive market may also be inefficient. The resources may not be put to their best or most effective use, so welfare is not maximised. Society would prefer more resources to be allocated to the production of these goods and the price to be lower. Also, if there is little or no competition, the costs of a monopolist may be higher than they could be, perhaps due to excessive advertising or overstaffing, further wasting resources.

So, the existence of monopoly and monopoly power can lead to market failure and a misallocation of resources through being both inequitable and inefficient. However, there are other factors that may affect the situation. Large firms may be able to take advantage of economies of scale and use their profits to invest in research and development, making market failure less likely to occur. This may also be the case if the firm is run by the state and prices are kept low, although state-run monopolies are not always efficient.

Why the immobility of factors of production can lead to market failure

Mobility of factors of production refers to the ability of resources to move from one place or type of work to another. **Immobility of factors of production** is where resources find it difficult to move from one place or type of work to another. It can be divided into two types – geographical and occupational immobility.

Geographical immobility of labour is when workers find it difficult to move to jobs in a different area, region or country. For example, this may be because of family ties to an area, or being unable to afford to live in the other place. **Occupational mobility of labour** is when workers find it difficult to move from one type of job to another. This is most likely to be because they lack the skills or training needed for the other job. Both types of immobility could be partly due to information failure, with individuals not knowing where there are suitable jobs.

If factors of production such as labour are immobile, this may lead to market failure. For example, if a worker lacks the skills needed to find work in an expanding industry and is unemployed, this is a waste of scarce resources. Alternatively, resources may be used inefficiently. Also, if firms are unable to recruit suitable workers, they may find it difficult to increase their output to meet demand.

Why price instability may be a source of market failure

Some prices, especially of primary products such as agricultural crops, may be unstable. This may also result in unstable incomes of producers. Agricultural prices can fluctuate considerably in the short term since the supply partly depends on the weather. If supply falls, this may lead to a large rise in price, particularly if demand is also inelastic, as shown in Figure 5.5.3.

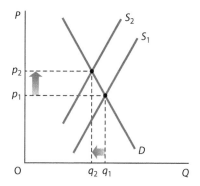

▲ Figure 5.5.3: Price instability

As supply falls from S_1 to S_2, there is a more than proportionate rise in price from p_1 to p_2 because demand is inelastic. Price acts as both a signal and an incentive in the market. However, if the price changes by large amounts (particularly if in different directions) in short time periods, these signals can be confusing. It may lead to firms either overproducing or underproducing in the short term. Also, there may be too little or too much investment in the longer term, resulting in an inefficient allocation of resources.

Information failure may add to the problem. For example, if there are many farmers all changing their plans in response to a large change in price, not knowing the full impact of their combined decisions on

Key terms

Geographical immobility of labour: when workers find it difficult to move to jobs in a different area, region or country.

Occupational mobility of labour: when workers find it difficult to move from one type of job to another.

the market, this may cause another large change in price. If there is speculation in the market, this could make the problem even worse.

Case study: The price of cocoa

Cocoa beans have been used to make chocolate and drinks for thousands of years. The Ivory Coast is the largest producer of cocoa beans, followed by Ghana and Indonesia. Table 5.5.1 shows the average daily prices of cocoa in selected months of a particular year.

▼ **Table 5.5.1:** Average daily prices of cocoa in selected months (figures relate to 2018)

https://icco.org/statistics/cocoa-prices/monthly-averages. html; accessed 1 December 2019

Month	Price (US$ per tonne)
January	1951.97
March	2503.95
May	2659.94
July	2357.05
September	2195.09

1   What is the difference in dollars between the highest and lowest monthly prices?

2   What was the percentage increase in price between January and March, to **one** decimal place?

3   Calculate the mean average daily price of cocoa for these five months, to **the nearest dollar**.

4   How might the price changes shown in the table lead to market failure?

▲ **Figure 5.5.4:** Cocoa beans

5.6 An inequitable distribution of income and wealth

This section will develop your knowledge and understanding of:

→ the difference between income and wealth

→ the distinction between equality and equity

→ why, in the absence of government intervention, the market mechanism is likely to result in a very unequal and inequitable distribution of income and wealth

→ why, in a market economy, an individual's ability to consume goods and services depends upon their income and wealth, and an inequitable distribution of income and wealth leads to a misallocation of resources and market failure.

The difference between income and wealth

Income

Income is a flow of money, received by an economic agent over a period of time. The income may be received by an individual, a firm or the country as a whole. For an individual, this includes income from work (earned income) and unearned income such as interest on savings, or dividends from owning shares. It also includes pension income, which may result from someone's job (occupational pension) or be paid by the government after people reach a certain age. Other welfare benefits paid by the state are also classified as income.

Wealth

Wealth is a stock of assets owned by an economic agent at a point in time. For many people, their most valuable asset is their home but some people own many properties, which they may rent to others. Assets also include savings in a bank or shares in a company. Individuals may have assets as part of their pension fund. Wealth often generates income; for example, savings in a bank may earn interest.

The distinction between equality and equity

Equality

The distribution of income and wealth refers to how it is divided between people or regions. This affects people's economic welfare. Equality is when everyone has, or is treated, the same. This may apply to the distribution of income or wealth. A distinction may also be made about whether there is equality of opportunity, and if so, inequality of income or wealth may not be inequitable.

Equity

Equity is about fairness. The degree of inequality can be measured but whether a given distribution of income is equitable (fair and just) involves a value judgement. This is a view about what is right or wrong, good or bad. People will differ in their opinions about whether the distribution of income or wealth should be more or less equal.

Link

Income and wealth were introduced in 2.1 "The demand for goods and services", as factors that determine the demand for a good or service, and equity was mentioned in 1.5 "Economic methodology", in the context of normative statements.

Key terms

Earned income: income from a job or self-employment.

Unearned income: income from the ownership of property or other assets, not from employment.

Welfare benefits: money paid by the state to people on low incomes.

Key terms

Distribution of income and wealth: how income or wealth is divided between people or regions.

Equality: when everyone has, or is treated, the same.

Get it right

Equity and equality are often confused. If income is unequally distributed, this does not necessarily make the situation inequitable.

Progress questions

1 For each of the following, state whether it is an example of income or wealth:

    i.   a state pension

    ii. the salary of a bank manager

    iii. a piece of land

    iv. a valuable painting

    v. the profits of a firm

    vi. a car

    vii. a diamond ring.

2 Will a statement about whether something is equitable or not be a normative or positive statement?

Why the market mechanism is likely to result in an unequal distribution of income and wealth

In a free market economy, in the absence of government intervention, the distribution of income and wealth is likely to be very unequal. This can be seen in many countries.

There are many reasons why income may be unequally distributed. For example, people have different skills and abilities, which will affect how much they are paid. Some people will be unable to work for different reasons, including age. Also, those people who have more income will find it easier to save and increase their wealth.

Wealth may be unequally distributed due to, for example, inheritance or people building up successful businesses. If wealth is unequally distributed, this will also contribute to the inequality of income.

Why an inequitable distribution of income and wealth leads to a misallocation of resources and market failure

As stated above, in a market economy, income and wealth are likely to be very unequally distributed. The allocation of goods and services in this type of economy is on the basis of ability and willingness to pay, with prices determined by the free market forces of supply and demand.

Individuals' ability to buy and consume goods and services will depend on their income and wealth. In a free market economy, their spending is a "vote" for more of that good to be supplied. Those with little or no income and wealth will not be able to buy as much, and may not even be able to buy the basic necessities. If the distribution of income is inequitable, there is a misallocation of resources and market failure.

People will differ in their views about whether a particular level of inequality of income or wealth is inequitable and this may depend on the extent of the inequality. Some economists, who believe free markets work best (**free-market economists** or non-interventionists), generally believe that an unequal distribution of income and wealth provides incentives for people to create more income and wealth, and is not necessarily a cause of market failure.

Activity

Find some numerical data for the distribution of income and/or wealth in your country in recent years. Has the distribution become more or less equal?

Progress questions

3 Explain how inequalities in wealth contribute to the inequality of income.

4 Is inequality of income and wealth always inequitable?

Key term

Free-market economists: those who believe that competitive markets and minimal government intervention are best for an economy.

This section will develop your knowledge and understanding of:

→ why the existence of market failure, in its various forms, provides an argument for government intervention in markets

→ how governments influence the allocation of resources in a variety of ways, including through public expenditure, taxation and regulations

→ how governments have a range of objectives and these aims affect how they intervene in a mixed economy to influence the allocation of resources

→ the use of indirect taxation, subsidies, price controls, buffer stocks, pollution permits, extension of property rights, state provision and regulation to correct market failure.

Why market failure provides an argument for government intervention

The existence of market failure, whatever its form or cause, results in a misallocation of resources. If left to the market forces of supply and demand, the quantity provided of some products is too little or too much for the benefit of society as a whole. The price may be too high, too low or fluctuate too much. There is a welfare loss due to an inefficient and/or inequitable allocation of resources.

Resources are not put to their best use, so welfare is not maximised. Society would benefit from a different allocation of resources. This may involve more or less of the good or service being produced and/or allocating it to consumers in a different way.

Market failure arises when the private sector, with no government intervention, results in too many or too few resources allocated to some products. This failure of free markets to allocate resources in the best way for society as a whole provides an argument for government intervention in markets.

How governments influence resource allocation

Governments often intervene in markets to correct market failure. They can influence the allocation of resources in a variety of ways. Three main ways in which governments intervene are through public expenditure, taxation and regulation.

Public expenditure is spending by the government, which may be by central or local government. This includes spending on public goods such as defence, merit goods such as education, benefits for those on low incomes, or on anything else that may increase the welfare of society and help to reduce inefficiency or inequity.

Taxation is money that must be paid to the government by individuals or firms. As well as providing money for public expenditure, other uses of taxation are to reduce inequalities in income and wealth and to increase the price of some goods to reduce their consumption.

> **Link**
>
> The types and causes of market failure have been covered earlier in Chapter 5.

> **Get it right**
>
> Public expenditure is spending by the government or public sector. It is not the spending of households or the general public.

> **Key terms**
>
> **Public expenditure:** spending by the government, which may be by central or local government.
>
> **Taxation:** money that must be paid to the government by individuals or firms.

Key term

Regulation: rules or laws that control the behaviour and activities of individuals and firms.

Regulation involves rules or laws that control the behaviour and activities of individuals and firms. Regulation may involve, for example, a ban or limit on some activities, or forcing people or firms to do something that they would not do otherwise. If laws are broken, there may be fines or other penalties.

How governments have a range of objectives that affect how they intervene in a mixed economy

In a mixed economy, some decisions about what to produce and who should benefit are left to the market and some decisions are made by the government. Some countries leave most decisions to buyers and sellers, with limited intervention by the government. In other countries, the government controls most of the major industries.

Key term

Interventionist economists: those who believe that governments need to take action to correct market failures to increase the welfare of the people.

Free-market economists believe that competitive markets generally work well, through signalling and incentives providing the mix of goods and services that people want. They believe that minimal government intervention is best for an economy. However, most free-market economists accept that governments need to provide public goods.

Interventionist economists argue that governments need to take action to correct market failures to increase the welfare of the people. This is because they believe that markets do not always work well and market failure is common.

How much governments intervene and in which areas is affected by moral and political judgements, and the likely consequences of their actions. Will government intervention help to correct market failure? Alternatively, could it make the situation worse or have unintended consequences? Will there be increased efficiency and/or equity or is it best left to the market? Governments have limited money. Resources are scarce and have alternative uses. Therefore, governments must make decisions about how best to use their money and resources.

▲ **Figure 5.7.1**: Traffic congestion: what should be done, if anything?

Governments have a range of objectives, relating both to parts of the economy and the economy as a whole. The aims of governments will affect how they intervene in a mixed economy to influence the allocation of resources.

Link

Mixed economies were explained in 1.3 "Scarcity, choice and the allocation of resources"; the impact of value judgements on decision making was covered in 1.5 "Economic methodology"; and free-market economists were introduced in 5.6 "An inequitable distribution of income and wealth".

Progress questions

1 Why should governments intervene in markets?

2 What are the **three** main ways that governments can intervene in markets?

3 Why do economists disagree about the amount of government intervention in markets?

The use of different policies to correct market failure

There are many ways in which governments can intervene to try to reduce or to prevent market failure. These include indirect taxation, subsidies, price controls, buffer stocks, pollution permits, extension of property rights, state provision and regulation.

Indirect taxes

An indirect tax is a tax/levy on spending. Firms have to pay this money to the government, which adds to their costs in the same way as higher raw material prices for example. This reduces supply.

Indirect taxes can be specific or ad valorem. **Specific taxes** are based on the quantity, not the price, of the good or service. For example, a tax of $1 per litre of petrol is an example of a specific tax. Alternatively, indirect taxes can be **ad valorem**, which means "according to value", where the tax is a percentage of the value. A 15% sales tax would be an example of an ad valorem tax.

As well as to raise revenue to pay for government spending, indirect taxes may be used to reduce the production and consumption of goods and services that generate negative externalities. Figure 5.7.2 shows the use of a specific indirect tax to correct the problem of negative externalities in production and Figure 5.7.3 shows its use to correct negative externalities in consumption.

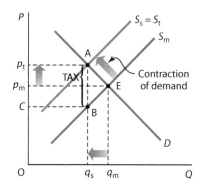

▲ **Figure 5.7.2:** Taxing negative externalities in production

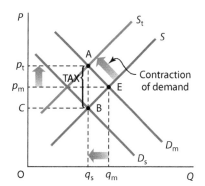

▲ **Figure 5.7.3:** Taxing negative externalities in consumption

Figure 5.7.2 shows a situation where there are harmful effects on third parties from production. For example, dust from a cement factory may affect the air quality of people living nearby. S_m is the supply curve when firms only consider their private costs (and benefits). However, there are negative externalities in production and the social costs are greater than the private costs. S_s shows the supply curve taking account of the social costs. Left to the market, the equilibrium is at E, where the price is p_m and the quantity sold is q_m.

To achieve the socially optimum output of q_s and therefore to remove the market failure of overproduction, a tax of AB is needed. This is equivalent to the external cost of that particular unit. The tax increases the private cost of the firms of producing this unit and they are then only willing to supply this quantity at a price of p_t instead of C. The

Key terms

Specific (tax or subsidy): based on the quantity, not the price of the good or service.

Ad valorem: according to value, a percentage of the value of the good or service.

market is now taking account of the full social cost, the external cost as well as the private cost.

The equilibrium moves from E to A as a result of the indirect tax of AB. The new equilibrium price increases to p_t and at this higher price, less is sold due to the resulting contraction of demand. The new equilibrium quantity is q_s, the social optimum. An indirect tax **internalises the externality** – making the firm's private costs or benefits equal to the social costs or benefits. This example also illustrates the **polluter pays principle** – the idea that that those who cause the pollution should pay for the costs to others.

Figure 5.7.3 shows a situation where there are harmful effects on third parties from consumption. For example, the smoking of demerit goods such as cigarettes can result in litter and increased health care costs, both for smokers and others. D_m is the demand curve when individuals only consider their private benefits (and costs). However, there are negative externalities in consumption and the private benefits are greater than the social benefits. D_s is the demand curve taking account of the social benefits.

Again, to achieve the socially optimum output of q_s and therefore to remove the market failure of overconsumption, a tax of AB is needed. This is equivalent to the external cost (or negative benefit) of consumption of that particular unit. The tax increases the private cost to the firms of producing this unit and they are then only willing to supply this quantity at a price of p_t instead of C.

The equilibrium moves from E to A as a result of the indirect tax of AB. The new equilibrium price increases to p_t and at this higher price, less is sold due to a contraction of demand. The new equilibrium quantity is q_s, the social optimum.

Advantages and disadvantages of indirect taxes

As well as reducing the quantity to the social optimum, the tax raises revenue for the government. The tax revenue, on both diagrams, is the area Cp_tAB, which is the tax per unit multiplied by the new quantity sold. Although this does not directly compensate those who suffer from the negative externalities, it may be used by the government to pay for other measures that help to reduce the problems caused, or to correct other market failures.

However, it is difficult to identify the "correct" amount of the tax. This requires the externality to be measured and given a money value, which is very difficult. If the tax is too high, it may raise the price too much and reduce the quantity to below the social optimum. If the tax is too low, it may not reduce production enough but at least the quantity provided will be closer to the social optimum than before.

The extent of the price increase as a result of the tax depends on the price elasticity of demand for the good or service. If demand is inelastic, most of the tax will be passed on to the buyers in the form of a higher price. In both diagrams, p_tp_m will be greater than p_mC. The **tax incidence** (how the tax is distributed between buyer and seller) falls mainly on the buyer. A large tax may be needed to reduce quantity to the social optimum. This may be inequitable if the product is a necessity, since the tax will be **regressive** – it will represent a larger percentage of a poorer person's income, and richer people may continue to buy a similar quantity to before.

Subsidies

A subsidy is a payment to producers to reduce costs. It enables firms to increase supply.

This will add to government spending but may be used to increase the production and consumption of goods and services that generate positive externalities. Figure 5.7.4 shows the use of a (specific) subsidy when there are positive externalities in consumption and Figure 5.7.5 shows its use for positive externalities in production.

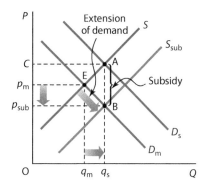

▲ **Figure 5.7.4**: Subsidising positive externalities in consumption

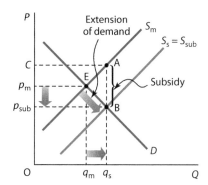

▲ **Figure 5.7.5**: Subsidising positive externalities in production

Figure 5.7.4 shows a situation where there are beneficial effects on third parties from consumption. For example, individuals and society as a whole benefit from good health care, which may be considered to be a merit good. The population will be more productive, others are less likely to become ill and there may be less need for government spending on health care. D_m is the demand curve when individuals only consider their private benefits (and costs). However, there are positive externalities in consumption and the social benefits are greater than the private benefits. D_s is the demand curve taking account of the social benefits.

To achieve the socially optimum output of q_s and therefore to remove the market failure of underconsumption, a subsidy of AB is needed. This is equivalent to the external benefit of that particular unit. The subsidy reduces the private cost to the firms of producing this unit and they are then willing to supply this quantity at a price of p_{sub} instead of C.

The equilibrium moves from E to B as a result of the subsidy of AB. The new equilibrium price falls to p_{sub} and at this lower price, more is sold due to the extension of demand. The new equilibrium quantity is q_s, the social optimum.

Figure 5.7.5 shows a situation where there are beneficial effects on third parties from production. For example, new technology developed by one firm may benefit other firms by lowering their costs.

S_m is the supply curve when firms only consider their private costs (and benefits). However, there are positive externalities in production and the private costs are greater than the social costs. S_s shows the supply curve taking account of the social costs. Left to the market, the equilibrium is at E, where the price is p_m and the quantity is q_m.

To achieve the socially optimum output of q_s and therefore to remove the market failure of underproduction, a subsidy of AB is needed. This is equivalent to the negative external cost (or external benefit) of that particular unit. The subsidy reduces the private cost to the firms of producing this unit and they are then willing to supply this quantity at a price of p_{sub} instead of C. The market is now taking account of the social cost not just the private cost.

The equilibrium moves from E to B as a result of the subsidy of AB. The new equilibrium price falls to p_{sub} and at this lower price, more is sold due to an extension of demand. The new equilibrium quantity is q_s, the social optimum.

Advantages and disadvantages of a subsidy

As well as increasing provision to the social optimum, a subsidy can make merit goods more affordable for the poor, improving both efficiency and equity in the market. However, unlike an indirect tax, a subsidy will cost the government money. It has a financial cost and an opportunity cost. Alternative uses of the money should be considered. The total spending by the government, on both diagrams, is area $p_{sub}CAB$, which is the subsidy per unit multiplied by the new quantity sold.

As with the tax, it is difficult to identify the "correct" amount for the subsidy. This again requires the externality to be measured and given a money value, which is very difficult. If the subsidy is too high, it may reduce the price too much and raise the quantity above the social optimum, resulting in an inefficient use of resources. If the subsidy is too low, it may not increase production enough but the quantity provided will be closer to the social optimum than before. Also, if firms are provided with a subsidy, they may have less incentive to try to be as efficient as before.

The extent of the fall in price depends on the price elasticity of demand for the product. If demand is inelastic, most of the subsidy will be passed onto the buyers in the form of a lower price. In both diagrams, $p_m p_{sub}$ will be greater than Cp_m. A large subsidy may be needed to increase quantity to the social optimum. A subsidy will reduce the price for all income groups, subsidising the rich as well as the poor.

Activity

Draw two versions of Figure 5.7.5, one with inelastic demand and the other with elastic demand. Compare what happens to price and quantity after a subsidy is provided.

Quantitative skills

When illustrating the appropriate tax or subsidy on an externality diagram, it is best to draw it as a vertical line between the two supply curves at the socially optimum level of output. This enables the total amount received from the tax, or spent on the subsidy, to be shown as well. However, if the tax or subsidy is specific (per unit, rather than ad valorem), the tax or subsidy per unit will be the same at all levels of output.

Case study: Flu vaccinations in Ireland

Influenza (flu) is an infectious disease that kills between 200 and 500 people in Ireland each year, mostly older people. Every year, about 10% of people in Europe catch flu. Vaccinations against flu in Ireland are available between October and April and people are encouraged to be vaccinated as soon as they can to be fully protected. Flu viruses change each year, so new jabs are needed.

The vaccination is available free for those in certain categories including people aged over 65, those with long-term health problems and those who work in health care. There are about a million people in total who qualify (about 20% of the country's population) but the vaccination is not compulsory. Others can choose to be vaccinated. The cost of a flu vaccination is approximately €20.

1. Why may the groups identified be offered a flu vaccination for free?

2. Should everyone in Ireland be given a flu jab for free?

3. What else could be done to encourage more people in Ireland to have a flu jab?

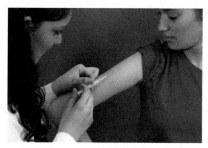

▲ Figure 5.7.6: Should flu vaccinations be free for all?

Price controls

Another way of trying to reduce or increase production and consumption is to use price controls. There are two types – minimum and maximum prices.

Minimum price

A **minimum price** (or price floor) is the lowest price that can be charged by law. This is used to increase the price of a good or service but a minimum price needs to be set above the current equilibrium to change the price.

In Figure 5.7.7, the equilibrium price is p where q is sold. If a minimum price is set at a higher level such as p_{min}, this results in an extension of supply and a contraction of demand, causing excess supply of $q_d q_s$. Normally, if there is excess supply, price will fall but with a minimum price, firms cannot sell legally at any price lower than p_{min}. Consumers are only willing to buy q_d at p_{min}, so consumption will fall from q to q_d.

Advantages and disadvantages of a minimum price

Whether the government intervenes further will depend on the reason for setting a minimum price. If it is used to reduce the provision of a product that is generating negative externalities in consumption or production, the higher price aims to reduce sales to the socially optimum level and no further action is likely to be taken. However, as with indirect taxes and subsidies, it is difficult to know what the socially optimum quantity is, and what price should be set to achieve this.

Alternatively, if a minimum price is used to increase the income of producers, perhaps of agricultural goods, the government will need to deal with the excess supply that results. In this case, the government may need to buy up the quantity AB, spending a total of $q_d ABq_s$.

If the government does not buy the excess, there may be an incentive for some firms to sell their surplus stock illegally below the minimum price. A minimum price must therefore be enforced, which will cost the government money.

> ### Key term
>
> **Minimum price:** the lowest price that can be charged by law.

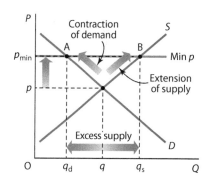

▲ Figure 5.7.7: Minimum price

> ### Link
>
> Intervention buying will be discussed in more detail in the next section on buffer stocks.

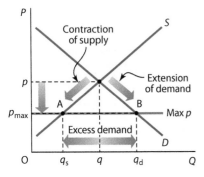

▲ Figure 5.7.8: Maximum price

Maximum price

A **maximum price** (or price ceiling) is the highest price that can be charged by law. This is used to reduce the price of a good or service but a maximum price needs to be set below the current equilibrium to change the price.

In Figure 5.7.8, the equilibrium price is p where q is sold. If a maximum price is set at a lower level such as p_{max}, this results in an extension of demand but a contraction of supply, causing excess demand of q_sq_d. Normally, if there is excess demand, price will rise but with a maximum price, firms cannot sell at any price higher than p_{max}. Sellers are only willing to supply q_s at p_{max}, so consumption will fall from q to q_s.

Advantages and disadvantages of a maximum price

A maximum price may be set for a good or service that is felt to be important and thought to be too expensive for those on low incomes if left to the free market. Again, as with a minimum price, it is difficult to know what price should be set or in which markets intervention may be appropriate. There is also the problem of how to ration the scarce goods and services, since this cannot be done through price rising in this case.

Some countries have rent controls, limiting how much people have to pay to live in their homes. Although some people will then be able to rent their homes more cheaply, there will not be enough of this housing to satisfy the demand. Also, some landlords may stop buying houses to rent. If the rent controls are on government-owned housing, there may be waiting lists and people may be forced to live in overcrowded accommodation while they wait for suitable housing to become available. The housing may be allocated on the basis of need or "first come, first served" (in order of application).

When shortages of products occur, this can also lead to a **black market**. A black market refers to products being bought and sold illegally, maybe to avoid price controls. For example, some landlords may rent their property to people willing to pay more than the maximum price. The term can also be applied to that part of an economy, also known as an underground or shadow economy, where trade occurs without government knowledge, perhaps to avoid paying tax. This trade is not recorded in the government's statistics.

Buffer stocks

A **buffer stock scheme** involves a government, international agency or organisation of producers buying and selling a commodity to stabilise price.

Some prices are unstable, especially of agricultural crops. Prices can fluctuate considerably in the short term since the supply partly depends on the weather. This may also result in unstable incomes for producers. Frequent large changes in price can lead to confusing signals and may cause firms to either overproduce or underproduce in the short term. There may also be too little or too much investment in the long term, resulting in an inefficient allocation of resources. Speculation may add to the problem. Supply is also relatively inelastic for minerals such as copper and tin, which may contribute to price fluctuations.

To reduce the fluctuations in price and incomes, a government or group of producers may set up a buffer stock scheme. This often involves setting a band of acceptable prices with action being taken if the market price falls outside this range.

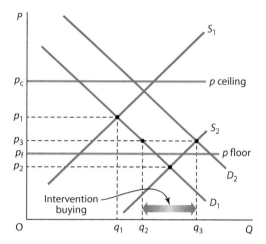

▲ Figure 5.7.9: Intervention buying

In Figure 5.7.9, p_c is the price ceiling, the highest acceptable price, above which intervention takes place and p_f is the price floor, the lowest acceptable price. Demand is D_1 and if supply is S_1, price will be p_1. This is between the highest and lowest acceptable prices, so no action is needed. As a result of favourable weather conditions, the supply, for example of wheat, then increases from S_1 to S_2.

Left to the market, price would fall below the price floor to p_2. The government or producers' organisation will need to intervene, buying wheat to increase demand, which will raise its price. If it buys enough wheat to increase the demand to D_2, price will rise above the price floor to p_3. At p_3, according to the market demand curve D_1, consumers are willing to buy q_2. The extra quantity q_2q_3 must be bought by the government or producers' organisation to raise demand enough to achieve an equilibrium price of p_3.

Figure 5.7.10 shows what happens after unfavourable weather conditions result in a poor harvest.

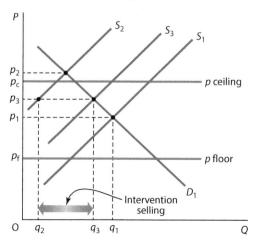

▲ Figure 5.7.10: Intervention selling

Link

Price instability as a source of market failure was explained in 5.5 "Market imperfections".

The poor weather reduces the supply of wheat from S_1 to S_2. If left to the market, price would rise above the price ceiling to p_2. The government or producers' organisation will need to intervene, selling wheat to increase supply, which will lower the price. If it sells enough wheat to increase the supply to S_3, price will fall below the price ceiling to p_3. At p_3, according to the market supply curve S_2, firms are willing to sell q_2. The extra quantity q_2q_3 must be sold from the buffer stock by the government to raise supply enough to achieve an equilibrium price of p_3.

Advantages and disadvantages of a buffer stock scheme

Buffer stock schemes help to stabilise prices for consumers and incomes for sellers, which can be important for essential items such as food. However, there are several possible problems.

It is difficult to know where to set the price ceiling and floor. There may be a tendency to set the price too high, which could result in excess supplies having to be bought in most years. Unless there is also a quota (a limit on quantity), a guaranteed high minimum price may encourage overproduction.

If the market price falls below the price floor, the government or producers' organisation will buy up the extra supplies. This costs money and there are also the problems of transport and storage, which may have to be in particular conditions to extend how long the product lasts. What if the product cannot be stored for long? Also, technological progress may result in substitutes for the product being developed, which will reduce demand in future.

Whether the organisation is set up by a group of producers or a group of producing countries, money is needed before the scheme starts. Will the members pay equal amounts or according to their market shares? What if some producers do not join the scheme? They could undercut the price of the buffer stock scheme, so even more has to be bought and stored. Alternatively, they may run out of stock if there are a few poor harvests.

The European Union ran buffer stock schemes for many agricultural products as part of its Common Agricultural Policy, paid for by money from its member countries. This was very expensive and led to large stocks of many foods building up. There is then the risk of waste, or if the products are given as aid outside the area covered by the scheme this could reduce the incomes of farmers in the countries receiving the aid. There have also been buffer stock schemes for rubber and tin, for example, but sooner or later they tend to fail.

Pollution permits

Pollution permits are licences or permits sold or allocated by a government or central authority to allow firms to emit a set quantity of pollution in a given time period. The permits are tradable – firms can buy and sell them on the free market. If firms do not need all their permits, they can be sold to other firms who need more, so a market for the permits will develop.

Pollution permits aim to reduce negative production externalities, particularly in industries that cause high levels of pollution or use large amounts of energy in the production process. The European Union's Emissions Trading Scheme is an example of carbon trading – a pollution permits scheme that targets carbon dioxide emissions.

Key term

Pollution permits: licences or permits sold or allocated by a government to allow firms to emit a set quantity of pollution in a given time period.

Pollution permits are sometimes called "cap and trade" schemes. The "cap" sets a limit on the total pollution of the industry. The government may reduce the allocated number of permits over time, giving firms an additional incentive to invest in new technology. The "trade" refers to the ability to buy and sell spare permits.

Advantages and disadvantages of pollution permits

The system aims to reduce pollution over time and gives individual firms some flexibility about when they make their production process less polluting, for example by installing cleaner technology. Some firms may be able to reduce their pollution quickly and cheaply but others may be less able to do this. Permits provide an incentive to make improvements that reduce the need for pollution permits. Otherwise, buying permits adds to firms' costs. A key benefit of the scheme is that it achieves the desired reduction in pollution at the least cost. This is because firms that can reduce pollution cheaply will do so to avoid having to buy permits.

A cap and trade scheme is a market-based approach to reducing pollution. Once the scheme is in place, the government or controlling body needs to monitor the situation. Firms that pollute beyond their limit, without enough permits, will have to pay an appropriate fine. Over time, as fewer permits are issued, it is likely that their price will rise, which will increase the incentive to become less polluting.

Although the total amount of pollution from the industry will fall, this may not apply to all geographical areas. However, if the government sells the permits, this can raise money to help to clean up the environment.

Progress questions

7   If demand for a product is inelastic, does this make it more or less likely that intervention will be needed in a buffer stock scheme and why?

8   List **three** problems of operating a buffer stock scheme.

9   Explain **two** advantages and **two** disadvantages of a pollution permits scheme.

Case study: Pollution permit schemes – European Union, California and China

The European Union Emissions Trading System (EU ETS) started in 2005. It aims to reduce global warming and is the world's largest multi-country greenhouse gas emissions cap and trade scheme. It operates in all the EU countries plus three others and covers about 45% of their greenhouse gas emissions. It applies to about 11,000 power stations and factories using large quantities of energy, plus the airlines that operate between these countries. By 2016, the emissions targeted by the EU ETS had fallen by 26%, although at times the price of permits on the market has been too low to encourage firms to invest in cleaner technology.

There is another scheme in California, USA, which has cut its carbon dioxide emissions by 8.8% between its start in 2013 and 2016. Also, in 2015, California attracted 68% of all US clean-tech investment while billions of dollars from the sale of permits have been put into a range of environmental schemes including a high-speed rail project.

China started its emissions trading system in 2017 and it is expected to become the world's largest scheme. The first phase applied to the power sector that covers 1,700 mostly state-owned firms, generating about a third of China's carbon emissions. It is due to be extended to other industries including chemicals and iron and steel. When this phase is complete, over 20% of the world's emissions will be covered by cap and trade schemes.

1   How can the success of a pollution permit scheme be judged?

2   What does the success of a pollution permit scheme depend on?

▲ Figure 5.7.11: A major source of pollution

Link

The tragedy of the commons was explained in 5.2 "Private goods, public goods and quasi-public goods" and other problems caused by a lack of property rights were covered in 5.3 "Positive and negative externalities in consumption and production".

Key term

Extension of property rights: allocating the ownership of more resources to people or firms, who can then determine how those resources are used.

Key term

Patent: a legal right to stop others from making or selling a new product for a number of years.

Link

Public goods were explained in 5.2 "Private goods, public goods and quasi-public goods" and merit goods were covered in 5.4 "Merit and demerit goods".

Extension of property rights

The **extension of property rights** is another way of internalising the externality and enabling markets to work more efficiently and equitably. It involves allocating the ownership of more resources to people or firms, who can then determine how those resources are used. If people own a resource, they have an economic incentive to look after the resource and to stop it from being polluted.

The extension of property rights can apply to physical resources such as land, sea or air or to creations such as books, songs or inventions. Without property rights, natural resources may be overused. For example, overfishing in some parts of the world is reducing fish stocks for the future. However, it is difficult to extend property rights to some resources, such as the air.

A law may be passed giving people or firms the right to use or sell the property, and control what use others can make of it. For example, a water company may be given the right to charge others who pollute a river or sea but it may be difficult to identify who is responsible. If there is a dispute, it could cost individuals too much money to take legal action to gain enough compensation.

Extending property rights could either force the producer of the external costs to pay the person or firm affected or may enable the two parties to reach an agreement, so one can be compensated for the external costs they have suffered, or pay for the benefits they have received.

The extension of intellectual property rights applies to what people have created, such as a book or a song. If a book is sold or a piece of music is used in a performance, the writer may be entitled to receive royalties, a small sum of money paid to the owner of the asset. An inventor may take out a **patent**, which is a legal right to stop others from making or selling the product for a number of years. Intellectual property rights such as royalties and patents encourage people to come up with new ideas since they can benefit financially from others paying for their use. Without this protection, there will be fewer new products and other creations.

State provision

Some goods and services may be provided by the state free at the point of use and paid for by taxation. This may be necessary if there is a missing market, for example, with public goods such as street lighting.

Public goods are non-excludable and non-rival in consumption, so private sector firms are very unlikely to supply them since they have little chance of making a profit. If these goods and services are considered to be important, for example the police force for public safety, then the state must provide them.

There may be other goods and services, which are not public goods, that some governments will also provide free of charge. This may apply to some merit goods. A government may consider that there are significant external as well as private benefits to be gained from their consumption but those on lower incomes may be unable to afford the market price. For example, many countries offer free education up to a certain age and free health care.

However, provision of goods and services will have a large financial and opportunity cost. It is also difficult to know what quantity to supply to achieve the social optimum. If the optimum quantity is provided by the government, it does not guarantee that it will be consumed. For example, university education may be provided free but not everyone will take advantage of this.

Regulation

Regulation may force individuals or firms to take a particular action or stop them from doing something that is considered bad for them or others. Regulation may be used to enforce the consumption of merit goods or to reduce production and/or consumption if it results in negative externalities. Regulation is therefore another method of correcting market failure.

Regulation needs to be backed by penalties for those who break the laws. For example, children under a certain age may be required by law to go to school. Those in a car may be required to wear seatbelts. As well as age limits, some activities, such as smoking, may only be allowed in certain areas. There needs to be a fine, or other penalty, for those who break the law, and this needs to be high enough to persuade people or firms not to.

Many countries, for example Sweden, offer free vaccination for the main infectious diseases, to reduce the number of people likely to catch and spread the illness. In Poland, vaccination is compulsory but in 2016, only 95.5% of people had received their first vaccination against mumps, measles and rubella (MMR), even though those refusing to be vaccinated can be fined.

Some people in Poland think they should have the right to choose whether to be vaccinated or not and believe the government is being too **paternalistic**. This means that the government is making decisions for other people that it believes will benefit them.

Monopoly and monopoly power can lead to market failure through both inefficiency and inequity. Countries are likely to have a **competition policy**, which includes regulations to control the activities of firms to protect consumers, to make markets more competitive and to encourage an efficient use of resources. This may include price controls but firms also have to follow other rules, for example about the safety of their products. This can add to their costs and increase prices.

However, different governments will make different rules about what can be done where and by whom. One advantage of regulation is that it is easy to understand, but to be effective it must be monitored and enforced. As with some other solutions to market failure, regulation may lead to a black market.

Other solutions

As well as passing laws and using measures that change prices, the government may also use other policies to help to correct market failures. To reduce information failure, it may advertise or promote certain activities to increase people's awareness, for example providing more information about possible jobs to those seeking work.

Activities

1 Make a list of **five** goods or services that are provided free by the government in your country.

2 For **two** of these, explain why the government provides it free of charge.

Key terms

Paternalistic: where a government makes decisions for other people that it believes will benefit them.

Competition policy: government measures to control the activities of firms to protect consumers, to make markets more competitive and to encourage an efficient use of resources.

New Zealand runs a number of health promotions at different times of year, for example "Diabetes Awareness Week" in November. Governments may also try to increase people's awareness of the harmful longer-term effects of consuming demerit goods, such as cigarettes. However, providing more information does not guarantee that people change the way they behave.

To reduce inequalities in income and/or wealth, the provision of merit goods such as education and health care, either free or subsidised, enables those on low incomes to have access to these vital services. If they had to pay the full price, these services would be underconsumed and those on low incomes would have less opportunity to increase their future incomes.

Progressive taxes may also be used. A **progressive** income tax is where, as income rises, so does the percentage paid in tax. This will involve those with higher incomes paying a higher percentage of their income in tax. They pay more money and a higher rate of tax, narrowing the gap between rich and poor.

The money obtained by the government could then be used to finance welfare benefits. These may be **means-tested**, where entitlement to benefits depends on a person's income and/or wealth, and on his or her needs. Means-tested benefits may be more difficult and costly to administer than giving money to everyone in a certain situation (universal benefits), for example to everyone with a child under the age of 16. However, the money goes to those who need it most and so these benefits involve paying less money in total.

As with other measures to correct market failures, it is difficult to know what tax rates to use and at which income levels, since it is important that people have sufficient incentives to work and to save. High income tax rates may reduce the incentive to work, for example. Also, benefits need to be high enough to help those who need support without creating a disincentive to work. There needs to be a balance between equity and efficiency.

Case study: Universal basic income experiment – Kenya

Despite rapid economic growth, inequalities are growing in many countries. This has led some people to suggest that there should be a universal basic income (UBI), a cash payment to everyone to cover their basic needs. There have been a few small-scale schemes tried by governments in a variety of countries including Canada, Finland and Namibia.

GiveDirectly, a non-profit organisation, has been running a basic income experiment for several years in 295 villages in Kenya. The aim is to investigate the effects of different options. The organisation divided people into four groups: those who receive a monthly income for 12 years, others who only receive it for two years, some who receive a one-off payment and others who receive nothing. Some recipients, for example, have used the money for seeds and education, others to improve their homes.

At the end of the 12-year period, there can be a full assessment of the experiment. This could include the effects on income, assets and incentives to work.

1 How might a UBI help to reduce inequality?

2 What problems might there be if a government provides a UBI?

▲ Figure 5.7.12: Could a guaranteed basic income help to reduce inequality?

This section will develop your knowledge and understanding of:

→ how government failure occurs when government intervention in the economy leads to a worse allocation of resources and a fall in economic welfare

→ why inadequate information, inappropriate or conflicting objectives, administrative costs and corruption are possible sources of government failure

→ how government intervention can lead to unintended consequences.

How government intervention can lead to government failure

Market failure is when there is an inefficient and/or inequitable allocation of resources if left to the market forces of supply and demand. At the market output, welfare is not maximised – there is a welfare loss.

Governments will often intervene to try to improve the allocation of resources. However, for a variety of reasons, government intervention in the economy does not always correct the market failure and could lead to a worse allocation of resources and a fall in economic welfare. This is known as **government failure**.

This may be caused by a lack of information or those making the decisions may have other motives for intervening. It may also be too costly to intervene or there may be unintended consequences, where different problems arise. Whatever the cause, there is a net welfare loss.

Sources of government failure

Sources of government failure include:

- inadequate information
- inappropriate or conflicting objectives
- administrative costs
- corruption.

Inadequate information

To make the best decision about when and how much to intervene to correct market failure requires complete and correct information. The information available to a government may be out of date or inadequate. This may cause the government to intervene too soon or too late, or too much or too little. This could mean that the costs are greater than the benefits, leading to a welfare loss and government failure. It is impossible for the government to know everything, for example, about people's changing preferences.

Inappropriate or conflicting objectives

Governments have a number of objectives and they are not always compatible. Taking action to correct one market failure may make

> **Key term**
>
> **Government failure:** when government intervention in the economy leads to a worse allocation of resources and a fall in welfare.

> **Get it right**
>
> Government failure can only occur as a result of government intervention. If the government does not intervene to correct market failure, there cannot be government failure.

another worse. Objectives of decision makers may not necessarily be in the best interests of society. An inappropriate objective can lead to a worse allocation of resources even if the objective is achieved.

For example, the government might introduce a policy to reduce inequality but this may also reduce incentives. The net result could mean that most people are worse off even if inequality is reduced. Banning cars using petrol within 10 years could have more costs than benefits.

A policy may be expensive in the short run but bring long-term benefits. Sometimes, short-term policies are chosen over longer-term solutions. This policy myopia may be because a government wants to take action that will produce benefits while it is still in power. Should roads be widened to ease congestion or should more high-speed rail links be built? Policies to change people's attitudes to public transport may take a long time to show significant benefits.

In a free market economy, the government may choose a programme to increase voters' income, such as a cut in income tax, rather than spending on training and environmental protection, especially before an election. In a centrally planned economy, resources may be inefficiently allocated if the price mechanism is not used to enable consumers to show their preferences for different goods and services. There may also be a lack of incentive to increase productivity and innovation, for example.

Administrative costs

In order to produce a solution to a market failure, it will take time and money to investigate the problem and to weigh up alternative solutions. The scheme may be expensive to administer or monitor. For example, if regulation is used to protect the environment, it must be checked that individuals and firms are not breaking the law. The benefits may be more than offset by the costs of introducing and running the policy, leading to a net welfare loss and government failure.

Corruption

Sometimes, decision makers may act in their self-interest not the benefit of society as a whole. Politicians want to be re-elected or may try to gain more money for their government department, choosing policies that will achieve this. They may be persuaded by certain groups to act, or not act, in a way that would help to correct market failure. For example, an organisation representing wheat farmers may persuade the government to subsidise wheat but this money might be better spent on something else. If bribes are involved, this would be an example of corruption.

In some countries where major industries, such as suppliers of electricity or rail services, are operating as monopolies in the private sector, there may be a regulatory organisation monitoring their activities and limiting how much prices can increase each year. The monopolies may be able to persuade the regulator to let them increase prices more than necessary, making it more difficult for those on low incomes to afford important services.

The idea that regulatory agencies may operate in the industry's interest rather than in the interest of the consumers they are trying to protect is known as **regulatory capture**. However, this is not always deliberate and does not necessarily involve corruption. The regulatory agency may work closely with the industry and be sympathetic to its problems.

Even if regulatory capture does not occur, supporters of **deregulation** (the removal of rules, particularly those that restrict competition) argue that some regulatory activity is unnecessary and just adds to the costs of firms and consumers.

How government intervention can lead to unintended consequences

When the government intervenes to correct market failures, there may also be unintended consequences, unexpected effects of an action. It is sometimes known as the **law of unintended consequences** when the actions of the government (or others) lead to unanticipated effects.

Unintended consequences may be good, bad or even lead to the opposite effect of that intended. These effects happen for a number of reasons. It is difficult to anticipate everything that could happen and previous experience may no longer apply. The problem may not even be serious enough to justify intervention. In 1990, cycle helmets were made compulsory in the Australian state of Victoria. The number of head injuries fell but this was because fewer young people were riding bicycles, since helmets were considered unfashionable. If fewer people were cycling, this may have led to more cars on the roads, causing additional problems.

Sometimes, the unintended consequences may even outweigh the advantages. For example, a government may give benefits to those on low incomes to reduce inequality, but if they are too high they may act as a disincentive for people to look for work.

Putting a high indirect tax on demerit goods, such as cigarettes, to reduce negative externalities will raise their price. For poorer people, the increase in tax is a greater percentage of their income. This is a particular problem when demand is inelastic. Although efficiency may be improved, the outcome could be considered inequitable. It may also lead to an increase in crime if more cigarettes are sold illegally to avoid the tax.

To reduce overfishing, limits may be put on the number or size of fish that can be caught. If too many are caught or they are too small, this may lead to large numbers of fish being dumped, wasting scarce resources. Also, in many cities suffering from congestion, including Seoul and Boston, adding extra roads seems to have made the problem worse, not better as expected.

Ultimately, in deciding whether government intervention to correct a market failure should take place, a judgement must be made about whether the risk of government failure outweighs the problems caused by the market failure.

Key terms

Regulatory capture: the idea that regulatory agencies may operate in the industry's interest rather than in the interest of the consumers they are trying to protect.

Deregulation: the removal of rules, particularly those that restrict competition.

Link

Unintended consequences were introduced in 2.7 "How markets and prices allocate resources".

Key term

Law of unintended consequences: the idea that the actions of the government (or others) lead to unexpected effects.

Progress questions

1 Explain why taxing a demerit good, such as cigarettes, is a particular problem when demand is inelastic.

2 What might have been an unintended consequence when the United States subsidised the use of corn to produce ethanol (for fuel), to reduce greenhouse gas?

Case study: Government failure

It is 2020, and the country of Failuria is facing a number of problems. With a rapidly growing population, congestion and pollution are increasing but productivity remains low. In 2015, bad weather led to poor wheat and potato harvests and some basic food prices rose to levels that many could not afford. The Failurian government launched an investigation. Three years later, the investigation was completed and the report was published, at a cost of $30 million.

Meanwhile, both rich landowners and small farmers have been pressing the government to introduce policies to increase their incomes and to stabilise prices. On the basis of the report, the government is now considering a buffer stock scheme for all agricultural products. The Prime Minister, who owns 1000 hectares of farmland in the west of the country, is keen to introduce the policy and plans to set up a regulatory body to oversee the running of such a scheme before next year's election. The government has also recently announced a reduction in the rates of income tax.

Use the data to identify as many potential causes of government failure as possible.

▲ **Figure 5.8.1**: Market failure or government failure?

Exam-style questions

1 Which one of the following indicates government failure? A situation where

   A beneficial unintended consequences result.

   B intervention leads to a net welfare loss.

   C the social costs are greater than private costs.

   D there is a missing market.   [1 mark]

2 In the diagram below, D_1 shows demand only taking account of the private benefits and D_2 shows demand taking account of the social benefits of a particular good.

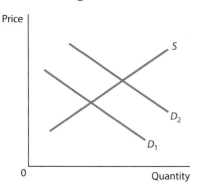

   This shows that the good has

   A negative externalities in consumption.

   B negative externalities in production.

   C positive externalities in consumption.

   D positive externalities in production.   [1 mark]

3 Which one of the following is a characteristic of a private good?

   A Consumption by one person reduces its availability to others

   B Free riders are able to enjoy the benefits

   C It is non-excludable

   D It is only supplied by firms in the private sector   [1 mark]

4 Define "quasi-public good".   [3 marks]

5 The government is considering building a new hospital. The table below shows the expected private and external costs and benefits.

	Private cost ($m)	External cost ($m)	Private benefit ($m)	External benefit ($m)
Hospital	100	20	70	80

   Calculate the net social benefit of the hospital. You are advised to show your working.   [3 marks]

6 The table below shows the average income and wealth in a country over an eight-year period.

Year	Income ($)	Wealth ($)
2011	2,000	6,000
2013	1,980	6,100
2015	2,010	6,300
2017	2,060	6,500
2019	2,120	7,000

(i) Explain why changes in the average income might affect the average wealth.   [6 marks]

(ii) To what extent do the data suggest that changes in average income affect the average wealth? Use the data in the table to support your answer.   [6 marks]

7 With the help of a diagram, explain how setting a minimum price will affect the market for rice.   [9 marks]

8 Analyse the likely effects on the market for a demerit good of improving information.   [12 marks]

9 Use the information in the case study on education in Argentina and Chile (in 5.4 "Merit and demerit goods") and your knowledge of Economics to assess whether a government should intervene to provide free education for people up to the age of 21.   [20 marks]

6 The measurement of macroeconomic performance

The national economy in a global environment

This section will develop your knowledge and understanding of:

→ the main objectives of government macroeconomic policy: economic growth, price stability, minimising unemployment and a stable balance of payments on current account

→ conflicts that might arise when attempting to achieve these objectives

→ how the importance attached to the different objectives will affect the policies adopted by the government.

Key terms

Macroeconomics: the study of the economy as a whole.

Policy objectives: what the government is trying to achieve, or its aims.

Fiscal policy: the use of government spending and taxation to influence the economy and help the government achieve its objectives.

Monetary policy: the use of interest rates, the supply of money and the exchange rate to influence the economy and help the government achieve its objectives.

Supply-side policies: measures to increase economic incentives, make markets work better and increase the productive capacity of the economy.

Policy instruments: tools the government can use to help it achieve its objectives.

Economic growth: the rate at which the total output of all goods and services produced by an economy is increasing.

This chapter and the chapters that follow are about **macroeconomics**. Macroeconomics looks at the economy as a whole, rather than individual markets. For example, macroeconomists are interested in what determines the total output of the economy rather than what determines the output of a particular industry. They try to explain why the average price of all goods and services changes rather than what determines the price of one good or service. Macroeconomics studies the aggregate or total values of variables such as unemployment, output, consumption, investment and exports.

The main macroeconomic policy objectives

The objectives, or aims, of government economic policy are what the government is trying to achieve. Governments have microeconomic and macroeconomic **policy objectives**. It is not always easy to distinguish between microeconomic and macroeconomic objectives partly because changes to the microeconomy can affect macroeconomic performance and the macroeconomy often affects what is happening in individual markets.

Most governments have four main macroeconomic policy objectives. They are to:

- achieve a satisfactory rate of economic growth
- keep prices stable
- keep unemployment low
- have a stable balance of payments on current account.

Governments have a variety of policies they can use to achieve their aims, including **fiscal policy**, **monetary policy** and **supply-side policies**. Each of these policies has several **policy instruments** that can be used to help the government achieve its aims.

Link

The instruments of government macroeconomic policy are explained in Chapter 9 "Macroeconomic policy".

Economic growth

Economic growth is the rate at which the total output of all goods and services produced by an economy is increasing. If total output falls, the rate of economic growth is negative. It is usually expressed

▲ **Figure 6.1.1**: Unemployment is a waste of scarce resources

as a percentage. For example, India's economic growth was estimated to be 7.8% in 2019. Achieving a stable rate of economic growth is a fundamental macroeconomic policy objective because an increase in output means more needs and wants can be satisfied. This should help to improve the standard of living.

Link

Economic growth is discussed in more detail in 8.1 "Economic growth and the economic cycle".

What is judged to be a satisfactory rate of economic growth for one country may not be acceptable for another country. In general, what is viewed to be an acceptable rate of economic growth for an already developed economy is usually lower than for a less developed economy. Also, if a country's population is growing rapidly, a higher rate of economic growth is needed to maintain living standards than for a country with a population that is only growing slowly.

Price stability

For most countries, having price stability as an objective means they want to prevent the price level rising too fast and to avoid the price level falling. The price level is the average price of all goods and services in an economy. A persistent rise in the price level is known as inflation. A fall in the price level is known as deflation. Most governments' objective is to achieve a low, stable rate of inflation rather than no change in the price level. In Vietnam, the target for the inflation rate in 2019 was 4% and in South Korea it was 2%.

High rates of inflation can be harmful for an economy as people have to pay more for the things they buy and inflation can make exports uncompetitive. Unstable prices make it difficult for economic agents to plan and can damage an economy.

Low unemployment

Unemployment is the total number of people who are willing and able to work but who cannot to find a job. In an economy where the demand for different products is changing, some unemployment is unavoidable. The aim for most governments is to keep unemployment as low as possible. Unemployment is a waste of scarce resources and means the economy is producing fewer goods and services than it could. More needs and wants could have been satisfied. Diagrammatically, unemployment can be illustrated by a point inside a country's production possibility boundary (PPB).

Unemployment is not only a waste of scarce resources, it also causes other economic and social problems. People who are unemployed for a long time may be unable to afford basic necessities and their families may live in poverty. High levels of unemployment can lead to an unequal and inequitable distribution of income. However, many people who lose their job soon find another job. It is not just the number of people who are out of work that matters, it is also for how long they are unemployed.

Key terms

Standard of living: the ability of people to satisfy their needs and wants, including health care and education.

Price level: the average price of all goods and services in an economy.

Inflation: an increase in the price level.

Deflation: a fall in the price level.

Inflation rate: the percentage increase in the price level.

Link

What determines living standards is covered in the A2 part of the course.

Link

The effects of inflation and deflation are covered in the A2 part of the course.

Key term

Unemployment: the number of people who are willing and able to work but who cannot to find a job.

Link

The use of production possibility diagrams is explained in 1.4 "Production possibility diagrams".

Link

The causes of unemployment are explained in 8.2 "Employment and unemployment".

▲ **Figure 6.1.2**: Exports and imports transported by ship

The balance of payments on current account

The balance of payments records all the financial transactions between one country and the rest of the world. The current account is part of the balance of payments. For most countries, **exports** and **imports** of goods and services are a large part of the current account of the balance of payments.

Activities

Identify four products that you or your family buys that have been imported from abroad.

1   In which country was each of these products made?
2   For each product, explain why you, or your family, bought a product made abroad rather than from your own country.

Link

What is included in the current account is explained in 8.4 "The balance of payments on current account".

Key terms

Balance of payments: a record of a country's financial transactions with the rest of the world.

Exports: goods and services that are sold to other countries.

Imports: goods and services that are bought from other countries.

Balance of payments deficit: when the value of imports is greater than the value of exports.

Balance of payments surplus: when the value of exports is greater than the value of imports.

Exchange rate: the price at which one currency can be converted into another currency.

A country has a **balance of payments deficit** when the value of imports is greater than the value of exports and a **balance of payments surplus** is when the value of exports is greater than the value of imports. Value means the total amount spent on either exports or imports. For most countries, their balance of payment on current account is stable if they run either a small surplus or a small deficit. However, some countries are able to run large surpluses or deficits without any serious problems.

If a country has a large balance of payments deficit on current account, it is not earning enough money from its exports to pay for the imports it is buying. This is likely to result in an increase in borrowing from abroad so that it can get the foreign currency it needs to pay for its imports. It can also lead to a fall, or depreciation, in its **exchange rate**, which makes imports more expensive. However, if the country is able to attract investment from foreign companies, or if it receives foreign aid, a large current account deficit may not be a serious problem, provided it does not last too long. A large surplus can lead to a rise, or appreciation, in its exchange rate. This makes its products less competitive compared to foreign goods in both its home and export markets. As a result, there may be an increase in unemployment.

Link

The effects of a balance of payments deficit or surplus on an economy are fully explained in the A2 part of the course. The effects of changes in the exchange rate are explained in 9.4 "Monetary policy".

Get it right

Do not confuse a balance of payments deficit with a budget deficit. The balance of payments is about exports and imports. The budget is about government spending and taxation.

Progress questions

1   What is meant by "an objective of economic policy"?
2   What are the four main objectives of macroeconomic policy?
3   Explain the difference between macroeconomics and microeconomics.
4   What is a policy instrument?
5   What is meant by "economic growth"?
6   What is meant by "inflation"?
7   What is a balance of payments deficit?

Other macroeconomic policy objectives

Many governments will also have other macroeconomic policy objectives and these may change over time. Examples of other policy objectives include:

- balancing the budget to prevent the national debt growing too fast
- achieving an equitable, or fair, distribution of income
- protecting the natural environment.

Balancing the government's budget

Some governments aim for a balanced budget to prevent the national debt growing too fast. The national debt is the amount of money the government owes, it is the sum of past borrowing. The government's budget is concerned with government spending and taxation. A balanced budget is where government spending equals tax revenue. If the government has a budget deficit, where government expenditure is greater than the money gained through taxation, it will have to borrow. This will increase the national debt. A budget surplus is where taxation is greater than government spending. The surplus can be used by the government to repay some of the money it owes. This will reduce the national debt. A balanced budget, or a budget surplus, often becomes a macroeconomic policy objective when the country's national debt has been growing quickly. For example, the global financial crisis of 2007–2008, which led to a large increase in the national debt of some countries, persuaded the governments of several of these countries to aim to balance their budgets.

Achieving an equitable distribution of income and wealth

Most governments intervene in the economy to influence the distribution of income and wealth. The aim is to achieve an equitable, or fair, distribution of income and wealth. This can be viewed as an objective of both microeconomic and macroeconomic policy. The government can use microeconomic policies to affect the distribution of income and wealth. However, if the government is able to reduce unemployment, a macroeconomic policy objective, this will also help to reduce inequality.

Protecting the natural environment

Protecting the natural environment is another objective of most governments. Both microeconomic and macroeconomic policies can help to achieve this aim. With growing concern about global warming, climate change and the destruction of the natural environment, this has become a much more important aim for most governments.

Possible conflicts between macroeconomic policy objectives

A conflict between policy objectives exists when the government uses measures that lead to an improvement in one policy objective but result in a worse outcome for a different policy objective. For example, if the government increases its spending to boost aggregate demand and this reduces unemployment but leads to higher inflation, there is a conflict between reducing unemployment and the objective of price stability. An increase in aggregate demand will encourage firms

Key terms

Balanced budget: when government spending is equal to the amount the government receives from taxation.

Budget deficit: when government spending is greater than the amount the government receives from taxation.

Budget surplus: when the amount the government receives from taxation is greater than government spending.

National debt: the total amount the government owes. It is the accumulated total of the amount borrowed by the country's governments in previous years. It is the stock of outstanding government debt.

Link

The government's budget and the national debt are discussed in more detail in 9.2 "Fiscal policy".

Link

The distribution of income and wealth is considered in more detail in 5.6 "An inequitable distribution of income and wealth", and in 5.7 "Government intervention in markets".

Key terms

Conflict between policy objectives: when an improvement in one policy objective leads to a worse outcome for a different policy objective.

Aggregate demand: total planned spending on all goods and services produced in the domestic economy.

Link

The effects of government policy on its macroeconomic objectives are explained in 8 "Economic performance" and 9 "Macroeconomic policy".

Get it right

There is not a conflict between all policy objectives, some are compatible with each other.

Link

The characteristics of a depression are explained in 8.1 "Economic growth and the economic cycle".

Key term

Depression: when the economy has very high unemployment and total output is much lower than the productive capacity of the economy. There is a large amount of spare capacity that continues for a number of years.

to produce more and employ more workers. However, rising demand may also encourage firms to raise prices. In this example, there is a **policy trade-off** between unemployment and inflation. The cost of lower unemployment is higher inflation.

There is not always a conflict between policy objectives. There are **compatible policy objectives**. For example, measures to reduce unemployment are likely to be compatible with reducing inequality.

Some policy objectives may conflict in the short run but may be compatible in the long run. Rising economic growth may lead to an increase in imports in the short run. To produce more goods, firms may import more raw materials and rising incomes may allow people to buy more foreign products. Rising imports will lead to a larger deficit on the current account of the balance of payments.

However, in the long run, economic growth may mean that home-produced goods replace imports and the country may be able to export more. This will reduce the current account deficit, or perhaps lead to a surplus. This is likely to happen if economic growth is caused by improvements in efficiency.

Whether policy objectives conflict or are compatible with each other may also depend on the present state of the economy. For example, if the government adopts policies to increase aggregate demand to reduce unemployment when the economy is **recession**, there is spare capacity and firms may not raise prices until the economy has recovered.

How the importance attached to different objectives will affect economic policy

How much importance a government attaches to each policy objective will vary depending on the government in power. Some governments may attach more importance to achieving high economic growth than keeping inflation low. Another government may believe that price stability is more important than other policy objectives.

How much importance a government attaches to a particular objective will be affected by many factors, including the problems facing the economy and the beliefs and values of the government. If the economy has been suffering from high unemployment for several years, the government may make its main objective to reduce unemployment. Some governments, and economists, believe that unless inflation is kept low and stable, other policy objectives will not be achieved in the long run. This has led some governments to have low inflation as their most important policy objective.

During the 1930s, the world economy was in a **depression** with high unemployment. After the Second World War, many governments of the more economically developed economies adopted achieving full employment as their main policy objective. However, in the 1970s, in some of these economies, inflation reached high and worrying levels. Keeping inflation low became the main objective for many of these governments.

When living standards are low, the government may consider that achieving a high rate of economic growth is the most important objective. If living standards improve, the importance attached to the different policy objectives may change. Although a high rate of economic growth helps to improve living standards and reduce poverty, it may damage the natural environment. Increasing pollution and environmental problems may lead to more importance being attached to this objective. The government and the population may be willing to accept a lower rate of economic growth to protect the environment.

Some people believe that rich economies should aim for zero growth. As the effects of global warming have become more obvious and well known, the importance many governments attach to protecting the environment has increased. However, it is not only economic events that affect the importance attached to the different macroeconomic policy objectives, it is also influenced by value judgements. Different governments may have different priorities because they have different views about what is right. The importance attached to each policy objective will affect the policies used to manage the economy.

Link

Macroeconomic policies are explained in Chapter 9 "Macroeconomic policy". Value judgements are explained in 1.5 "Economic methodology".

Case study: Economic growth and inflation in Malaysia, 2014–2018

▼ **Table 6.1.1**: Economic growth and inflation in Malaysia 2014–2018

Year	Growth Rate (%)	Inflation (%)
2014	6.01	3.14
2015	5.09	2.10
2016	4.22	2.08
2017	5.90	3.80
2018	4.72	0.97

Source: www.statista.com; accessed 4 October 2019

1 Draw a bar chart to show the growth rate **and** the rate of inflation in Malaysia between 2014 and 2018.
2 Explain why the data in the table show that there is a trade-off between the growth rate and inflation in Malaysia between 2014 and 2018.

▲ **Figure 6.1.3**: Kuala Lumpur, capital of Malaysia

Progress questions

8 What is meant by "a trade-off between policy objectives"?
9 If two policy objectives are compatible with each other, what does that mean?
10 Explain why an increase in aggregate demand is likely to reduce unemployment.
11 Why might a high rate of economic growth harm the environment?

This section will develop your knowledge and understanding of:

→ data that is commonly used to measure the performance of an economy: real GDP, real GDP per capita, the Gini coefficient, the Consumer Price Index, measures of unemployment, productivity and the balance of payments on current account

→ how index numbers are calculated including the base year and weights.

Link

National income is explained in 7.1 "The circular flow of income".

Activity

Find out the GDP of your country last year and the rate of economic growth over the past five years.

Statistics that are used to measure the current or past performance of an economy are known as economic indicators. Governments publish data that measure an economy's performance in relation to each of the main macroeconomic objectives. They also publish a variety of other data to show what is happening to other aspects of economic performance. As well as helping to assess how well an economy is performing, such data are also used to test and develop economic theories that aim to explain how an economy works.

Measuring economic growth

The most commonly used indicator of economic growth is the percentage change in real gross domestic product, usually shortened to real GDP. GDP is a measure of national income. National income measures the monetary value of the total output of an economy. It is measured over a period of time, for example over one year or a quarter of a year. If GDP is measured in real terms, it means that the effects of inflation have been removed from the figures.

Over time, GDP can increase because the total output of the economy has increased and/or because prices have risen. Changes in nominal GDP (or money GDP) show the change in the monetary value of total output, including the effects of inflation. Since economic growth is the change in the total output of the economy, to calculate economic growth the effects of inflation must be removed. If real GDP has risen, this means the volume, or quantity, of goods and services produced by the economy has increased.

If the real GDP of an economy increased from $250 billion in 2018 to $260 billion in 2019, the growth rate in 2019 is calculated as follows.

$$\text{Economic growth in 2019} = \frac{\text{Change in real GDP}}{\text{Original real GDP}} \times 100$$

$$= \frac{260 - 250}{250} \times 100$$

$$= 4\%$$

Real GDP per capita

The change in real GDP per capita is the most frequently used measure of changes in living standards. Real GDP per capita is the average amount of real GDP per person. It is calculated by dividing real GDP by the size of the country's population. An increase in real GDP per capita means that average output per person has increased. Therefore, on average, there are more goods and services for each person to consume. Real GDP per capita is also known as real GDP per head.

If a country's population increases more quickly than its real GDP increases, real GDP per capita will fall. Even though the country has experienced economic growth, average output per person has fallen, indicating a fall in living standards.

The Gini coefficient

The Gini coefficient is used to measure inequality in income. A Gini coefficient of zero means that the income is distributed equally between individuals: everyone has exactly the same income. A Gini coefficient of 1 represents the largest degree of inequality possible. The higher the value of the Gini coefficient the more unequal the distribution of income. The Gini coefficient is also used to measure inequality in wealth.

The Gini coefficient is sometimes shown as a percentage ranging from 0 to 100, where the higher the percentage the greater the inequality.

▼ **Table 6.2.1**: World Bank estimates of the Gini coefficient for selected countries

Country	Gini coefficient	Year estimated
Australia	35.8	2014
Chile	46.6	2017
France	32.7	2015
Indonesia	38.1	2017
Norway	27.5	2015
South Africa	63.0	2014
USA	41.5	2016

Source: World Bank; https://data.worldbank.org; accessed 4 October 2019

Measuring unemployment

An individual is **unemployed** when he or she is out of work and actively seeking work. Not everyone who is out of work is included in the unemployment figures. For example, measures of unemployment do not include people who stay at home to look after their children and those who are retired. Measuring unemployment accurately is difficult in countries where many people work in the **informal economy**, often in rural areas.

There are two main ways of measuring unemployment. Many countries use the International Labour Organisation (ILO) measure of unemployment. This method estimates unemployment by asking a large sample of the population to complete a survey. People are counted as unemployed if they are out of work, have been looking for work and are able to start work within the next two weeks.

The other main method of measuring unemployment counts people claiming unemployment benefits. This method usually underestimates the true level of unemployment because some people who are unemployed are not eligible to claim unemployment benefits.

Get it right

Make sure you know the difference between nominal or money GDP and real GDP.

Link

The measurement of living standards is covered in the A2 part of the course.

Link

The Gini coefficient is explained in more detail in the A2 part of the course.

Key terms

Unemployed: people who are out of work and actively seeking work.

Informal economy: part of the economy that is not regulated or protected by government. People and firms operating in the informal economy rarely pay taxes and barter may be used to exchange goods and services.

Case study: Unemployment and the labour force

The population of a country is 30 million. The number of people in employment is 18 million, 2 million are self-employed and 1 million are looking for work.

1 Calculate the size of the country's labour force.

2 What is the unemployment rate for this country? Give your answer to **two** decimal places.

Link

The effects of productivity on other macroeconomic policy objectives is explained in more detail in Chapter 8 "Economic performance".

Link

The current account of the balance of payments is explained in 8.4 "The balance of payments on current account". The significance of balance of payments deficits and surpluses is covered in the A2 part of the course.

Unemployment is often measured as a percentage of the total labour force. This is the **unemployment rate**. The **labour force** includes people who are working and those who are unemployed and looking for work. It is the number of people who are available for work.

Measuring productivity

Productivity is a measure of efficiency. It measures how much is produced by a unit of a factor of production in a given time. Labour productivity is how much is produced by one worker in a given time, for example each hour or each day. It is the most commonly used measure of productivity. Labour productivity is calculated by dividing total output produced, in a given time, by the number of workers. For example, if a factory produces 50 chairs in an hour and employs 20 workers, labour productivity in this factory is 2.5 chairs per hour.

Productivity should not be confused with production. Production is the amount produced in a given time. In the previous example, production was 50 chairs per hour.

Productivity is an important indicator of the performance of an economy. An increase in labour productivity means that more output can be produced by the same labour force. Improvements in productivity usually lead to economic growth. Improvements in productivity, and efficiency, will make the country more competitive in its home and export markets and should improve the balance of payments.

Balance of payments on current account

The size of the deficit or surplus on a country's balance of payments on current account is another important indicator of the performance of the economy. For example, if a country has a large deficit, it might mean that it is less competitive than other countries. However, there might be other reasons for the deficit. When assessing the significance of the deficit, or surplus, it is best to measure it as a percentage of GDP. An annual current account deficit of $5 billion for a country with a small economy might be a serious problem. However, a deficit of $5 billion might not be a problem for a much bigger economy.

Progress questions

1 What does GDP measure?

2 A country's nominal GDP increased by 15% but, over the same time period, its real GDP only increased by 8%. Explain why this is possible.

3 Over a period of 10 years, the Gini coefficient showing the distribution of income in a country increased from 30.5 to 37.1. Has inequality fallen or risen?

4 State the **two** main methods of measuring unemployment.

5 Explain the difference between production and productivity.

6 If a firm employs 200 workers and produces 3,600 baskets each day, calculate the average labour productivity of each worker.

Index numbers

Index numbers are used to measure changes in, or to compare, a selection of related variables. The starting point for an index number has a base value of 100. Economists often use index numbers when making comparisons over time.

Changes in the price level, and hence inflation, are measured using index numbers. The most commonly used measure of inflation is the **Consumer Price Index (CPI)**. The CPI measures changes in the average price of a weighted basket of consumer goods and services purchased by households.

The first stage is to determine which goods and services should be included in the index. This is usually done by getting a selection of households to record their expenditure over a period of time. The products on which people in the average household spend most of their money are included in the **basket of goods**.

The products included in the basket will change over time. For example, 20 years ago compact discs (CDs) were the main way in which many people bought music but today many people download their music from the internet. Therefore, CDs have been replaced in the basket by music downloaded from the internet.

The pattern of consumer spending also determines the **weight** attached to each item in the basket. The greater the percentage of total spending on an item, the larger its weight. The sum of the weights attached to all items is often set at 1000, therefore if the typical household spends 12.3% of its total income on an item, it will be given a weight of 123.

Weights are used to ensure that the relative importance of the different items in the index is taken into account. For example, food is likely to have a higher weight than petrol. The use of weights means that a given percentage increase in the price of food would have a greater impact on the overall price index than the same percentage increase in the price of petrol.

The **base year** is the starting point for an index. The price of each item is given a value of 100 in the base year. This means that the average price of all items, the overall price index, will also have a value of 100 in the base year. As the price of each item changes, the index for that item is recalculated. For example, if the base year was 2017 and the price of a chicken increased from $3.00 in 2017 to $3.60 in 2020, the index for the price of chicken in 2020 would be calculated as follows.

$$\text{New price index} = \frac{\text{new price}}{\text{original price}} \times 100$$

$$= \frac{3.60}{3.00} \times 100$$

$$= 120$$

The following example shows how a simple price index for four items might be calculated. In the example, Year 1 is the base year. Average monthly expenditure on each of the items is as follows: coffee $15, milk $10, sugar $5 and tea $20. Since total expenditure on coffee is

Key terms

Index number: a statistic, with a base value of 100, that is used to measure changes in a selection of related variables.

Consumer Price Index (CPI): a measure of the price level and inflation.

Basket of goods: the goods and services that are included in a price index.

Weight: a way to reflect the relative importance of each item in an index.

Activity

Choose six goods and services that you would include in a basket of goods used to calculate the rate of inflation for yourself or your family. Estimate the weight that you would attach to each of the items.

Key term

Base year: the starting point for an index, where its value is 100.

Quantitative skills

Make sure that you know how to calculate the new price index for an individual item after a change in the price of that item.

three times the total expenditure on sugar, the weight attached to coffee must be three times the weight attached to sugar. In this simple example, the sum of the weights is fixed at 100, but it could have been some other value, for example 50 or 1000. What matters is that the weights reflect the relative importance of each item. In a price index, this is determined by the relative amount spent on each item.

▼ **Table 6.2.2**: Constructing a weighted price index

Item	Price in Year 1	Index in Year 1	Price in Year 2	Index in Year 2	Weight	Index in Year 2 × Weight
Coffee	$2.00	100	$2.20	110	30	3300
Milk	$0.80	100	$1.00	125	20	2500
Sugar	$1.20	100	$0.96	80	10	800
Tea	$1.50	100	$1.95	130	40	5200
				Total	100	11800
				Overall price index		118

For each item, the figure in the final column of the table is calculated by multiplying the "Index in Year 2" by its "Weight". The overall price index is calculated by dividing the sum of the final column of the table, by the sum of the weights: 11800 ÷ 100 = 118.

The initial stages in constructing a price index, such as the CPI, can be summarised as follows.

- Decide which goods and services should be included in the basket.
- Decide on the base year, the starting point for the index.
- Find out the price of each item in the base year.
- Find out the percentage of income that a typical household spends on each item.
- Use the pattern of expenditure to determine the weight attached to each item.
- Give a value of 100 to the base year price of each item.
- For each item, multiply the base year index by the weight attached to the item.
- Add up the resulting totals and divide by the sum of the weights, this must result in a base year index of 100.

This is how to calculate the new price index for the current year.

- Find the price of each item in the current year.
- Calculate the new index for each item.
- Multiply the new index by the weight.
- Add up the totals and divide by the sum of the weights.
- This will give the weighted index for the current year.

Quantitative skills

Make sure you can calculate a weighted price index for a small number of items.

Case study: Changing patterns of expenditure in China affect the CPI

▲ **Figure 6.2.1**: Food prices have less effect on the CPI

In 2016, the National Bureau of Statistics (NBS) in China made changes to the basket of goods used to calculate inflation. It reduced the weight given to the category "food, tobacco and alcohol". The income elasticity of demand for food is much lower than for many other products. As a result, rapid economic growth in China has meant that the proportion of income spent on food has fallen, even though more food is being consumed. However, the weights given to "housing" and to "transport and communication" rose. At the same time, the base year for the index was changed from 2010 to 2015.

1   How might the National Bureau of Statistics decide which products to include in the basket of goods that are used to calculate inflation?

2   Explain why the weight given to "transport and communication" has risen.

3   How might a change in the weights given to different products affect the rate of inflation, as measured by the CPI?

4   How will changing the base year from 2010 to 2015 affect the CPI?

Using a price index to remove the effects of inflation

Data that is given as a monetary value can be expressed in either nominal (money) terms or real terms. Changes in the price level can make it difficult to interpret what is happening to an economic variable. For example, if the nominal value of government spending has risen by 20%, this might be because prices have risen and/or because the government is providing more goods and services to people. Data measured in real terms has the effects of inflation removed and shows what has happened to the quantity, or volume, of goods and services. The following example illustrates how data can be converted from nominal to real terms. Table 6.2.3 shows government spending in nominal terms and a price index showing the change in the prices of the goods and services the government buys.

▼ **Table 6.2.3**: Changes in government spending, 2017–2019

Year	Government spending	Price index
2017	$500 million	100
2018	$560 million	108
2019	$600 million	112

To remove the effects of inflation it is necessary to measure the variable, in this case government spending, using the same year's prices. For example, government spending in 2018 and 2019 could be measured in 2017 prices.

The following formula can be used to calculate the value of a variable, for example government spending, measured using the prices in the base year.

Progress questions

7   What is meant by the "base year"?

8   Explain why items in an index are often given a weight.

9   What does the CPI measure?

Spending in current year at base year prices

$$= \text{Spending in the current year} \times \frac{\text{Base year price index}}{\text{Current year price index}}$$

Using the figures in Table 6.2.3, the value of government spending in 2018 at 2017 prices is calculated as follows.

Government spending in 2018 at 2017 prices

$$= \text{Government spending in 2018} \times \frac{\text{2017 price index}}{\text{2018 price index}}$$

$$= \$560 \times \frac{100}{108}$$

$$= \$518.52 \text{ million}$$

In nominal terms, government spending increased by $60 million (12%) between 2017 and 2018 but in real terms it only increased by $18.52 million (3.7%). The value of government spending in 2019 in 2017 prices is $600 million $\times \frac{100}{112} = \$535.71$ million, showing an increase of 7.14% in real terms since 2017.

Using index numbers to show changes in economic variables

Index numbers are used to show changes in a wide selection of economic indicators. For example, they can be used the show changes in production, the value of exports, and consumer spending. Most economic variables can be presented as index numbers.

Index numbers do not have units. For example, even if the original data is expressed in $ million or tonnes, when converted into index number form, there are no units.

Using index numbers can make it easier to understand and compare the changes that are taking place. Table 6.2.4 shows the real GDP for the UK economy between 2014 and 2018 in £ million and as index numbers, with a base year of 2015. It is much easier to interpret the changes in the index numbers than the figures shown in £ million.

▼ **Table 6.2.4**: Real GDP for the UK, 2014–2018

Year	Real GDP (£ million)	Index of real GDP
2014	1,912,866	97.70
2015	1,957,920	100.00
2016	1,995,478	101.92
2017	2,033,234	103.85
2018	2,061,408	105.29

Source: Office for National Statistics (UK); www.ons.gov.uk; accessed 10th October 2019

However, care is still needed when using the figures. It is correct to say that real GDP increased by 1.92% between 2015 and 2016, or by 5.29% over the period 2015 to 2018. However, although the index of real GDP increased by 1.44 between 2017 and 2018, this is not the percentage change in real GDP. The percentage change is only the same as the difference between the two figures when starting from the base year, when the original value is 100. The percentage change in real GDP in 2018, or the growth rate, is calculated as follows.

Percentage change in real GDP

$$= \frac{\text{Change in the index of real GDP}}{\text{Index of real GDP in the original year}} \times 100$$

Percentage change in real GDP in 2018

$$= \frac{\text{Index in 2018} - \text{Index in 2017}}{\text{Index in 2017}} \times 100$$

$$= \frac{1.44}{103.85} \times 100$$

$$= 1.39\%$$

Index numbers can also be used to make comparisons at a point in time. For example, they might be used to compare productivity between countries.

▼ **Table 6.2.5**: Index of labour productivity in four countries, 2020

Country A	Country B	Country C	Country D
90	100	113	127

In this example, the base value is given to a country rather than a date. In Table 6.2.5, it is easy to compare productivity in Country B with the other three countries. For example, it can be seen that labour productivity in Country A is 10% lower than in Country B but labour productivity in Country D is 27% higher than in Country B.

Quantitative skills

Make sure you understand how to interpret data presented as index numbers.

Activity

Find out what has happened to the value of goods exported by your country over the past five years. Put the figures in a three-column table showing: the year, the monetary value of exports and the index of the value of exports. When calculating the index, use the third year as the base year.

Progress questions

10 What is the formula for converting the money, or nominal, value of a variable to its real value?

11 Between 2015 and 2020, consumer spending in an economy increased from $240 billion to $380 billion. If the base year for the index of consumer spending is 2015, what is the index of consumer spending in 2020?

12 Using the figures in question 11, state the percentage increase in consumer spending between 2015 and 2020.

Exam-style questions

1 Which one of the following is an objective of government macroeconomic policy?

  A A high Gini coefficient

  B High interest rates

  C Low labour productivity

  D Stable economic growth   [1 mark]

2 The unemployment rate is

  A the number of people claiming unemployment benefits.

  B the number of people out of work.

  C unemployment as a percentage of the labour force.

  D unemployment as a percentage of those who are working.   [1 mark]

3 The weight given to housing in a country's Consumer Price Index (CPI) has increased. This means that

  A house prices are increasing faster than the prices of other products.

  B spending on housing as a percentage of total spending has increased.

  C the price of houses has increased.

  D the total amount spent on housing has risen.   [1 mark]

4 (i) Define "base year".   [3 marks]

  (ii) Define "inflation rate".   [3 marks]

5 The table below shows the imports of a country in $ billion and the index of import prices for that country between 2016 and 2019.

Year	Value of imports ($ billion)	Index of import prices (2018 = 100)
2016	754	92
2017	790	97
2018	842	100
2019	915	109

You are advised to show your working for the calculations below.

  (i) Calculate, to **one** decimal place, the percentage increase in the average price of imports between 2016 and 2017.   [2 marks]

  (ii) Calculate, to the nearest $ billion, the real value of imports in 2019 in 2018 prices.   [4 marks]

7 How the macroeconomy works

The national economy in a global environment

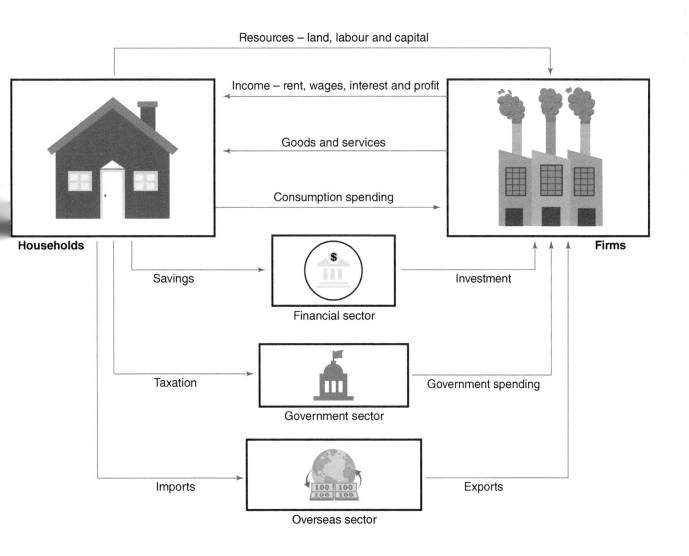

This section will develop your knowledge and understanding of:

→ what national income measures

→ the difference between nominal (money) and real income

→ real national income as an indicator of economic performance

→ the circular flow of income model, the equation income = output = expenditure and the concepts of equilibrium and full employment income

→ the difference between injections and withdrawals into the circular flow of income

→ the effects of changes in injections and withdrawals on national income.

This chapter will develop a model of how the economy works. The economic model explained in this chapter allows different views of the operation of the macroeconomy to be explored. The model will explain the important factors that affect the macroeconomic policy objectives and it will provide a framework for understanding how government policies can help to achieve these objectives.

What national income measures

National income measures the monetary value of all the goods and services that are produced by an economy in a given period of time, usually a year. It also measures total income and total expenditure. National income is a flow; it is what is produced over a period of time.

The output method of measuring national income

One way of measuring national income is the output method. Statisticians calculate the output of each industry or sector of the economy, including services such as retail, hairdressing and insurance. The total value of output, or national income, is calculated by summing the value added by each industry to total output.

Value added is the difference between the value of an industry's output and the value of the inputs it buys from other firms. Value added is used to avoid double counting. For example, sugar is used to make biscuits. If the total value of the output of firms producing sugar and the total value of the output of firms producing biscuits is added together, the value of the sugar is counted twice.

Output is measured in monetary terms because money is a common unit of measurement. It is not possible, for example, to add the number of laptops to the tonnes of tea produced unless both are converted into their monetary value.

The income method of measuring national income

Output creates income for the factors of production producing that output. The income created will include wages for the workers and rent paid to the owners of the factory, office or shop. It will also include interest paid to the suppliers of capital. What is left will be profit, which is income for the entrepreneur. The monetary value of output must create an equal amount of income. Therefore, national income can also be calculated by adding up all the income earned by the factors of production.

The expenditure method of measuring national income

Output also equals expenditure. After output has been produced, someone will buy that output. Therefore, the value of expenditure must equal the monetary value of output. If, in a particular year, some of the output is not sold, firms' **stocks** of unsold products will increase. **Inventory** is another name for stocks held by firms. An increase in stocks is treated as firms buying their own output. Similarly, if expenditure is greater than output, stocks will fall and this is treated as negative expenditure by firms. This adjustment for the change in stocks means that the value of expenditure must equal the value of output. Therefore, national income can also be calculated by adding up the total value of expenditure on the output produced.

Expenditure is usually divided into different categories: consumer expenditure, investment expenditure, government expenditure and exports. However, some of the expenditure in each of these categories will be on foreign goods. Therefore, the value of imports must be subtracted when calculating the total expenditure on **domestic output**.

Consumer expenditure (C), or consumption, is spending on goods and services by households. **Investment expenditure** (I) is spending by firms on capital goods but also includes changes in stocks of finished and unfinished goods. When calculating national income, government expenditure (G) includes the spending by governments on goods and services but does not includes **transfer payments** such as pensions. Exports (X) are goods and services that are sold to people abroad. Imports (M) are goods and services that are purchased from abroad.

When statisticians calculate national income using the expenditure method, they add up the value of the different categories of expenditure: $C + I + G + X - M$.

National income can be calculated in three ways. If calculated accurately, they must be equal because **output = income = expenditure**. However, there are always statistical errors. Usually the output method is the most accurate, but sometimes an average is taken.

The difference between GDP, GNP and NNP

Gross domestic product (GDP) measures the value of output produced within a country. Gross national product (GNP) is GDP plus net income from abroad. **Net income from abroad** is the difference between the income domestic residents earn from abroad and the income earned by foreign residents from in the domestic economy. An example is interest earned on money deposited in a foreign bank.

GNP = GDP + net income from abroad

▲ Figure 7.1.1: Inventory

Key terms

Stocks or inventory: products that firms have in store, they could be raw materials, semi-finished or finished goods.

Domestic output: goods and services produced within an economy.

Consumer expenditure: spending by households on goods and services.

Investment expenditure: spending by firms on capital goods.

Transfer payments: money paid to an individual without a service having been provided, for example money taken from tax-payers and given, by the government, to people receiving welfare benefits.

Net income from abroad: the income domestic residents earn on their assets abroad **minus** the income earned by foreign residents on their assets in the domestic economy.

The difference between GNP and NNP is **depreciation**, or capital consumption, which is subtracted from GNP to calculate NNP. Over time, a country's capital stock depreciates. Some of the output produced is used to replace capital that has worn out or is **obsolete**.

$$NNP = GNP - depreciation$$

National income can also be measured at market prices or factor cost. Indirect taxes increase the market price of products and subsidies reduce market prices compared to the factor cost. Therefore, indirect taxes are subtracted and subsidies are added to national income at market prices to get to national income at factor cost.

National income at factor cost = national income at market prices – indirect taxes + subsidies

For example, NNP at factor cost = NNP at market prices – indirect taxes + subsidies.

NNP at factor cost is also known as net national income (NNI). NNI per capita is often used as an indicator of living standards.

Case study: Farina's Footwear

Farina's Footwear started trading in 1997. In 2019, its sales were $15 million. Inputs bought from other firms included leather, rubber, glue and electricity. In 2019, the total cost of these inputs was $4.5 million.

On 1 January 2010, the firm bought a machine for $46,000. The machine worked well for many years, but recently it has often broken down. Also, in the last few years changes in technology meant that other companies, using newer machines, were able to make their shoes more cheaply. In 2019, the old machine was replaced by a more efficient machine.

1 Calculate the contribution Farina's Footwear made to national income in 2019.

2 If the machine that was bought in 2010 was sold for $1,000 on the 1 January 2019, calculate the average annual depreciation.

3 Explain **two** reasons why the machine depreciated.

▲ Figure 7.1.2: Shoes for sale

The difference between nominal national income and real national income

Nominal national income is also known as money national income. As explained in Chapter 6, changes in nominal national income can result from changes in output and/or changes in the price level. If national income is measured in real terms, the effects of inflation, or deflation, have been removed. Nominal national income values output at the current year's prices, whereas real national income values output at the prices in the base year. Changes in real national income show changes in the total output of the economy.

Real national income as an indicator of economic performance

Economic growth should always be measured by changes in real and not nominal national income. An increase in real national income indicates that more goods and services have been produced and therefore more needs and wants can be satisfied. This indicates an improvement in the performance of the economy. However, if the population has increased, average living standards may not have risen. When using national income to measure changes in living standards, real national income per capita is used.

Although real national income is an important indicator of economic performance, there are many other factors that affect economic development and people's well-being. For example, an individual's well-being is affected by the person's health, education and the environment in which he or she lives. An increase in real national income does not always mean that there has been an improvement in healthcare or education. Inequality is another objective of economic performance. An increase in real national income may not mean that everyone is better off, it might just mean that the already rich are getting richer.

Get it right

When measuring economic growth or changes in living standards, use real national income and not nominal national income.

Link

The use and limitations of national income as an indicator of economic development are covered in the A2 part of the course.

Progress questions

1. What does national income measure?
2. How is national income calculated when using the expenditure method?
3. What is investment expenditure?
4. Explain what is meant by "depreciation".

Activity

Choose **two** countries and for each country find out:

i. real GDP and real GDP per capita five years ago
ii. real GDP and real GDP per capita last year.

The circular flow of income model

Income is a flow, which means it is produced over a period of time. When firms produce goods and services, this creates the same amount of income for the factors of production producing the goods and services. Since economic agents will buy the output produced:

national output ≡ national income ≡ national expenditure

The model of the circular flow of income is a theory of how the national economy works. In the simplest version of the model, there are just two sectors, households and firms. In this simple model, households supply factors of production to firms and the firms use these factors of production to produce goods and services. In return for supplying factors of production, households receive income, which they spend on the goods and services produced by the firms. This is a continuous process representing how a simple economy works.

In Figure 7.1.3, the red lines show the "real flows" of factors of production and good and services. The blue lines show the "money flows" of income and expenditure.

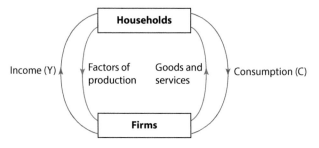

▲ **Figure 7.1.3**: A simple two-sector model of an economy

Introducing injections and withdrawals

The previous very simple model assumes that households spend all their income and firms only produce goods and services for consumers. The model represented in Figure 7.1.4 shows households saving part of their income. Saving is a **withdrawal** (W) from the circular flow of income. A withdrawal is part of income that is not spent on goods and services produced by the economy. A withdrawal is also known as a leakage from the circular flow of income. It is money taken out of the circular flow of income.

This model also includes two types of expenditure, consumption and investment. Investment is firms buying capital goods, such as machinery. In this model, investment does not depend on the income received by households. It is an **injection** (J) into the circular flow of income. An injection is an expenditure that increases the circular flow of income in an economy. It is money that is added to the circular flow of income. Consumption is not an injection because it comes out of household income.

Figure 7.1.4 still represents a simple two-sector economy. It shows a closed economy without a government sector. In a **closed economy**, there is no foreign trade, there are no exports or imports.

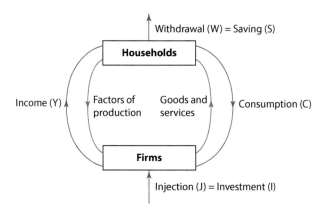

▲ **Figure 7.1.4**: A simple two-sector model of an economy, with saving and investment

Equilibrium income in a two-sector economy

As explained earlier, income must equal output. If households are saving some of their income, household consumption expenditure is not large enough to buy everything that has been produced. However, the injection of investment expenditure adds to the demand for the output of firms. In this two-sector model, aggregate demand, total demand or spending, is equal to consumption plus investment (C + I).

If C + I = Y, everything that has been produced will be sold. Aggregate demand is sufficient to buy all the goods and services produced. There is no reason why firms should change the amount they are producing. National income will be in equilibrium. **Equilibrium income** is when national income is stable and does not change from one time period to the next time period. If aggregate demand is equal to national output (or income), withdrawals from the circular flow of income *must* equal injections into the circular flow. In a two-sector economy, national income is in equilibrium when saving = investment.

In a two-sector economy, if aggregate demand (C + I) is less than current output, firms will have unsold stocks of goods and services. Therefore, they will reduce output to stop stocks increasing. As output falls, national income also falls. National income will be in disequilibrium. If aggregate demand is less than current output, the withdrawals from the circular flow of income must be greater than the injections. In a two-sector economy, national income will fall if S > I.

If aggregate demand (C + I) is greater than current output, firms will not be able satisfy demand unless they have stocks that were produced in an earlier time period. To make sure they can satisfy demand and to stop stocks falling, they will increase output. Again, national income will be in disequilibrium but will be rising rather than falling. National income will increase if injections are greater than withdrawals. In a two-sector economy, national income will rise if I > S.

Equilibrium income in an economy with government and foreign trade sectors

The government affects the circular flow of income by its spending and by taxing economic agents. Government spending (G) increases aggregate demand, and since the amount of government spending does not depend on household income, it is an injection into the circular flow of income. Taxation reduces household incomes and is a withdrawal from the circular flow. Taxation will reduce consumer spending and aggregate demand.

An economy that trades with other economies is known as an **open economy**. Exports are an injection into the circular flow because exports increase spending on the output produced by domestic firms, exports increase aggregate demand. The value of exports is not affected by domestic national income but will be affected by the national income of other economies.

Imports are a withdrawal from the circular flow of income. If households buy foreign goods, some of the income earned is not passed on in the circular flow of income. Spending on imports reduces the amount of income that households spend on goods and services produced by domestic firms.

Key terms

Equilibrium income: when national income is stable and does not change from one time period to the next time period.

Key term

Open economy: an economy that trades with other economies. There are exports and imports.

Activity

Estimate how much of your income, or your family's income, was withdrawn from the circular flow of income last month.

Figure 7.1.5 represents an open economy with a government sector. In this economy, there are three withdrawals: saving, taxation and imports (S + T + M). There are also three injections: investment, government spending and exports (I + G + X).

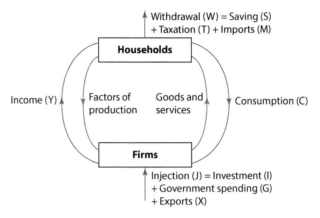

▲ **Figure 7.1.5:** A model of an open economy with a government sector

In this economy, aggregate demand is equal to consumption spending plus the injections into the circular flow of income (AD = C + I + G + X). However, the equation for aggregate demand is usually written as:

$$\textbf{AD = C + I + G + X – M}$$

If consumption and the injections include spending on imports, this has to be subtracted to calculate aggregate demand. Aggregate demand is total planned spending on **home-produced** goods and services.

The aggregate demand equation is sometimes written as **AD = C + I + G + (X – M)**. This emphasises the effect changes in net exports (X – M), have on aggregate demand. If exports are greater than imports, foreign trade increases aggregate demand. If imports are greater than exports, foreign trade reduces aggregate demand.

In this model of the economy, national income is still in equilibrium when aggregate demand equals national output or when injections equal withdrawals. Two conditions for this economy to be in equilibrium are:

Aggregate Demand (AD) = National Output (Y)

I + G + X = S + T + M [Injections (J) = Withdrawals (W)]

If one of these conditions is true, the other condition must also be true.

If aggregate demand is greater than national output, firms will increase production and national income will increase. If aggregate demand is less than national output, firms will reduce production and national income will fall.

Full employment income

An economy may be in equilibrium but that does not mean that it is at **full employment**. Sometimes an economy can get stuck producing a level of output well below that needed for full employment. Full employment is when the economy creates enough jobs so that

Key terms

Home-produced: made by firms in the domestic economy.

Net exports: the value of exports minus the value of imports.

Key term

Full employment: when everyone who is willing and able to work at current market wage rates has a job.

everyone who is willing and able to work at current market wage rates is employed. The output of an economy will affect the level of employment. When output rises more jobs are created. When output falls, employment falls and unemployment rises. **Full employment income** is the level of national income/output that creates enough jobs for everyone who is willing and able to work at current market wage rates.

If the equilibrium level of national income is below the full employment level of national income, there will be some **involuntary unemployment**.

Get it right

Make sure you understand why there may still be involuntary unemployment when an economy's national income is in equilibrium.

Link

The causes of unemployment are explained in 8.2 "Employment and unemployment".

The effects of changes in injections and withdrawals on national income

An increase in injections into the circular flow of income will cause an increase in aggregate demand. For example, an increase in investment will increase the demand for goods produced by firms making machines and other capital goods. More spending by the government and/or more exports will also increase the demand for goods and services.

An increase in withdrawals will reduce aggregate demand. If, for example, households increase the proportion of their income that is saved, other things being equal, consumption of home-produced goods and services will fall. Higher taxes and more spending on imports will also reduce the consumption of home-produced goods and services.

If aggregate demand rises, firms will increase their output and unemployment will fall. The equilibrium level of national income will increase. If injections fall, or withdrawals increase, aggregate demand will fall. This will reduce the equilibrium level of national income.

Injections and withdrawals are affected by a variety of factors including producer and consumer confidence. Fluctuations in injections and withdrawals will cause fluctuations in equilibrium income.

Get it right

An increase in injections (I, G or X), or a fall in withdrawals (S, T or M) will lead to a rise in equilibrium income. If injections fall or withdrawals increase equilibrium income will fall.

Key terms

Full employment income: the level of national income/output that creates enough jobs for everyone who is willing and able to work at current market wage rates.

Involuntary unemployment: when people are willing and able to work at current market wage rates but are unable to find employment.

Link

The causes of fluctuations national income are explained in 8.1 "Economic growth and the economic cycle".

Case study: Indonesia's economy survives the world financial crisis

The 2007–2008 world financial crisis caused many countries around the world to go into recession, with the effects felt beyond 2008. Some economies were affected more than others, suffering large falls in national income. The financial crisis led to reductions in consumption and investment. In some countries, government expenditure was also cut. Many countries in North America, South America and Europe were badly affected.

Some countries in Asia were not as badly affected. In 2009, Indonesia's national income grew by 4.7%. Total exports were $139.3 billion in 2008 but had fallen to $115.6 billion in 2009. Imports fell more than exports. Total imports fell from $116.0 billion in 2008 to $86.6 billion in 2009.

Source: this summary of Indonesia's economy is based on information from https://countryeconomy.com and www.economywatch.com.

1   Explain why the changes in consumption, investment and government spending after the world financial crisis caused the national income of some economies to fall.

2   Calculate the change in net exports for Indonesia between 2008 and 2009.

3   Explain how this change in net exports may have affected Indonesia's national income.

▲ **Figure 7.1.6**: Indonesia

Quantitative skills

Make sure you can interpret and analyse information presented in a numerical form.

Progress questions

5   Name the **three** injections into the circular flow of income.

6   Name the **three** withdrawals from the circular flow of income.

7   Explain why national income will increase if aggregate demand is greater than current output.

8   What is meant by "the full employment level of national income"?

Changes in the price level are represented by movements along the AD and AS curves

The aggregate demand and aggregate supply model is used to illustrate and help explain causes of developments in the macroeconomy. For example, it can be used to help analyse the causes of unemployment, inflation, economic growth and fluctuations in economic activity.

Movements along the AD curve

The **aggregate demand (AD) curve** shows the relationship between the price level and total spending in an economy. The AD curve slopes downwards from left to right. This shows that a fall in the price level will cause a rise in aggregate demand. It is drawn on the assumption that other things that affect aggregate demand remain unchanged – the *ceteris paribus* assumption.

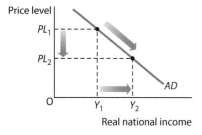

▲ **Figure 7.2.1**: The AD curve

In Figure 7.2.1, a fall in the price level from PL_1 to PL_2 causes aggregate demand to increase from Y_1 to Y_2. There is an inverse relationship between the price level and aggregate demand.

The following are two reasons why a fall in the price level is likely to increase aggregate demand.

• If the price level falls, home-produced goods and services will become relatively cheaper than foreign goods in both the home and export markets. Imports should fall and exports rise, increasing aggregate demand.

• A fall in the price level will increase the real value of assets that have a fixed monetary value, for example money saved in a bank

> **Key term**
>
> **Aggregate demand (AD) curve:** shows the relationship between the price level and total spending in an economy.

> **Get it right**
>
> A movement along the AD curve is caused by a change in the price level.

> **Quantitative skills**
>
> An inverse relationship is when two variables move in opposite directions, for example, a fall in one variable leads to an increase in the other variable.

account. This increase in wealth should lead to an increase in spending.

Movements along the AS curve

The **aggregate supply (AS) curve** shows the relationship between the price level and the total amount of goods and services that firms are willing to produce, as measured by real national income/output. The AS curve slopes upwards from left to right. This shows that a rise in the price level will encourage firms to increase their output. The AS curve is drawn on the assumption that other things that affect aggregate supply remain unchanged – the *ceteris paribus* assumption. If other things remain unchanged, a rise in the price level means it is more profitable to produce. As result, firms will have an incentive to increase output.

Key term

Aggregate supply (AS) curve: shows the relationship between the price level and the total amount of goods and services that firms are willing to produce.

Get it right

A movement along the AS curve is caused by a change in the price level.

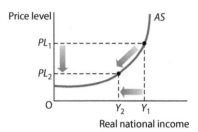

▲ **Figure 7.2.2:** The AS curve

In Figure 7.2.2, when the price level falls from PL_1 to PL_2, firms cut production because it is less profitable. National income/output falls from Y_1 to Y_2. There is a direct relationship between the price level and aggregate supply.

Quantitative skills

A direct relationship is when two variables move in the same direction, for example, a fall in one variable leads to a fall in the other variable.

At low levels of output the AS curve is horizontal (as shown in Figure 7.2.2). When there is a lot of spare capacity in the economy, firms will not need the incentive of higher prices to encourage them to increase output. An increase in aggregate demand will encourage firms to produce more, even if the price level remains the same.

The AS curve becomes vertical when the economy reaches full capacity. At full capacity, firms are unable to increase production in response to an increase in aggregate demand. In the short run, national income cannot increase beyond this level of output. In the long run, the productive capacity of the economy may increase.

Link

Causes of long-run changes in productive capacity are explained in 8.1 "Economic growth and the economic cycle".

Most of the time, economies produce on the upward-sloping section of the AS curve. Therefore, when using AD/AS diagrams to analyse the performance of the economy, the following AS curve is often used.

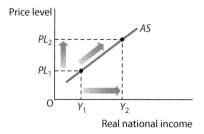

▲ **Figure 7.2.3:** Upward-sloping section of the AS curve

In Figure 7.2.3, an increase in the price level from PL_1 to PL_2 encourages firms to increase output and real national income rises from Y_1 to Y_2.

Factors that shift the AD curve and the short-run aggregate supply (SRAS) curve

Shifts in the AD and short-run aggregate supply (SRAS) curves are caused by factors that affect aggregate demand or aggregate supply, other than a change in the price level.

Shifts in the AD curve

There are many factors that will affect aggregate demand other than a change in the price level, for example changes in consumer confidence, producer confidence or a change in taxes on income. If the change leads to a fall in aggregate demand, the AD curve shifts to the left. This shows that less is demanded at any given price level. If the change leads to an increase in aggregate demand, the AD curve will shift to the right. This shows that more is demanded at any given price level.

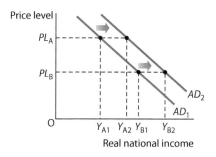

▲ **Figure 7.2.4:** A shift in the AD curve

In Figure 7.2.4, the shift to the right from AD_1 to AD_2 shows an increase in aggregate demand. This might have been caused by a variety of factors, for example an increase in government spending or growth in the world economy, leading to an increase in exports. If the price level was PL_A, aggregate demand would increase from Y_{A1} to Y_{A2}. If the price level was PL_B, aggregate demand would increase from Y_{B1} to Y_{B2}. Anything that causes an increase in aggregate demand, other than a fall in the price level, will mean more goods and services are demanded at any given price level.

A shift of the AD curve to the left, from AD_2 to AD_1, means less is demanded at any given price level. If, for example, a fall in confidence

Get it right

If you want to illustrate the effect of an event on an economy that is in recession or working at full capacity, use the AS curve drawn in Figure 7.2.2. Otherwise, you can use the upward sloping AS curve shown in Figure 7.2.3.

Get it right

When illustrating an individual market, you should use a demand and supply diagram. When illustrating the effect of an event that affects the economy as a whole, you should use an AD/AS diagram.

Quantitative skills

The vertical axis on an AD/AS diagram is labelled "Price level" and the horizontal axis is labelled "Real national income" or "Real GDP".

about the future caused firms to reduce investment spending, this would shift the AD curve to the left.

Shifts in the SRAS curve

The main cause of a shift in the SRAS curve is a change in costs of production. Costs of production are mainly affected by raw material prices, wages, indirect taxes and productivity. At any given price level, an increase in costs will reduce firms' profits. Some firms are likely to cut production and less will be produced, unless the price level changes. This increase in costs is represented by a leftward shift in the SRAS curve, less is produced at any given price level.

If costs fall, profits will increase and firms will be willing to produce more at any given price level. This is shown by a rightward shift in the SRAS curve.

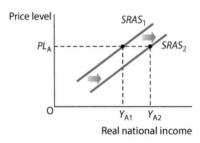

Price level

$SRAS_1$

PL_A

$SRAS_2$

O Y_{A1} Y_{A2}

Real national income

▲ **Figure 7.2.5:** A shift in the SRAS curve

In Figure 7.2.5, the SRAS curve has shifted from $SRAS_1$ to $SRAS_2$. For example, the price of oil may have fallen, reducing energy, transport and other costs. Figure 7.2.5 shows that if the price level is PL_A, the output firms want to produce will rise from Y_{A1} to Y_{A2}.

Progress questions

1   What are the vertical and horizontal axis labels for an AD/AS diagram?
2   What causes a movement along the AD curve?
3   What causes the AD curve to shift to the left?
4   What might cause the SRAS curve to shift to the left?

Factors that affect long-run aggregate supply

The long-run aggregate supply (LRAS) curve shows the amount that can be produced at the economy's **normal capacity level of output**. In the short run, an economy may be able to produce more than its normal capacity level of output but the economy cannot continue to produce this level of output in the long run. If an economy is producing more than its normal capacity level of output, there will be shortages of labour and other factors of production. Excess demand for factors of production will cause factor prices to rise. This will lead to rising inflation.

An economy's normal capacity level of output, its productive capacity, is determined by the supply of factors of production in the economy and the productivity of these factors. If an economy is producing at its

Get it right

It is important to remember that what happens to price level and real national income after an event such as a fall in the price of oil depends on aggregate demand and aggregate supply.

Key term

Normal capacity level of output: the maximum output that an economy can continue to produce in the long run.

Link

The causes of inflation are explained in 8.3 "Inflation and deflation".

normal capacity level of output, it is also producing on its production possibility boundary (PPB).

In Figure 7.2.6, Y_N is the normal capacity level of output. The vertical LRAS curve means that, other things unchanged, Y_N is the output the economy will tend to produce in the long run, but in the short run it may produce more or less than this output. The normal capacity output of Y_N is compatible with any price level.

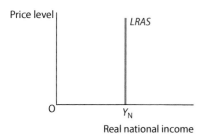

▲ **Figure 7.2.6:** The LRAS curve

Why underlying economic growth is represented by a rightward shift in the LRAS curve

The underlying rate of economic growth is also known as the trend rate of economic growth. In the long run, an economy cannot grow more quickly than the productive capacity of the economy is increasing. If there is an increase in the normal capacity level of output of the economy, this is represented by a rightward shift in the LRAS curve. An economy's underlying rate of economic growth is estimated by taking an average of the actual rate of growth over a number of years, perhaps 20 or more. Ideally, in the first and last year, the amount of spare capacity in the economy should be the same.

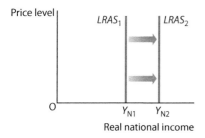

▲ **Figure 7.2.7:** A rightward shift in the LRAS curve shows underlying economic growth

The rightward shift of the LRAS curve in Figure 7.2.7, from $LRAS_1$ to $LRAS_2$, shows an increase in the normal capacity level output of the economy from Y_{N1} to Y_{N2}. There has been underlying growth in this economy. A rightward shift in the PPB also shows underlying growth.

An increase in the productive capacity of the economy can be caused by two factors:

- an increase in the supply of the factors of production
- an increase in the productivity of these factors.

Key term

Underlying rate of economic growth: the annual percentage increase in the productive capacity of an economy.

Activities

1 Find out the actual rate of economic growth for your country during each of the past 30 years and put the figures in a two-column table.

2 Estimate the underlying rate of economic growth over this period.

3 Do you consider that the underlying rate of economic growth has risen, fallen or stayed the same in the last 15 years compared to the previous 15 years?

Link

The use of a production possibility diagram to illustrate economic growth is explained in 8.1 "Economic growth and the economic cycle".

Progress questions

5   What is meant by the normal capacity level of output of an economy?

6   Why will investment in new machinery shift the LRAS curve to the right?

7   What else might shift the LRAS curve to the right?

If there is an increase in the labour force or more capital, this will increase the amount of goods and services that the economy is capable of producing. The discovery of a new supply of raw materials, such as oil or copper, will also increase the productive capacity of the economy.

An improvement in productivity will allow more to be produced from the same amount of factors of production. Increases in productivity can, for example, result from improvements in technology or better organisation of production.

The use of AD/AS diagrams to illustrate macroeconomic equilibrium

The macroeconomy is in equilibrium when the planned level of aggregate demand equals current output. In an AD/AS diagram it is where aggregate demand equals aggregate supply. In Figure 7.2.8, the economy is in equilibrium when real national income is Y_e and the price level is PL_e. Firms are selling what they are producing.

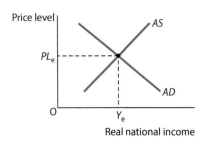

▲ **Figure 7.2.8:** The equilibrium price level and real national income

In Figure 7.2.8, if the price level was above PL_e, aggregate demand would be less than the amount firms are willing to produce at that price level. Firms would have unsold stocks. Prices would be reduced to encourage economic agents to buy the surplus stock. The fall in the price level would cause an extension in aggregate demand and a contraction in aggregate supply. The economy would stabilise at a price level of PL_e and where national income is Y_e.

If the price level was below PL_e, there would be excess aggregate demand and the price level would rise. This would cause a contraction in aggregate demand and an extension in aggregate supply, until equilibrium was restored.

The effect of a shift in aggregate demand on macroeconomic equilibrium

There are many reasons why aggregate demand might increase or decrease. For example, an increase in aggregate demand might be caused by a reduction in taxes on income. Figure 7.2.9 illustrates the effect of an increase in aggregate demand on macroeconomic equilibrium.

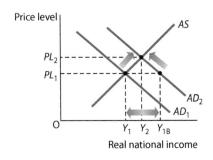

▲ **Figure 7.2.9:** The effect of an increase in aggregate demand on macroeconomic equilibrium

In Figure 7.2.9, the macroeconomy is originally in equilibrium at $PL_1 Y_1$. The increase in aggregate demand from AD_1 to AD_2 causes excess AD of $(Y_{1B} - Y_1)$ at the original price level of PL_1. As a result, the price level will rise, causing an extension in aggregate supply and a contraction in aggregate demand. Macroeconomic equilibrium is restored at PL_2Y_2. Both the price level and real national income have risen.

The effect of a shift in short-run aggregate supply on macroeconomic equilibrium

Shifts in aggregate supply result from changes in costs of production. If production costs rise, SRAS shifts to the left. If production costs fall, SRAS shifts to the right. Figure 7.2.10 illustrates the effect of a decrease in aggregate supply on macroeconomic equilibrium.

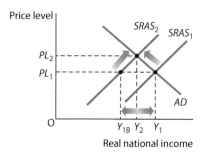

▲ **Figure 7.2.10:** The effect of a decrease in aggregate supply on macroeconomic equilibrium

In Figure 7.2.10, the macroeconomy is originally in equilibrium at PL_1Y_1. The decrease in AS from AS_1 to AS_2 causes excess aggregate demand of $(Y_1 - Y_{1B})$ at the original price level of PL_1. As a result, higher prices are offered, causing an extension in aggregate supply and a contraction in aggregate demand. Macroeconomic equilibrium is restored at PL_2Y_2. The price level has risen and real national income has fallen.

Drawing an AD/AS diagram to illustrate the effect of an economic event

These are the stages to go through when drawing an AD/AS diagram to illustrate the effect of an economic event on the macroeconomy.

1. Draw the diagram to show the initial equilibrium.
2. Check that you have:
   a. labelled both axes correctly: "Price level" and "Real national income"
   b. labelled both curves
   c. drawn the dotted lines to show the equilibrium price level and real national income
   d. labelled the equilibrium points.
3. Decide whether the event affects aggregate demand or aggregate supply.
4. Decide whether the new curve should be shifted left (decrease) or right (increase).
5. Draw the new curve and label it.
6. Draw the new dotted lines to show the new equilibrium price level and real national income.
7. Label the new equilibrium points.

> ### Get it right
>
> AD/AS diagrams can be used to illustrate the effect of economic events on the price level and real national income of an economy. Where appropriate, use them to support written explanations – and always refer to them in the text.

Progress questions

8   What is meant by the equilibrium level of national income?

9   State **two** conditions for an economy to be producing at its equilibrium level of national income.

10 Draw a diagram to illustrate the effect of an increase in government spending on an economy's equilibrium level of national income.

Key term

Demand-side shock: an event that leads to sudden or unexpected change in aggregate demand.

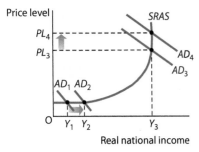

▲ **Figure 7.2.11:** The effects of a positive demand-side shock

Key term

Supply-side shock: an event that leads to a sudden or unexpected change in aggregate supply.

When you have completed the diagram, make sure that you refer to it and use it in your written explanation of the effect of the event on the macroeconomy.

The effects of demand-side and supply-side shocks on the macroeconomy

The effects of a demand-side shock

A **demand-side shock** results from an event that leads to a sudden or unexpected change in aggregate demand. If it leads to an increase in aggregate demand it is a positive demand-side shock, the AD curve shifts to the right. If it leads to a decrease in aggregate demand, it is a negative demand-side shock, the AD curve shifts to the left.

Examples of demand-side shocks include:

- a change in consumer confidence or producer confidence
- an unexpected and significant change in interest rates
- unexpected changes in taxation or government spending
- a change in property prices that affect households' wealth
- a change in the growth of the world economy that affects exports.

A positive demand-side shock will tend to increase real national income and the price level. The extent to which it affects real national income, or the price level, will depend on the current state of the economy and the elasticity of aggregate supply. For example, if the economy is in recession, with plenty of spare capacity, a positive demand-side shock will usually increase national income and have little effect on the price level. However, if the economy is already working at full capacity, a positive demand-side shock will increase the price level and have little effect on real national income.

If the economy is producing at Y_1 in Figure 7.2.11, there is a lot of spare capacity. A positive demand-side shock that increases aggregate demand from AD_1 to AD_2 is likely to increase real national income and will have little effect on the price level.

However, if the economy is producing at Y_3 in Figure 7.2.11, there is no spare capacity. A positive demand-side shock that increases aggregate demand from AD_3 to AD_4 will increase the price level and will have little effect on real national income.

A negative demand-side shock will tend to reduce real national income and the price level. The extent to which real national income and the price level are affected by the shock will depend on the current state of the economy.

The effects of a supply-side shock

A **supply-side shock** results from an event that affects production costs and shifts the SRAS curve. If production costs fall, it is a positive supply-side shock that leads to an increase in short-run aggregate supply. The SRAS curve shifts to the right. If production costs rise, it is a negative supply-side shock that leads to a decrease in SRAS. The SRAS curve shifts to the left.

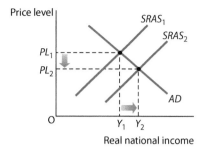

▲ **Figure 7.2.12:** The effects of a positive supply-side shock

As can be seen from Figure 7.2.12, a positive supply-side shock will increase real national income and reduce the price level. If costs of production fall, firms' profits will increase. Supply will increase and there will be pressure for prices to fall. The shift in aggregate supply to the right from $SRAS_1$ to $SRAS_2$ leads to a fall in the price level from PL_1 to PL_2 and an increase in real national income from Y_1 to Y_2.

A negative supply-side shock will increase the price level and reduce real national income. As costs and the price level rise, aggregate demand will fall. As demand falls, firms will reduce production.

Examples of supply-side shocks include:

- a change in the world market price of oil, for countries importing oil
- a change in other commodity prices, for countries importing these commodities
- an unexpected change in money wages
- the introduction of a national minimum wage or a significant change in the existing minimum wage
- unexpected changes in indirect taxes or subsidies to producers
- a change in productivity.

Progress questions

11 What is a negative demand-side shock?

12 Explain how an increase in exports would be likely to affect real national income and inflation in an economy that has a lot of spare capacity.

13 Draw a diagram to illustrate the effects of a negative supply-side shock on the macroeconomy.

14 Explain why an improvement in productivity is a positive supply-side shock.

Case study: Falling commodity prices will help to keep inflation low

The IMF's Primary Commodity Price Index fell by 6.9% between August 2018 and February 2019, mainly due to a fall in energy prices, including the price of oil, natural gas and coal. Lower commodity prices should help to keep inflation low in consuming countries such China, Germany, India and the United States. If commodity prices continue to fall, other things being equal, this will also help to increase the growth of real GDP in these economies. However, falling commodity prices will lead to a negative demand-side shock for those countries who are the major producers of the commodities.

1 Draw an AD/AS diagram to show the effect of falling world commodity prices on the macroeconomy of countries that import these products.

2 Explain why falling commodity prices are a negative demand-side shock for countries that produce and export commodities.

▲ **Figure 7.2.13:** Natural gas pipeline

The meaning and components of aggregate demand

Aggregate demand is the total planned expenditure on goods and services in an economy. It is the amount spent on home-produced goods and services. Therefore, it must be adjusted to remove spending on imports. For example, some household spending will be on foreign goods and this must be removed when calculating aggregate demand.

Aggregate demand is split into a number of different components. They are consumer expenditure, investment expenditure, government expenditure and exports. If the amount spent on these components includes imports, aggregate demand is calculated as:

$$AD = C + I + G + X - M$$

Each of these components is affected by different factors. For example, what determines the value of exports sold will be different from what determines consumer expenditure. Therefore, when attempting to forecast aggregate demand, economists will usually forecast each component separately.

Consumer expenditure, or consumption, is spending by households on goods and services. Investment is spending by firms on capital goods. The government usually provides a variety of goods and services but which goods and services it provides and how much will vary between countries. Exports are spending by foreign residents on domestic output and therefore exports increase aggregate demand.

Determinants of consumption, investment, government spending, exports and imports

Economists have different theories, or models, to explain what determines each of these components of aggregate demand. The importance of each of these components of aggregate demand will vary between countries. For example, household consumption as a percentage of GDP is typically around 65% in the UK, 60% in India, 55% in Japan and 43% in Norway. These percentages will vary over time but in many countries, consumption is the largest single component of aggregate demand.

Activity

Find out the percentage of total spending that was on each of the components of aggregate demand in your country's economy last year.

Determinants of consumption

Household consumption is affected by a number of factors, including:

- income
- wealth
- taxation
- consumer confidence
- interest rates
- the availability of credit.

Income

Other things being equal, as national income increases, it is likely that household consumption will also increase. The **marginal propensity to consume (MPC)** measures the proportion of a change in income that is spent on consumption, it is measured by the following formula.

Marginal propensity to consume (MPC) = change in consumption ÷ change in income

This is also written as: $\dfrac{\Delta C}{\Delta Y}$ where Δ means "change in"

For example, if the MPC is 0.6, a $100 million increase in national income would result in a $60 million increase in consumption.

Wealth

Household wealth also affects consumption. If households are wealthier, they are likely to increase their spending. Rising house prices or an increase in the price of shares are two examples of reasons why household wealth might increase. An increase in wealth makes people more confident and may also make it easier for households to borrow to purchase consumer durables. **Consumer durables** are goods that provide a service to people over a period of time, for example furniture, a washing machine or a car. Consumer durables can be expensive and many households borrow to help pay for them.

Taxation

Taxation can affect households' **disposable income** and/or the price of products. Taxation is a withdrawal from the circular flow of income. An increase in taxation will reduce spending. If the government reduces income tax or indirect taxes, households are likely to increase their spending and consumption will rise.

Disposable income = gross income + cash welfare benefits – taxes on income

Consumer confidence

Confidence in the future is an important determinant of consumption. If people believe that their job and future income is secure, they are more likely to spend than if they think they might lose their job. Confidence, and expectations about the future, can have a significant effect on household consumption.

Key terms

Rate of interest: the price of money, which is the cost of borrowing and the reward for saving.

Availability of credit: how easy, or difficult, it is to find a bank or other organisation that is willing and able to lend.

Link

The use of monetary policy to affect consumption and other components of aggregate demand is explained in 9.1 "Monetary policy".

Interest rates

The rate of interest is the price of money, it is the cost of borrowing and the reward for saving. The rate of interest paid to savers is usually lower than the rate charged to borrowers. There are many different interest rates in an economy but they often move up and down together. If interest rates increase, it is more rewarding for people to save and this will tend to reduce consumption. An increase in interest rates also makes it more expensive to borrow because the amount that has to be repaid to the lender increases. A rise in interest rates will tend to reduce household spending on consumer durables. When interest rates fall, other things being equal, consumption tends to increase.

The availability of credit

It is not only the cost of borrowing that affects consumption but also the availability of credit. There are times when interest rates are low but some households may find it difficult to find a bank or other organisation that is willing and able to provide credit. When credit is widely available, consumption will tend to rise. When credit is not easily obtained, consumption will tend to fall.

Monetary policy is often used to affect interest rates and the availability of credit, and hence household consumption.

Case study: A slowdown in the growth of household consumption is forecast

Household spending is expected to be supported by the steady growth of disposable income and lower interest rates. However, problems in the world economy have led some people to predict that unemployment will rise. High levels of household debt mean people are expected to be cautious and, as a result, they are likely to increase savings and reduce borrowing. Therefore, next year, consumers' spending in many countries is expected to grow more slowly than disposable income.

1 State **two** reasons why household consumption is forecast to rise.

2 State **two** reasons why household consumption may not increase very much.

▲ Figure 7.3.1: Cars for sale

Determinants of investment

Investment is spending by firms on capital goods such as machinery and buildings. Governments also invest but, in the aggregate demand equation, investment by the state is usually included as part of government expenditure. Firms invest to replace capital that has depreciated because it has worn out or is obsolete. They also invest to increase the size of the capital stock and increase productive capacity. Gross investment is the total value of investment spending. Net investment is gross investment after subtracting the amount of investment needed to replace the part of the capital stock that has depreciated.

Net investment = gross investment – depreciation

In the private sector, firms invest if they believe that investment will be profitable but many of the costs and revenues that result from investment are uncertain. Estimates will be affected by firms' expectations of the future state of the economy.

Investment is affected by a number of factors, including:

- interest rates
- the cost of the capital
- expectations and confidence
- the growth of national income
- the amount of spare capacity
- changes in technology
- profits and the availability of finance
- taxes and subsidies.

Interest rates

When considering whether an investment is likely to be profitable, a firm will need to consider whether the **rate of return** on the investment is sufficient to cover the cost of funds used to finance the project. The rate of return is the profit expressed as a percentage of the cost of the project (or the cost of capital). For example, if the investment is expected to have an annual rate of return of 15% but the rate of interest on the money borrowed to finance the project is 18%, the project is not worthwhile. However, if the rate of interest is 7%, the investment is worthwhile.

A rise in interest rates increases the cost of borrowing to finance investment. This means that fewer investment projects will be worthwhile. Also, if interest rates are high, firms may, for example, prefer to save any surplus funds with a bank rather than use them to finance capital investment. Even if the firm does not need to borrow to finance investment, the opportunity cost of funds needs to be considered. The effect of a rise in interest rates is shown in Figure 7.3.2.

The **marginal efficiency of investment (MEI)** is the rate of return on an additional unit of investment. In Figure 7.3.2, if the rate of interest is R_1 then I_1 investment projects are worthwhile. However, if the rate of interest falls to R_2 then I_2 projects are expected to be profitable. A project will be profitable if the expected rate of return, the MEI, is higher than the cost of funds. In summary, other things being equal, a fall in interest rates will lead to an increase in investment because more projects will be profitable.

The cost of capital

If the cost of capital rises, the rate of return on the project will fall. The cost of capital might include how much it costs to build a new factory or buy a piece of machinery. An increase in the cost of capital will mean that fewer investment projects are worthwhile. An increase in the cost of capital is illustrated by a leftward shift in the MEI curve.

> **Key term**
>
> Rate of return: the profit expressed as a percentage of the cost of the project.

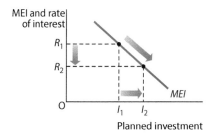

▲ Figure 7.3.2: The effect of a fall in interest rates on planned investment

> **Key term**
>
> Marginal efficiency of investment (MEI): the rate of return on an additional unit of investment.

> **Get it right**
>
> Other things being equal, an increase in interest rates will reduce investment, and a reduction in interest rates will encourage firms to increase investment.

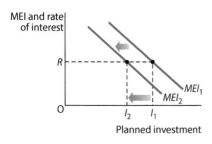

MEI and rate of interest

R

O

I_2 I_1

Planned investment

MEI_1

MEI_2

▲ **Figure 7.3.3**: The effect of a fall in the marginal efficiency of investment on planned investment

Key term

Animal spirits: human emotions and instincts that affect decision-making.

▲ **Figure 7.3.4**: John Maynard Keynes

In Figure 7.3.3, an increase in the cost of capital shifts the MEI curve to the left. At a rate of interest R, planned investment falls from I_1 to I_2.

Expectations and confidence

Expectations and confidence about the future will affect the expected rate of return on an investment project. If firms are optimistic about the future, they will expect a higher rate of return than if they believe that the economy is likely to go into a recession. Confidence about the future can change very quickly and is often irrational. The English economist, John Maynard Keynes, believed that entrepreneurs' changing "animal spirits" meant that investment is a more unstable component of aggregate demand than consumption. When firms are confident about the future, the MEI curve shifts to the right, causing an increase in investment. When firms are pessimistic about future economic prospects, the MEI curve shifts to the left and investment falls.

The growth of national income

When national income is growing, aggregate demand will increase. As spending rises, firms will want to increase production to meet the increase in demand. In these circumstances, firms are more likely to invest in new capital to increase their productive capacity. When national income and aggregate demand are falling, very few firms will need to invest to increase their capacity.

Link

See also the basic accelerator process, a theory of investment explained later in this section.

The amount of spare capacity

If firms have plenty of spare capacity, investment spending is likely to be low. Investment may be needed to replace worn-out capital and to increase efficiency but it is not needed to allow firms to meet demand. When the economy is operating close to full capacity, firms will need to invest to meet any increase in demand for their goods or services. When an economy is recovering from a recession, investment is likely to be low but as the economy approaches full capacity, investment is likely to increase.

Changes in technology

Changes in technology can also lead to an increase in investment spending. Improvements in technology mean that firms may need to invest to improve their efficiency. For example, investment in robotic manufacturing systems may be essential if a firm is to remain competitive. When new products are developed, this also requires investment.

Profits and the availability of finance

Investment can be very expensive and firms must be able to raise the money to finance it. Investment is often financed by using profits that have been retained in the business. It can also be financed by issuing new shares or by borrowing. When profits are low or when banks and other financial institutions are reluctant to lend, even projects that seem very profitable may not take place.

Taxes and subsidies

Governments can also affect aggregate investment. Reducing taxes on company profits will help firms finance investment and provide a greater incentive to invest. Many governments subsidise some types of investment. Changes in taxes and subsidies can affect the amount of investment that takes place. However, cutting taxes on profits and subsidising investment may reduce government spending on other projects and/or lead to an increase in other taxes.

Determinants of government spending

The amount a government spends is determined largely by social and political factors. The government might increase its spending to improve public services such as education and healthcare, or to help people on low incomes. The government's spending is also affected by the amount it can or is willing to raise in taxes, and by its ability and willingness to borrow.

There are times when a government changes how much it spends because it wants to influence aggregate demand. For example, in a recession, when aggregate demand is falling, the government might increase its spending to offset a fall in household consumption and investment by firms.

Link

The use of government spending to affect aggregate demand is explained in 9.2 "Fiscal policy".

Determinants of exports

Exports are an injection of demand into the circular flow of income. Goods and services sold abroad add to domestic demand and create income for factors of production in the domestic economy. The factors that determine the volume and value of exports will be affected by the types of products that are exported. For example, the value of exports for a country exporting primary products will depend on the world market price of these commodities. Commodity prices often fluctuate significantly over time. The prices of manufactured goods and services tend to be more stable.

Factors influencing the value of exports include:

* relative prices
* the exchange rate
* quality and other non-price aspects of competitiveness
* national income and rate of growth in the major export markets
* restrictions on international trade.

Progress questions

1 What are the main components of aggregate demand?
2 If the national income of a euro area country falls by €300 million and its marginal propensity to consume is 0.75, what will be the effect on consumer spending?
3 Why does the amount of spare capacity in an economy affect investment?

Key terms

Volume of exports: the quantity of exports.

Value of exports: the amount spent on exports, determined by the price and quantity.

Link

The causes of fluctuations in commodity prices is explained in 2.5 "The determination of market prices".

Key terms

Relative prices: the price of one good compared to another.

Exchange rate: the price at which one currency can be converted into another currency.

Relative prices

A country's exports usually have to compete with goods and services produced by other countries. Relative prices will affect the demand for a country's exports. Other things being equal, if inflation has been higher than in other countries, exports are likely to fall as they become less competitive. People abroad will start to buy products from countries whose prices are lower or from domestic firms. It is the relative rate of inflation that matters.

The exchange rate

A change in the exchange rate will usually lead to a change in the foreign currency price of a country's exports. If the exchange rate falls, the foreign currency price of exports will fall. Other things being equal, this should lead to an increase in the quantity of exports sold. However, if a country has had a period of high inflation, the fall in the exchange rate might just compensate for the decline in competitiveness caused by the high rate of inflation.

Quality and other non-price aspects of competitiveness

However, competitiveness is not only affected by relative prices. The design and quality of products will also affect exports. Reputation and the standard of the service provided are other factors to consider. Brand loyalty, successful advertising and product differentiation may mean that some countries' products continue to sell well, even when prices have increased.

National income and rate of growth in the major export markets

The value of exports will also be affected by the rate of growth in the country's main export markets. If countries are growing rapidly and incomes are increasing, the demand for foreign goods is likely to increase. If national income is falling, both firms and consumers will reduce their spending, including spending on foreign goods. When the world economy is growing rapidly, most countries will benefit from an increase in demand for their exports.

Restrictions on international trade

Since the end of the Second World War in 1945, many restrictions on international trade, such as tariffs, have been reduced or removed. As a result, the growth in world trade has been faster than the growth in world GDP. However, if such restrictions increase, this will tend to reduce the growth in exports.

Determinants of imports

The factors that affect the amount of imports a country can buy are similar to those that affect its exports. For example, if a country has had a higher rate of inflation than in other countries, home-produced goods will become relatively more expensive and domestic residents will start buying more imports and fewer home-produced goods.

A fall in the exchange rate will increase the price of imports in terms of domestic currency. This will tend to reduce the demand for imports. If the exchange rate rises, the price of imports in terms of domestic currency will fall, increasing the demand for foreign goods. However, the demand for imports also depends on non-price factors, such as quality and design.

The demand for imports is also affected by the rate of growth of the domestic economy. If the economy is growing rapidly, consumers will spend more and some of the extra spending will be on foreign goods and services. Domestic firms will be producing more. As their output increases, they will import more raw materials and components.

If the economy becomes more open and restrictions on trade are reduced, imports are likely to increase. If the government imposes tariffs and **quotas** on foreign goods, imports will fall.

Determinants of savings

Savings are a withdrawal from the circular flow of income. Other things being equal, if households increase the proportion of income that they save, aggregate demand will fall. However, savings also help finance investment spending and contribute to economic growth. When households save, they forgo current consumption so that they can consume more in the future. Some saving is short term, for example to pay for a holiday. Households might save long term to provide money to spend in old age. Many of the factors that affect household consumption will also affect savings. Factors that affect total savings include:

* income
* interest rates
* expectations and confidence
* age
* taxation
* government provision of welfare
* the financial structure of the economy
* social attitudes.

Income

People vary in their attitudes to saving but, in general, household savings increases as income increases. However, rising income does not necessarily mean that the proportion of income saved increases. The proportion of disposable income that is saved is known as the **savings ratio**. The savings ratio varies significantly between countries and over time.

Key term

Quota: a limit on the number or value of a product that can be imported.

Progress questions

4   A country's exchange rate has increased. Why will this affect the volume of exports?

5   If the world economy is growing much faster than the domestic economy, how is this likely to affect a country's net exports?

▲ Figure 7.3.5: Saving

Key term

Savings ratio: household savings as a percentage of household disposable income.

Activity

Find out the savings ratio in your country in each of the past 10 years. Is there a clear trend? Can you explain the variations from one year to another?

Interest rates

Interest rates are the reward for saving and forgoing current consumption. A rise in the rate of interest makes saving more rewarding and should increase household saving. However, it is important to distinguish between the nominal and real rate of interest. The real rate of interest removes the effect of inflation. If the nominal rate of interest is 5% and inflation is 3%, the real rate of interest is 2%. In money terms, the amount in the savings account will be 5% higher at the end of the year than at the start of the year. However, what can be bought with the money will only be 2% higher. Rational households will consider the real rate of interest rather than the nominal rate, but people do not always act rationally.

Real rate of interest = nominal rate of interest – rate of inflation

Expectations and confidence

One reason why people save is to protect themselves against a fall in their income. When people are confident about the future and believe that their job and income are secure, the savings ratio tends to fall. In a recession, when unemployment is rising, many households are more cautious and the savings ratio tends to increase. Expectations about the future can have a significant effect on the savings ratio.

Age

People save to provide themselves with an income in old age. When working, many people will put money into a pension fund that will give them an income when they stop working. Older people often use their savings to support their consumption after they have stopped working. In many countries, the proportion of the population that is over 65 is increasing and this is expected to reduce the savings ratio.

Taxation and government provision of welfare

Taxation affects households' disposable income and hence their ability to save. Government provision of welfare and other services can also affect savings. If the state provides unemployment benefits when people lose their job and pays generous pensions for those in retirement, people have less need to save. The provision of services such as healthcare and education can also affect the need for people to save to provide for future needs.

The financial structure of the economy

A developed financial system can make it easier for people to save. If people have trust in banks and other financial institutions, and it is easy to deposit and withdraw money, it will encourage people to save. However, it may also allow people to borrow more. Borrowing is negative savings and reduces the saving ratio.

Social attitudes

Attitudes towards saving and borrowing can also affect the savings ratio. In some societies saving is seen as being good and borrowing foolish. In these societies, saving is likely to be higher than in societies with a different attitude to saving and borrowing.

Progress questions

6 Define the savings ratio.

7 Nominal interest rates rise from 4% to 7% and inflation rises from 1% to 6% in a country. Why might this reduce the amount households save?

The marginal propensities to consume, save, tax and import

As explained earlier, the marginal propensity to consume (MPC) measures how a change in income affects consumption.

The marginal propensity to save (MPS)

The marginal propensity to save (MPS) measures how a change in income affects savings.

$$MPS = \frac{\Delta S}{\Delta Y}$$

For example, if the MPS is 0.15 and national income rises by $200 million, then savings would increase by $30 million. The equation to calculate the change in savings is:

Change in savings = change in income × MPS or $\Delta S = \Delta Y \times MPS$

The MPS is not the same as the savings ratio. The MPS measures the effect of a change in income whereas the savings ratio measures the proportion of total disposable income that is saved.

In a closed economy without a government sector, the MPC + MPS must equal 1. The proportion of any increase in income that is not consumed must be saved. For example, if people consume 0.9 of any change in income, they must save 0.1 of the change in income.

The marginal propensity to tax

The marginal propensity to tax (MPT) is also known as the marginal rate of taxation. It measures the effect of a change in income on the amount of revenue the government raises in taxes.

$$MPT = \frac{\Delta T}{\Delta Y}$$

For example, if national income falls by $500 million and the MPT is 0.3, tax revenue will fall by $150 million. The equation to calculate the change in taxation is:

Change in taxation = change in income × MPT or $\Delta T = \Delta Y \times MPT$

The marginal propensity to import

The marginal propensity to import (MPM) measures the effect of a change in income on the amount that is spent on imports.

$$MPM = \frac{\Delta M}{\Delta Y}$$

For example, if national income increases by $400 million and the MPM is 0.25, spending on imports will increase by $100 million. The equation to calculate the change in imports is:

Change in imports = change in income × MPM or $\Delta M = \Delta Y \times MPM$

In an open economy with a government sector, the MPC + MPS + MPT + MPM must equal 1. Any change in income must be spent on home-produced goods, saved, taxed or spent on imports.

Key terms

Marginal propensity to save (MPS): the proportion of a change in income that is saved.

Marginal propensity to tax (MPT): the proportion of a change in income that is taxed.

Marginal propensity to import (MPM): the proportion of a change in income that is spent on imports.

Get it right

The marginal propensities to consume, save, tax and import measure how a *change in income* affects each of these variables.

Case study: How will a growing economy affect the budget balance and net exports?

In 2019, national income for an economy was $800 billion. In 2020, national income was expected to grow by 5%. The government wants to know how this is likely to affect the budget balance and net exports. Table 7.3.1 provides selected data for the economy in 2019.

▼ **Table 7.3.1:** Government spending, tax revenue, exports and imports in 2019

	$ billion
Government spending	400
Tax revenue	360
Exports	130
Imports	150

The government has decided to keep its spending at $400 billion in 2020 but expects exports to increase to $135 billion. It is estimated that the marginal propensity to tax is 0.3 and the marginal propensity to import is 0.25.

1 Calculate the expected budget balance (government spending – tax revenue) in 2020.

2 Calculate the expected value of net exports in 2020.

▲ **Figure 7.3.6:** How will the budget balance change?

Link

The budget balance was explained in 6.1 "The objectives of government macroeconomic policy".

Get it right

In Economics, when people buy shares, they are saving. However, when a company issues new shares, it will provide the firm with money that it might decide to invest in capital equipment.

Key term

Marginal capital–output ratio (MCOR): the amount that has to be spent on capital to produce a given increase in annual output.

The difference between saving and investment

Saving is a withdrawal from the circular flow of income. It is that part of households' disposable income that is not spent. People save in different ways. For example, they might put money in a bank account to earn interest, they might buy shares or they might put money into a pension fund to provide them with income when they retire.

The financial institutions who receive people's savings often use the money saved to lend to firms who wish to invest in new capital, for example to build a new office or buy computers. Investment is an injection into the circular flow of income and increases aggregate demand.

The basic accelerator process

The accelerator process is a theory of investment. It is not a complete explanation of what determines investment in an economy but explains one important influence on investment.

The theory explains why changes in the level of national income affect investment. If national income increases, aggregate demand will also increase. If firms are working close to full capacity, they will not be able to meet the increase in demand unless they invest to increase their productive capacity. How much they need to invest depends on the **marginal capital–output ratio (MCOR)**. The MCOR is the amount that has to be spent on capital to produce a given increase in annual output. For example, if investing an extra $30,000 on new machinery results in annual output increasing by $10,000, the MCOR is 3:1. The investment is likely to continue producing output for many years. For many countries the MCOR is approximately 3:1.

The MCOR determines the *accelerator coefficient*. If the MCOR is 4:1, the accelerator coefficient is 4.

Since the marginal capital-output ratio is greater than 1, it means that when national income increases it will require a larger amount of investment to allow firms to meet the increase aggregate demand. The following formula shows how an increase in national income will affect the amount firms will need to invest to enable them to produce the extra output.

Investment = α × change in national income   I = α × ΔY

α is the accelerator coefficient.

For example, if the MCOR in an economy is 2.5:1, the accelerator coefficient is 2.5. If national income and aggregate demand increase by $500 million, the theory predicts that $1,250 million of extra investment will be required.

Limitations of the accelerator theory

The accelerator theory is most likely to provide an explanation of investment when the economy is approaching full capacity. If the economy is recovering from recession and firms have spare capacity, they will be able to meet the extra demand without investing in new capital.

Firms will only invest in new capacity if they expect the higher level of demand to continue. If the increase in national income is not expected to continue, firms will not spend large sums of money on new capital. Expectations and confidence are also important.

Some investment is needed to replace existing capital as it wears out or becomes obsolete. The accelerator theory does not consider replacement investment.

> **Quantitative skills**
>
> Make sure that you understand ratios and can calculate and use them.

> **Key term**
>
> Replacement investment: investment to replace capital that is worn out or obsolete.

> **Progress questions**
>
> 8 What is the difference between savings and investment?
>
> 9 Why is the accelerator coefficient likely to be greater than 1?
>
> 10 In an economy, national income increased by $300 million and the marginal capital–output ratio is 2.5. What is the amount of investment that would be predicted by the accelerator theory?
>
> 11 Why is the accelerator theory unlikely to provide a satisfactory explanation of investment when the economy has plenty of spare capacity?

> **Get it right**
>
> The accelerator theory explains only one factor that affects investment, there are many others.

This section will develop your knowledge and understanding of:

→ the role of aggregate demand in influencing the level of economic activity

→ the multiplier process.

The role of aggregate demand in influencing the level of economic activity

Economic activity involves the production, consumption, exchange and distribution of goods and services. Real GDP is the main indicator of economic activity. If real GDP is rising, more goods and services are being produced, consumed and exchanged. The levels of employment and unemployment in an economy are also indicators of economic activity. If employment is increasing, output is also likely to be rising. A fall in employment and rising unemployment usually mean that output, and hence economic activity, is falling.

In the short run, the main determinant of economic activity is aggregate demand. An increase in aggregate demand will encourage firms to increase output to meet the increase in demand. Employment is also likely to increase as firms will need more workers. There is a direct relationship between output and employment. If output is rising, firms will employ more people to enable them to increase production. If output is falling, firms will start to reduce employment as fewer workers are needed.

Provided there is spare capacity in the economy, an increase in aggregate demand is likely to lead to an increase in output and employment. However, as the economy approaches full capacity, firms will find it difficult to increase production and the price level is likely to increase instead. Too much aggregate demand will cause inflation.

Quantitative skills

If two variables have a *direct relationship* with each other, an increase in one of the variables is associated with an increase in the other variable. If two variables have an *inverse relationship* with each other, an increase in one of the variables is associated with a decrease in the other variable.

Link

The causes of inflation are explained in 8.3 "Inflation and deflation".

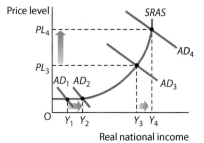

▲ **Figure 7.4.1:** The effect of an increase in aggregate demand on the level of economic activity

In Figure 7.4.1, real national income, shown on the horizontal axis, indicates the level of economic activity. At Y_1 the economy has a lot of spare capacity. If aggregate demand increases from AD_1 to AD_2, real national income will rise from Y_1 to Y_2. The increase in aggregate demand only affects economic activity. However, if the economy is at Y_3, there is very little spare capacity. The increase in aggregate demand from AD_3 to AD_4 has little effect on economic activity. Real national income increases from Y_3 to Y_4 but the main effect is on inflation. The price level rises from PL_3 to PL_4.

In the long run, production can only continue to increase if productive capacity is increasing. Increases in productive capacity result from **supply-side improvements** in the economy. For example, investment in new capital and improvements in labour productivity will increase the productive capacity of an economy.

However, aggregate demand can affect economic activity in the long run. If aggregate demand is high enough to allow firms to produce close to capacity, investment is likely to be high, leading to a long-run increase in productive capacity and economic activity. However, if aggregate demand is too high, inflation will rise. High inflation is likely to lead to instability and firms will be reluctant to invest.

If aggregate demand is low and the economy is producing below capacity, firms are less likely to invest in new capital, or spend money on training workers or on research and development. Most governments attempt to manage aggregate demand to try to keep the economy producing close to its full capacity level of output.

The multiplier process

In macroeconomics, the **multiplier** is the extent to which a change in injections affects national income. For example, if government spending increases by $100 million and this results in national income increasing by $300 million, the multiplier is 3.

Initially, an injection into the circular flow of income will increase national income by the amount of the injection. If the demand for exports increases by $200 million, firms will increase output to meet the increase in aggregate demand. This will create $200 million of income for the factors of production producing the exports. The increase in expenditure = the increase in national output = the increase in national income. The increase in income will then lead to a further increase in aggregate demand.

The size of this increase in demand will depend on the marginal propensity to consume (MPC). For example, if the MPC is 0.6 the $200 million rise in income will lead to a $120 million increase in consumption (0.6 × $200 million). The increase in consumer spending leads to an increase of $120 million in output of consumer goods and a $120 million rise in national income. This increase in income results in another increase in aggregate demand, national output and national income. The increase is (0.6 × $120 = $72 million). Since the MPC is less than 1, the increase in aggregate demand and national income gets smaller each time and eventually becomes insignificant.

The larger the MPC, the larger the size of the multiplier. If the MPC were 0.8, an increase in exports of $200 million would increase consumption by $160 million and then by $160 × 0.8 = $128 million, and so on.

The size of the multiplier can be calculated by the following formula.

$$\text{Multiplier} = \frac{1}{(1 - \text{MPC})}$$

> ### Key term
>
> **Supply-side improvements:** increases in productivity and reductions in costs that improve efficiency, productive capacity and competitiveness.

> ### Get it right
>
> Aggregate demand mainly affects economic activity in the short run. However, it may have some effect on the rate at which productive capacity and economic activity increase in the long run.

> ### Key term
>
> **Multiplier:** the extent to which a change in injections affects national income.

If the MPC is 0.6, the multiplier = 1 ÷ (1 – 0.6) = 1 ÷ 0.4 = 2.5

If the MPC is 0.8, the multiplier = 1 ÷ (1 – 0.8) = 1 ÷ 0.2 = 5

The following formula can be used to calculate the change in income (Y) that results from an injection (J) into the circular flow of income.

$$\Delta Y = \Delta J \times multiplier$$

For example, if government spending increased by $5 billion and the MPC was 0.75 the effect on national income would be:

ΔY = $5 billion × [1 ÷ (1 – 0.75)]

= $5 billion × (1 ÷ 0.25)

= $5 billion × 4

= $20 billion

In the example, the multiplier is 4. The $5 billion injection of government spending has increased national income by $20 billion, that is $15 billion more than the original injection. If the MPC had been smaller, the multiplier effect would have been smaller.

In a *closed economy without a government*, the MPC + the MPS equals 1. For example, if people consume 80% of an increase in their income, they must save 20%. Therefore (1 – MPC) = MPS and the formula for the multiplier is also

$$Multiplier = \frac{1}{MPS}$$

In an *open economy with a government sector*, the (MPC + MPS + MPT + MPM) = 1. Therefore (1 - MPC) = (MPS + MPT + MPM) and the formula for the multiplier is:

$$Multiplier = \frac{1}{(MPS + MPT + MPM)}$$

For example, if investment in an economy increases by $900 million and the MPS = 0.1, the MPT = 0.3 and the MPM = 0.2, the effect on national income would be:

ΔY = $900 million × [1 ÷ (0.1 + 0.3 + 0.2)]

= $900 million × (1 ÷ 0.6)

= $900 million × 1.67

= $1,500 million

Get it right

The multiplier effect means that an increase in injections will lead to a larger rise in national income and a decrease in injections will lead to a larger fall in national income.

When people's incomes increase, some of the money is taxed, some is spent on imports and some is saved. These withdrawals reduce the size of the multiplier because they reduce the amount spent on home-produced goods and services.

It is also important to remember that a fall in injections will also have a multiplier effect. If, for example, exports fall by $150 million and the multiplier is 2, national income will fall by $300 million.

While the multiplier effect is normally associated with changes in injections into the circular flow of income, it can start with any change in aggregate demand. For example, a rise in consumption can lead to a larger increase in national income, due to the multiplier effect. An increase in withdrawals, for example more spending on imports, can lead to a larger fall in national income.

In Figure 7.4.2, an injection of government spending initially increases aggregate demand from AD_1 to AD_2 and real national income from Y_1 to Y_2. The multiplier effect of the injection of government spending leads to a further increase in aggregate demand, to AD_3. The higher level of government spending and its multiplier effect eventually increase real national income to Y_3.

However, if the economy is close to full capacity, an increase in injections and the associated multiplier effect will not have much effect on real national income. The increase in aggregate demand is likely to increase the price level rather than national output.

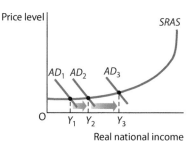

▲ **Figure 7.4.2:** The multiplier effect

Get it right

Do not confuse the multiplier and accelerator processes. The multiplier process explains the effect of a change in injections, including investment, upon national income. The accelerator process explains the effect of a rise in national income upon investment.

Progress questions

1 What is the main indicator of economic activity?

2 Why will a fall in aggregate demand reduce economic activity in the short run?

3 If the government reduces its spending by $12 billion and the MPC is 0.5, calculate the effect on national income.

Case study: What will happen to the economy?

Last year, national income for an economy was $1,200 billion. Firms are confident and optimistic about the future of the economy. Economists have forecast that investment will increase by $40 billion and that exports will rise by $25 billion. However, the government has decided to reduce its spending by $5 billion. The marginal propensity to save is 0.1, the marginal propensity to tax is 0.4 and the marginal propensity to import is 0.3.

1 Calculate the effect of these changes on the country's national income.

2 What is the expected increase in consumption?

▲ **Figure 7.4.3:** Investment in new machinery

This section will develop your knowledge and understanding of:

→ why the price level and production costs are the main determinants of short-run aggregate supply

→ why changes in costs, including money wage rates, raw material prices, indirect taxes and productivity will shift the SRAS curve.

The price level and production costs are the main determinants of short-run aggregate supply

In the short run, the productive capacity of the economy does not change. The amount that firms are willing to supply will depend on whether or not it is profitable for them to sell the goods and services they produce. Other things being equal, a rise in the general price level will lead to higher profits and therefore output is likely to increase. When firms are producing close to full capacity, the extra cost of increasing output rises. Therefore an increase in the price level may be needed to make it profitable for firms to increase production. This is represented by a movement along the SRAS curve.

Why changes in costs will shift the SRAS curve

If firms' costs increase, at any given price level, producing and selling goods and services is less profitable. The SRAS curve will shift to the left. If firms' costs decrease, at any given price level, producing and selling goods and services is more profitable and the SRAS curve will shift to the right.

In Figure 7.5.1, before the increase in costs, firms were willing to supply an output of Y when the price level was PL_1. However, after costs increase, firms will only supply an output of Y if the price level rises to PL_2. After an increase in the costs of production, the price level will have to increase to persuade firms to produce any given level of output.

An increase in money wages or a rise in raw material prices will increase firms' costs and shift the SRAS curve to the left. If indirect taxes increase, firms will have to pay more to the government. Therefore, to persuade firms to produce the same output, the price level will have to rise. An indirect tax is a cost of production for firms.

If firms' costs of production fall, they will be willing to produce any given level of output at a lower price level. Reductions in money wages, raw material prices and indirect taxes will shift the SRAS curve to the right.

An increase in productivity will also reduce firms' costs of production. If each worker is paid $9 per hour and each worker produces two items per hour, the unit labour cost is $4.50. If labour productivity increases and each worker produces three items per hour, unit labour costs fall to $3.00 per item. An increase in productivity will also shift the SRAS curve to the right.

Link

Figures 7.2.2 and 7.2.3 illustrate the effects of changes in the price level on aggregate supply.

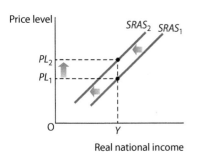

▲ **Figure 7.5.1**: An increase in costs shifts the SRAS curve to the left

Progress questions

1 How is the effect of a fall in the price level shown on the SRAS curve?

2 How would an increase in indirect taxes affect the SRAS curve?

3 Why would an increase in labour productivity shift the SRAS curve to the right?

This section will develop your knowledge and understanding of:

→ the fundamental determinants of long-run aggregate supply

→ why the position of the vertical LRAS curve represents the normal capacity level of output of the economy.

The fundamental determinants of long-run aggregate supply

In the long run, the amount an economy is able to produce is determined by the supply of the factors of production and their productivity. The supply of land, the capital stock, the size of the labour force and entrepreneurial skills of the population will help to determine what the economy is capable of producing. Productivity, the amount that can be produced by each unit of a factor of production, is also important. An increase in the supply of factors of production and/or improvements in productivity will increase an economy's productive capacity.

Since the Second World War, some countries have benefited from an increase in the number of women in the labour force and from improvements in technology. An increase in the **female participation rate** increases the supply of labour and improvements in technology lead to an increase in productivity. Investment increases in the size of the **capital stock** and increases productivity. Some investment is needed to replace capital that has depreciated but investment has also increased the capital stock, increasing the productive capacity of economies around the world.

Attitudes to work and adaptability to change can affect the supply of labour and the productivity of the labour force. Economies are constantly changing and how well people adapt to change will affect the number of people employed and their productivity. The types of goods and services people buy changes frequently. Developments in technology affect methods of production as well as what we buy. Over time, some industries will grow while others decline. The mobility of labour will affect the number of people who are unemployed as a result of such changes. If people are occupationally immobile, when jobs are lost in declining industries they will take a long time to find work in another industry. If they are geographically immobile, unemployment may remain high in places where jobs have been lost.

Economic incentives also affect the supply of labour, for example. The **replacement ratio** affects the incentive to work. The replacement ratio is the income received by a person when unemployed compared to the income that person receives when in work. If the replacement ratio is high, the economic incentive to find work is low. If taxes on the income people earn when working are high and the government provides generous unemployment benefits, the incentive to find work may be weak.

Key terms

Female participation rate: the percentage of women of working age who are working or actively seeking work.

Capital stock: the value of machinery, buildings and other human-made factors of production that exist at a point in time.

Activity

Find out what has happened to the female participation rate in your economy over the past 25 years. What are the reasons for the trend you have found?

Key term

Replacement ratio: the income received when unemployed as a ratio of the income received when in work.

Some economists believe that high taxes and high levels of welfare benefits, not only unemployment benefit, reduce the supply of labour and reduce the productive capacity of the economy.

In summary, the productive capacity of the economy is affected by supply-side factors such as:

- the capital stock
- technology
- the size of the working population
- mobility of labour
- attitudes to work and enterprise
- economic incentives
- productivity.

The vertical LRAS curve represents the normal capacity level of output of the economy

The normal capacity level of output is the maximum output that an economy can continue to produce in the long run without experiencing inflationary pressures. An economy can produce more than this output for a short period of time but there will be excess demand for factors of production. Labour shortages are likely to result in wages increasing. The price of other factors of production will also rise. For example, there may be shortages of factories and offices, leading to rising property prices and rents. This increase in costs of production will cause firms to raise the prices of goods and services. Firms may also find it difficult to meet the demand for their products and this excess demand will allow them to increase prices and profits.

In Figure 7.6.1, the economy is in short-run equilibrium at Y_e but the economy will not be able to continue to produce this level of output in the long run. There will be inflationary pressures and real national output/income will fall.

However, if the economy benefits from long-run economic growth, the normal capacity level of output will increase. The LRAS curve will shift to the right as shown in Figure 7.2.7. The increase in the supply of factors of production, and/or productivity, will allow the economy to produce more goods and services without experiencing inflationary pressures.

> **Get it right**
>
> An increase in productivity shifts the SRAS curve to the right because it reduces production costs. An increase in productivity also shifts the LRAS curve to the right because it increases the normal capacity level of output of the economy.

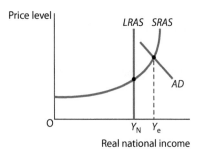

▲ **Figure 7.6.1:** An economy producing more than its normal capacity level of output in the short run

> **Progress questions**
>
> 1 What is the difference between investment and the capital stock?
> 2 Why might a fall in the replacement ratio shift the LRAS to the right?
> 3 Why is an economy unlikely to be able to continue producing beyond its normal capacity level of output in the long run?

Case study: The female participation rate in different countries

▼ Table 7.6.1: Female participation rate, selected countries, 1991 to 2019

Country	1991	2005	2019
Australia	52.0%	57.0%	59.6%
India	30.0%	32.2%	23.4%
Nigeria	47.1%	47.8%	50.6%
Peru	43.5%	64.0%	70.2%
UK	51.8%	54.7%	57.1%
Vietnam	72.7%	71.7%	72.5%

Source: these figures are based on information from the World Bank; https://data.worldbank.org

1   Which country's female participation rate has fallen most between 1991 and 2019?

2   Which country's female participation rate has risen most between 1991 and 2019?

3   Which country's female participation rate has been most stable between 1991 and 2019?

4   Explain how the change in Australia's female participation rate is likely to have affected the productive capacity of Australia's economy between 1991 and 2019.

▲ Figure 7.6.2: Indian women in the labour force

Exam-style questions

1 Which one of the following is an injection into the circular flow of income?

A Consumption   **C** Investment

B Imports   **D** Savings   [1 mark]

2 The marginal propensity of import (MPM) measures the

A proportion of income spent on imports.

B proportion of an increase in consumption spent on imports.

C proportion of a change in income spent on imports.

D ratio of imports to exports.   [1 mark]

3 In an economy, the marginal propensity to consume (MPC) is 0.6. If exports increase by $100 million and investment falls by $120 million, national income will fall by

A $8 million.   **C** $48 million.

B $20 million.   **D** $50 million.   [1 mark]

4 Define "aggregate demand".   [3 marks]

5 In 2019, the national income of an economy was $160 billion and the value of imports was $25 billion . The marginal propensity to import (MPM) is 0.24. In 2020, national income was $168 billion. Calculate, to **one** decimal place, the value of imports for the economy in 2020.   [4 marks]

6 The table below shows how national income and investment in an economy changed between 2016 and 2020.

Year	National income ($bn)	Investment ($bn)
2016	530	84
2017	560	97
2018	605	122
2019	600	87
2020	612	83

(i) Explain why changes in national income might affect investment.   [6 marks]

(ii) To what extent do the data suggest that changes in national income affect investment? Use the data in the table to support your answer.   [6 marks]

7 With the help of a diagram, explain how an increase in exports is likely to affect the equilibrium national income of an economy.   [9 marks]

8 Analyse the effects of an improvement in technology on the normal capacity level of output of an economy.   [12 marks]

8 Economic performance

The national economy in a global environment

Economic growth and the economic cycle

This section will develop your knowledge and understanding of:

→ the difference between short-run and long-run growth

→ various demand-side and supply-side determinants of short-run growth of real national income and the long-run trend rate of economic growth

→ the economic cycle and the use of a range of economic indicators, including real GDP, the rate of inflation, unemployment and investment, to identify the various phases of the economic cycle

→ the difference between positive and negative output gaps

→ how demand-side and supply-side shocks in the national and global economy affect domestic economic activity.

Link

Economic growth was introduced in Chapter 6 "The measurement of macroeconomic performance".

The difference between short-run and long-run growth

Achieving a stable rate of economic growth is an important objective of macroeconomic policy. Economic growth usually leads to an improvement in living standards because the economy is producing more goods and services. However, it is important to distinguish between short-run economic growth and long-run economic growth.

Short-run economic growth is the percentage change in the total output of an economy from one time period to the next. The time period is usually one year. For example, if real GDP for an economy was $500 billion in 2019 and $525 billion in 2020, the short-run rate of growth in 2020 would be 5%. However, although economists usually compare annual rates of economic growth, many countries also publish quarterly growth rates. Short-run economic growth is also known as the actual rate of economic growth.

Long-run economic growth is the average annual percentage change in the productive capacity of an economy over a number of years. Long-run economic growth is also known as the underlying rate of economic growth or the trend rate of economic growth.

Short-run economic growth is concerned with the rate of increase in national output, usually in one year, whereas long-run economic growth is concerned with the average annual increase in the productive capacity of an economy over a number of years. It is not easy to measure accurately changes in national output but it is even more difficult to measure changes in the productive capacity of an economy. The growth in productive capacity is usually estimated by taking an average of a country's short-run growth rate over many years; for example, the average might be taken over 10, 20 or 50 years. In the first and last year, the amount of spare capacity in the economy should be the same.

Illustrating the difference between short-run and long-run economic growth

Production possibility diagrams are often used to illustrate the difference between short-run and long-run growth. The production possibility boundary (PPB) shows the various combinations of goods and services that can be produced with the current state of technology, when the country's resources are fully and efficiently employed.

Link

The use of production possibility diagrams to illustrate features of the fundamental economic problem was explained in 1.4 "Production possibility diagrams".

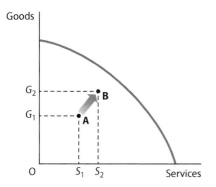

▲ **Figure 8.1.1**: Short-run economic growth

In Figure 8.1.1, the movement of the economy from point A to B shows short-run economic growth. At point A, the economy is producing G_1 goods and S_1 services. At point B the economy is producing G_2 goods and S_2 services, the output of goods and services has increased. This is short-run economic growth, because the productive capacity of the economy has not changed, the PPB has not shifted. The movement from inside the PPB to a point closer to the boundary shows short-run economic growth. The output of the economy has increased because more factors of production are employed or they are being used more efficiently.

The most likely reason for an economy moving from A to B is an increase in aggregate demand. An increase in aggregate demand will encourage firms to employ more factors of production to increase output to meet the increase in demand.

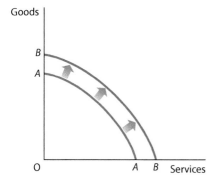

▲ **Figure 8.1.2**: Long-run economic growth

In Figure 8.1.2, long-run economic growth is shown by a rightward shift of the PPB. A rightward shift of the PPB means that the productive capacity of the economy has increased. This results from supply-side improvements. There may be more factors of production and/or a rise in productivity, perhaps as a result of improvements in technology.

As explained earlier, long-run or underlying economic growth can also be illustrated by a rightward shift in the long-run aggregate supply curve (LRAS).

Link

The LRAS curve was explained in 7.2 "Aggregate demand and aggregate supply analysis".

Short-run economic growth is limited by the productive capacity of the economy. If an economy has spare capacity, an economy can grow more quickly than the underlying rate of economic growth but this cannot continue.

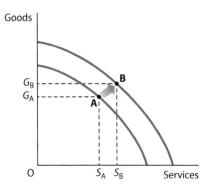

▲ **Figure 8.1.3**: Short-run and long-run economic growth

In Figure 8.1.3, the economy is initially at point A where there is no spare capacity. Supply-side improvements shift the PPB to the right, showing long-run growth. At the same time aggregate demand increases, moving the economy to point B on the new PPB. The movement from A to B shows both long-run and short-run growth.

Supply-side improvements lead to long-run growth but if aggregate demand does not change, firms will not increase production and there will be spare capacity. In Figure 8.1.3, the economy would remain at point A.

Demand-side and supply-side determinants of economic growth

Short-run economic growth is affected by changes in aggregate demand whereas long-run growth is affected by changes to the supply-side of the economy.

Demand-side determinants of short-run economic growth

In the short run, the rate of economic growth depends on the rate of growth of aggregate demand. If aggregate demand increases, firms will increase output leading to growth in real GDP. The increase in aggregate demand could result from an increase in any or all of the components of aggregate demand. For example, an improvement in consumer confidence and producer confidence may lead to an increase in consumption and investment. This increase in consumption and investment will have a multiplier effect that will lead to further increases in aggregate demand and output.

Short-run growth can continue until the economy approaches its normal capacity level of output. As the economy gets closer to its normal capacity level of output, rising aggregate demand is likely to cause the price level to rise and will not have much effect on national output. An increase in aggregate demand without an increase in the economy's productive capacity will not lead to sustainable economic growth.

Get it right

When using a production possibility diagram to illustrate the macroeconomy, the axes should reflect the output of the whole economy. Examples of reasonable axis labels are: "Goods and services", "Consumer goods" and "Capital goods", or "Public sector goods" and "Private sector goods". It does not matter which label is on the vertical axis and which label is on the horizontal axis.

Quantitative skills

To achieve an increase in the short-run rate of economic growth, for example from 4% to 5%, aggregate demand must be growing at a faster rate than before. If aggregate demand increases, but at a slower rate, short-run economic growth is likely to fall.

Increases in government spending and exports can also lead to short-run economic growth. As part of fiscal policy, governments may increase their spending to boost the economy. This is often done to help the economy recover from a recession or to compensate for a reduction in the other components of aggregate demand.

Economic growth means incomes are rising. Some of the increase in income will be spent on imports, leading to a deterioration in the balance of payments. The deterioration in the balance of payments may mean that the government has to reduce aggregate demand and the growth of the economy. To solve this problem, many governments aim for **export-led growth**. An increase in exports, an injection into the circular flow of income, will have a multiplier effect and increase national output. It will lead to short-run economic growth. Imports will increase but if the growth in aggregate demand is caused by an increase in exports, an unsustainable balance of payments deficit should be avoided. Countries such as China and Germany that have benefited from export-led growth have experienced high rates of economic growth and balance of payments surpluses. The profits companies earn from exports can be invested. If this happens, it will increase productive capacity and long-run growth.

If aggregate demand falls, this is likely to lead to **negative short-run economic growth**. If aggregate demand falls, firms will reduce production to stop the stocks of unsold goods increasing and real GDP will fall.

Supply-side determinants of the long-run trend rate of economic growth

The long-run trend rate of economic growth is mainly determined by changes in the supply-side performance of an economy, but aggregate demand may also have some effect on long-run growth.

Improvements in the supply-side performance of any economy may be the result of market forces and the actions of individuals and firms in the private sector. However, the actions and policies of governments can also produce significant improvements in the supply-side performance of an economy.

When firms invest in new capital, it increases the productive capacity of the economy. Spending on research and development can lead to technological change. Technological change improves productivity and leads to the development of new and better products. When firms train their workers, this also increases productivity and contributes to long-run growth.

If the government spends money on infrastructure, the productive capacity and productivity of the economy increases. New transport links reduce journey times and improve efficiency. Government spending on education and training improves the skills, adaptability and productivity of workers. Government funding of research and development is another example of a way in which government supply-side policies can affect the trend rate of economic growth.

Link

The causes of increases in the price level are explained in 8.2 "Inflation and deflation".

Key terms

Export-led growth: where a significant part of the increase in a country's real GDP results from exporting goods and services abroad.

Negative short-run economic growth: when real GDP is falling.

Link

Conflicts between economic growth and other macroeconomic policy objectives are explained in 8.5 "Possible conflicts between macroeconomic policy objectives".

Progress questions

1   Explain the difference between short-run and long-run economic growth.

2   In Year 1, a country's real GDP was $600 billion and in Year 2, its real GDP was $615 billion. Calculate the country's short-run rate of economic growth in Year 2.

3   Explain why aggregate demand affects the short-run rate of economic growth.

Get it right

Investment is an injection into the circular flow of income and affects aggregate demand but investment also creates capacity and affects aggregate supply.

Link

Factors that influence the supply-side performance of an economy are explained in more detail in 9.3 "Supply-side policies".

Link

The accelerator theory of investment was explained in 7.3 "Determinants of aggregate demand".

Get it right

If aggregate demand is growing too slowly or too fast, it is likely to affect the supply-side performance of the economy and reduce the trend rate of economic growth.

Although the trend rate of economic growth depends on improvements in the supply-side performance of an economy, aggregate demand can also have an effect. Investment is affected by the level and rate of growth in aggregate demand. If aggregate demand is rising, firms are likely to make more profit and need to invest in new capacity. The accelerator theory explains why increasing aggregate demand is likely to lead to a more than proportionate increase in investment. When aggregate demand is increasing and profits are rising, firms are also likely to spend more on research and development, and on training. A steady, stable growth of aggregate demand is likely to encourage firms to take actions that improve the supply-side performance of the economy.

If aggregate demand falls, investment is also likely to fall. When aggregate demand is falling, firms will want to cut costs and may reduce spending on research and development, and on training. This will damage the supply-side performance of the economy. However, if aggregate demand is too high, it can be unsustainable, causing inflation and balance of payments problems. This will reduce investment and damage the supply-side performance of the economy.

Case study: Exports support the growth of China's economy

▲ **Figure 8.1.4**: Exports can help economies grow

Since the Second World War, exports have contributed significantly to the development and growth of many countries around the world, including China, Germany, Ireland, Japan, Mexico, Singapore and South Korea. Between 1990 and 2018, the average annual rate of growth in Chinese exports was over 15%.

China became a member of the World Trade Organisation in 2001 and between 2001 and 2008, export growth averaged over 25% a year. During this period, exports increased from just over 20% of GDP to more than 35% of GDP. This rise in exports increased short-run growth and created employment, but it also encouraged investment. Investment by private companies and the government have helped to increase productive capacity and long-run growth.

In recent years, exports have grown more slowly and domestic consumption has made a bigger contribution to the growth of aggregate demand. In the first decade of the 21st century, economic growth in China averaged over 10% a year. In the second decade, the average growth rate was lower at approximately 7%, but still much higher than in most other countries. Although the growth in exports has slowed down, China continues to have a substantial surplus on its balance of trade in goods and services. Net exports continue to support aggregate demand.

1 Explain why the rise in exports has increased employment and short-run economic growth in China.

2 Explain why an increase in exports may also have led to an increase in the productive capacity of China's economy.

3 Explain how a change in net exports affects aggregate demand.

The main phases of the economic cycle

Economies do not grow at the same rate each year, most economies experience fluctuations in the level of economic activity. These fluctuations in economic activity are caused by a variety of factors and can be unexpected. The **economic cycle** is the periods of **expansion** and **contraction in economic activity** around an economy's long-run trend rate of economic growth.

There are four main phases of the economic cycle. They are:

- boom
- recession (or downturn)
- depression (or slump)
- recovery.

However, when economic activity fluctuates, it does not always go through all of these phases of the economic cycle. For example, an economy might recover from a recession without suffering from a slump.

Boom

In a boom, the economy is producing more than its normal capacity level of output. Aggregate demand is very high, unemployment is low. Inflation is high and rising, and firms are making large profits. Wages increase rapidly and firms find it difficult to recruit workers. There are shortages of labour and other factors of production. In a boom, many economies suffer from increasing balance of payments deficits as inflation makes exports less competitive and rising incomes lead to more spending on imports.

Recession

A boom is unsustainable and is followed by a recession or just a slowdown in the rate of growth in real GDP. In a recession, aggregate demand and economic activity are falling. Unemployment rises as output falls and wages increase more slowly or may fall. The fall in aggregate demand means that the rate of inflation falls and firms make less profit. Some firms will go out of business. An economy is in a **technical recession** when it experiences two consecutive quarters of negative economic growth.

Depression

A depression (or slump) does not happen very often. Economies often move from a recession to recovery without suffering from a depression.

In a depression, firms and households are pessimistic about the future, leading to low aggregate demand and economic activity. The economy has plenty of spare capacity and unemployment is high. Wages are low and may be cut as firms struggle to survive. Deflation is a common feature of a depression.

Recovery

A recovery begins when economic activity and real GDP start to increase after a recession or depression. A rise in aggregate demand

Key terms

Economic cycle: fluctuations in economic activity around an economy's long-run trend rate of economic growth.

Expansion in economic activity: when aggregate demand, output and employment are increasing.

Contraction in economic activity: when aggregate demand, output and employment are falling.

Technical recession: when an economy has two consecutive quarters of negative growth of real GDP.

encourages firms to increase output and, before long, firms start to employ more workers and unemployment falls. When the recovery has been going on for a while, inflation and wages start to increase. As firms become more confident about the future, investment will increase to replace capital that has depreciated and to increase productive capacity.

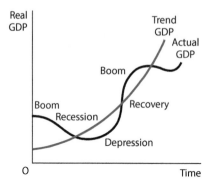

▲ **Figure 8.1.5**: The economic cycle

Figure 8.1.5 shows how real GDP changes over time, where real GDP is used as the main indicator of economic activity. The fluctuations in actual GDP around trend GDP show the economic cycle. The line showing trend GDP is upward sloping, indicating that the productive capacity of the economy is increasing.

Activity

Investigate the fluctuations in the growth in real GDP and unemployment in your country's economy during the past 30 years. Can you identify different phases in the economic cycle?

Economic indicators used to identify the phases of the economic cycle

Real GDP

The change in national output (real GDP) is the most important indicator of the economic cycle. In a recession, real GDP is falling. In a depression, real GDP may be stable but it is well below the normal capacity level of output of the economy. In the recovery phase, real GDP is increasing. This will continue into the boom phase of the cycle but, in this phase of the cycle, the growth in real GDP is limited by the long-run trend rate of growth of the economy.

Unemployment

Unemployment is another indicator of the economic cycle. The change in unemployment usually comes after the change in real GDP. For example, unemployment begins to fall several months after the recovery in the economy has started, and unemployment starts to rise several months after the start of the recession phase of the cycle. Unemployment is known as a **lagging indicator**. There is a **time lag** between the change in output and the change in unemployment, and employment.

Inflation

When the economy is in the boom phase, the rate of inflation usually increases. Aggregate supply cannot keep up with the increase in aggregate demand and demand-pull inflationary pressures will emerge. When the economy goes into recession and aggregate demand is falling, the rate of inflation usually falls; there will be **disinflation**. If the economy gets stuck in a depression, the price level may fall and the economy may experience a period of deflation. In the recovery phase, inflationary pressures are likely to reappear. In most economic cycles, inflation is a lagging indicator.

Investment

Investment is probably the most volatile component of aggregate demand. In a recession or slump, firms will cut back on investment because aggregate demand and profits are falling. In a boom, profits are rising and firms find it difficult to meet the demand for their products. They will invest to increase productive capacity. Changes in the level of investment can provide a useful indicator of the different phases of the economic cycle.

The difference between positive and negative output gaps

An economy has an output gap when the economy's equilibrium level of national income is not the same as its normal capacity level of national income/its productive potential.

Output gap = equilibrium level of national income **minus** the normal capacity level of national income

$$= (Y_e - Y_N)$$

The output gap can be either positive or negative.

A positive output gap

A **positive output gap** is when the economy's equilibrium level of national income is greater than its normal capacity level of national income. A positive output gap occurs in the boom phase of the economic cycle. If the positive output gap continues for too long, the economy is likely to experience **accelerating inflation** and a deterioration in its balance of payments on current account.

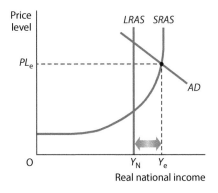

▲ **Figure 8.1.6**: An economy with a positive output gap

In Figure 8.1.6, the normal capacity level of output, or its productive potential, is Y_N. The short-run equilibrium level of national income is Y_e. Since Y_e is greater than Y_N, the economy has a positive output gap which, in the diagram, is equal to $(Y_e - Y_N)$. This situation is unlikely to continue for long as inflation is likely to accelerate. A rising rate of inflation is likely to reduce aggregate demand leading to a fall in the equilibrium level of national income. To prevent inflation accelerating, the **central bank** may act, using monetary policy to reduce aggregate demand. The government might also use contractionary fiscal measures to control inflation.

A negative output gap

A **negative output gap** is when the economy's equilibrium level of national income is less than its normal capacity level of national income. A negative output gap occurs when the economy is in recession or a depression. The size of the negative output gap will fall in the recovery phase of the economic cycle. If the negative output gap lasts for a long time, the economy will experience disinflation and perhaps deflation.

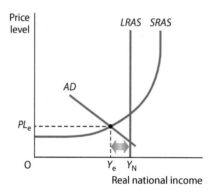

▲ **Figure 8.1.7**: An economy with a negative output gap

In Figure 8.1.7, the normal capacity level of output/its productive potential, is Y_N. The short-run equilibrium level of national income is Y_e. Since Y_e is less than Y_N, the economy has a negative output gap, which in Figure 8.1.7 is equal to $(Y_e - Y_N)$. If the negative output gap persists, there will be a depression and a long period of high unemployment. **Keynesian economists** believe that unless the government uses policies to increase aggregate demand this situation may continue for many years.

However, **neoclassical economists** believe that market forces will prevent an economy from remaining in a slump for very long and that market forces will automatically create incentives for the economy to move towards its normal capacity level of output, without government intervention.

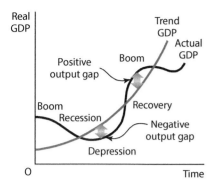

▲ **Figure 8.1.8**: An economic cycle diagram showing a positive and negative output gap

In Figure 8.1.8, the vertical distance between the trend GDP line and the actual GDP line shows the size of the output gap. If trend GDP is above actual GDP there is a negative output gap. If trend GDP is below actual GDP there is a positive output gap.

How demand-side and supply-side shocks affect economic activity

Economic shocks are an important reason why the level of economic activity fluctuates. An economic shock can start within or outside the domestic economy and might affect aggregate demand or aggregate supply.

How a demand-side shock within the domestic economy can cause economic activity to fluctuate

A stable, growing economy can be sent into a recession by a sudden, unexpected fall in aggregate demand. Confidence about future economic prospects can change quickly. If consumers and firms within the domestic economy lose confidence and become pessimistic about the economy, they will reduce spending. This is an internal, demand-side shock. Firms will cut investment and households will reduce spending on consumer durables and will start to save more. This fall in aggregate demand will cause a downward multiplier effect and national income will fall by more than the original reduction in aggregate demand. Falling aggregate demand and national income may also have an accelerator effect, leading to further falls in investment. When aggregate demand is falling, firms do not need to invest to increase their productive capacity. An economy that was growing steadily will then go into a recession.

When confidence returns, aggregate demand will start to increase. The initial increase in aggregate demand will have a multiplier effect and the economy will move into the recovery phase of the economic cycle.

▲ **Figure 8.1.9**: Hyman Minsky

Rising aggregate demand will encourage firms to invest to replace capital that has worn out and an accelerator effect is also likely. Once the recovery has started, multiplier and accelerator effects can cause a rapid increase in aggregate demand and may result in the economy moving into the boom phase of the economic cycle.

Changes in consumer confidence and producer confidence are not the only causes of demand-side shocks from within the domestic economy. Unexpected changes in interest rates, taxation or government spending can also result in significant changes in aggregate demand. Problems in the country's financial system can affect the availability and cost of credit, which will reduce spending and lead to a fall in economic activity.

Activity

The American economist Hyman Minsky said that financial crises are an important reason for fluctuations in economic activity. Find out all you can about Minsky's financial instability hypothesis.

How a demand-side shock outside the domestic economy can cause economic activity to fluctuate

Demand-side shocks can also start in the global economy. For many countries, exports are a large part of aggregate demand. If growth in the world economy slows down, this will affect the demand for a country's exports. A fall in exports will have a multiplier effect and may drive the economy into recession. Similarly, an increase in global growth will increase exports and aggregate demand. This will help the economic recovery and may lead the economy into the boom phase of the economic cycle. This is an example of an external demand-side shock that can lead to a change in economic activity in the domestic economy.

How supply-side shocks cause fluctuations in economic activity

Supply-side shocks that shift the short-run aggregate supply (SRAS) curve can also cause economic activity to fluctuate. During the past 50 years, changes in the world market price of oil have had significant effects on economic activity in oil-consuming economies. When the world market price of oil increases, economic activity in the oil-consuming countries falls. The rise in the price of oil means that consuming countries have to spend more on imports. Imports are a withdrawal from the circular flow of income and economic activity slows down. When oil prices fall, spending on imports falls and households in oil-consuming countries have more money to spend on other goods and services, increasing aggregate demand.

Figure 8.1.10 shows the effect of a rise in the world market price of oil on oil-consuming countries. Higher oil prices increase the cost of producing many products, such as petrol and plastic. The increase in costs shifts the SRAS curve to the left. Higher costs lead to higher prices and there is a movement along the AD curve. Real national income falls from Y_1 to Y_2. Economic activity has fallen and the economy has gone into a recession. The negative supply-side shock has also caused some inflation as costs and prices rise. However, in the long run, the fall in economic activity will reduce inflationary pressures.

Get it right

The impact of both positive and negative demand-side shocks on economic activity are increased by the multiplier and accelerator effects.

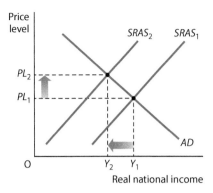

▲ **Figure 8.1.10**: A rise in the world market price of oil reduces economic activity in oil-consuming countries

Get it right

The impact of events in the global economy do not necessarily have the same effect on every country.

Link

Causes of changes in commodity prices are explained in 2.5 "The determination of market prices".

The impact of a rise in the world market price of oil on oil producers is very different. Since the price elasticity of demand for oil is inelastic, the increase in the world market price will lead to an increase in export revenue for the oil producers. This is an injection into the circular flow of income for the oil-producing countries and will increase aggregate demand and economic activity.

Changes in the prices of other commodities can also affect economic activity in consuming and producing countries. However, the impact of changes in oil prices on consuming countries is usually much greater than the impact of changes in the prices of other commodities.

Case study: The 1973 oil crisis

▲ **Figure 8.1.11**: Barrels of oil

In October 1973, the Organisation of Oil Exporting Countries (OPEC), restricted the supply of oil to countries that had supported Israel in the Yom Kippur War. This led to the price of a barrel of oil rising by almost 400%. This is known as the "first oil shock".

In the early 1970s, many countries were suffering from high inflation and the increase in the price of oil made inflation worse. It also caused some economies to go into recession. In the UK, the recession lasted from 1973 to 1975 and during that time, real GDP fell by over 3%. The unemployment rate rose from 3.6% in 1973 to 5.6% in 1977. Other countries that depended on imports of oil also suffered from falling real GDP and rising unemployment.

1   Explain what is meant by a recession.
2   Why did the increase in the price of oil cause inflation **and** unemployment to rise in many countries?
3   Explain why unemployment often continues to rise after a recovery begins.

The Kondratieff Wave

A positive supply-side shock will increase economic activity. The Russian economist Nikolai Kondratieff believed that new inventions and innovation would lead to long periods of rising economic activity. Innovation can increase productivity and reduce costs, shifting aggregate supply to the right. It also leads to new products that can

▲ **Figure 8.1.12**: Nikolai Kondratieff

increase aggregate demand. The development of the steam engine and the railway system is an example of such a development in the 19th century. More recently, developments in information technology and biotechnology have helped to increase economic activity.

In times when only a few new technologies are developed, Kondratieff said that economic activity would grow more slowly and might fall. Kondratieff believed that each cycle, known as a Kondratieff Wave, lasts between 40 and 60 years.

Fluctuations in economic activity are not only caused by economic shocks

Although fluctuations in economic activity are sometimes started by economic shocks, there are other reasons why periods of prosperity and economic depression come to an end. The rate of growth in real GDP is limited by the increase in productive capacity. In a boom, confidence is high and excess aggregate demand will cause inflation to rise. High inflation affects confidence and aggregate demand is likely to fall. The economy will go into recession.

In a depression, there will come a time when capital and consumer durables have to be replaced. Investment and consumption should increase. This will have a multiplier effect and the economy should start to recover.

Case study: The global financial crisis 2007–2008

▲ **Figure 8.1.13**: Banks in crisis

In 2007–2008, problems in the world's financial markets led to the worst economic crisis many countries had experienced since the Great Depression of the 1930s. The collapse of the housing market in the United States caused some large financial institutions, such as Lehman Brothers, to go bankrupt. People lost confidence in the banks and governments in some countries had to support them. The problems in the financial system meant that banks reduced their lending and interest rates increased. Households and firms lost confidence and found it hard to borrow. Household consumption fell and firms reduced investment.

In China, growth slowed but the government acted quickly. It took measures to increase aggregate demand and the recovery in China helped other countries, particularly in Asia.

1 Briefly explain **two** reasons why problems in financial markets might cause an economy to go into recession.

2 Explain the significance of the multiplier for an economy after aggregate demand starts to fall.

3 Why might the increase in aggregate demand in China have helped other countries recover from the effects of the global financial crisis?

Activity

Find out how the global financial crisis in 2007–08 affected the economy of your country.

This section will develop your knowledge and understanding of:

→ measuring unemployment, including the International Labour Organisation (ILO) measure

→ cyclical, structural, frictional and seasonal unemployment

→ the distinction between unemployment and underemployment

→ how employment, unemployment and underemployment may be determined by both demand-side and supply-side factors

→ global influences upon employment and unemployment.

Measuring unemployment

A person is unemployed when he or she is out of work and looking for a job. Not everyone who is not working is unemployed. For example, students and people who have retired would not be included when measuring unemployment. There are two main ways of measuring unemployment:

- counting people who are registered as unemployed and are claiming unemployment benefits
- using a survey to estimate the number of people who are out of work and looking for work.

Counting those who are registered as unemployed usually underestimates the true level of unemployment. Some people are unemployed but not eligible to claim unemployment benefits. In the UK, the claimant count was the official measure of unemployment until the late 1990s. China uses the urban registered jobless rate and the United States counts people claiming unemployment insurance.

Most countries, including the UK, China and the United States, also calculate unemployment using a household survey. Although surveys are estimates of unemployment and have sampling errors, they are usually more accurate than measures of unemployment that count people claiming unemployment benefits.

The International Labour Organisation (ILO) labour force survey method is used by many countries. The sample size is large, usually over 50,000 people. To be considered as unemployed a person must:

- be out of work
- have been looking for work during the past four weeks
- be able to start work within two weeks.

When comparing unemployment between countries, the unemployment rate is normally used. This is because the size of the population varies considerably. Comparing unemployment rates for different countries is more accurate if the countries use the same ILO labour force survey method of measuring unemployment.

> ### Link
>
> Unemployment was introduced in Chapter 6 "The measurement of macroeconomic performance".

▲ **Figure 8.2.1:** Jobs available

Cyclical, structural, frictional and seasonal unemployment

There are different types of unemployment and the measures that should be used to reduce unemployment depend on the type of unemployment that is affecting the economy.

Cyclical unemployment

Cyclical unemployment occurs when an economy goes into a recession. The main cause of an increase in cyclical unemployment is a fall in aggregate demand. In a recession or depression, aggregate demand is less than the quantity of goods and services that the economy is capable of producing, and cyclical unemployment will be high. Cyclical unemployment is also known as demand-deficient unemployment or Keynesian unemployment.

When aggregate demand falls, firms reduce output and the number of people they employ. When output falls, firms do not need as many workers. When aggregate demand falls, firms' profits also fall and they will reduce the number of people they employ to reduce their costs of production. Cyclical unemployment occurs when there is a negative output gap.

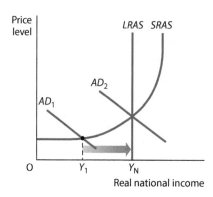

▲ **Figure 8.2.2**: Reducing cyclical unemployment

In Figure 8.2.2, real national income is initially at Y_1. The economy is producing below its normal capacity level of output and there is cyclical unemployment. If measures are taken to increase aggregate demand to AD_2, real national income will increase to Y_N. The increase in output will mean that more jobs will be created and cyclical unemployment will fall.

Structural unemployment

Structural unemployment affects particular industries, types of workers or regions of the country. Unlike cyclical economy, it does not affect all parts of the economy. Structural unemployment is long term and is caused by changes in the economy. With structural unemployment there are jobs available but the skills needed are different from the skills of those workers who are unemployed, and/ or the places where the jobs are located are different from the places where workers are unemployed. It occurs when the skills and location of the unemployed workers do not match the jobs available.

Over time, economies change in a variety of ways. These changes to the structure of the economy can lead to unemployment. Causes of structural unemployment include:

- changes in technology
- changes in the pattern of demand
- foreign competition
- exhaustion of a natural resource.

Changes in technology

This type of structural unemployment is often known as technological unemployment. Improvements in technology can lead to more efficient methods of production that increase labour productivity. Unless the demand for the product increases, fewer workers will be needed. Also, the skills required may be different and some people may be unable or unwilling to adapt to these changes. The introduction of robots and artificial intelligence (AI) are examples of changes in technology that have led to structural unemployment.

Changes in technology also lead to the development of new products. These products may cause the demand for other products to fall. For example, technologies that have enabled people to download or stream music have led to a fall in the demand for physical media such as compact discs and records. Some people who were employed in these industries will have become structurally unemployed.

Changes in the pattern of demand

The products people buy change over time. The pattern of demand is affected by, for example, fashion, advertising, relative prices, competition and changes in peoples' tastes and preferences. Changes in the pattern of demand can cause structural unemployment. If the demand for a product falls, people will be made unemployed and they may be unable or unwilling to learn the skills needed by the industries that are growing. Also, the growing industries may be located in a different part of the country and people may find it hard to move to a different region.

Foreign competition

An important cause of structural unemployment is foreign competition. This is sometimes known as imported unemployment. Over time, the competitiveness of different countries and the pattern of comparative advantage change. This can lead to some firms going out of business or starting to produce their products in other countries. For example, the market share of European shipbuilders began to decline in the 1960s when they faced competition from Japan. More recently, Japan has lost work to South Korea and China. People employed in shipbuilding have particular skills and the jobs are concentrated in particular regions. If the industry declines, some workers will find it hard to get work in other industries. The decline in a localised industry will also affect other firms in the region. There will be a downward regional multiplier effect

Key terms

Technological unemployment: a type of structural unemployment that is caused by developments in technology.

Pattern of demand: the types of goods and services people buy.

Imported unemployment: a type of structural unemployment that is caused by foreign competition.

Localised industry: an industry that is located in a particular area or region of a country.

Link

The principle of comparative advantage is explained in the A2 part of the course.

▲ **Figure 8.2.3**: Copper mine

Link

Policies a government might use to reduce unemployment are explained in Chapter 9 "Macroeconomic policy".

Progress questions

1 What are the two main ways of measuring unemployment?

2 What is the main cause of cyclical unemployment?

3 State **three** different causes of structural unemployment.

4 Explain why occupational **and** geographical mobility of labour affect structural unemployment.

5 What is meant by "frictional unemployment"?

that could lead to many job losses in the local area. There may be plenty of jobs in other regions but some people will be unwilling or unable to move to these jobs.

Exhaustion of a natural resource

Jobs in mining industries such as extracting coal, minerals and precious metals will be lost when the raw material runs out or becomes uneconomic to mine. Mining industries are localised and the closure of a mine often leads to structural unemployment.

Structural unemployment and the mobility of labour

If labour was perfectly mobile, there would not be any structural unemployment. If people were perfectly occupationally mobile, they would be willing and able to accept work in other industries when the industry in which they were working declined. If they were perfectly geographically mobile, people would immediately move from regions where there was unemployment to regions that had **job vacancies**. Occupational and geographical immobility of labour can cause structural unemployment to last for many years.

Frictional unemployment

Frictional unemployment is short-term unemployment when people are between jobs. Economies are always changing and this means that factors of production need to be reallocated in response to the changes that are taking place. People change jobs for many reasons and may be out of work for a short period of time. People do not always start a new job immediately after they have left their previous job. Frictional and structural unemployment exist because labour is not perfectly mobile. The main difference between frictional and structural unemployment is that frictional unemployment does not last long whereas someone who is structurally unemployed will be out of work for many months or perhaps several years.

Seasonal unemployment

Seasonal unemployment is when people are unemployed at particular times of the year; for example, unemployment may be higher in the winter than in the summer. In the summer, there might be lots of jobs in the tourist industry that do not exist in the winter. In the winter, bad weather may mean that there are fewer jobs in the construction industry.

Seasonally adjusted unemployment

Most governments publish seasonally adjusted unemployment figures. The seasonal adjustment removes the regular short-term seasonal variations from the figures. For example, if unemployment in the winter is normally higher than in the summer, the seasonally adjusted figures will be lower than the actual figures in the winter months and higher than the actual figures in the summer months. This makes it easier to see the underlying long-run changes in unemployment.

Distinction between unemployment and underemployment

Unemployment is when someone is looking for work but cannot find a job. Underemployment is when a person is working but would like to work more hours, or is overqualified for his or her job and has skills that are not fully used.

If there is underemployment, there is spare capacity in the economy and labour is underused. The economy could produce more goods and services and increase living standards.

However, underemployment is better than unemployment. People who are underemployed have some income with which to support themselves. Aggregate demand does not fall as much as would happen if people were unemployed, and the government will not have to spend as much on welfare benefits.

When economic activity falls, unemployment increases and underemployment also increases. The increase in unemployment does not fully reflect the extent of the fall in economic activity. In a recovery, unemployment and underemployment fall. Some people who were working in part-time jobs are able to find full-time employment. As the demand for labour increases, it is more likely that people can find a job that makes good use of their skills.

How employment, unemployment and underemployment are affected by both demand-side and supply-side factors

When the number of people in employment increases, it does not necessarily mean that the number of people who are unemployed will fall. If the size of the labour force increases by more than the increase in the number of people finding work, both employment and unemployment will rise.

An increase in employment will lead to an increase in national output, unless labour productivity falls. If labour productivity increases, national output will increase even if the number of people in employment does not change.

The productive capacity of the economy is influenced by the size of the labour force and labour productivity. If the size of the labour force increases and/or productivity increases, the amount the economy is capable of producing will increase.

Changes in productivity, employment and underemployment will affect the actual level of output. If labour productivity is unchanged, an increase in employment and/or a reduction underemployment will lead to an increase in national output. If the level of employment is unchanged, an increase in labour productivity will result in an increase in national output. If underemployment falls, other things being equal, national output will increase.

▲ **Figure 8.2.4**: A part-time job

Key term

Underemployment: when a person is working but would like to work more hours, or is overqualified for his or her job and has skills that are not fully used.

Get it right

The productive capacity of the economy is influenced by the size of the labour force and labour productivity. The level of national output is affected by changes in productivity, employment and underemployment.

Demand-side influences on employment, unemployment and underemployment

An increase in aggregate demand will increase the number of people in employment and is likely to reduce unemployment. An increase in aggregate demand will encourage firms to increase output to meet the demand. An increase in output, other things being equal, will mean firms need more workers. As aggregate demand and output increase, firms may ask people who were underemployed to work more hours. When aggregate demand increases, people will find it easier to get a job that makes good use of their skills.

A fall in aggregate demand will lead to a fall in employment and an increase in both unemployment and underemployment. In the short run, some firms may continue to employ the same number of workers but underemployment will increase. It is expensive to train people and to recruit new employees. Many firms will not reduce the number of people they employ unless they believe that aggregate demand is going to stay low. Instead, the number of hours people work may be reduced.

A fall in aggregate demand leads to involuntary unemployment. There are people who are willing and able to work at current market wage rates but no jobs are available. Some people would also like to work longer hours but employers are not willing to provide them with more work.

Supply-side influences on employment, unemployment and underemployment

Unemployment is not always caused by insufficient aggregate demand. Structural and frictional unemployment still exist when the economy is at its normal capacity level of output and firms are finding it difficult to recruit workers. Supply-side causes of unemployment include:

- a high replacement ratio
- immobility of labour
- technological change
- minimum wage laws
- trade unions.

A high replacement ratio

The replacement ratio is the income people receive when they are unemployed as a proportion of the income they receive when they are working. If the replacement ratio is high, the incentive to find work is low. A high replacement ratio means people are not much better off when they are working than when they are unemployed. The replacement ratio is affected by the level of welfare benefits and taxes on income. If taxes on income and welfare benefits are high, it will reduce the incentive to work. A high replacement ratio is likely to increase frictional and structural unemployment. However, if out-of-work benefits are low, people who cannot find work will have a poor standard of living.

Unemployment caused by a high replacement ratio is a form of voluntary unemployment. There are jobs available but people are not willing to accept them at current market wage rates.

> **Key term**
>
> **Voluntary unemployment:** when there are jobs available but people are not willing to work at current market wage rates.

Immobility of labour

If labour is occupationally and geographically immobile, when an industry or region of a country declines, people will remain unemployed even if there are plenty of jobs in other industries and regions. People may be occupationally immobile because they do not have **transferable skills** or because there are not many opportunities to retrain and learn new skills. People may be geographically immobile because they do not want to move to another part of the country. For example, they might have friends and family who live close by. Poor transport and communication links may make it difficult for people to travel to work. Also, in parts of the country where there is plenty of work, it might be difficult for people to find somewhere to live that they can afford.

Government policy can help to improve labour mobility. The government could pay for the retraining of workers. It could spend money on improving the transport and communication system or it could provide affordable housing in regions where there are lots of job vacancies. However, some of these measures are expensive and may lead to higher taxes.

Technological change

A fast rate of technological change will lead to the decline in some industries and the growth of others. Even if an industry is growing, developments in technology may result in job losses. When technology is changing fast, frictional and structural unemployment are likely to increase. The long-run effect on unemployment will depend on the adaptability of the population and the mobility of labour.

Minimum wage laws

In some countries, the government has set a national **minimum wage** that all firms must pay. Firms can pay more than the minimum wage but not less than the minimum wage. A minimum wage can make it more attractive for people to look for work but it can lead to job losses in some industries.

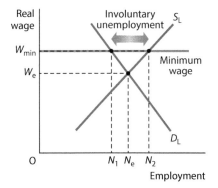

▲ Figure 8.2.5: The effect of a minimum wage on employment and unemployment

Figure 8.2.5 shows the demand and supply of labour in an individual labour market, for example the market for unskilled factory workers. S_L is the supply of labour. S_L slopes upwards from left to right because an increase in the real wage will lead to more people being willing to do this job. D_L is the demand for labour. D_L slopes downwards from left to right because a fall in the real wage will encourage firms to employ more workers. In a free market, the wage would be W_e because, at this wage, the number of workers firms want to employ is the same as the number of people who are willing to work.

If a national minimum wage is set at W_{min}, it is above the free market equilibrium wage in this industry. At a wage of W_{min}, N_2 workers would be willing to work but, at this higher wage, firms would only be willing to employ N_1 workers. There would be involuntary unemployment equal to $(N_2 - N_1)$ workers. The number of jobs lost depends on the elasticity of demand for labour. If the demand for labour is very inelastic in response to a change in the wage rate, the fall in employment will be small.

The minimum wage will mainly affect those jobs where the free market equilibrium wage is below the minimum wage. However, it might lead to higher wages in other occupations as well.

A higher minimum wage may not lead to job losses if there is an increase in labour productivity. Some economists believe that an increase in wages will, for example, encourage people to work harder and persuade firms to train their workers. If productivity rises, firms' labour costs might not increase and there will be little effect on employment.

Trade unions

In some countries, trade unions negotiate with employers to agree the wage paid to particular groups of workers. If the negotiation leads to the wage being set above the free market equilibrium wage, the effects will be the same as shown in Figure 8.2.5 and explained above. However, trade unions often cooperate with employers and can help to improve labour productivity. The impact of trade unions on employment and unemployment is affected by the level at which the wage is set and the relationship between the unions and employers.

Global influences on employment and unemployment

Since the Second World War the volume of international trade has grown much faster than the growth in world GDP. Many economies are much more dependent on exports and imports that they were 25 years ago. As a result, developments in the global economy can have an important effect on employment and unemployment in a country's economy.

World economic growth

When the global economy is growing rapidly, countries will export more goods and services. This will increase employment in export industries and the multiplier effect will help to create jobs in other industries. Firms exporting goods will often buy components from local firms, and workers will spend some of their income on goods and services produced in the domestic economy. An increase in exports will help to increase employment throughout the economy.

If the world economy goes into recession, this will have the opposite effect on open economies that export a significant proportion of the goods and services they produce. Jobs will be lost in the export industries and the negative multiplier effect will mean that other firms in the domestic economy will reduce the number of people they employ.

Competitiveness

Competitiveness is how well a firm or economy is performing in the marketplace compared to other firms or economies. Competitiveness is not only about price but is also affected by the design and quality of products. The ability to deliver on time and after-sales service will affect competitiveness. Productivity, invention and innovation will influence the competitiveness of an economy.

The exchange rate is another factor that affects competitiveness. A fall in the exchange rate reduces the foreign currency price of exports and increases the price of imports in the domestic currency. This makes domestic products more competitive abroad and in the domestic market.

In global markets, firms compete for business with firms located in other economies. The competitiveness of the firms in an economy will affect net exports (X – M) and aggregate demand. If the competitiveness of an economy improves, exports will increase and imports will fall. An improvement in competitiveness will create jobs and reduce unemployment.

Restrictions on international trade

Since the Second World War, there has been a significant reduction in the restrictions on international trade. This has helped to increase the volume of world trade.

However, more recently, there has been an increase in **protectionism**. For example, in 2018, President Trump imposed tariffs on a variety of Chinese exports and China retaliated by imposing tariffs on some goods exported by the United States. The United States has also imposed tariffs on some goods exported from Canada, Mexico and the European Union. These countries retaliated by imposing tariffs on some exports from the United States.

An increase in tariffs and other restrictions on international trade will reduce exports and can increase unemployment. These restrictions might protect jobs in the country imposing the tariffs but this usually leads to **retaliation** and can start a **trade war**. If there is a trade war, all the countries involved will experience a fall in exports and unemployment is likely to increase in the industries affected.

> **Link**
>
> How changes in the exchange rate affect the prices of exports and imports is explained in 8.4 "The balance of payments on current account".

> **Key terms**
>
> **Competitiveness:** how well a firm or economy is performing in the marketplace compared to other firms or economies.
>
> **Protectionism:** a government policy of protecting domestic firms by restricting imports using tariffs, quotas, subsidies and regulations.
>
> **Retaliation:** when a country imposes tariffs, or other restrictions, on the exports of a country in response to that country imposing tariffs, or other restrictions, on its exports.
>
> **Trade war:** two or more countries imposing tariffs, or other restrictions, on each other's exports.

> **Link**
>
> The arguments for free trade and protectionism are explained in the A2 part of the course.

Progress questions

6 What is the difference between unemployment and underemployment?

7 What is the replacement ratio?

8 Explain why a fall in the replacement ratio might reduce unemployment.

9 Explain how competitiveness might affect the level of employment in an economy.

Case study: Unemployment in Spain is falling

▲ **Figure 8.2.6**: Jobs in the service sector

In 2007, Spain's unemployment rate was around 8% but after the global financial crisis it rose rapidly, peaking at over 26% in 2013. Since then, the Spanish economy has recovered and the unemployment rate in 2019 was under 14%. In 2019, the number of unemployed workers was just over 3.2 million. The reduction in unemployment was helped by the growth in exports. Exports increased from just over a quarter of GDP in 2007 to over a third of GDP in 2019. Spain has had a surplus on the current account of its balance of payments since 2013. Between 2013 and 2019, total employment increased from around 17 million to just under 20 million. Part-time employment reached an all-time record of nearly 3 million in the third quarter of 2019. Since 2013, jobs have been created in the service sector but employment in manufacturing and agriculture has fallen.

1 What is meant by the "unemployment rate"?

2 Estimate the size of the labour force in Spain in 2019.

3 Explain why the growth in exports has helped to reduce unemployment in Spain.

4 Why might the record level of part-time employment indicate that there is underemployment in Spain?

5 What has happened to the pattern of employment in Spain since 2013?

This section will develop your knowledge and understanding of:

→ inflation, deflation and disinflation

→ demand-pull and cost-push influences on the price level

→ how external events may affect domestic inflation including changes in world commodity prices

→ how changes in the exchange rate affect inflation.

Inflation, deflation and disinflation

Since the Second World War, most countries have experienced inflation. Inflation occurs when the price level is rising but it is also when the value of money is falling and the **cost of living** is rising. The rate of inflation has varied at different times during the past 75 years and from one country to another. The rate of inflation is the percentage increase in the price level. It is helpful to distinguish between **creeping inflation** and **hyperinflation**. Keeping inflation low is an important objective of government economic policy because high inflation can be very harmful for an economy.

Get it right

Do not confuse the cost of living with the standard of living. Inflation leads to an increase in the cost of living. When the price level is rising, people have to spend more money to maintain the same standard of living. However, if incomes are rising faster than the rate of inflation, people may be better off.

Creeping inflation is when there is a low rate of inflation that continues for many years. Even a low rate of inflation can be harmful. Inflation affects the distribution of income. People whose wages increase by more than inflation become better off in real terms but people whose wages increase by less than inflation become worse off. If the rate of inflation is higher than in other countries, domestic products become uncompetitive in home and export markets. It can also create uncertainty and might reduce economic growth and lead to higher unemployment. However, a low, predictable rate of inflation does not necessarily have these effects and can have some benefits.

Hyperinflation is when the rate of inflation is very high. Germany experienced hyperinflation in 1923 and Zimbabwe suffered from hyperinflation during the first decade of the 21st century. The highest month-on-month rate of inflation in Zimbabwe has been estimated to be nearly 80 billion per cent. A monthly inflation rate of 50% or more is usually regarded as hyperinflation. Hyperinflation is always harmful. The value of money falls rapidly and people may use barter to exchange goods and services. Foreign currencies, such as the US dollar, are often used instead of the domestic currency. In a period of hyperinflation, economic activity falls significantly. Once the rate of inflation starts to rise, it can increase rapidly unless the government or central bank takes action to keep it low. This is why keeping inflation under control is the most important macroeconomic policy objective in some countries.

Link

Inflation was introduced in Chapter 6 "The measurement of macroeconomic performance".

Key terms

Cost of living: how much a person has to spend to maintain the same standard of living. When there is inflation, the cost of living is rising.

Creeping inflation: when there is a low rate of inflation that continues for many years.

Hyperinflation: when the rate of inflation is very high.

▲ **Figure 8.3.1**: A fall in the value of money

Key terms

Malign deflation: bad deflation that occurs in a slump and is caused by low aggregate demand.

Benign deflation: good deflation that is caused by improvements in technology, efficiency and productivity.

Deflationary policies: measures used by the government to reduce aggregate demand.

Reflationary policies: measures used by the government to increase aggregate demand.

Deflation is when the price level is falling. It is most likely to occur in a slump or during a bad recession. Deflation is usually caused by very low, or falling, aggregate demand. This type of inflation is sometimes known as **malign deflation**. When aggregate is low and prices are falling, people lack confidence and may reduce spending even more because they believe goods will be cheaper in the future. Governments and central banks want to prevent malign deflation as well as high inflation.

A fall in the price level is not always bad. **Benign deflation** is when a fall in the price level is caused by improvements in technology, efficiency and productivity. When improvements in technology lead to lower prices, economic activity usually increases and people are better off. However, when prices are falling, whatever the reason, it might cause some people to delay spending and reduce aggregate demand.

A sustained period of deflation is fairly unusual, although Japan has experienced several periods of deflation since the 1990s. Some other countries, for example Greece, have also experienced a period of deflation. The annual rate of inflation in Greece was negative between 2013 and 2015.

In a recession, disinflation is much more common than deflation. When an economy goes into recession, aggregate demand and the rate of inflation fall. Falling output and rising unemployment mean that firms are less likely to increase prices and wages start to increase more slowly.

Disinflation is often caused by a slower rate of increase in aggregate demand and not always by a fall in aggregate demand. If the growth of aggregate demand falls below the current rate of inflation, output and the rate of inflation are likely to fall.

Keynesian economists distinguish between **deflationary policies** and **reflationary policies**. Deflationary policies are monetary and fiscal measures to reduce the growth in aggregate demand. If the government uses policies that deflate the economy, it is using policies to reduce aggregate demand. Deflationary policies often result in disinflation but do not often cause deflation.

If the government uses policies to reflate the economy, it is using policies to increase aggregate demand. Reflationary policies often result in a rise in the rate of inflation but they rarely cause hyperinflation.

Case study: Inflation in India, 2000–2018

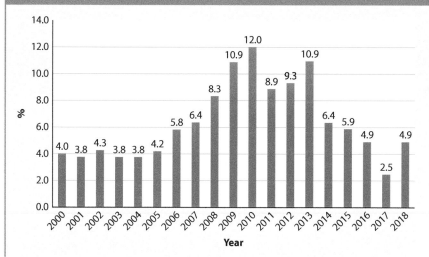

▲ **Figure 8.3.2**: Consumer Price Index (CPI) inflation in India, 2000–2018

Source: The World Bank, https://data.worldbank.org, accessed 13 December 2019

India has a population of over 1.3 billion. Since 2000, its annual rate of economic growth has averaged over 6.5%

but its rate of inflation has fluctuated and this led to the government introducing an inflation target of 4% in 2016.

1 Describe the main changes in inflation in India between 2000 and 2018.

2 In which years was there disinflation in India?

3 Calculate the mean annual rate of inflation, to **one** decimal place, over the period.

4 Would you describe the inflation in India between 2000 and 2018 as creeping inflation? Explain your answer.

Demand-pull and cost-push influences on the price level

Economists usually distinguish between **demand-pull inflation** and **cost-push inflation**. Demand-pull inflation is when the rise in the price level is caused by an increase in aggregate demand. Cost-push inflation is when the rise in the price level is caused by an increase in the costs of production. In a period of sustained inflation, aggregate demand and production costs are likely to be rising. Many economists believe that inflation cannot continue for long without aggregate demand increasing.

Demand-pull inflation

Demand-pull inflation is most likely to occur when an economy is close to full capacity. If there is plenty of spare capacity, the increase in aggregate demand can be met by increasing output. That does not mean that prices will not rise at all but, if there is spare capacity, the rate of inflation is likely to stay low.

The rise in aggregate demand could come from any of the components of aggregate demand and will be increased by the multiplier effect. When aggregate demand is increasing, firms will be able to increase prices to make more profits. They will also demand more factors of production and may have to pay higher wages to attract workers and pay higher prices for raw materials. As costs increase, firms will raise prices even further. As long as aggregate demand keeps rising, this process will continue. If prices keep rising, consumers, workers and firms will come to expect inflation. **Inflationary expectations** will encourage workers to demand higher money wages to compensate for inflation

> ## Key terms
>
> **Demand-pull inflation**: when the rise in the price level is caused by an increase in aggregate demand.
>
> **Cost-push inflation**: when the rise in the price level is caused by an increase in the costs of production.

> ## Key term
>
> **Inflationary expectations**: the rate of inflation that households, firms and other economic agents believe will occur in the future.

and maintain their **real wages**. Firms will expect costs to rise and will raise prices to stop profits falling. Once inflation has become established, it can be difficult to reduce it without an increase in unemployment.

The demand-pull inflationary process is shown in Figure 8.3.3.

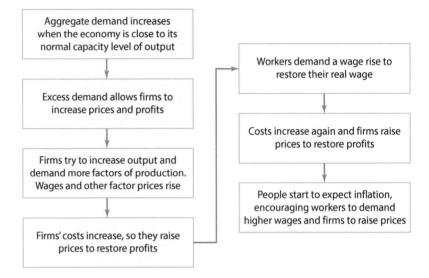

▲ **Figure 8.3.3**: The demand-pull inflationary process

Demand-pull inflation is often shown using an AD/AS diagram. In Figure 8.3.4, the increase in aggregate demand is illustrated by a rightward shift in the AD curve. The upward sloping SRAS curve indicates that the economy is close to the normal capacity level of output of the economy.

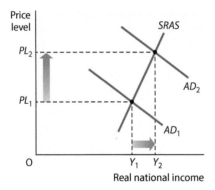

▲ **Figure 8.3.4**: Demand-pull inflation

In Figure 8.3.4, the increase in aggregate demand leads to some increase in output, real national income increases from Y_1 to Y_2, but the main effect is on the price level, which rises from PL_1 to PL_2. When an economy is close to capacity, firms will find it hard to increase output and the increase in aggregate demand is likely to cause inflation. If aggregate demand continues to increase more rapidly than the economy's underlying rate of economic growth, demand-pull inflation will continue and may accelerate.

The monetarist view

Monetarist economists believe that inflation is always caused by the money supply increasing too quickly. They believe that there is a stable, long-run relationship between the growth of the money supply and the growth in aggregate demand. If the money supply is allowed to increase too quickly, they believe that aggregate demand will increase too quickly and the result will be inflation. To prevent inflation, monetarists believe that the rate of growth of the money supply must **not** be allowed to increase more quickly than the underlying rate of growth in the productive capacity of the economy. If it does, the result will be excess aggregate demand and inflation. As a simple rule, monetarists believe that the rate of inflation will be approximately equal to the difference between the rate of growth in the money supply and the growth in the productive capacity of the economy. For example, if the productive capacity of the economy is growing at 3% per annum and the money supply increases by 5% per annuum, inflation will be around 2% per annum.

The monetarist view is that inflation is always caused by too much demand and that too much demand can only be caused by the money supply increasing too quickly.

Milton Friedman was an influential American monetarist economist who helped to make the monetarist view of the cause of inflation very popular in the 1970s and 1980s. It is a view that still influences some policymakers.

▲ **Figure 8.3.5**: Milton Friedman

Cost-push inflation

Cost-push inflation starts with an increase in costs of production. When costs increase, firms' profits fall. Firms are likely to increase prices to restore their **profit margins**. Rising prices will mean that workers' real wages fall and they will ask for higher wages. The rise in wages will lead to further cost and price increases. It will also mean workers and firms start to expect inflation, which will affect their behaviour. Inflationary expectations will encourage further wage and price rises.

The cost-push inflationary process is shown in Figure 8.3.6.

Key terms

Profit margin: profit as a percentage of the price of the product.

Imported inflation: a type of cost-push inflation that starts with an increase in the price of commodities imported from abroad.

Wage-push inflation: a type of cost-push inflation that starts with an increase in workers' wages.

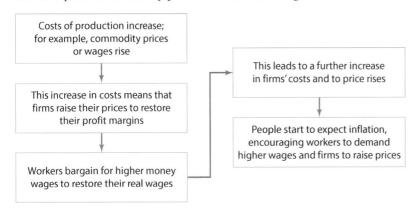

▲ **Figure 8.3.6**: The cost-push inflationary process

An important cause of cost-push inflation is an increase in the world market price of oil and other commodities such as copper, timber and cement. Countries that use commodities often import them and this type of cost-push inflation is sometimes known as **imported inflation**.

Wage-push inflation is another type of cost-push inflation. This type of inflation is often linked with strong trade unions trying to improve the real wages of their members. Wages are often the largest cost of production. If trade unions and workers are able to obtain large wage rises, firms' costs will increase and this may start a cost-push inflationary process.

Progress questions

1 What is meant by "disinflation"?

2 What is meant by "deflationary policies"?

3 What is the difference between demand-pull and cost-push inflation?

4 Explain why a large increase in money wages may cause inflation.

Cost-push inflation can also be shown using an AD/AS diagram. In Figure 8.3.7, the increase in costs of production is illustrated by a leftward shift in the SRAS curve from $SRAS_1$ to $SRAS_2$.

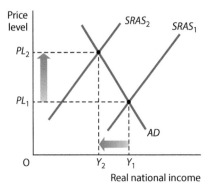

▲ **Figure 8.3.7**: Cost-push inflation

In Figure 8.3.7, the increase in production costs means firms increase prices to try to restore their profit margins. The SRAS curve shifts to the left and the price level rises from PL_1 to PL_2. The increase in the price level leads to a contraction in aggregate demand, a movement along the AD curve. This contraction in aggregate demand causes a decrease in output and real national income falls from Y_1 to Y_2.

The fall in national income and rising unemployment may mean that the increase in costs will not continue unless there is also an increase in aggregate demand. Some economists believe that an increase in costs can cause inflation in the short-run but that inflation cannot continue unless there is a sustained increase in aggregate demand.

How external events may affect domestic inflation

The rate of inflation in country can be affected by events in the global economy. For example, food prices may be affected by weather conditions in those parts of the world that supply food. If bad weather leads to poor harvests, the world market price of food will increase. This will add to cost-push inflationary pressure.

A change in the world market price of oil, and other commodities, will affect inflation in many countries. A rise in commodity prices can start a cost-push inflationary process in consuming countries. When commodity prices fall, this will help to reduce inflation.

The rate of growth of the global economy will affect the volume of exports and aggregate demand in economies that are open to foreign trade. If the global economy is growing fast, countries that depend on exports may find that they experience demand-pull inflationary pressures. The increase in exports will have multiplier and accelerator effects that may lead to a level of aggregate demand that is greater than the economy's normal capacity level of output.

If the global economy is growing fast, the demand for commodities will also increase. Since the supply of commodities is inelastic, particularly in the short run, the world market price of commodities will increase substantially. This is another reason why a fast-growing global economy is likely to increase inflation in many countries.

When the global economy slows down, the demand for exports and commodity prices will fall and this will lead to disinflation in many countries. However, it must be remembered that the rate of inflation is affected by internal as well as external influences.

How changes in the exchange rate affect inflation

The exchange rate is the rate at which one currency can be exchanged for another. For example, US $1 = €0.90 was the $/€ exchange rate on 12 December 2019. If the exchange rate falls, it means that the currency will buy fewer units of foreign currency than before. This is known as a **depreciation in the exchange rate**. An increase in the value of the currency is an **appreciation in the exchange rate**.

A depreciation in the exchange rate is likely to increase inflationary pressures and an appreciation of the exchange rate will reduce inflationary pressures. If the exchange rate depreciates, the foreign currency price of exports falls and the domestic currency price of imports rises.

There are three main reasons why a depreciation in the exchange rate is likely to increase inflation.

- The fall in the price of exports and the rise in the price of imports will make domestically products more competitive in both the foreign and domestic markets. This will increase aggregate demand and will add to demand-pull inflationary pressures.
- The rise in the price of imports will increase the price of raw materials and components bought from abroad. This will lead to a rise in firms' costs of production and add to cost-push inflationary pressures.
- Some imported products are included in the Consumer Price Index (CPI), therefore the rise in the price of imports will increase inflation as measured by the CPI.

If the exchange rate appreciates, aggregate demand and the price of imports will fall. This will reduce demand-pull and cost-push inflationary pressures.

Key terms

Depreciation in the exchange rate: a fall in the value of the currency; it buys fewer units of foreign currency.

Appreciation in the exchange rate: a rise in the value of the currency; it buys more units of foreign currency.

Link

Why a change in the exchange rate affects the foreign currency price of exports and the domestic currency price of imports is explained in 8.4 "The balance of payments on current account".

Progress questions

5 Why will a high rate of global economic growth increase inflationary pressures in some countries?

6 Explain **two** reasons why an appreciation in a country's exchange will reduce inflationary pressures in the country.

This section will develop your knowledge and understanding of:

→ the importance of international trade for an economy

→ the balance of payments as a record of a country's financial transactions with the rest of the world

→ how the current account comprises trade in goods, trade in services, primary income and secondary income

→ the meaning of a deficit and a surplus on current account

→ factors that influence a country's current account balance including productivity, inflation, the exchange rate, and economic activity at home and abroad.

Link

The balance of payments was introduced in Chapter 6 "The measurement of macroeconomic performance".

Key term

International trade: the exchange of goods and services between countries.

Link

The costs and benefits of international trade are covered in detail in the A2 part of the course.

Key terms

Debit items: items that lead to an outflow of foreign currency.

Credit items: items that lead to an inflow of foreign currency.

The importance of international trade for an economy

International trade is the exchange of goods and services between countries. International trade makes up a high proportion of the GDP of many countries. In 1960, total world exports were 11.9% of world GDP but in 2017 exports were 29.4% of world GDP. World trade has grown faster than world GDP and many more people now depend on international trade for their job and income.

International trade allows countries to specialise in producing those goods and services they are best at producing and to import those products they cannot produce efficiently. This should lead to a better allocation of the world's scarce resources. Improvements in efficiency mean that it should be possible to increase output and make everyone better off. Also, international trade allows countries to import products that they cannot produce themselves and it provides consumers with a greater variety of products. The competition that results from the growth in world trade should encourage firms to increase productivity, reduce prices and improve their products.

However, international trade does not benefit everyone. Foreign competition may mean that some workers lose their job. People may buy foreign goods instead of home-produced goods. If labour is occupationally and geographically immobile, workers who lose their job might be structurally unemployed for a long time.

International trade allows firms to sell their products on the world market. If sales increase, more jobs will be created. Exports are an injection into the circular flow of income and will boost aggregate demand and GDP. However, imports are a withdrawal from the circular flow of income and if imports are greater than exports, net trade (X – M) will reduce aggregate demand.

The balance of payments account

The balance of payments is a record of a country's financial transactions with the rest of the world during a given period of time, for example one year. **Debit items** on the account are those that lead to an outflow of foreign currency, for example spending on imports. **Credit items** lead to an inflow of foreign currency, for example exports of goods and services.

The balance of payments account has **four** main sections:

- the current account
- the capital account
- the financial account
- net errors and omissions.

The current account records income flows. The capital and financial accounts record changes in assets and liabilities. Net errors and omissions is a figure showing the sum of the statistical errors that have been made when trying to record all the transactions that should be included on the balance of payments account.

The current account of the balance of payments

The current account has four main sections, each of which records a different type of income flow. The **four** main sections of the current account are:

- trade in goods
- trade in services
- primary income
- secondary income.

Trade in goods

The balance of trade in goods is the difference between the value of goods exported and the value of goods imported. Goods are products that can be seen and touched. They include a large variety of products including cars, washing machines, rice, copper, computers, machinery and oil. They are sometimes known as visible exports and visible imports. The balance of trade in goods is also known as the visible balance.

If the value of goods imported is greater than the value of goods exported, the balance of trade in goods is in deficit. If the value of goods exported is greater than the value of goods imported, there is a surplus on the balance of trade in goods.

Trade in services

Services that are traded between countries include financial services, insurance, transport, tourism, construction services, sport and music. There are also many others. The balance of trade in services is the difference between the value of services exported and the value of services imported.

A service is an export if it results in money coming into the country. Exports are credit items. A service is an import if it results in money going out of the country. Imports are debit items. For example, a French resident travelling in a Singapore Airlines plane would be an export, or credit item, for Singapore but an import, or debit item, for France. An Australian tourist staying in a hotel in Japan would be a Japanese export. A Canadian business insuring its lorries with a UK insurance company would be an export for the UK. However, if the insurance company had to pay out because one of the lorries had an accident, the payment made to the Canadian business would be a debit item on the UK balance of payments.

Link

The capital account, the financial account and net errors and omissions are explained in the A2 part of the course.

Key terms

Balance of trade in goods or **visible balance**: the difference between the value of goods exported and the value of goods imported.

Balance of trade in services: the value of services exported **minus** the value of services imported.

An important figure on the current account of the balance of payments is the balance of trade in goods and services, which is the difference between the value of goods and services exported and the value of goods and services imported.

Primary income

Primary income is the flow of income from residents of one country to another in return for investment and labour services.

Many countries own assets abroad. These assets earn income that might be interest, dividends, profits or rent. The difference between the amount of income domestic residents earn on their assets abroad and the amount of income paid to foreign residents on their assets in the domestic economy is called net investment income. Net investment income is for many countries the largest part of the primary income balance.

Income flows out of the domestic economy to foreign residents who provide labour services in the domestic economy. Money comes into the domestic economy from abroad when domestic residents provide labour services in other countries. The difference between these two flows is another part of the primary income balance.

Secondary income

Secondary income is when money is transferred from the residents of one country to another without any goods or services given in return. Some transfers are made by governments, for example foreign aid. These are known as official transfers. Other transfers are made by private individuals, for example a gift sent to a member of the family living in another country. These are known as private transfers.

The meaning of deficits and surpluses on the current account

Deficits and surpluses refer to a particular part of the balance of payments account. Overall, the balance of payments account must balance but, for example, there might be a deficit on the balance of trade in goods and a surplus on the current account.

A deficit on a part of the balance of payments means that the money leaving the country is greater than the money coming in, or debits are greater than credits. A surplus is when the money coming into the country is greater than the money going out, or credits are greater than debits. For example, a country has a surplus on its balance of trade in goods if the value of the goods it exports is greater than the value of the goods it imports. A country has a deficit on its balance of trade in goods if the value of the goods it imports is greater than the value of the goods it exports. If it has a deficit on the balance of trade in goods it is not receiving enough money from selling its exports of goods to pay for the goods it is importing. However, it may have a surplus on its trade in services.

In Table 8.4.1, the country has a surplus on its balance of trade in goods because the value of its exports of goods is greater than the

▼ Table 8.4.1: An example of the current account of the balance of payments

	$ billion	$ billion
Exports of goods	800	
Imports of goods	650	
Balance of trade in goods	150	
Services balance	−200	
Balance of trade in goods and services		−50
Primary income balance		100
Secondary income balance		−30
Current account balance		20

value of the goods imported. The surplus is $150 billion. However, there is a deficit on its balance of trade in goods and services because the deficit on its trade in services of $200 billion is greater than the surplus on its trade in goods. The primary and secondary income balances are added to the balance of trade in goods and services to calculate the **current account balance**. In Table 8.4.1, the current account shows a surplus of $20 billion.

Key term

Current account balance: the sum of the balance of trade in goods and services + the primary income balance + the secondary income balance.

The current account is in surplus if the total amount of money coming into the country from all current account transactions is **greater than** the total amount of money going out of the country from all current account transactions. Credits are greater than debits on this part of the account.

The current account is in deficit if the total amount of money coming into the country from all current account transactions is **less than** the total amount of money going out of the country from all current account transactions. Credits on the current account are less than debits.

The importance of each of the sections of the current account will vary from one country to another. For example, some countries might export lots of goods and others might specialise in selling services. Some countries might own lots of assets abroad and receive large amounts of investment income. Other countries may receive large transfers of money from their citizens living in other countries.

Progress questions

1 What does the balance of payments show?
2 What are the **four** main sections of the current account of the balance of payments?
3 What is meant by a deficit on the balance of trade in goods and services?
4 What is the difference between primary and secondary income on the current account of the balance of payments?

Case study: The US current account balance in the 3rd quarter of 2019

The US current account deficit was $125.2 billion in the 2nd quarter of 2019. The deficit improved in the 3rd quarter, mainly due to a smaller deficit in trade in goods and a larger surplus on the primary income balance.

In the 3rd quarter of 2019, exports of goods were $413.8 billion and imports of goods were $633.4 billion. Exports of services were $212.0 billion and imports of services were $149.8 billion. The primary income surplus was $68.7 billion and the secondary income deficit was $35.4 billion. Although there was an improvement, the US current account deficit was still 2.3% of GDP in the 3rd quarter of 2019.

Source: adapted from US Bureau of Economic Analysis; www.bea.gov; accessed 21 December 2019

▲ **Figure 8.4.1**: Tourism helps the balance of payments

1 Calculate the US balance of trade in goods in the 3rd quarter of 2019.

2 Calculate the US balance of trade in services in the 3rd quarter of 2019.

3 Calculate the US current account balance in the 3rd quarter of 2019.

4 Describe what happened to the US current account balance between the 2nd and 3rd quarters of 2019.

Factors that influence a country's current account balance

A country's balance of payments on current account can change very quickly. It is affected by a variety of factors in the domestic and global economies.

The balance of trade in goods and services, a large part of the current account, is affected by the competitiveness of domestic firms. An improvement in international competitiveness should result in an increase in exports and a fall in imports. Competitiveness is affected by:

- productivity
- inflation
- the exchange rate
- non-price factors.

Productivity

Improvements in productivity reduce firms' costs and allow firms to reduce prices. If the rate of productivity growth is faster than in other countries, it should help to improve the country's international competitiveness.

Inflation

The rate of inflation in the domestic economy compared to other economies will affect competitiveness. If inflation in the domestic economy is 3% higher than in other economies, other things being equal, domestic firms will, on average, become 3% less price competitive each year. The volume of exports is likely to fall and the volume of imports is likely to increase.

The exchange rate

A fall in the exchange rate makes exports cheaper in foreign currency and imports more expensive in domestic currency. A fall in the exchange rate will help to improve competitiveness and will usually lead to an improvement in the balance of payments on current account.

However, if inflation is higher in the domestic economy than in other economies, a fall in the exchange rate might not improve competitiveness but only help to restore it. For example, if inflation is 2% higher in the UK than Japan, a 2% depreciation of the pound sterling compared to the Japanese yen would leave the price competitiveness of UK and Japanese products unchanged.

Non-price factors

International competitiveness is not only affected by the relative prices of exports and imports, non-price factors are also important. The quality and design of products affect competitiveness. Innovation and product development are important in helping firms outdo their competitors. Reputation and reliability of the suppliers will also be taken into account when deciding which products to buy.

The level of economic activity in the domestic market, and in the global economy, also affect the current account of the balance of payments.

Domestic economic activity

If the domestic economy is growing, the demand for imports is likely to increase. Rising household incomes will lead to an increase in the consumption of home-produced and foreign goods. Also, as output increases, firms are likely to buy more raw materials and components from abroad. The increase in imports will be affected by the size of the change in income and the marginal propensity to import. For a given change in income, the larger the marginal propensity to import, the larger the increase in imports. Other things being equal, an increase in economic growth is likely to result in an increase in imports and a deterioration in the current account of the balance of payments.

However, if economic growth has been caused by an improvement in competitiveness and increased exports, the current account of the balance of payments may improve rather than deteriorate. Many countries aim for export-led growth.

Global economic activity

Economic growth in the world economy will affect the value of a country's exports. If a country's main export markets are growing, the country is likely to benefit from an increase in exports and an improvement in the current account of its balance of payments. The increase in exports will be affected by the country's competitiveness, the rate at which the global economy is growing and marginal propensities to import in other economies.

Get it right

Domestic economic growth usually leads to an increase in imports and a deterioration in the current account of the balance of payments. Global economic growth usually leads to an increase in exports and an improvement in the current account of the balance of payments.

Primary and secondary income flows affect the current account of the balance of payments

Changes in primary and secondary income flows can lead to significant changes in the current account of the balance of payments. For example, changes in foreign aid will affect the current account of both donor and recipient countries. Over time, the amount of foreign investment will affect the income received. If a country has a current account surplus and invests the money abroad, it will earn income on its investments in the future. Also, the income from foreign investment will be affected by, for example, interest rates and the profits companies are making.

Progress questions

5   Explain how inflation affects the current account of the balance of payments.

6   A country's national income increases by $30 billion and its marginal propensity to import is 0.27. Other things being equal, calculate the effect of the increase in the country's national income on the current account of its balance of payments.

7   Explain why overseas investment affects the current account of a country's balance of payments.

This section will develop your knowledge and understanding of:

→ how economic growth may affect the environment, the distribution of income, unemployment and the budget balance

→ how negative and positive output gaps relate to unemployment and inflationary pressures

→ how economic policies may be used to try to reconcile possible policy conflicts both in the short run and the long run.

Governments have a variety of policy objectives. Some of these objectives are compatible with each other but others may conflict. Some conflicts between policy objectives may occur in the short run but not in the long run. Governments also have a variety of policy instruments that they can use to try to overcome conflicts between objectives.

> **Link**
>
> The instruments of government economic policy are explained in Chapter 9 "Macroeconomic policy".

Economic growth may affect the environment, the distribution of income, unemployment and the budget balance

Achieving a stable rate of economic growth is the most important macroeconomic policy objective for many governments. If the rate of economic growth exceeds the growth of the country's population, real GDP per capita will increase. This should improve living standards. However, economic growth can impose costs on a society.

Economic growth and the environment

Economic growth means that production and consumption are increasing. More production means that more non-renewable resources and renewable resources are being used. If these natural resources are used too quickly, it will affect economic growth and living standards in the future.

Some non-renewable resources can be conserved through recycling but too often non-renewable resources are not recycled. If renewable resources are used too quickly, they can also be used up. For example, overfishing in some parts of the ocean means that the stock of fish is too small to replace itself by natural means. Deforestation is another consequence of economic growth in some parts of the world. Trees absorb carbon dioxide and if forests disappear, global warming and harmful climate change will occur more quickly.

As resources run out the price should increase, which will encourage recycling and the development of substitutes. However, the economic incentives that this produces may not be sufficient and government intervention is needed to compensate for market failure.

Increased production may also lead to more negative externalities such as pollution, damage to the countryside and increased congestion. The failure of markets to deal effectively with externalities means that government action is needed to limit the damage to the environment that can result from increasing production.

> **Key term**
>
> **Recycling:** the process of recovering and changing waste materials into materials that can be used again.

Link

Causes of market failure and government policies to deal with market failure were explained in Chapter 5 "Market failure and government intervention in markets".

Link

Economic growth and the environment are considered in more detail in the A2 part of the course.

▲ **Figure 8.5.1**: Deforestation can increase global warming

Increasing consumption also means an increase in waste. As societies get richer, products are often discarded and replaced, rather than repaired. Some people believe that a fundamental change in society and in people's attitudes and values is needed as well as intervention by governments.

However, as societies get richer, they can afford to devote more resources to caring for the environment. Economic growth can also lead to changes in technology that can help to reduce the damage to the environment that may be caused by growth.

Progress questions

1 Explain the difference between non-renewable and renewable resources.
2 Explain **two** ways in which economic growth can damage the environment.
3 Explain how market forces might help to slow down the use of a non-renewable resource, such as tin.

Economic growth and the distribution of income

Economic growth should mean that, on average, people get richer. However, it does not mean that everyone is better off. When the rate of economic growth in a country first starts to increase, some people do not benefit. As a result, the distribution of income becomes more unequal.

When an economy is growing, older industries are often replaced by new ones. This causes structural unemployment to increase. The immobility of labour means that some people may stay unemployed for a long time. High levels of structural unemployment can affect a region where a declining industry is concentrated and help to make the distribution of income unequal.

Inequality might be needed to create the economic incentives required to create economic growth. The chance of making large profits might be needed to encourage people to start up a business and to take risks. High wages might be needed to persuade some people to learn new skills and to work longer hours.

However, economic growth does not always lead to greater inequality. Growth can provide opportunities for many people in society to earn a higher income. When the economy is growing, the government might decide to spend more on merit goods such as healthcare and education, benefiting most people. The government might also decide to provide cash welfare benefits to people who are not very well off, such as the elderly, those who are unemployed or have large families to support. The distribution of income is fairly even in some rich societies but uneven in others.

Economic growth and unemployment
Economic growth creates jobs for people. An increase in output means that more people will be employed producing goods and services. Therefore, the macroeconomic policy objectives of economic growth and low unemployment are usually compatible with each other.

However, if labour productivity increases by more than the increase in output, employment will fall. Although this is possible, economic growth usually results from an increase in employment and productivity.

Since economic growth usually means that the economy is changing, it often leads to some frictional and structural unemployment. The amount of unemployment depends on the amount of change taking place and the mobility of labour. If people are adaptable and governments adopt policies to help the occupational and geographical mobility of labour, unemployment may not be too serious.

Economic growth and the budget balance
The budget balance is the difference between government expenditure and the amount of money the government raises in taxes. A budget deficit is when the government is spending more than it is raising in taxes. A budget surplus is when the government is spending less than it is raising in taxes. When government spending equals tax revenue the government has a balanced budget. Many governments spend more money than they raise in taxes. If the budget deficit is large, they might want to reduce the size of the deficit. However, increasing taxes and reducing government spending is unpopular.

Economic growth will lead to an increase in tax revenues. Economic growth means that household income, firms' profits and household spending are increasing. An increase in household income and firms' profits will lead to an increase in the revenue raised from direct taxes. An increase in household spending will mean that the government also raises more money from indirect taxes.

Economic growth will also reduce some types of government spending. As more jobs are created and people's income increases, the government will not have to spend as much money on welfare benefits to support people who do not have much money.

> **Key term**
>
> Direct taxes: these are taxes on income and wealth. Unlike an indirect tax, the burden of a direct tax cannot be passed on to someone else.

▲ **Figure 8.5.2:** Government spending on the railways

Since economic growth increases tax revenues and reduces some types of government spending, it is compatible with the macroeconomic policy objective of reducing the government's budget deficit and balancing the budget.

However, to increase the rate of economic growth, the government may choose to increase its spending. For example, it might spend more money on education and training, transport and communication, and financing research and development. It might also choose to cut tax rates to create incentives for people to work hard and for firms to invest and grow. Therefore, some policies that might help to increase economic growth may lead to a larger budget deficit. The objective of achieving a higher rate of economic growth and reducing the budget deficit may conflict, at least in the short run.

Progress questions

4   Give **two** reasons why economic growth might lead to a more unequal distribution of income.

5   Why does economic growth usually lead to more jobs being created?

6   Why might economic growth lead to an increase in structural unemployment?

7   Explain why economic growth should help to reduce a government's budget deficit.

How output gaps relate to unemployment and inflationary pressures

When an economy is producing at its normal capacity level of output, the economy is likely to have some frictional and structural unemployment but there is not any cyclical (demand-deficient) unemployment.

How a negative output gap relates to unemployment and inflation

A negative output gap is when the economy is producing less than its normal capacity level of output. Aggregate demand is not high enough to create jobs for everyone who would like to work, so there is involuntary unemployment. When there is a negative output gap there will be some demand-deficient unemployment but also some frictional and structural unemployment. There will be both voluntary and involuntary unemployment.

When there is a negative output gap, there is some spare capacity and this is likely to moderate inflationary pressures. A negative output gap means that the economy is in a slump, a recession or in the recovery phase of the economic cycle. If the economy is in a slump, the low level of aggregate demand may mean there is deflation. In a slump, even if there is not deflation, inflation will be very low. If the economy is in recession, it is likely that it is also experiencing disinflation since aggregate demand is falling. In the recovery phase, inflation is likely to be low but is likely to increase as the negative output gap falls and the economy approaches its normal capacity level of output.

How a positive output gap relates to unemployment and inflation

A positive output gap is when the economy is producing above its normal capacity level of output. When there is a positive output gap, there will not be any demand-deficient unemployment but this does not mean that there will not be any unemployment. Real wage, structural, frictional and some voluntary unemployment are likely to exist. Even in the boom phase of the economic cycle, there will be some unemployment.

When there is a positive output gap, there is excess aggregate demand and demand-pull inflationary pressures. Firms will find it hard to meet demand and are likely to increase prices to increase their profits. Firms will also find it difficult to find enough workers and wages will be bid upwards as firms compete with each other to recruit the workers they need. Skilled workers will be particularly hard to find. Property prices and the prices of components are also likely to rise. Firms' costs will rise, leading to further price increases. As long as the positive output gap remains, inflation is likely to accelerate.

Use of economic policies to reconcile conflicts between policy objectives

Governments have a variety of policy instruments that they can use to help them achieve their objectives. Monetary policy is mainly used to influence aggregate demand. Fiscal policy can be used to influence aggregate demand too but is also used to affect the supply side of the economy. Governments can affect the supply side of the economy in other ways as well.

Economic growth, unemployment and inflation

In the short run, governments can reduce cyclical unemployment by using monetary and fiscal measures to increase aggregate demand and reduce a negative output gap. Lower interest rates, increased government spending and lower taxes can be used to increase aggregate demand. Increasing aggregate demand will also increase short-run economic growth but is likely to add to inflationary pressures. However, unless the productive capacity of the economy increases, there is a limit to which increasing aggregate demand can

> **Link**
>
> The use of macroeconomic policy instruments is considered in more detail in Chapter 9 "Macroeconomic policy".

reduce unemployment and increase economic growth. If aggregate demand is increased too much, the economy is likely to experience accelerating inflation. If inflation accelerates, the economy is likely to go into recession and unemployment will increase. Also, an increase in aggregate demand will not eliminate structural, frictional and voluntary unemployment.

Supply-side policies can be used to try to reduce structural, frictional and voluntary unemployment. If successful, supply-side policies will increase the economy's long-run rate of economic growth, shifting the LRAS curve to the right. They help to overcome the short-run conflict between inflation and reducing unemployment and achieving economic growth.

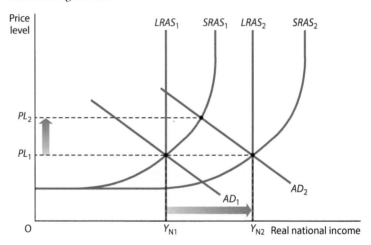

▲ **Figure 8.5.3**: Supply-side policies can help to reduce the conflict between inflation and unemployment

In Figure 8.5.3, supply-side policies have succeeded in shifting the LRAS curve to the right, from $LRAS_1$ to $LRAS_2$. This has allowed the economy to grow without inflation. If supply-side policies had not been used, the increase in aggregate demand from AD_1 to AD_2 would have led to a short-run increase in real national income but the price level would also have increased from PL_1 to PL_2. In the long run, accelerating inflation would probably cause the economy to go into recession.

Link

Supply-side policies and supply-side improvements are considered in more detail in 9.3 "Supply-side policies".

However, the increase in aggregate demand combined with the shift in long-run aggregate supply has increased real national income from Y_{N1} to Y_{N2} and the price level has remained at PL_1. Supply-side improvements allow the economy to grow and unemployment to fall without inflation. Supply-side improvements can result from supply-side policies but can also result from the independent actions of firms, for example investment in human and physical capital.

Economic growth and the balance of payments

Economic growth leads to rising real national income and an increase in aggregate demand. As national income increases, spending on imports will also increase and the balance of payments is likely to deteriorate. In the short run, there is often a conflict between economic growth and a satisfactory balance of payments. If economic growth is accompanied by a high rate of inflation, the economy may become uncompetitive and the balance of payments could move into a long-run deficit.

Supply-side policies can be used to try to improve competitiveness and achieve long-run growth with low inflation. Allowing the exchange rate to fall can also help to restore competitiveness. A depreciation in the exchange rate will increase aggregate demand and help to support economic growth. However, a depreciation in the exchange rate adds to inflationary pressures and may mean that the improvement in competitiveness is temporary.

Get it right

Economics studies human behaviour, which can be unpredictable and can change. Economic theory usually starts with the assumption that "other things remain the same" but often, in the real world, many changes are taking place at the same time. Predicting the effect of economic events and policies is difficult. There will always be some uncertainty. When explaining the economic effects of events and policies, phrases such as "it is likely to" or "assuming that" or "the most probable outcome is" are worth considering.

Use of supply-side policies to reconcile conflicts between policy objectives

Policies that increase aggregate demand can help to solve some economic problems but may make other problems worse. For example, in a serious recession, an increase in aggregate demand is needed to encourage firms to produce more and to reduce unemployment. However, increasing aggregate demand alone will not reduce some types of unemployment or produce long-run, sustainable economic growth, and it may lead to inflation and balance of payments deficits.

If successful, supply-side policies can help to resolve conflicts between macroeconomic policy objectives. They aim to increase productive capacity, improve productivity and efficiency, and reduce firms' costs. They also aim to make firms and workers more adaptable, helping the economy to adjust to change. Structural unemployment will not be eliminated but people who lose their job in one industry should be able to find a new job more easily. The economy should be able to cope with an increase in aggregate demand without serious inflationary pressures.

However, supply-side policies are not always successful. Governments do not always know what is best for the economy. They may, for example, spend money on projects that have little economic benefit or spend on training people in the wrong skills. People may not respond in the way that is expected and some supply-side measures may lead to policy conflicts. For example, reducing regulations on business to encourage investment may lead to more damage to the natural environment. Also, unless there is enough aggregate demand, people and other resources will remain unemployed.

Case study: The Hungarian economy: selected economic indicators, 2016–2018

In 2018, Hungary was one of the fastest growing economies in Europe. The economy was producing above its normal capacity level of output, unemployment was low and wages were growing rapidly. Growth is expected to slow down and this should prevent inflation rising too rapidly. Supply-side reforms should also help the Hungarian economy to continue to grow without inflation getting out of control.

▼ **Table 8.5.1:** Selected economic indicators for Hungary, 2016–2018

	2016	2017	2018
Percentage change in real GDP	2.2	4.3	5.1
Output gap (% of potential GDP)	−1.7	−0.2	1.2
Average unemployment rate (%)	5.1	4.2	3.7
CPI inflation rate	0.4	2.4	2.8
Balance of payments on current account (US $ million)	5,845	3,150	−678

Source: IMF 2019 Article IV Consultation – IMF Country Report no 19/357; https://www.imf.org; accessed 27 December 2019

1   Explain how the data in the table show that, between 2016 and 2018, there was a short-run conflict between economic growth and the balance of payments on current account in Hungary.

▲ **Figure 8.5.4:** Budapest, the capital of Hungary

2   Describe the change in the output gap of the Hungarian economy between 2016 and 2018.

3   Describe the relationship between unemployment and inflation in Hungary between 2016 and 2018.

4   Explain why "supply-side reforms should help the Hungarian economy to continue to grow without inflation getting out of control".

Activity

Find out what has happened to economic growth, unemployment, inflation and the balance of payments on current account in Hungary since 2018.

Exam-style questions

1   Which one of the following is most likely to occur during the recovery phase of the economic cycle?

A   A fall in business confidence   C   A rise in cyclical unemployment

B   A fall in the budget deficit   D   A rise in spare capacity   [1 mark]

2   In the diagram below, D_L shows the demand for labour and S_L shows the supply of labour in a free market. A minimum wage is introduced at W_{min}.

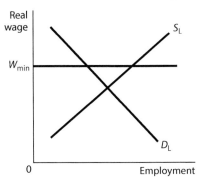

Which one of the following is most likely to result from the introduction of a minimum wage at W_{min}?

A   The number employed will rise

B   There will be excess demand for labour

C   There will be no effect on the wage rate

D   Unemployment will increase   [1 mark]

3   Which one of the following is a cause of structural unemployment?

A   A lack of aggregate demand

B   Changes in the pattern of demand

C   Lower demand at certain times of year

D   People between jobs for a short time   [1 mark]

4   Define "deflation".   [3 marks]

5   The table below shows details of the balance of payments on current account for a country over two years.

	Balance of trade in goods ($bn)	Exports of services ($bn)	Imports of services ($bn)	Primary income balance ($bn)	Secondary income balance ($bn)
Year 1	150	70	90	80	−20
Year 2	?	80	70	100	−30

You are advised to show your working for the calculations below.

(i) Calculate the balance of trade in goods and services in Year 1.   [2 marks]

(ii) If the current account balance in Year 2 was a surplus of $200 billion, calculate the balance of trade in goods.   [4 marks]

6 The table below shows economic growth, the annual percentage change in real GDP, and the inequality of income, as indicated by the Gini coefficient, in a country over an eight-year period.

Year	Economic growth	Gini coefficient
2008	1.7	0.403
2010	7.5	0.394
2012	7.2	0.393
2014	1.0	0.370
2016	3.4	0.365

(i) Explain why economic growth might affect the inequality of income. [6 marks]

(ii) To what extent do the data suggest that economic growth affects the inequality of income?
Use the data in the table to support your answer. [6 marks]

7 With the help of a diagram, explain how a rise in government spending can reduce a negative output gap. [9 marks]

8 Use the information in the case study on the 1973 oil crisis (in 8.1 Economic growth and the economic cycle, page 215) and your knowledge of economics to discuss the likely effects of an increase in oil prices on the economy of an oil-consuming country. [20 marks]

9 Macroeconomic policy

The national economy in a global environment

This section will develop your knowledge and understanding of:

→ how monetary policy involves the central bank acting to influence interest rates, the supply of money and credit, and the exchange rate

→ the objectives and targets of monetary policy

→ the use of interest rates to control inflation and affect economic activity

→ how changes in the exchange rate affect aggregate demand and the various macroeconomic policy objectives

→ other instruments of monetary policy, including quantitative easing.

Key terms

Supply of money: the total amount of money in circulation in an economy, it includes notes, coins and bank deposits.

Supply of credit: the total value of loans outstanding (loans that have not yet been repaid).

The central bank's monetary policy

One of the main functions of a central bank is to implement monetary policy. Monetary policy involves the central bank acting to affect interest rates, the **supply of money** and **credit**, and the exchange rate. Central banks have a number of measures that they can use to influence these variables.

The most important objective of monetary policy is to maintain the value of money and confidence in the currency. This means that inflation must be kept low.

In some countries, central banks implement monetary policy independently of the government. However, the government usually sets the target for inflation that the central bank is expected to achieve. In other countries, the central bank consults with and advises the government but the government can reject the advice given. When the government makes the final monetary policy decisions it can make sure that monetary policy does not conflict with other economic policies.

▲ **Figure 9.1.1:** Central Bank of Argentina

The rate of interest is the main instrument of monetary policy. The rate of interest is the cost of borrowing and the reward for saving. There are many different interest rates in an economy. The actions of the central bank can affect the overall level of interest rates but cannot determine the rate of interest paid on every savings scheme or the rate of interest charged on every loan. The central bank affects the overall level of interest rates by varying the rate of interest it charges when lending to other banks. This is the **central bank's discount rate**. It is sometimes known as the central bank's base rate of interest.

If the central bank increases its discount rate it makes it more expensive for other banks to borrow from the central bank and signals to the other banks that they should increase their interest rates. Changes in the central bank's discount rate mainly affect short-term interest rates but changes in short-term rates will also have some effect on long-term interest rates.

Interest rates affect the amount of money people save and borrow. The levels of saving and borrowing affect aggregate demand and inflation. If savings fall and/or borrowing increases, aggregate demand will increase. If aggregate demand is growing too fast, the economy will experience inflation and the value of money will fall. To achieve stable prices, the central bank will need to keep aggregate demand growing at the same rate as the output of the economy is growing.

In Figure 9.1.2, long-run economic growth is shown by the shift in the LRAS curve from $LRAS_1$ to $LRAS_2$. If the central bank uses monetary policy to manage aggregate demand so that it increases from AD_1 to AD_2, this should prevent inflation. If the government is willing to allow some inflation, aggregate demand can grow more quickly. Most governments set a target for a low, positive rate of inflation. For example, **the inflation target** in the UK is 2% and in India it is 4%. In practice, it is difficult to predict the long-run rate of economic growth and to precisely control the rate of growth in aggregate demand.

The rate of growth in the supply of money and credit are monitored by central banks because the growth in money and credit affect aggregate demand. The rate of growth in the money supply and credit provides an indicator of the rate of growth in aggregate demand. The central bank can use interest rates to affect the rate of growth of the money supply and credit. If the central bank wishes to reduce the rate of growth of the money supply and credit, it will increase interest rates. This will make it more expensive to borrow and reduce the demand for loans, leading to a fall in the rate of growth of the money supply and credit.

The central bank has other ways of affecting the rate of growth of money and credit. For example, some central banks set reserve ratios for other banks. If the central bank increases the required reserve ratio, it will make it harder for banks to lend. Quantitative easing is another instrument a central bank can use to affect the growth of money and credit.

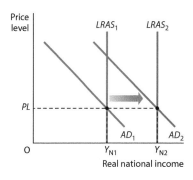

▲ **Figure 9.1.2**: Managing aggregate demand to prevent inflation

The exchange rate is also affected by interest rates and other actions of the central bank. For example, other things being equal, an increase in interest rates will tend to increase the exchange rate and a cut in interest rates will tend to reduce the exchange rate.

In summary, **contractionary monetary policy** means the central bank increases interest rates, restricts the rate of growth of the supply of money and credit, and increases the exchange rate. As explained, an increase in interest rates will help to restrict the growth of money and credit and achieve an appreciation in the exchange rate. The aim of contractionary monetary policy is to reduce aggregate demand and reduce inflation.

An **expansionary monetary policy** involves reducing interest rates, increasing the rate of growth of the supply of money and credit, and attempting to achieve a depreciation in the exchange rate. The aim of expansionary monetary policy is to increase aggregate demand, economic activity and inflation.

The objectives and targets of monetary policy

The objective of monetary policy is the overall aim, or outcome, that the government wishes to achieve through the use of monetary policy. There might be more than one objective of monetary policy. **Targets of monetary policy** are the variables that the central bank tries to influence in order to achieve its monetary policy objectives. For example, the objective might be low inflation. To achieve that objective the central bank might target the rate of growth of the money supply because it believes that inflation is affected by the rate of growth of the money supply. Other possible targets of monetary policy include the exchange rate, the supply of credit and the rate of interest.

In most countries, the main objective of monetary policy is to maintain the value of the country's currency by achieving price stability. In practice, this usually means keeping inflation low rather than aiming for a zero rate of inflation. However, monetary policy is also used to support other macroeconomic policy objectives, for example helping to achieve a sustained, stable rate of economic growth and low unemployment. In the UK, the Banking Act of 1998, stated that "in relation to monetary policy, the objectives of the Bank of England shall be:

i. to maintain price stability; and

ii. subject to that, to support the economic policy of Her Majesty's Government, including its objectives for growth and employment."

The use of interest rates to control inflation and affect economic activity

Interest rates affect aggregate demand. A change in aggregate demand affects inflation and economic activity. A rise in interest rates will tend to reduce aggregate demand and a cut in interest rates will tend to increase it. The ways in which monetary policy affects aggregate demand, inflation and economic activity are known collectively as the **monetary policy transmission mechanism**.

Reasons why an increase in interest rates tends to reduce aggregate demand

A rise in interest rates makes it more rewarding to save rather than spend. Therefore, some people will decide to save more and spend less.

A rise in interest rates also increases the cost of borrowing and this will tend to reduce the demand for expensive consumer durables. For example, since many people borrow to buy a new car, an increase in interest rates will increase the monthly repayments and the total cost of the loan, reducing the demand for new cars. An increase in the cost of borrowing will mean some people will reduce their spending on consumer durables.

People usually finance the purchase of a house by taking out a mortgage. As with other loans, an increase in interest rates will increase people's mortgage repayments. For many households, the mortgage repayment is a large percentage of their disposable income. If mortgage repayments rise, households may have to reduce their purchases of other products.

Many firms finance investment by borrowing. A rise in interest rates increases the cost of financing investment, making it less profitable. A fall in investment reduces the demand for capital goods.

A rise in interest rates will, other things being equal, tend to cause the exchange rate to appreciate. A rise in interest rates makes it more attractive for overseas residents to save money in the country's banks and to buy interest-bearing securities such as government bonds. To do this, they need to buy the country's currency. An increase in the demand for the currency increases the price of the currency and the exchange rate will appreciate. An appreciation in the value of the currency makes exports more expensive and imports cheaper. The demand for exports will fall and the demand for imports will rise, leading to a fall in net exports and aggregate demand.

A rise in interest rates tends to cause the price of assets, such as houses and shares, to fall. House prices fall because the increase in mortgage repayments reduces the demand for houses. If interest rates are high, some people will purchase interest-bearing securities rather than shares. The fall in the demand for shares tends to reduce the price of shares. As a result, the wealth of some households falls. This **wealth effect** leads to a reduction in spending as people are less well off. Some households might increase their savings to try to increase their wealth.

However, it should be remembered that when interest rates rise, people earn more money on their savings and this may cause some people with savings to spend more. Nevertheless, in most situations a rise in interest rates leads to a fall in aggregate demand.

How interest rates are used to control inflation

Central banks increase their discount rate when inflation is expected to rise above the inflation target. An increase in the central bank's discount rate usually causes other interest rates to rise and leads to a fall in aggregate demand. High inflation is usually caused by too much aggregate demand. A fall in aggregate demand reduces demand-pull inflationary pressures. If aggregate demand falls: firms are less likely to

▲ **Figure 9.1.3**: Buying a house is expensive

Key term

Wealth effect: the effect of a change in wealth on aggregate demand.

increase prices; unemployment is likely to rise; and wages will increase more slowly or perhaps fall. This means that firms' costs are not rising as much as they were, reducing cost-push inflationary pressures.

If the rise in interest rates leads to an appreciation in the exchange rate, this reduces the price of imports. Lower import prices help to reduce cost-push inflationary pressures.

An increase in interest rates reduces borrowing and the growth in the supply of money and credit. Some economists believe that inflation is always caused by the money supply increasing too quickly.

In Figure 9.1.4, without an increase in interest rates, aggregate demand would have increased from AD_1 to AD_2 and the price level would have risen from PL_1 to PL_2. An increase in interest rates means that aggregate demand only increases to AD_3 and the price level rises more slowly, from PL_1 to PL_3. The diagram illustrates how a rise in interest rates, contractionary monetary policy, can reduce inflation.

If inflation is expected to be below the inflation target, the central bank will cut its discount rate leading to an increase in aggregate demand. This is likely to cause the price level to increase more quickly and this should help to prevent inflation falling below the target.

In many countries, the inflation target is given as a range. For example, the target rate of inflation might be 3% plus or minus 2%. This means that the central bank is expected to use monetary policy to keep inflation between 1% and 5%.

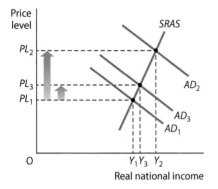

▲ **Figure 9.1.4**: The effect of a rise in interest rates on inflation

Central banks usually act before inflation goes outside the target range. This means that they have to try to predict what is likely to happen to inflation in the future. To predict the future rate of inflation they will consider a variety of indicators. These include what is happening to the different components of aggregate demand and the long-run growth in the productive capacity of the economy. They will also consider the amount of spare capacity and unemployment. The rate at which wages and commodity prices are rising will be taken into account because they affect cost-push inflationary pressures. What is happening to the exchange rate and the rate of growth of the money supply and credit affect inflation and will be considered.

How interest rates affect economic activity

When using monetary policy, central banks are usually expected to consider the effects of their actions on economic activity as well as inflation. For example, in the United States, the Federal Reserve Bank has the dual objective of promoting maximum employment and stable prices. Sometimes these objectives can conflict, at least in the short run.

An increase in economic activity means that the total output of the economy and employment are increasing. A cut in interest rates will increase aggregate demand and should encourage firms to increase output and employ more people. The initial increase in aggregate demand will have an upward multiplier effect, leading to a further increase in economic activity. If it is producing below its normal capacity level of output, the economy is usually able to grow without too much effect on inflation. However, when there is not much spare capacity, cutting interest rates to increase aggregate demand is likely to increase inflation. It is not always easy to determine the amount of spare capacity and this can make it difficult for the central bank to decide whether it should raise or lower interest rates, or leave them unchanged.

Monetary policy and interest rates have a role to play in reducing fluctuations in economic activity and stabilising the economy. In a recession, cutting interest rates can help to increase aggregate demand and prevent output and employment falling. In a boom, when the economy is overheating, a rise in interest rates can help to reduce aggregate demand and prevent inflation accelerating.

How the exchange rate affects aggregate demand and macroeconomic policy objectives

The central bank can influence the exchange rate by changing interest rates and by buying and selling its currency on the foreign exchange market. Actions taken by the central bank to influence the exchange rate are part of monetary policy.

Changes in the exchange rate affect the government's macroeconomic policy objectives. A change in the exchange rate affects the economy because it changes the foreign currency price of the country's exports and the domestic currency price of imports. This can be illustrated by a numerical example.

If the price of a pair of Italian shoes exported to the United States is €80 and the euro/US dollar exchange rate falls from € 1= $1.50 to €1 = $1.00, the dollar price of the Italian shoes exported to the United States will fall from $120 to $80. The fall in the euro/US dollar exchange rate has reduced the foreign currency price of Italian exports to the United States.

If the price of an American computer that is imported by Italy is $900 and the euro/US dollar exchange rate falls from €1 = $1.50 to €1 = $1.00, the euro price of the American computer imported by Italy will increase from €600 to €900. The fall in the euro/US dollar exchange rate has increased the domestic currency price of Italian imports from the United States.

A fall (depreciation) in a country's exchange rate will increase aggregate demand. The fall in the price of exports will increase the demand for its exports. The rise in the price of imports will encourage domestic residents to buy more home-produced products and fewer imports. Net exports (X – M) will increase.

A rise (appreciation) in a country's exchange rate will reduce aggregate demand because that country's exports will be more expensive abroad and imports will be cheaper. Net exports will fall.

The main way in which changes in the exchange rate affect the government's macroeconomic policy objectives is through the effect on aggregate demand.

Progress questions

4 State **two** reasons why a fall in interest rates is likely to increase aggregate demand.

5 Why will a cut in interest rates tend to increase inflation?

6 Why will an increase in interest rates tend to reduce economic activity?

Link

The ways in which a central bank can influence the exchange rate are explained in the A2 part of the course.

Get it right

A change in the exchange rate affects the economy because it affects the foreign currency price of exports and the domestic currency price of imports. When explaining how the exchange rate affects the economy, start your analysis by stating how the exchange rate affects the prices of exports and imports.

Get it right

Net exports (X – M) affect aggregate demand, which is total spending on home-produced goods and services. AD = C + I + G + (X – M), so an increase in exports will increase aggregate demand. If people spend more on imports, aggregate demand will fall.

How changes in the exchange rate affect economic growth

A depreciation in the exchange rate makes a country's products more competitive in its home and export markets. As a result, aggregate demand will increase, leading to an increase in output and short-run economic growth, provided there is some spare capacity. A fall in the exchange rate also makes it cheaper for foreign firms to invest in the economy. If investment increases, the productive capacity of the economy will increase. Therefore, a fall in the exchange rate might also help to increase the economy's long-run rate of economic growth.

Monetary policy measures leading to an appreciation in the value of the currency will tend to reduce aggregate demand and the economy's rate of economic growth.

How changes in the exchange rate affect unemployment

A depreciation in the exchange rate makes exports more competitive abroad and should result in an increase in the demand for exports. This will lead to more jobs in industries that export goods and services. The increase in exports is an injection into the circular flow of income and will have a positive multiplier effect. It will also increase incomes and employment in other parts of the economy.

The depreciation in the value of the currency increases the domestic currency price of imports. As a result, some consumers will buy home-produced products rather than the more expensive imports. This will create jobs in import-competing industries.

Monetary policy measures leading to an appreciation in the value of the currency will make home-produced goods and services less competitive. Firms will sell fewer exports and imports will increase, jobs will be cut and, other things being equal, unemployment will increase.

How changes in the exchange rate affect inflation

A depreciation in the exchange rate will increase inflationary pressures and an appreciation in the exchange rate will reduce inflationary pressures. There are two main reasons why a fall in the exchange rate increases inflationary pressures. First, it leads to an increase in aggregate demand and adds to demand-pull inflationary pressures. Second, it increases the price of imports and adds to cost-push inflationary pressures. Firms have to pay more for the raw materials and components that they import, increasing their costs of production. Households have to pay more for the goods and services they buy from abroad, directly increasing the Consumer Prices Index (CPI).

An appreciation in the exchange rate reduces aggregate demand and the domestic currency price of imports falls, reducing demand-pull and cost-push inflationary pressures.

How changes in the exchange rate affect the balance of payments

A depreciation in the exchange rate will tend to improve the balance of trade in goods and services and the current account balance. The fall in the foreign currency price of exports will increase the demand for exports. Provided the percentage increase in the quantity sold

Key term

Import-competing industries: domestic industries that produce goods and services that are substitutes for goods and services imported from abroad.

Get it right

A depreciation in the exchange rate tends to increase output and employment but adds to inflationary pressures. An appreciation in the exchange rate leads to a fall in output and employment but reduces inflationary pressures.

is greater than the percentage fall in the price, the foreign currency value of exports will increase.

The rise in the domestic currency price of imports will reduce the demand for imports. Provided the percentage decrease in the quantity sold is greater than the percentage rise in the price, the domestic currency value of imports will fall.

Since the fall in the exchange rate makes exports more competitive and imports less competitive, it will usually lead to an improvement in the balance of trade in goods and services and the current account.

An appreciation in the exchange rate makes exports less competitive in overseas markets and imports more competitive in the domestic market. This will reduce the demand for exports and increase the demand for imports. It is likely to result in a deterioration in the balance of trade in goods and services and the current account.

Other instruments of monetary policy, including quantitative easing

The rate of interest is the main instrument of monetary policy but there are other instruments that a central bank can use. They include:

- Setting required reserve ratios
- Quantitative easing.

Required reserve ratios

Central banks often set a **reserve ratio** that other banks must follow. A reserve ratio is the **liquid assets** that a bank must hold expressed as a percentage of its **deposits**. A **cash ratio** is an example of a reserve ratio. A cash ratio is the ratio between the amount of cash a bank holds and its deposits. If the cash ratio is set at 8% and a bank's total deposits are $100 million, the bank must keep $8 million in cash. Cash includes notes and coins and any money that a bank has deposited with the country's central bank.

Even if the central bank does not set a required reserve ratio, banks must hold some cash so that they can pay customers who want to take their money out of the bank.

Bank deposits are part of the money supply because they can be used to buy goods and services. Banks can create deposits by lending money to its customers. When the bank gives a customer a loan, it adds to the deposits in the customer's account. If the cash ratio is increased, unless it is able to obtain more cash, the bank will have to reduce the amount of deposits it creates.

If the central bank increases required reserve ratios, this will make it more difficult for banks to create deposits and is likely to reduce bank lending. This limits the growth of the money supply and credit and is an example of contractionary monetary policy.

If the central bank reduces reserve ratios, the supply of money and credit is likely to increase, leading to an increase in aggregate demand. This is an example of expansionary monetary policy.

Link

A more detailed explanation of how a change in the exchange rate affects the balance of payments is included in the A2 part of the course.

Progress questions

7 A car manufactured in the United States has a price of $25,000. What would happen to the price of the car in China if the yuan/US dollar exchange rate appreciated from ¥1 = $0.15 to ¥1 = $0.20?

8 Why will an appreciation in a country's exchange rate tend to reduce economic activity in that country?

9 State **two** reasons why a fall in the exchange rate will tend to increase inflation.

Key terms

Reserve ratio: the ratio between the amount of liquid assets a bank holds and its deposits.

Liquid assets: cash or other assets that can be easily converted into cash.

Deposits: money that customers have in their bank accounts; it is money the bank owes to its customers.

Cash ratio: the ratio between the amount of cash a bank holds and its deposits.

Key terms

Quantitative easing: when the central bank makes large scale purchases of government and/or corporate bonds.

Government bonds: a security representing a loan to the government that pays interest to the holder until it matures.

Corporate bonds: a security representing a loan to a company that pays interest to the holder until it matures.

Unconventional monetary policy: measures used by central banks when the usual instruments of monetary policy are ineffective.

Stimulate the economy: measures to increase aggregate demand and economic activity.

Activity

Find out why Japan used quantitative easing in 2001.

The central banks in most countries set required reserve ratios but there are some exceptions including the UK, Canada, Sweden and Australia.

In China and many other countries, changes to required reserve ratios are an important instrument of monetary policy.

Get it right

If a central bank requires other banks to increase their reserve ratio, this is an example of contractionary monetary policy. A cut in the required reserve ratio is an example of expansionary monetary policy.

Quantitative easing

Quantitative easing is when the central bank makes large scale purchases of **government bonds**. It can also involve the purchase of **corporate bonds**, or other financial assets, by the central bank. Quantitative easing was first used by Japan in 2001 and is a form of expansionary monetary policy. The United States, the UK, the European Central Bank (ECB) and a few other countries used quantitative easing to stimulate their economies after the 2007–2008 financial crisis.

Government bonds are securities that are issued when the government needs to borrow money to help to pay for government expenditure. The government borrows when government spending is greater than the money it raises in taxes. Government bonds usually pay a fixed rate of interest to the owner (or holder) of the bond until it matures. The money borrowed (the face value of the bond) is repaid to the holder when the bond matures.

Quantitative easing is an example of an **unconventional monetary policy** and is used when the usual instruments of monetary policy are ineffective. For example, if an economy is in recession and short-term interest rates are already close to zero per cent, short-term interest rates cannot be cut much more but the central bank may still want to **stimulate the economy**.

Case study: The Bank of Zambia increases the Statutory Reserve Ratio

The annual inflation rate in Zambia rose from 7.5% in March 2019 to 10.8% in November 2019. In December 2019, the country's central bank, the Bank of Zambia, increased the Statutory Reserve Ratio (SRR) from 5% to 9%. This means that banks in Zambia are required to increase the value of deposits they hold as statutory reserves with the central bank. It is hoped that this increase in the SRR will help to reduce inflation and support macroeconomic stability. It is likely to lead to a reduction in bank lending and an increase in interest rates. Businesses and households will be affected.

1. Explain why an increase in the SRR from 5% to 9% should help to reduce inflation.
2. How might the increase in the SRR affect businesses in Zambia?

▲ **Figure 9.1.5**: Borrowing is affected by the cash ratio

Two ways in which quantitative easing helps to increase aggregate demand are by making it easier for banks to lend and by reducing long-term interest rates.

If the central bank buys bonds from banks and other financial institutions, it will make them more liquid. The banks will have more cash reserves and will be able to create more loans, which should help to increase aggregate demand.

When the central bank buys large quantities of bonds, the increase in the demand for bonds will lead to an increase in the price of bonds. It will reduce the yield on the bond. This means that long-term interest rates fall. It will then be cheaper for economic agents to finance their spending – for example, firms that want to invest in new capital and people who want to buy a house using a mortgage.

The following example illustrates why an increase in the price of bonds will reduce the yield. If a bond pays the holder $5 each year and the price of the bond increases from $100 to $125, the rate of return, or yield, falls from 5% to 4%. As a result, economic agents, such as large companies, who want to borrow will be able to do so more cheaply.

When the economy starts to recover and the central bank wants to **tighten monetary policy**, it could start to sell its holdings of government bonds. This reduces the liquidity of the banks and increases long-term interest rates. It is known as **quantitative tightening** and is an example of unconventional contractionary monetary policy.

Activity

Find out about other ways in which quantitative easing might affect aggregate demand.

Key terms

Tighten monetary policy: monetary policy measures that reduce aggregate demand. The same as contractionary monetary policy.

Quantitative tightening: when the central bank sells its holdings of government bonds.

Activity

Find out all you can about the way in which your country's central bank implements monetary policy. Does it have an inflation target? Does it have other objectives besides controlling inflation? Does it set a required reserve ratio? Has it used quantitative easing?

Case study: Monetary policy in Canada

The Bank of Canada is Canada's central bank and its main role is to "to promote the economic and financial welfare of Canada". Its Governing Council has six members who jointly make decisions about interest rates eight times a year. Changes in the Bank of Canada's official interest rate will affect interest rates set by other financial institutions in the economy, which will in turn affect saving, mortgages and other loans.

The aim is to keep inflation low, stable and predictable. The current inflation-control target is 2%, with an allowable range of 1% to 3%, which shows that the Bank is concerned about deflation as well as inflation. The flexible exchange rate can help to deal with both internal and external shocks and help the Bank achieve its inflation target while supporting economic activity.

▲ **Figure 9.1.6**: Maintaining the value of the Canadian dollar

Changes in interest rates typically take between 18 months and 2 years to have their full effect on inflation. So, like many other central banks, the Bank of Canada has to be forward looking, trying to anticipate what might happen in the near future in order to make the right decision about when and by how much to change its official interest rate.

1   Explain how changes in the official interest rate are likely to affect saving, mortgages and other loans.
2   Apart from the current inflation rate, explain **four** factors that might encourage the Governing Council of the Bank of Canada to increase its official interest rate.
3   Explain how a flexible exchange rate helps the Bank of Canada achieve its inflation target and support economic activity.

This section will develop your knowledge and understanding of:

→ how fiscal policy involves the manipulation of government spending, taxation and the budget balance

→ how fiscal policy can have both macroeconomic and microeconomic functions

→ how fiscal policy can be used to influence aggregate demand

→ how fiscal policy can be used to influence aggregate supply

→ how government spending and taxation can affect the allocation of resources and the pattern of economic activity

→ direct and indirect taxes

→ progressive, proportional and regressive taxes

→ the relationship between the budget balance and the national debt

→ cyclical and structural influences on the budget balance.

The government's fiscal policy

Fiscal policy is the use of government spending and taxation to influence the economy. Changes in government spending and taxation affect the budget balance, which can influence aggregate demand. Since the Great Depression of the 1930s and the work of the economist John Maynard Keynes, governments have made more use of fiscal policy to help them manage aggregate demand and achieve their macroeconomic policy objectives.

Expansionary fiscal policy is when the government increases its spending and/or reduces the amount of money it raises in taxes. Fiscal policy is expansionary when the budget surplus is falling or the budget deficit is increasing.

Contractionary fiscal policy is when the government reduces its spending and/or increases the amount of money it raises in taxes. Fiscal policy is contractionary when the budget surplus is increasing or the budget deficit is falling.

Other things being equal, a budget deficit is expansionary and will tend to increase aggregate demand and stimulate economic activity. A budget surplus is contractionary and will tend to reduce aggregate demand and reduce economic activity.

The macroeconomic and microeconomic functions of fiscal policy

As already explained, changes in government spending affect aggregate demand. Changes in aggregate demand affect economic growth, unemployment, inflation and the balance of payments. The government can use fiscal policy to manage aggregate demand and help prevent large fluctuations in economic activity and inflation. If the economy is in recession, the government can use fiscal policy to increase aggregate demand, helping the economy to recover from recession. If the economy is growing too rapidly and inflation is rising, the government can use fiscal policy to reduce aggregate demand and prevent inflation getting out of control.

Key terms

Expansionary fiscal policy: an increase in government spending and/or a reduction in taxation to increase aggregate demand.

Contractionary fiscal policy: a decrease in government spending and/or an increase in taxation to reduce aggregate demand.

However, some governments prefer to use monetary policy to manage aggregate demand and only use fiscal measures when monetary policy is not having enough effect. For example, if the economy is in recession and interest rates are very low but demand is not increasing, a rise in government spending might be needed to stimulate the economy.

Fiscal policy can also be used to help the government achieve its microeconomic objectives and correct market failure. For example, the government could increase the tax on demerit goods such as tobacco to reduce demand. The government might provide, or subsidise, merit goods such as education and healthcare. Governments can use fiscal measures to reduce inequalities in the distribution of income and wealth. For example, it could impose high taxes on the rich and give cash welfare benefits to support people with low incomes. Providing services such as education and healthcare free to everyone also helps to reduce inequality.

Changes in taxation and government spending will have both macroeconomic and microeconomic effects. When changing taxes and government spending, the government will consider the consequences for individual markets and the economy as a whole.

The use of fiscal policy to manage aggregate demand

Keynesian economists emphasise the role of fiscal policy in managing aggregate demand to prevent large fluctuations in economic activity. When private sector spending is falling, Keynesians believe the government should use expansionary fiscal policy to prevent the economy from going into recession. When private sector spending is rising too fast, Keynesians believe that the government should use contractionary fiscal policy to prevent inflation accelerating.

Using fiscal policy to increase aggregate demand

A recession is usually caused by a fall in aggregate demand. A depression occurs when aggregate demand is too low, leading to high unemployment and spare capacity. In such circumstances, Keynesian economists would recommend that the government increases its spending, cuts taxes and deliberately runs a budget deficit. Keynesians believe that without government intervention, there is a risk that the economy can get stuck with high unemployment and a low level of economic activity for many years.

Government spending (G) is a component of aggregate demand $(AD = C + I + G + X - M)$ and an injection into the circular flow of income. If the government spends more, it will increase aggregate demand and lead to an increase in output and employment. As incomes increase, there will be a further increase in aggregate demand, leading to more output and employment. The increase in government spending has a multiplier effect on national income.

Taxation is a withdrawal from the circular flow of income. If the government cuts taxes, the withdrawals from the circular flow of income will fall, leading to an increase in aggregate demand, output

Link

The multiplier effect is explained in 7.4 "Aggregate demand and the level of economic activity".

263

and employment. A cut in income tax will increase households' disposable income and increase consumption. A cut in taxes on business will increase company profits and may lead to an increase in investment. An increase in consumption and investment will also have a multiplier effect on national income.

When aggregate demand is low, Keynesians usually prefer to increase government spending rather than cut taxation. In a recession, households and firms may lack confidence and the reduction in taxation might be saved and not spent. If this happens, there will not be much effect on aggregate demand, or the economy.

Increasing government spending (G) and reducing taxation (T) affects the budget balance. When aggregate demand is low, Keynesians argue that the government should deliberately run a budget deficit (G > T). A budget deficit is a net injection into the circular flow of income. The government is injecting more money into the circular flow of income than it is withdrawing through taxes. This will increase aggregate demand and lead to an increase in output, employment and national income.

Using fiscal policy to reduce aggregate demand

If aggregate demand is growing faster than the underlying increase in the productive capacity of the economy, there will be demand-pull inflationary pressures. When the economy is in a boom and inflation is accelerating, a contractionary fiscal policy will reduce aggregate demand and should help to prevent the economy from overheating.

To reduce aggregate demand, the government could reduce its spending and increase taxes. A reduction in government spending (G) and an increase in taxation (T) will reduce a budget deficit and may lead to a budget surplus (T>G). A budget surplus is a net withdrawal for the circular flow of income and will reduce aggregate demand. A cut in government spending and an increase in taxation will have a multiplier effect on the economy, leading to further reductions in aggregate demand.

In Figure 9.2.1, the rightward shift in the LRAS curve from LRAS$_1$ to LRAS$_2$ shows underlying growth in the economy. If aggregate demand increases from AD$_1$ to AD$_2$, the price level would rise from PL$_1$ to PL$_2$. However, if the government used contractionary fiscal policy, reducing its spending and/or increasing taxation, inflation would be lower. If the contractionary fiscal policy reduced the increase in aggregate demand to AD$_3$, the price level would only increase from PL$_1$ to PL$_3$.

Although fiscal measures can be used to manage demand and control inflation, most countries prefer to use monetary policy to control inflation. However, when the central bank is deciding whether to increase or reduce interest rates, it will consider how the government's fiscal policy is affecting aggregate demand and hence inflation.

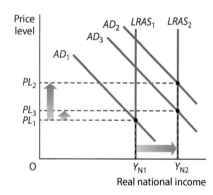

▲ **Figure 9.2.1**: The use of fiscal policy to reduce inflation

Get it right

A budget deficit is a net injection of demand into the circular flow of income and is expansionary fiscal policy. A budget surplus is a net withdrawal of demand from the circular flow of income and is contractionary fiscal policy.

Using fiscal policy to influence aggregate supply

Aggregate supply is the total output of an economy. The position of the LRAS curve shows the potential output of an economy. It is the maximum amount an economy is capable of producing without inflation accelerating. Improvements in the supply-side of an economy lead to underlying economic growth and shift the LRAS curve to the right.

Fiscal policy can be used to try to shift the LRAS curve to the right. For example, government spending on infrastructure can increase the efficiency and productive capacity of an economy. Government spending on education and training can help to increase labour productivity. Cuts in income tax rates may increase the incentive to work and increase the number of people in the labour force. Cutting taxes on company profits may increase investment and spending on research and development. Fiscal policy measures that are used to try to shift the LRAS curve to the right are examples of supply-side policies.

However, fiscal policy measures designed to influence aggregate supply are unlikely to have much effect in the short run and the long-run consequences cannot be predicted with any certainty. Whereas, at least in the short run, the effect of fiscal policy measures to influence aggregate demand are more predictable.

Using fiscal policy to influence the pattern of economic activity

The pattern of economic activity is concerned with how an economy's factors of production are allocated between different uses. The pattern of economic activity changes when there is a change in the types of goods and services the economy is producing. For example, if an economy is allocating more of its scarce resources (factors of production) to supplying healthcare and fewer resources to building houses, the pattern of economic activity has changed.

As well as affecting the level of economic activity, government spending and taxation can influence the pattern of economic activity. If the government decides to spend more money on healthcare, more resources will be needed to provide the service. More hospitals will be built and more doctors and nurses will be trained and employed. If the government reduces its spending on building roads, other things being equal, fewer factors of production will be employed in the construction industry. Changes in the pattern of public spending will affect the allocation of resources and pattern of production.

Taxation also affects the pattern of economic activity and the allocation of resources. If the government increases the tax on a demerit good, such as tobacco, the price will rise and the demand is likely to fall. Fewer factors of production will be employed producing tobacco. If it wants to do so, the government can affect the pattern of demand, and therefore the pattern of production, by having different tax rates on different products.

Activity

Find out your government's budget balance for each of the past five years. Does the change in the budget balance indicate that the government has adopted a more expansionary or a more contractionary fiscal policy? Explain your conclusion.

Link

Supply-side policies are explained in 9.3 "Supply-side policies".

Key terms

Pattern of economic activity: how an economy's factors of production are allocated between different uses.

Get it right

The level of economic activity changes when the total output of the economy increases or decreases. The pattern of economic activity changes when there is a change in the types of goods and services the economy is producing. The different phases of the economic cycle reflect changes in the level of economic activity.

Government spending and taxation can be used to protect the environment. If the government subsidises the production of solar panels and wind turbines, more resources will be used to produce these goods and it is likely that fewer resources will be used in producing fossil fuels. High taxes on petrol and diesel are likely to encourage more people to use public transport and buy electric cars. Government fiscal measures can be used to help the government achieve its environmental objectives. Taxes and subsidies can be used to encourage a change in the pattern of economic activity, creating incentives for firms and households to reduce their use of products that damage the environment.

Progress questions

1 Explain why a large increase in taxes on tobacco has both micro and macroeconomic effects.
2 Explain why a budget surplus is contractionary fiscal policy.
3 If an economy is in a depression and suffering from deflation, why might it be more effective to increase government spending rather than cut taxes?
4 Explain why a large increase in government spending on education will affect the pattern of economic activity.

Direct and indirect taxes

The main reason governments **levy taxes** is to pay for government expenditure. As already explained, taxes can also be used to influence the pattern and level of economic activity. Taxes are often classified as either direct taxes or indirect taxes.

Direct taxes

Direct taxes are taxes on income and wealth. The burden of a direct tax cannot be passed on to others. The person who is liable to pay the tax cannot pass it on to someone else.

Income tax, taxes on company profits, taxes on property, capital gains tax and taxes on inheritance are examples of direct taxes levied by many governments.

The effects of a decrease in a direct tax on the macroeconomy are usually illustrated by shifting the AD curve to the right. For example, if income tax is reduced, households have more disposable income and are likely to increase consumption.

In Figure 9.2.2, the fall in income tax leads to an increase in consumption and the AD curve shifts from AD_1 to AD_2. This leads to an increase in the price level and real national income. If the economy has plenty of spare capacity the increase in aggregate demand will not have much effect on the price level but should increase real national income and employment. If the economy is close to full capacity, the price level will increase but there will be little effect on real national income.

In the long run, a reduction in income tax may also affect the incentive to work. If a reduction in income tax leads to people being

Key term

Levy taxes: to impose taxes on economic agents, including firms and households.

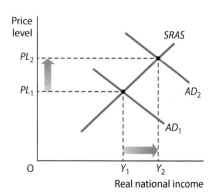

▲ **Figure 9.2.2**: The effect of a reduction in income tax

willing to work more hours and to an increase in the number of people in the labour force, the productive capacity of the economy will increase and the LRAS curve will shift to the right.

Indirect taxes

Indirect taxes are taxes on spending. It may be possible for the person who pays an indirect tax to pass the burden on to other people. For example, a firm may have to pay the tax levied on its products to the government but it may be able to pass on some of the burden of the tax to consumers. It does this by increasing the price of the products on which the tax is levied. How the burden of the tax is shared between the producers and consumers is known as the incidence of the tax.

Value added tax (VAT), customs duties and taxes on tobacco and petrol are common examples of indirect taxes.

In Figure 9.2.3, the increase in the sales tax increases firms' costs and makes production less profitable at any given price level. This is represented by a leftward shift in the SRAS curve. As a result, the price level will increase as firms pass on some of the tax to consumers. The rise in the price level will, other things being equal, lead to a reduction in aggregate demand (shown by a movement along the AD curve) and a fall in real national income.

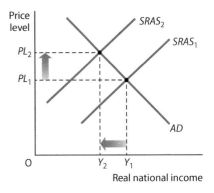

▲ **Figure 9.2.3**: The effect of an increase in a sales tax on the macroeconomy

Link

Some of the effects of indirect taxes were explained in 5.7 "Government intervention in markets".

Activity

Make a list of the main taxes levied by your government. Your list should have two columns with the headings "Direct taxes" and "Indirect taxes". Try to find out how much money was raised from each of these taxes last year.

Progressive, proportional and regressive taxes

A tax is progressive when as income increases the percentage of income taken in tax also increases. Progressive taxes help to make the distribution of income more equal.

A **proportional tax** is when the percentage of income taken in tax is the same at all levels of income. A proportional tax does not affect the distribution of income. The degree of inequality in income before and after the tax is the same.

A tax is regressive when as income increases, the percentage of income taken in tax decreases. Regressive taxes increase inequality. The distribution of income after a regressive tax has been paid is more unequal than before the tax.

Key term

Proportional tax: when the percentage of income taken in tax is the same at all levels of income.

▼ **Table 9.2.1**: Progressive, proportional and regressive taxes

Income	Tax A		Tax B		Tax C	
	Tax	% of income	Tax	% of income	Tax	% of income
$10,000	$500	5%	$1,000	10%	$1,000	10%
$20,000	$2,000	10%	$2,000	10%	$1,800	9%
$50,000	$8,000	16%	$5,000	10%	$4,000	8%
$100,000	$25,000	25%	$10,000	10%	$7,000	7%

In Table 9.2.1, tax A is progressive, tax B is proportional and tax C is regressive. With tax C, although the amount of tax increases as income rises, the percentage of income taken in tax falls as income increases.

Table 9.2.2 shows that with a regressive tax (tax C), the distribution of income after the tax has been paid is more unequal than before the tax.

▼ **Table 9.2.2**: A regressive tax makes the distribution of income more unequal

| Income before tax | Tax C | | |
	Tax	% of income taken in tax	Income after tax
$10,000	$1,000	10%	$9,000
$20,000	$1,800	9%	$18,200
$50,000	$4,000	8%	$46,000
$100,000	$7,000	7%	$93,000

In Table 9.2.2, before the tax, a person earning $100,000 is 10 times better off than a person earning $10,000. After the tax, the person earning $100,000 is 10.33 times better off than the person earning $10,000 ($93,000 ÷ $9,000 = 10.33).

In the case of tax A, after the tax, a person earning $100,000 is only 7.89 times better off than a person earning $10,000 ($75,000 ÷ $9,500 = 7.89). This shows that a progressive tax such as tax A, makes the distribution of income more equal.

When levying taxes to finance public expenditure, governments will usually consider the effect of the tax on the distribution of income. Direct taxes in many countries, particularly income tax, are often progressive. People on low incomes may not pay any income tax, whereas people with high incomes will pay a much higher rate of tax on the income they earn.

Indirect taxes are often regressive. With a specific indirect tax, each buyer pays the same amount of tax when he or she buys a product. The tax is a much smaller percentage of a rich person's income than a poor person's income.

Even if an ad valorem sales tax is levied on all products, it will still tend to be regressive because the rich tend to save more of their income than the poor. As a result, the percentage of total income paid in tax will be lower for someone on a high income than a low income. This is shown in Table 9.2.3.

▼ **Table 9.2.3**: Why an ad valorem tax may be regressive

Income	Spending	Saving	Tax – 10% of spending	Tax as a % of income
$10,000	$10,000	$0	$1,000	10%
$50,000	$45,000	$5,000	$4,500	9%

In Table 9.2.3, an indirect tax of 10% is levied on all spending. People earning $10,000 cannot afford to save and spend all of their income. This means the indirect tax accounts for 10% of their income. People earning $50,000 save $5,000 and spend the rest of their income. They pay $4,500 in indirect tax, which is 9% of their income. The indirect tax takes a higher percentage of the income of people who have the lower income.

However, not all indirect taxes make the distribution of income less equal. Governments could levy higher rates of tax on luxury goods that are bought mainly by people with high income and make necessities exempt from tax.

Case study: Income tax in South Africa

The tax year in South Africa starts on the 1 April and ends on the 31 March. In the tax year 2019–20, individuals could earn R79,000 (R = South African rand) before they started paying income tax. Income above R79,000 is taxed at rates shown in Table 9.2.4.

▼ **Table 9.2.4:** Income tax bands in South Africa, 2019–2020

Taxable income (South African rand)	Tax rates
R1 to R195,850	18% of taxable income
R195,851 to R305,850	R35,253 + 26% of taxable income above R195,850
R305,851 to R423,300	R63,853 + 31% of taxable income above R305,850
R423,301 to R555,600	R100,263 + 36% of taxable income above R423,300
R555,601 to R708,310	R147,891 + 39% of taxable income above R555,600
R708,311 to R1,500,000	R207,448 + 41% of taxable income above R708,310
R1,500,001 and above	R532,041 + 45% of taxable income above R1,500,000

1 How much income tax would a person earning R68,000 pay?
2 How much income tax would a person earning R300,000 pay?
3 How much money would person earning R300,000 have left to spend after paying income tax?
4 Calculate, to **two** decimal places, the average amount of income that a person earning R300,000 has to pay in income tax.

Taxes affect incentives

Governments need to consider the effect of different taxes on the distribution of income but they also need to consider the effects on incentives to work and enterprise.

If income tax rates are too high, people may have little financial incentive to work and this could lead to a smaller working population and voluntary unemployment. High rates of income tax may mean that some people are unwilling to work longer hours or to do overtime. Also, high rates of income tax may deter people from spending the time needed to improve their knowledge and skills. People who have skills that are scarce and in high demand may move abroad to find work in countries where tax rates are lower. A very progressive tax system may have significant disincentive effect for people who are in highly paid jobs. However, while people work to earn money, it is not the only reason why people work.

In the private sector, an important reason for setting up a business is to make a profit. High taxes on company profits reduce the incentive to set up businesses and to invest in expanding the business. A large, transnational company will consider the rates of tax on company profits when deciding where to expand its operations. If a country has high rates of tax on company profits, it may reduce inward foreign direct investment (FDI) and economic growth.

Key terms

Transnational company: a business that operates in more than one country.

Foreign direct investment (FDI): when a firm sets up, expands or buys a business in a different country.

Progress questions

5   What is the main reason why governments levy taxes?

6   Is a sales tax a direct tax or an indirect tax? Explain why.

7   How does a proportional tax affect the distribution of income?

8   A person's income before tax is $20,000 and tax-free pay is $8,000. How much income tax will the person have to pay if the government levies a 15% rate of income tax on taxable income between $1 and $30,000?

Indirect taxes are usually regressive and make the distribution of income less equal. However, they do not reduce the incentives for work and enterprise as much as direct taxes. In some countries, governments have increased indirect taxes and reduced rates of direct taxation to make work and enterprise more rewarding. The aim is to increase employment and economic growth. However, increasing indirect taxes adds to cost-push inflationary pressures and as prices rise, real incomes may fall.

The relationship between the budget balance and the national debt

The budget balance is the difference between government expenditure and the revenue the government receives from taxation in a financial year. A budget deficit is when government spending is greater than taxation (G > T). The budget deficit shows the amount of money the government needs to borrow in the financial year to pay for government expenditure that has not been financed through taxation.

A budget surplus is when taxation is greater than government spending (T > G). If the budget is in surplus in a financial year, the government is able to repay money that it has borrowed in previous years.

A balanced budget is when government spending equals tax revenue (G = T). In the financial year, the government has raised just enough money through taxation to pay for its spending.

Case study: Changes to taxation in Singapore

The Republic of Singapore is a small state in Southeast Asia. It has a population of 5.6 million and in 2018 the country had the third highest GDP per capita in the world.

Before 1986, both its corporate tax rate and its highest rate of personal income tax were 40%. Singapore's government believed that these direct tax rates were uncompetitive. It decided to change its tax system so that it relied more on indirect taxes and less on direct taxes for its revenue.

A Goods and Services Tax (GST) was introduced in 1994 at a rate of 3% on most goods and services, including imports. At the same time, the corporate tax rate and highest income tax rate were both cut by 3%, the corporate tax rate to 27% and income tax rate to 30%. Both have fallen further since. When GST was raised to 7% in 2007, the government increased many welfare benefits to offset the effects of the higher prices on those on low incomes.

GST is now due to be increased to 9% at some point between 2021 and 2025 to provide more money for infrastructure and to help support the ageing population.

1   Explain the difference between:
    i.   direct and indirect taxes
    ii. progressive and regressive taxes.

2   Discuss the effects of changing the tax system so that the government relies more on indirect taxes and less on direct taxes for its revenue.

▲ **Figure 9.2.4**: The Merlion Statue – a symbol of Singapore

The national debt is the accumulated total of past government borrowing. It is the stock of government debt that is outstanding at a point in time. It is the total amount of money that the government owes at a point in time.

The national debt is a stock, it is the amount owed at a point in time. The budget balance is a flow over a period of time, usually one year. A budget deficit shows the increase in the national debt that occurs in one year. For example, if the national debt was $550 billion at the start of the financial year and the budget deficit during the year was $30 billion, the national debt would be $580 billion at the end of the year. A budget surplus shows the reduction in the national debt in one year.

The national debt is money that the government has borrowed and is not necessarily owed to people and financial institutions in other countries. The main way in which governments borrow is by issuing bonds that pay interest to the people who own the bonds. The main holders of government bonds are banks and other financial institutions such as insurance companies and pension funds.

Does the size of a country's national debt matter?

Considering data showing a country's national debt as a percentage of its GDP is the main way of comparing the national debt of different countries. Japan has the largest ratio of national debt to GDP of any country in the world. Table 9.2.5 shows the percentage of national debt to GDP for a selection of countries at the end of 2018.

▼ **Table 9.2.5**: Government debt as a percentage of GDP for selected countries, December 2018

Country	Government debt to GDP (%)
Japan	238.2
Greece	181.2
Mozambique	113.0
United States	106.1
Egypt	90.5
UK	80.8
India	68.3
China	50.5
Mexico	46.0
Norway	36.3

Source: https://tradingeconomics.com; accessed 22 January 2020

When assessing the significance of a country's national debt, it is also important to consider how much of the money the government owes has been borrowed from abroad. Only a small proportion of the Japanese government's debt has been borrowed from abroad whereas over a quarter of US national debt is overseas debt.

If a country has a high national debt, other things being equal, the interest that the government has to pay on the debt will be higher. In the future, the government may have to increase taxes or cut other types of government spending to pay the interest on the debt.

Get it right

The budget deficit is a flow and represents the amount of extra money that the government needs to borrow in a financial year. The national debt is the stock of money that the government owes at a point in time.

Also, if banks and other financial institutions believe that there is a risk that the government will be unable to repay bond holders when the bonds mature, the rate of interest the government has to pay to attract people to buy its bonds will increase.

Although the government can increase aggregate demand by running a budget deficit, if the deficit and the national debt get too large, interest rates may increase and this may result in a fall in consumption and investment.

However, when interest rates are low, the government can borrow cheaply to finance spending on investment, for example on infrastructure. This should help to increase the underlying rate of growth of the economy.

Cyclical and structural influences on the budget balance

The size of the budget deficit or surplus is affected by the economic cycle and long-term structural influences. If the government has a budget deficit caused by cyclical factors, the deficit will disappear when the economy recovers but a structural deficit will not correct itself automatically.

Cyclical influences on the budget balance

The budget balance is affected by cyclical fluctuations in economic activity. When an economy goes into recession, the budget balance deteriorates; for example, if the government is already running a budget deficit, the deficit will get larger. If at the start of the recession there was a budget surplus, the size of the surplus would fall or the budget might move into deficit.

In a recession, household spending falls, unemployment increases and firms make less profit. As a result, the government tax revenue falls. The reduction in spending reduces the revenue raised from indirect taxes on sales, such as VAT. The reduction in employment means that the revenue received from taxes on income falls. Lower profits mean that the tax on firms' profits also falls. The increase in unemployment and fall in household incomes results in the government spending more money on cash welfare payments. The reduction in revenue from direct and indirect taxes, and the increase in government spending on welfare, causes the budget balance to deteriorate. This is known as the **cyclical budget deficit**.

In a recession, the government might also decide to increase government spending and cut tax rates to try to increase aggregate demand. This will lead to a further deterioration in the budget balance.

When the economy recovers, the revenue from both indirect and direct taxes will rise as spending, household incomes and firms' profits increase. Government spending on cash welfare benefits will fall and the budget balance will improve. For example, the budget deficit will fall or the budget may move from a deficit to a surplus. This is known as the **cyclical budget surplus**. As the economy approaches full capacity, the government might also cut government spending and

Key terms

Cyclical budget deficit: the deterioration in the budget balance that is caused by the decline in economic activity when an economy goes into a recession.

Cyclical budget surplus: the improvement in the budget balance that is caused by the increase in economic activity when an economy recovers.

increase tax rates to prevent aggregate demand increasing too quickly and causing inflation. This will also improve the budget balance.

Get it right

When economic activity falls the cyclical budget balance deteriorates, for example the budget deficit increases. When economic activity increases the cyclical budget balance improves, for example the budget deficit falls.

Structural influences on the budget balance

The **structural budget balance** is the underlying budget deficit or surplus after the effects of cyclical fluctuations in economic activity upon government spending and taxation have been removed. It is the budget deficit or surplus that exists when the economy is operating at its normal capacity level of output.

The size of any structural deficit or surplus, depends on the government's tax and spending policies. For example, the government may deliberately run a budget deficit because it wishes to increase spending on infrastructure to improve the efficiency and productive capacity of the economy but does not want to increase taxes. If the government wants to cut taxes but is unwilling to reduce its spending, this may also lead to a **structural budget deficit**. An ageing population may also lead to a structural deficit. An ageing population means that the government has to spend more on pensions and healthcare while the revenue from taxation falls because fewer people are working. A government may plan to have a structural budget deficit to achieve its objectives or it might result from poor management of the government's finances.

The overall budget balance is determined by both structural and cyclical influences. For example, if a country has an overall budget deficit of $90 billion, $60 billion might be structural and $30 billion because the economy is in recession. When the economy recovers, the cyclical deficit will disappear but, unless the government acts to reduce government spending or increase taxes, the structural deficit will remain.

However, if the economy is benefiting from underlying long-run economic growth, taxes revenues will increase and, unless the government increases its spending, the structural deficit should fall.

Key terms

Structural budget balance: the underlying budget deficit or surplus after the effects of cyclical fluctuations in economic activity upon government spending and taxation have been removed.

Structural budget deficit: when government expenditure is greater than taxation after the effects of cyclical fluctuations in economic activity on government spending and taxation have been removed.

Progress questions

9   What is the difference between the budget deficit and the national debt?

10 At the start of 2019, a country's national debt was $254 billion. In 2019, its budget surplus was $17 billion. What was the amount of its national debt at the end of 2019?

11 Explain the likely effects of the recovery in an economy on the government's budget balance.

Activity

Find out what has happened to the national debt to GDP ratio in your country during the past 15 years. What has caused the ratio to change?

Case study: A Greek tragedy

Greece became a member of the European Union (EU) in 1981 and adopted the euro as its currency in 2001. Average living standards improved rapidly after Greece joined the EU but the global financial crisis of 2007–2008 led to GDP per head falling. GDP per head peaked at around $32,000 in 2007 but was just over $25,000 in 2018.

The problems the Greek economy experienced after 2007 have been blamed on economic mismanagement. By 2009, Greece had the largest budget deficit and national debt to GDP ratio in the EU. The 2009 budget deficit was 15.7% of GDP. The size of the deficit was partly caused by the recession that followed the global financial crisis but it was also a structural problem.

Between, 2007 and 2011 the Greek national debt increased from just over 100% of GDP to more than 170% of GDP. Bondholders feared that the Greek government would not be able to repay the money borrowed when the bonds matured. As a result, interest rates increased and the Greek government was unable to borrow on financial markets to finance its budget deficit. Instead, the government had to borrow from the European Central Bank (ECB) and the International Monetary Fund (IMF). As a condition for granting the loans, the ECB and IMF insisted that the Greek government cut its spending and increased taxes.

1   Explain why the recession that followed the global financial crisis contributed to the increase in the Greek government's budget deficit.

2   Explain the main reasons why the Greek national debt as a percentage of GDP rose rapidly between 2007 and 2011.

3   "The ECB and IMF insisted that the Greek government cut its spending and increased taxes." What effects would this have had on the economy of Greece?

▲ **Figure 9.2.5**: The Parthenon in Athens

This section will develop your knowledge and understanding of:

→ the difference between supply-side policies and supply-side improvements in the economy

→ how supply-side policies can help to achieve supply-side improvements in the economy

→ how supply-side policies, including tax changes designed to change incentives, may increase the potential output of the economy and increase the underlying trend rate of economic growth

→ how supply-side policies can affect unemployment, inflation and the balance of payments on current account

→ supply-side policies including government spending on education and training, investment in infrastructure, welfare reforms, deregulation and industrial policy.

The difference between supply-side policies and supply-side improvements

Supply-side improvements in an economy lead to a rightward shift in the LRAS curve, increasing the productive capacity of the economy. Supply-side improvements cause underlying economic growth and/or reduce unemployment. Supply-side improvements can result from the actions of individuals, businesses and governments.

Improvements in productivity and efficiency are examples of supply-side improvements in an economy. Supply-side improvements also involve improvements in the quality of products and enabling the economy to supply the goods and services people need and want. Supply-side improvements result from improvements in labour mobility, creating new infrastructure and invention and innovation. Increased willingness to work and to set up and expand businesses also lead to supply-side improvements in an economy.

Government supply-side policies can help to generate supply-side improvements in the economy but supply-side improvements can occur independently of the government. When firms invest in physical capital, such as machines and buildings, it is likely to increase efficiency, productivity and productive capacity. If a firm trains its workers, this **investment in human capital** should increase labour productivity and the quality of goods and services produced. Individuals who develop their skills and abilities or set up their own business improve the supply side of the economy.

However, government policies can create an environment in which supply-side improvements are more likely to take place or may directly improve the supply side of an economy.

How supply-side policies can lead to supply-side improvements in the economy

After the end of the Second World War, in 1945, until the early 1970s, the economic policies of many governments around the world focused on using fiscal policy to manage aggregate demand, with the main objective of keeping unemployment low. This approach to economic

> ### Key terms
>
> **Human capital:** the knowledge, skills, abilities and experience of people.
>
> **Investment in human capital:** spending on education and training to improve the knowledge, skills and abilities of people.

Key terms

Free-market supply-side policies: measures to increase incentives to work and enterprise, and to make markets more competitive by reducing government involvement, with the aim of shifting the LRAS curve to the right.

Interventionist supply-side policies: measures taken by the government to deal with the weaknesses of the free-market, with the aim of shifting the LRAS curve to the right.

management was based on the ideas of John Maynard Keynes. However, rising inflation and unemployment led people to question whether a different approach to managing the economy was needed.

Some economists, particularly in the United States, argued that government policy should focus on the supply side of the economy. At first, supply-side economists emphasised the role of markets and the need to make markets work better. They argued for less government intervention and for measures that increase incentives to work and enterprise. However, another group of supply-side economists favour a more interventionist approach. They emphasise the need for government action to overcome the failures of the free market.

Most governments use a combination of **free-market supply-side policies** and **interventionist supply-side policies** to try to achieve an improvement in the supply-side performance of the economy. Free-market supply-side policies involve minimising government involvement in the economy. Free-market supply-side economists argue for low taxes to increase incentives to work and expand businesses. They believe in competitive markets and private enterprise and are in favour of deregulation to allow markets to operate freely without government involvement. Interventionist supply-side economists point to imperfections in markets and emphasise the need for government intervention to deal with the weaknesses of the free market.

Free-market supply-side policies lead to supply-side improvements by increasing incentives to work and enterprise and by reducing restrictions that prevent markets from working well. Interventionist supply-side policies lead to supply-side improvements by the government acting to remedy some of the weaknesses of the free market by, for example, supplying public goods, providing education and training and subsidising research and development.

Supply-side economists emphasise the importance of measures to improve the performance of the supply side of the economy and some free-market supply-side economists argue that the government does not need to be concerned about aggregate demand. These economists argue that "supply creates its own demand", a quotation attributed to the 18th century French economist Jean-Baptiste Say, and known as "Say's Law of Markets". Since output creates the same amount of income, there should not be a shortage of demand. However, it cannot be guaranteed that all the income will be spent. John Maynard Keynes argued that injections into the circular flow of income do not necessarily equal the amount withdrawn and so aggregate demand does not necessarily equal aggregate supply.

Most economists believe that managing aggregate demand to make sure that the economy stays close to full capacity is also necessary and is a responsibility of the government.

▲ **Figure 9.3.1**: Jean-Baptiste Say

Progress questions

1   What is the difference between supply-side improvements and supply-side policies?

2   What is meant by "investment in human capital"?

3   Explain how investment in human capital is likely to improve the supply-side performance of an economy.

How supply-side policies increase the potential output and growth of an economy

The main aim of supply-side policies is to increase the supply of factors of production and their productivity. These policies should also help to make the economy more adaptable, support enterprise and encourage innovation. Effective supply-side policies support markets in improving quality and in supplying the products that consumers need and want.

How tax reform can improve the supply-side performance of an economy

Free-market supply-side economists are in favour of low taxes. High tax rates can reduce incentives to work and enterprise but cutting taxes may mean reducing government spending to avoid a large budget deficit. However, free-market supply-side economists are in favour of limiting government involvement in the economy. Also, if low taxes lead to an increase in economic activity, tax revenue should increase.

High rates of income tax reduce the financial rewards from work and can have a variety of disincentive effects. High income tax rates may cause voluntary unemployment, particularly if unemployment benefits are also high. People in work may be unwilling to work extra hours. Progressive taxes, with high rates of tax on high incomes, may deter people from spending the time needed to acquire the knowledge and skills required for highly paid jobs. They may also lead to some people being unwilling to accept jobs that are highly paid but more demanding.

In a market economy, differences in earnings are important in allocating resources and increasing labour mobility. If the demand for a product rises, higher wages may be needed to persuade people to change jobs and to acquire the skills needed to make the product. High rates of taxation can inhibit the required reallocation of resources.

Although high tax rates can be a disincentive to work, high tax rates might mean that some people may choose to work more hours to achieve the income they want. Also, earning money is not the only reason why people work, people are motivated by a variety of other factors.

High taxes on firms can be a disincentive to enterprise. In a market economy, people set up businesses because they expect to make a profit. If taxes on firms' profits are high, it will deter people from starting and expanding firms. High taxes on profits will also reduce the funds available to finance investment, restricting the growth of firms and their ability to invest in developing new products and training workers. They may also reduce investment in the economy from abroad.

Supply-side economists believe that cutting taxes should increase economic activity but recognise that taxes are needed to pay for government spending. Most supply-side economists would prefer that the revenue needed to pay for government spending is raised by

Activity

Find out all you can about the Laffer curve.

levying indirect rather than direct taxes. However, although indirect taxes may have fewer disincentive effects, they are usually regressive and increase inequality.

How government spending can improve the supply-side performance of an economy

There are many ways in which government spending can help to increase the productive capacity of an economy. Most free-market supply-side economists believe that some goods would be undersupplied if the government did not provide them. For example, government spending on infrastructure such as road and rail improves efficiency and reduces transport costs.

Interventionist supply-side economists believe that private companies do not invest enough into projects that are beneficial in the long run. They argue that private companies are more concerned with earning profits in the short run so they can keep their shareholders happy. Interventionist supply-side economists believe that without government support, investment and spending on research and development would be too low.

Inequality and the existence of positive externalities means that without government spending too few resources would be devoted to education and training. Investment in human capital is a very important source of economic growth.

Interventionist supply-side economists believe that government ownership of some businesses is required to meet the needs of the economy. For example, industries supplying water, steel and power benefit from economies of scale and this leads to large firms. In the private sector, large firms with monopoly power may exploit consumers. Free-market supply-side economists are in favour of the privatisation of government-owned firms because they believe that such firms are inefficient.

> **Key term**
>
> Privatisation: when a government-owned business is sold and becomes a private sector business.

> **Link**
>
> The case for and against government ownership of firms is covered in the A2 part of the course.

> **Get it right**
>
> Government can affect aggregate demand by changing the total amount of government spending, taxation and the budget balance. This will affect how much of the existing capacity of the economy is used. Governments can also affect the productive capacity of the economy by changing taxes and government spending to try to achieve a more efficient, productive economy. Supply-side fiscal measures designed to increase productive capacity do not necessarily involve changes in the total amounts that governments tax and spend.

How other supply-side policies can improve the supply-side performance of an economy

Governments can make sure that taxes do not create significant disincentive effects, and some types of government spending can support supply-side improvements in an economy. However, there is also a variety of other supply-side policies that governments can use.

Free-market supply-side economists believe that markets should be deregulated. Regulations imposed on firms by governments increase costs and can reduce investment. Complying with the regulations can be costly for firms and governments have to employ people to make sure that firms obey the regulations. Deregulation reduces costs and may encourage new firms to enter the market. Some regulations may be unnecessary but others are important to make sure, for example, that people and the environment are protected. Health and safety regulations can save lives and protecting the environment is important for the future of all of us.

Reducing restrictions on imports and inward investment from abroad increases competition and can lead to improvements in productivity and efficiency. If successful, this will increase the growth of the economy. However, if domestic firms are unable to compete with overseas rivals, this may reduce GDP and increase unemployment.

Policies such as providing free or subsidised childcare can make it easier for women to return to work after having children. Promoting equal pay and equal opportunities for women can increase female participation rates and increase the size of the labour force.

Effective supply-side policies should increase the productive capacity of the economy and its underlying growth rate by increasing the supply of labour, encouraging new businesses, increasing investment and productivity. These benefits are illustrated by shifting the LRAS curve to the right.

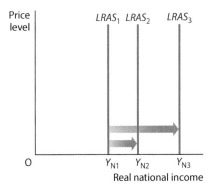

▲ **Figure 9.3.2**: The effect of supply-side policies on the potential output and the growth of the economy

In Figure 9.3.2, without supply-side policies, improvements in supply-side performance would have increased the productive capacity of the economy from Y_{N1} to Y_{N2}. However, successful supply-side policies lead to a faster underlying rate of economic growth and the economy's productive capacity increases from Y_{N1} to Y_{N3}.

Supply-side policies can affect unemployment, inflation and the balance of payments on current account

Successful supply-side policies should contribute to reducing unemployment, keeping inflation low and improving the current account of the balance of payments. They help to remove some of the policy conflicts that can result from using monetary and fiscal measures to manage aggregate demand.

Progress questions

4   State **two** reasons why a cut in income tax rates may increase the supply of labour.

5   State **two** reasons why a cut in the tax on company profits may improve the supply-side performance of an economy.

6   How might a reduction in the rates of tax on income and company profits lead to an increase in tax revenue?

7   State **two** ways in which government spending can help to increase the productive capacity of an economy.

8   How might deregulation help to improve the productive capacity of an economy?

How supply-side policies can help to reduce unemployment

Supply-side policies can help to reduce both frictional and structural unemployment. Labour immobility causes frictional and structural unemployment and supply-side policies can improve labour mobility.

Frictional unemployment is when people are between jobs. They may have decided to change jobs or may have been made redundant but people who are frictionally unemployed are not out of work for very long. Supply-side policies to reduce frictional unemployment include:

- providing better information about job vacancies to help people find work quickly
- improvements to local transport systems so that people are able to get to jobs in other areas more easily
- reducing the replacement ratio, which may mean that people will start work again as soon as possible.

Reducing income tax and limiting out-of-work welfare benefits are supply-side measures that reduce the replacement ratio. However, cutting out-of-work welfare benefits can be unfair. It may mean that some people who have lost their job have a very low standard of living.

Supply-side policies to improve the occupational and geographical mobility of labour can help to reduce structural unemployment. They include:

- government spending on education to improve people's basic skills and make the workforce more adaptable
- retraining programmes to allow people who have lost their job in a declining industry to acquire the necessary skills to work in industries that are growing
- good local transport and communication links to allow people to travel to work in a different area
- fast, reliable national transport and communication links, which may also encourage people who are unemployed to move to a different part of the country to find work
- providing good quality, affordable housing in areas where there are labour shortages to make it easier for people to move from areas where unemployment is high.

Not only do supply-side policies contribute to reducing unemployment, they can also help to increase the size of the labour force by making it more attractive for people to work. Income tax cuts and providing good-quality, subsidised childcare are examples of such policies.

How supply-side policies can help to keep inflation low

Supply-side policies can help reduce cost-push and demand-pull inflationary pressures. If supply-side policies lead to an increase in productivity and efficiency, this will reduce firms' average cost of production and offset other cost increases. Supply-side improvements that increase productive capacity will help the economy respond to an increase in aggregate demand by increasing output rather than leading to an increase in the price level. As a result, demand-pull inflationary pressures are reduced.

In Figure 9.3.3, supply-side policies shift the LRAS curve from $LRAS_1$ to $LRAS_2$. If aggregate demand increases from AD_1 to AD_2, the price level will increase from PL_1 to PL_2. However, without the increase in productive capacity caused by the supply-side policies, the price level would have increased from PL_1 to PL_3. Successful supply-side policies help to reduce inflation.

However, it is unlikely that supply-side policies can be relied on to keep inflation low. Supply-side policies take time to affect the economy and aggregate demand can change very quickly. If aggregate demand starts to increase and the economy is close to full capacity, an increase in interest rates is more likely to be effective in eliminating the excess aggregate demand. Fiscal policy can also be used to affect aggregate demand but monetary policy is more flexible and most countries use monetary policy as the main way of controlling inflation.

In some situations, supply-side policies leading to supply-side improvements in the economy may lead to deflation. Improvements in productivity and efficiency reduce firms' costs and competition between firms may lead to lower prices. This is an example of benign deflation and results in an increase in real incomes and improvements in living standards. However, if prices keep falling it could lead to people delaying buying goods and services. If this becomes a problem, demand-side policies could be used to increase spending.

How supply-side policies can help to improve the current account of the balance of payments

Supply-side policies should help to improve the competitiveness of domestic firms. If supply-side policies increase productivity and efficiency, costs will fall and domestic firms will be more price competitive in their home market and overseas.

If the supply-side policies used by government encourage invention and innovation, they should also lead to better quality and more advanced products. Lower prices and better products should lead to an increase in exports and encourage domestic consumers to buy home-produced goods and services rather than imports.

Successful supply-side policies will result in new firms being set up and in the expansion of existing firms. The resulting increase in productive capacity should, provided there is enough demand, make it easier for domestic firms to supply export markets. It will also allow domestic firms to supply their home market and reduce the need to import goods and services. More exports and fewer imports improve the current account of the balance of payments.

Different types of supply-side policy

There is a variety of supply-side policies that governments can use. It can be useful to distinguish between free-market and interventionist supply-side policies, but there is not always a clear-cut difference between them. Most governments use both free-market and interventionist supply-side policies to try to improve the performance of their economies.

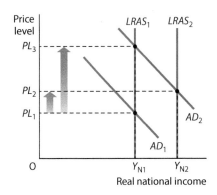

▲ **Figure 9.3.3**: The effect of supply-side policies on inflation

Get it right

An increase in aggregate demand can be satisfied by an increase in output and/or by a rise in the price level. If the economy is able to respond to an increase in aggregate demand by supplying more goods and services, the effect on inflation will be reduced.

Government spending is often used to improve the supply side of the economy. Some of the most important forms of government spending that focus on improving the supply side of the economy are:

- spending on education and training
- investment in infrastructure
- subsidising investment
- subsidising research and development
- financial and other support for new and expanding sectors of the economy.

Changes to the tax system to increase incentives to work and enterprise can also help to improve the supply side of the economy. Changes to the tax system that focus on improving the supply side of the economy include:

- increasing the amount of income that people can earn before paying income tax
- reducing rates of income tax
- reducing rates of tax on company profits
- reducing the amount of revenue raised from direct taxes and increasing the amount raised from indirect taxes instead.

If the government increases its spending to try to improve the supply side of the economy, this will, at least in the short run, lead to higher taxes or a deterioration in the budget balance. Higher taxes could damage the supply-side performance of the economy.

Other supply-side policies include:

- changes to the welfare system designed to increase incentives to work
- privatisation of state-owned industries
- deregulation
- promoting competition and restricting the monopoly power of some large enterprises
- reducing taxes on imports and other restrictions on international trade
- industrial policy to support and develop manufacturing and other sectors of the economy
- provision of childcare and other measures that promote gender equality to increase female participation in the labour force.

Benefits of supply-side policies

Most economists agree that improving the supply-side performance of an economy is essential if people are to benefit from a sustained increase in their standard of living. If successful, the benefits of supply-side policies include:

- an increase in the underlying trend rate of economic growth
- an increase in real GDP per capita, leading to a higher standard of living
- a reduction in frictional and structural unemployment
- a reduction in both cost-push and demand-pull inflationary pressures

Key terms

Industrial policy: government intervention to support and develop particular sectors of the economy, often manufacturing.

- improvements in international competitiveness and the balance of trade in goods and services
- reducing the conflicts between macroeconomic policy objectives that can result from relying on demand-management policies, helping the economy to achieve non-inflationary growth
- improvements in the flexibility and adaptability of the economy that can help to reduce fluctuations in economic activity.

The limitations of supply-side policies

The effects of supply-side policies on an economy are uncertain and economists disagree about the relative advantages and disadvantages of interventionist and free-market supply-side policies. The limitations of supply-side policies include the following.

- It may take many years before the economy benefits. For example, it takes a long time before spending on education leads to supply-side improvements in the economy.
- The effects of supply-side measures cannot be guaranteed. For example, government subsidies for research and development might not lead to useful technological progress.
- Some supply-side measures are expensive, such as spending on infrastructure.
- There may be unintended consequences. For example, more spending on roads may increase the volume of traffic and increase pollution.
- Some free-market supply-side policies may lead to greater inequality, such as changes to the tax and benefit systems to increase the incentive to work or cutting taxes on the profits of large firms.

Case study: Norway – a success story

Norway is one of a few western European countries that is not part of the European Union (EU). It has a population of 5 million and, through persistent growth, it has achieved one of the highest GDP per capita figures in the world.

What has contributed to Norway's success? Over the past 50 years, it has benefited considerably from selling oil and gas from the North Sea. This has enabled the Norwegian government to invest some of the money earned to create a very large Oil Fund. The income from this fund will benefit the country's economy and its people for many years to come. Now however, 98% of Norway's domestic energy supply comes from renewable sources.

Education is aimed at diversifying the economy and the government has encouraged the study of STEM subjects – Science, Technology, Engineering and Mathematics. There are grants and tax incentives for research and development, particularly if the developments benefit society. Between 2013 and 2019, the rate of tax on corporate income was cut from 28% to 22%.

Norway does not have a minimum wage but workers are generally paid well. The government has also tried to narrow the gender gap, both in terms of income and opportunity. Childcare is heavily subsidised and since 2003 at least 40% of company board members must be women.

1   Identify **three** examples of supply-side policies in the case study **and** explain how they may help to increase Norway's potential output.

2   What else may have contributed to Norway's high GDP per capita figures?

▲ **Figure 9.3.4**: An important source of Norwegian income

Exam-style questions

1 Which one of the following is an example of expansionary monetary policy?

An increase in

A government spending

B interest rates

C the exchange rate

D the money supply [1 mark]

2 The table below shows the amount of income tax paid by an individual at different levels of income.

Income ($)	Income tax ($)
60,000	10,000
40,000	5,000
20,000	2,000

The type of tax shown in the table is

A flat rate.

B progressive.

C proportional.

D regressive. [1 mark]

3 Which one of the following is a supply-side policy?

A A rise in interest rates

B A fall in the tax on company profits.

C An increase in a sales tax

D The use of quantitative easing [1 mark]

4 Define "national debt" [3 marks]

5 If the exchange rate of the US dollar to the Japanese yen is $1 = ¥110, calculate, to the nearest US dollar, the price in US dollars of a Japanese car, priced at ¥2,000,000.

You are advised to show your working. [3 marks]

6 Analyse how supply-side policies can increase the potential output of an economy. [12 marks]

7 Use the information in the case study on monetary policy in Canada (in 9.1 "Monetary policy") and your knowledge of economics to assess the effectiveness of changes in interest rates in keeping inflation low and stable. [20 marks]

Glossary

A

Accelerating inflation: when the rate of inflation is increasing.

Ad valorem: according to value, a percentage of the value of the good or service.

Aggregate demand (AD) curve:: shows the relationship between the price level and total spending in an economy.

Aggregate demand: total planned spending on all goods and services produced in the domestic economy.

Aggregate supply (AS) curve: shows the relationship between the price level and the total amount of goods and services that firms are willing to produce.

Allocative efficiency: the combination of goods that best meets people's preferences.

Animal spirits: human emotions and instincts that affect decision making.

Appreciation in the exchange rate: a rise in the value of the currency; it buys more units of foreign currency.

Asset: something of value that is owned.

Asset bubble: when the price of a commodity or other asset increases quickly over a short period of time, usually due to speculation.

Asymmetric information: a form of imperfect information where one party has more or better information than the other.

Automation: using advanced technology to produce goods and services with little help from workers.

Availability of credit: how easy, or difficult, it is to find a bank or other organisation that is willing and able to lend.

Average cost or unit cost: the cost of producing each unit, total cost divided by the number of units produced.

Average fixed costs: fixed costs per unit of output.

Average revenue: the revenue per unit sold, calculated by dividing the total revenue by the number of units.

Average variable costs: variable costs per unit of output.

B

Balanced budget: when government spending is equal to the amount the government receives from taxation.

Balance of payments: a record of a country's financial transactions with the rest of the world.

Balance of payments deficit: when the value of imports is greater than the value of exports.

Balance of payments surplus: when the value of exports is greater than the value of imports.

Balance of trade in goods and services: the value of goods and services exported **minus** the value of goods and services imported.

Balance of trade in goods or visible balance: the difference between the value of goods exported and the value of goods imported.

Balance of trade in services: the value of services exported **minus** the value of services imported.

Barriers to entry: factors that make it difficult for new firms to come into a market.

Barter: the exchange of goods and services for other goods and services.

Base year: the starting point for an index, where its value is 100.

Basket of goods: the goods and services that are included in a price index.

Benign deflation: good deflation that is caused by improvements in technology, efficiency and productivity.

Black market: when products are bought and sold illegally.

Brand loyalty: where customers continue to buy products from a particular firm.

Budget deficit: when government spending is greater than the amount the government receives from taxation.

Budget surplus: when the amount the government receives from taxation is greater than government spending.

Buffer stock scheme: where a government (or organisation of producers) buys and sells a commodity to stabilise price.

C

Capital: human-made resources.

Capital stock: the value of machinery, buildings and other human-made factors of production that exist at a point in time.

Cash ratio: the ratio between the amount of cash a bank holds and its deposits.

Central bank: the financial institution responsible for monetary policy and maintaining a stable financial system.

Central bank's discount rate: the rate of interest the central bank charges when lending to other banks.

Centrally planned economy: where decisions about what to produce, how to produce it and who should benefit are taken by the government.

Closed economy: an economy that does not trade with other economies, there are no exports or imports.

Commodities: primary products – raw materials, agricultural or mining products.

Compatible policy objectives: an improvement in one policy objective is accompanied by an improvement in a different policy objective.

Competition policy: government measures to control the activities of firms to protect consumers, make markets more competitive and to encourage an efficient use of resources.

Competitive market: where there are many buyers and sellers, good market information and ease of entry.

Competitiveness: how well a firm or economy is performing in the marketplace compared to other firms or economies.

Complementary goods or goods in joint demand: products that are bought or used together – if the demand for one good increases, so will demand for the other. They are in joint demand.

Composite demand: a good which has more than one use.

Concentrated market: where a few firms, or possibly only one, have a high market share.

Concentration ratio: a measure of the combined share of the largest firms in an industry, usually as a percentage of the total.

Conflict between policy objectives: when an improvement in one policy objective leads to a worse outcome for a different policy objective.

Consumer durables: products households buy that last for several years.

Consumer expenditure: spending by households on goods and services.

Consumer Price Index (CPI): a measure of the price level and inflation.

Consumer sovereignty: when consumers determine what is produced through their spending.

Consumption externalities: effects on third parties due to the consumption of goods and services.

Contraction in economic activity: when aggregate demand, output and employment are falling.

Contractionary fiscal policy: a decrease in government spending and/or an increase in taxation to reduce aggregate demand.

Contractionary monetary policy: when the central bank increases interest rates, restricts the rate of growth of the supply of money and credit, and attempts to increase the exchange rate. The aim is to reduce aggregate demand and inflation.

Corporate bonds: a security representing a loan to a company that pays interest to the holder until it matures.

Cost of living: how much a person has to spend to maintain the same standard of living. When there is inflation, the cost of living is rising.

Cost-push inflation: when the rise in the price level is caused by an increase in the costs of production.

Credit items: items that lead to an inflow of foreign currency.

Creeping inflation: when there is a low rate of inflation that continues for many years.

Cross elasticity of demand: a measure of the percentage change in quantity demanded of one good as a result of a given percentage change in the price of another good, or simply, the responsiveness of quantity demanded of one good to a change in the price of another.

Current account balance: the sum of the balance of trade in goods and services + the primary income balance + the secondary income balance.

Cyclical budget deficit: the deterioration in the budget balance that is caused by the decline in economic activity when an economy goes into a recession.

Cyclical budget surplus: the improvement in the budget balance that is caused by the increase in economic activity when an economy recovers.

Cyclical unemployment: when the economy goes into recession and people cannot find work because aggregate demand is too low.

D

Debit items: items that lead to an outflow of foreign currency.

Deficit (on the balance of payments): the money leaving the country is greater than the money coming in, or debits are greater than credits.

Deflation: a fall in the price level.

Deflationary policies: measures used by the government to reduce aggregate demand.

Demand: the quantity that consumers are willing and able to buy at a given price in a given period of time.

Demand-pull inflation: when the rise in the price level is caused by an increase in aggregate demand.

Demand-side shock: an event that leads to sudden or unexpected change in aggregate demand.

Demerit good: a product that society or government judges is undesirable, too much is provided by the market for the benefit of society as a whole.

Deposits: money that customers have in their bank accounts; it is money the bank owes to its customers.

Depreciation: the fall in the value of an asset over a period of time.

Depreciation in the exchange rate: a fall in the value of the currency; it buys fewer units of foreign currency.

Depression: when the economy has very high unemployment and total output is much lower than the productive capacity of the economy. There is a large amount of spare capacity that continues for a number of years.

Deregulation: the removal of rules, particularly those that restrict competition.

Derived demand: where the demand for a factor of production results from the demand for the product it makes.

Direct taxes: these are taxes on income and wealth. Unlike an indirect tax, the burden of a direct tax cannot be passed on to someone else.

Diseconomies of scale: a rise in long-run average costs due to the growth of a firm or industry.

Disequilibrium: where there are forces at work that will lead to a change in a variable.

Disinflation: when inflation exists but the rate of inflation is falling; for example, when the rate of inflation falls from 7% to 4%.

Disintegration: where different parts of a production process are carried out by different firms.

Disposable income: what is left of a household's income after taxes on income have been paid; it includes any cash welfare benefits received from the government.

Distribution of income and wealth: how income or wealth is divided between people or regions.

Division of labour: when a worker performs one task or a narrow range of tasks as part of the production process.

Domestic output: goods and services produced within an economy.

Double coincidence of wants: having to find someone who has what you want and will accept what you have to trade.

E

Earned income: income from a job or self-employment.

Economic activity: the production, distribution and consumption of goods and services.

Economic agents: a person, firm, organisation or government that has a role in the economy.

Economic cycle: fluctuations in economic activity around an economy's long-run trend rate of economic growth.

Economic growth: an increase in productive potential or the rate at which the total output of all goods and services produced by an economy is increasing.

Economic indicators: statistics that are used to measure the current or past performance of an economy.

Economic model: a simplified representation of the economy, or part of the economy, that provides understanding of the real world.

Economic resources (factors of production): inputs into the production process, needed to produce goods and services.

Economics: the study of how we use our scarce resources to satisfy our many wants.

Economies of scale: a fall in long-run average costs due to the growth of a firm or industry.

Empirical evidence: evidence based on observation, experience and laboratory experiments.

Entrepreneur or enterprise: the person or group of people who takes risks, makes decisions and organises the production process.

Equality: when everyone has, or is treated, the same.

Equilibrium income: when national income is stable and does not change from one time period to the next time period.

Equilibrium price: the price where demand and supply for a product are equal.

Equilibrium quantity: the quantity where demand and supply for a product are equal.

Equity: fairness.

Exchange rate: the price at which one currency can be converted into another currency.

Excludable: where non-payers can be prevented from using the product.

Expansion in economic activity: when aggregate demand, output and employment are increasing.

Expansionary fiscal policy: an increase in government spending and/or a reduction in taxation to increase aggregate demand.

Expansionary monetary policy: when the central bank reduces interest rates, increases the rate of growth of the money supply and credit, and attempts to achieve a depreciation in the exchange rate. The aim is to increase aggregate demand, economic activity and inflation.

Export-led growth: where a significant part of the increase in a country's real GDP results from exporting goods and services abroad.

Exports: goods and services that are sold to other countries.

Extension of property rights: allocating the ownership of more resources to people or firms, who can then determine how those resources are used.

External economies of scale: a fall in long-run average costs due to the growth of an industry.

Externalities: effects on other people or firms (third parties) due to the consumption or production of goods and services.

F

Factor market: the market for buying and selling resources/factors of production.

Female participation rate: the percentage of women of working age who are working or actively seeking work.

Fiscal policy: the use of government spending and taxation to influence the economy and help the government achieve its objectives.

Fixed costs: costs that do not change with output.

Foreign direct investment (FDI): when a firm sets up, expands or buys a business in a different country.

Free-market economists: those who believe that competitive markets and minimal government intervention are best for an economy.

Free market economy: where decisions about what to produce, how to produce it and who should benefit are taken by buyers and sellers, with no involvement by government.

Free-market supply-side policies: measures to increase incentives to work and enterprise, and to make markets more competitive by reducing government involvement, with the aim of shifting the LRAS curve to the right.

Free-rider problem: where people can consume as much as they like of a good, without having to pay for it.

Frictional unemployment: short-term unemployment when people are between jobs.

Full capacity: when a firm, or an economy, is producing its maximum output from the available resources, given the current level of technology.

Full employment: when everyone who is willing and able to work at current market wage rates has a job.

Full employment income: the level of national income/output that creates enough jobs for everyone who is willing and able to work at current market wage rates.

Fundamental (or basic) economic problem: that scarce resources are not enough to satisfy our many wants.

G

Geographical immobility of labour: when workers find it difficult to move to jobs in a different area, region or country.

Goods/product market: the market for buying and selling goods and services.

Government bonds: a security representing a loan to the government that pays interest to the holder until it matures.

Government failure: when government intervention in the economy leads to a worse allocation of resources and a fall in welfare.

Gross domestic product (GDP): is a measure of national income, it measures the monetary value of the total output of an economy over a given period of time, for example, a year.

H

Home-produced: made by firms in the domestic economy.

Homogeneous goods: identical products.

Human capital: the knowledge, skills, abilities and experience of people.

Hyperinflation: when the rate of inflation is very high.

I

Immobility of factors of production: where resources find it difficult to move from one place or type of work to another.

Imperfect information: when buyers and/or sellers do not have all the necessary information to make the correct decision about a product.

Import-competing industries: domestic industries that produce goods and services that are substitutes for goods and services imported from abroad.

Imported inflation: a type of cost-push inflation that starts with an increase in the price of commodities imported from abroad.

Imported unemployment: a type of structural unemployment that is caused by foreign competition.

Imports: goods and services that are bought from other countries.

Incentive function: the idea that changes in price make producers or sellers of factors of production more or less likely to sell their goods or services.

Income: a flow of money, received by an economic agent over a period of time.

Income elasticity of demand: a measure of the percentage change in quantity demanded as a result of a given percentage change in income, or simply, the responsiveness of quantity demanded to a change in income.

Index number: a statistic, with a base value of 100, that is used to measure changes in a selection of related variables.

Indirect tax: a tax on spending.

Industrial policy: government intervention to support and develop particular sectors of the economy, often manufacturing.

Industry: all the firms involved in producing a particular good or service.

Inferior good: a product where demand decreases if income rises.

Inflation: an increase in the price level.

Inflation rate: the percentage increase in the price level.

Inflation target: the rate of inflation that the central bank is expected to maintain through its use of monetary policy. The target is often set by the government.

Inflationary expectations: the rate of inflation that households, firms and other economic agents believe will occur in the future.

Informal economy: part of the economy that is not regulated or protected by government. People and firms operating in the informal economy rarely pay taxes and barter may be used to exchange goods and services.

Information failure: where individuals or firms have incomplete or inaccurate information, resulting in wrong decisions.

Injection: expenditure that is added to and increases the circular flow of income in an economy.

Innovation: making changes to existing products by introducing new ideas that better meet existing needs or new requirements.

Intellectual property rights: the ownership of a creation of someone's mind.

Interdependence: when two things, for example individuals or firms, depend on each other.

Internal economies of scale: a fall in long-run average costs due to the growth of a firm.

Internalise an externality: make the firm's private costs or benefits equal to the social costs or benefits.

International trade: the exchange of goods and services between countries.

Interventionist economists: those who believe that governments need to take action to correct market failures to increase the welfare of the people.

Interventionist supply-side policies: measures taken by the government to deal with the weaknesses of the free-market, with the aim of shifting the LRAS curve to the right.

Invention: the creation of a new idea, product or process.

Investment: an increase in the capital stock.

Investment expenditure: spending by firms on capital goods.

Investment in human capital: spending on education and training to improve the knowledge, skills and abilities of people.

Involuntary unemployment: when people are willing and able to work at current market wage rates but are unable to find employment.

J

Job vacancies: where firms have jobs available but have not yet been able to find people to accept the jobs.

Joint supply: when the output of one good results in the output of another good.

K

Keynesian economists: followers of the influential English economist John Maynard Keynes who believe that the macroeconomy is unstable and that government intervention may be needed to prevent a slump lasting for many years.

L

Labour: human resources.

Labour force: the number of people available for work. It is the sum of those who are employed, self-employed and unemployed.

Labour productivity: how much a worker produces in a given time.

Lagging indicator: a statistic that comes after an event has taken place.

Land: natural resources.

Law of unintended consequences: the idea that the actions of the government (or others) lead to unexpected effects.

Levy taxes: to impose taxes on economic agents, including firms and households.

Liquid assets: cash or other assets that can be easily converted into cash.

Localisation: when an industry is concentrated in one or a few locations.

Localised industry: an industry that is located in a particular area or region of a country.

Long run: the time period when all factors of production are variable.

M

Macroeconomics: the study of the economy as a whole.

Malign deflation: bad deflation that occurs in a slump and is caused by low aggregate demand.

Marginal capital–output ratio (MCOR): the amount that has to be spent on capital to produce a given increase in annual output.

Marginal efficiency of investment (MEI): the rate of return on an additional unit of investment.

Marginal propensity to consume (MPC): the proportion of a change in income that is spent on consumption.

Marginal propensity to import (MPM): the proportion of a change in income that is spent on imports.

Marginal propensity to save (MPS): the proportion of a change in income that is saved.

Marginal propensity to tax (MPT): the proportion of a change in income that is taxed.

Market: all the buyers and sellers of a good or service.

Market failure: when if left to the market forces of supply and demand, there is an inefficient and/or inequitable allocation of resources.

Market forces: demand and supply, which determine the price and quantity sold of products in a market economy.

Market share: the percentage of an industry's sales accounted for by one or a few firms.

Market structure: the characteristics of an industry that affect the conduct of firms in that market.

Maximum price: the highest price that can be charged by law.

Means-tested: where entitlement to a payment depends on a person's income and/or wealth, and on his or her needs.

Medium of exchange: something not wanted for itself but to be used as a way of obtaining other goods and services.

Merit good: a product that society or government judges is desirable, too little is provided by the market for the benefit of society as a whole.

Microeconomics: the study of parts of the economy, including the behaviour of individuals, firms and industries.

Minimum price: the lowest price that can be charged by law.

Minimum wage: the lowest wage that can legally be paid to workers.

Misallocation of resources: the inefficient use of resources, where they are not put to their best or most effective use.

Missing market: where a market for a product does not exist.

Mixed economy: where some decisions about what to produce, how to produce it and who should benefit are taken by buyers and sellers, and some decisions are taken by the government.

Mobility of factors of production: the ability of resources to move from one place or type of work to another.

Monetarist economists: those who believe that inflation is always caused by the money supply increasing too quickly.

Monetary policy: the use of interest rates, the supply of money and the exchange rate to influence the economy and help the government achieve its objectives.

Monetary policy transmission mechanism: the ways in which monetary policy affects aggregate demand, inflation and economic activity..

Monopolistic competition: a market with a large number of small firms, selling similar but not identical products, and with few barriers to entry into and exit from the industry.

Monopoly: a market where one firm controls the supply of a good or service.

Monopoly power: the ability of a firm to influence price and output.

Multiplier: the extent to which a change in injections affects national income.

Myopic/myopia: short-sighted/shortsightness, focusing on the short-term effects rather than the longer-term consequences

N

National debt: the accumulated total of past government borrowing and the total amount of money that the government owes at a point in time.

National debt: the total amount the government owes. It is the accumulated total of the amount borrowed by the country's governments in previous years. It is the stock of outstanding government debt.

National income: the monetary value of all the goods and services that are produced by an economy in a given period of time.

Needs: goods and services required for people to survive.

Negative externalities/external costs: costs of consumption or production to third parties, for which they do not receive compensation.

Negative output gap: when the economy's equilibrium level of national income is less than its normal capacity level of national income.

Negative short-run economic growth: when real GDP is falling.

Neoclassical economists: those who believe that the market forces of supply and demand determine the allocation of resources, prices, output and the distribution of income. They also believe that market forces determine the level of national output, unemployment and economic growth.

Net exports: the value of exports minus the value of imports.

Net income from abroad: the income domestic residents earn from abroad *minus* the income earned by foreign residents from the domestic economy.

Net investment income: the difference between the amount of income domestic residents earn on their assets abroad and the amount of income paid to foreign residents on their assets in the domestic economy.

Nominal GDP (or money GDP): the monetary value of the total output of the economy without any adjustment for inflation.

Non-excludable: where non-payers cannot be prevented from using the product.

Non-price competition: using methods other than changes in price to outdo rival firms.

Non-renewable resources: resources that cannot be replaced naturally after use.

Non-rival in consumption: where consumption of a product by one person does not reduce the amount available to others.

Normal capacity level of output: the maximum output that an economy can continue to produce in the long run.

Normal good: a product where demand increases if income rises.

Normative statement: a statement based on a value judgement.

O

Obsolete: out of date and not used any more.

Occupational mobility of labour: when workers find it difficult to move from one type of job to another.

Official transfers: transfers made between countries by governments.

Oligopoly: a market where a small number of firms control the supply of a good or service.

Open economy: an economy that trades with other economies. There are exports and imports.

Opportunity cost: the next best alternative forgone.

Other things being equal (ceteris paribus): the assumption that nothing else changes.

Output gap: when the economy's equilibrium level of national income is not the same as its normal capacity level of national income.

P

Partial market failure: where a market exists for a product but it does not result in the socially optimum quantity being produced and consumed, causing a misallocation of resources.

Patent: a legal right to stop others from making or selling a new product for a number of years.

Paternalistic: where a government makes decisions for other people that it believes will benefit them.

Pattern of demand: the types of goods and services people buy.

Pattern of economic activity: how an economy's factors of production are allocated between different uses.

Perfect competition: a market with a large number of buyers and sellers, where products are identical, there is perfect information and there are no barriers to entry into or exit from the industry.

Perfect information: where anything that may affect a buyer's or seller's decision making is known and understood.

Policy instruments: tools the government can use to help it achieve its objectives.

Policy objectives: what the government is trying to achieve, or its aims.

Policy trade-off: the opportunity cost of achieving an improvement in a policy objective.

Polluter pays principle: the idea that those who cause the pollution should pay for the costs to others.

Pollution permits: licences or permits sold or allocated by a government to allow firms to emit a set quantity of pollution in a given time period.

Positive externalities/external benefits: benefits of consumption or production to third parties, for which they do not have to pay.

Positive output gap: when the economy's equilibrium level of national income is greater than its normal capacity level of national income.

Positive statement: a statement that can be tested against the facts or evidence.

Price elasticity of demand: a measure of the percentage change in quantity demanded as a result of a given percentage change in price, or simply, the responsiveness of quantity demanded to a change in price.

Price elasticity of supply: a measure of the percentage change in quantity supplied as a result of a given percentage change in price, or simply, the responsiveness of quantity supplied to a change in price.

Price level: the average price of all goods and services in an economy.

Price maker: a firm that has the power to set the price in the market.

Price mechanism: the way in which the prices of goods and services are determined by the free market forces of demand and supply.

Price taker: a firm that has to accept the price set by the market supply and demand.

Primary income: the flow of income from residents of one country to another in return for investment and labour services.

Primary sector: the part of the economy involved with extracting or acquiring raw materials.

Private benefits: the benefits to those involved in the transaction, the benefits to the firms and consumers involved.

Private costs: the costs to those involved in a transaction, the costs to the consumers and firms involved.

Private goods: products that are rival in consumption and excludable.

Private sector: the part of the economy not under government control.

Private transfers: transfers, or gifts, between countries made by private companies or individuals.

Privatisation: when a government-owned business is sold and becomes a private sector business.

Product differentiation: how firms make their goods and services appear different from other firms' products.

Production: turning inputs, such as raw materials, capital and labour, into final output.

Production externalities: effects on third parties due to the production of goods and services.

Production possibility boundary (also known as production possibility curve or production possibility frontier): a curve showing the quantities that can be produced of two goods or services with the current state of technology, when resources are fully used.

Productive efficiency: where it is not possible to produce more of one good or service without producing less of another.

Productive efficiency for a firm: where average costs are minimised, the lowest point of the AC curve.

Productivity: how much a factor of production produces in a given time.

Profit: total revenue minus total cost.

Profit margin: profit as a percentage of the price of the product.

Profit maximisation: producing where total revenue minus total cost is greatest.

Progressive tax: where, as income rises, so does the percentage of income paid in tax.

Property rights: the authority to determine how a resource is used. The ownership of land, sea, air or any resource on or within it.

Proportional tax: when the percentage of income taken in tax is the same at all levels of income.

Protectionism: a government policy of protecting domestic firms by restricting imports using tariffs, quotas, subsidies and regulations.

Public expenditure: spending by the government, which may be by central or local government.

Public goods: products that are non-rival in consumption and non-excludable.

Public sector: the part of the economy under government control.

Pure monopoly: when there is only one firm in the market.

Q

Quantitative easing: when the central bank makes large scale purchases of government and/or corporate bonds.

Quantitative tightening: when the central bank sells its holdings of government bonds.

Quasi-public good: when a public good has some characteristics of a private good.

Quota: a limit on the number or value of a product that can be imported.

R

Rate of interest: the price of money, which is the cost of borrowing and the reward for saving.

Rate of return: the profit expressed as a percentage of the cost of the project.

Rational behaviour: that people will consider alternative choices and make decisions that will provide them with the most benefit, welfare or satisfaction.

Rationing function: the allocation of scarce resources and finished goods to those able and willing to pay.

Real GDP per capita: the average, or mean, real GDP per person.

Real rate of interest: the rate of interest after the effects of inflation have been removed.

Real terms: when the effects of inflation have been removed from the economic variable.

Real wages: nominal, or money, wages after the effects of inflation have been removed.

Recession: when total output of the economy is falling and unemployment is rising.

Recycling: the process of recovering and changing waste materials into materials that can be used again.

Reflationary policies: measures used by the government to increase aggregate demand.

Regressive tax: where, as income rises, the percentage of income paid in tax falls.

Regulation: rules or laws that control the behaviour and activities of individuals and firms.

Regulatory capture: the idea that regulatory agencies may operate in the industry's interest rather than in the interest of the consumers they are trying to protect.

Relative prices: the price of one good compared to another.

Relative rate of inflation: the rate of inflation in one country compared to the rate of inflation in other countries.

Renewable resources: resources that can be replaced naturally after a period of time.

Replacement investment: investment to replace capital that is worn out or obsolete.

Replacement ratio: the income received when unemployed as a ratio of the income received when in work.

Research and development (R&D): using resources to design new or improved products.

Reserve ratio: the ratio between the amount of liquid assets a bank holds and its deposits.

Retaliation: when a country imposes tariffs, or other restrictions, on the exports of a country in response to that country imposing tariffs, or other restrictions, on its exports.

Rival in consumption: where consumption of a product by one person reduces the amount available to others.

S

Savings ratio: household savings as a percentage of household disposable income.

Scarce resources: factors of production that are limited in supply; there are not enough to satisfy our wants.

Seasonal unemployment: when people are unemployed at particular times of the year.

Secondary income: money transferred from the residents of one country to another without any goods or services given in return.

Secondary sector: the part of the economy involved with construction or manufacturing.

Self-interest: focusing on your own needs and wants.

Self-sufficient: providing for your own needs.

Short run: the time period when at least one factor of production is fixed in supply.

Shortage/excess demand: where demand is greater than supply at a given price.

Signalling function: the idea that changes in price provide information to buyers and sellers in a market.

Social benefits: the benefits or beneficial effects to those involved in the transaction and to any third parties affected.

Social costs: the costs or harmful effects to those involved in the transaction and to any third parties affected.

Social optimum: the quantity that maximises social welfare and reflects the social costs and benefits of an activity.

Social science: the study of society and the relationships between individuals in society.

Spare capacity: where a firm, or an economy, has some resources not fully employed.

Specialisation: where different firms, regions, countries or factors of production concentrate on the production of different goods or services.

Specific (tax or subsidy): based on the quantity, not the price of the good or service.

Speculation: the buying or selling of an asset to make a profit, by predicting that the price will rise or fall in the future.

Standard of living: the ability of people to satisfy their needs and wants, including health care and education.

Stimulate the economy: measures to increase aggregate demand and economic activity.

Stocks or inventory: products that firms have in store, they could be raw materials, semi-finished or finished goods.

Structural budget balance: the underlying budget deficit or surplus after the effects of cyclical fluctuations in economic activity upon government spending and taxation have been removed.

Structural budget deficit: when government expenditure is greater than taxation after the effects of cyclical fluctuations in economic activity on government spending and taxation have been removed.

Structural unemployment: long-term unemployment that occurs when the skills and location of the unemployed workers do not match the jobs available.

Subsidy: a payment to producers to reduce costs and increase supply.

Substitute goods or goods in competitive demand: alternative products – if the price of one good increases, so will demand for the other. They are in competitive demand.

Supply: the quantity that firms are able and willing to sell at a given price in a given period of time.

Supply of credit: the total value of loans outstanding (loans that have not yet been repaid).

Supply of money: the total amount of money in circulation in an economy, it includes notes, coins and bank deposits.

Supply-side improvements: increases in productivity and reductions in costs that improve efficiency, productive capacity and competitiveness.

Supply-side policies: measures to increase economic incentives, make markets work better and increase the productive capacity of the economy.

Supply-side shock: an event that leads to a sudden or unexpected change in aggregate supply.

Surplus (on the balance of payments): the money coming into the country is greater than the money going out, or credits are greater than debits.

Surplus/excess supply: where supply is greater than demand at a given price.

T

Targets of monetary policy: the variables that the central bank tries to influence in order to achieve its monetary policy objectives.

Tariff: an indirect tax on imports.

Tariff: a tax on imports.

Taxation: money that must be paid to the government by individuals or firms.

Tax incidence: how the tax is distributed between buyer and seller.

Technical economies: a fall in average costs due to the production process being carried out on a larger scale.

Technical recession: when an economy has two consecutive quarters of negative growth of real GDP.

Technological unemployment: a type of structural unemployment that is caused by developments in technology.

Tertiary sector: the part of the economy that provides services.

Tighten monetary policy: monetary policy measures that reduce aggregate demand. The same as contractionary monetary policy.

Time lag: a period of time between one event and another.

Total costs: all the costs of a business, fixed costs plus variable costs.

Total revenue: income from sales, calculated as price × quantity sold.

Trade-off: where two things cannot be achieved at the same time, one must be sacrificed for another.

Trade war: two or more countries imposing tariffs, or other restrictions, on each other's exports.

Tragedy of the commons: where individuals act in their own self-interest and this results in the depletion (using up) or degradation (damage) of a shared resource.

Transferable skills: skills and abilities that can be used in many different jobs and industries.

Transfer payments: money paid to an individual without a service having been provided, for example money taken from tax-payers and given, by the government, to people receiving welfare benefits.

Transnational company: a business that operates in more than one country.

U

Unconventional monetary policy: measures used by central banks when the usual instruments of monetary policy are ineffective.

Underemployment: when a person is working but would like to work more hours, or is overqualified for his or her job and has skills that are not fully used.

Underlying rate of economic growth: the annual percentage increase in the productive capacity of an economy.

Unearned income: income from the ownership of property or other assets, not from employment.

Unemployed: people who are out of work and actively seeking work.

Unemployment: the total number of people who are willing and able to work but who cannot to find a job.

Unemployment rate: the percentage of the labour force that is unemployed.

Unintended consequence: an unexpected effect of an action.

V

Value added: the difference between the value of an industry's output and the value of the inputs it buys from other firms.

Value judgement: a view about what is right or wrong, good or bad, in a moral sense.

Value of exports: the amount spent on exports, determined by the price and quantity.

Variable costs: costs that change with output – as output rises, so do variable costs.

Volume of exports: the quantity of exports.

Voluntary unemployment: when there are jobs available but people are not willing to work at current market wage rates.

W

Wage-push inflation: a type of cost-push inflation that starts with an increase in workers' wages.

Wants: goods and services that people would like but are not required for them to survive.

Wealth: a stock of assets owned by an economic agent at a point in time.

Wealth effect: the effect of a change in wealth on aggregate demand.

Weight: a way to reflect the relative importance of each item in an index.

Welfare: the satisfaction or utility obtained from consuming goods and services, which contributes to the standard of living and happiness of an individual or group.

Welfare benefits: money paid by the state to people on low incomes.

Withdrawal (or leakage): part of household income that is not spent on goods and services produced by the economy.

Answers

1.1 – Progress Questions, Case Studies

Progress Questions

1. The central purpose of economic activity is to produce goods and services to satisfy people's needs and wants.
2. Examples of economic activity – two of: production, distribution or consumption. Or two examples of one of these is also acceptable, such as making tables and cars.
3. Utility.
4. Example of inputs – two of workers/labour, equipment/raw materials/ capital, land or someone to organise/entrepreneur. Or two examples of one of these is acceptable, such as land for farming and land for factories.
5. Primary = **i.** drilling for oil, **v.** growing coconuts, **vii.** fishing; Secondary = **iii.** making tyres for a car, **iv.** working in a car-assembly factory, **viii.** building a hotel; Tertiary = **ii.** driving a taxi, **vi.** working as a market trader, **ix.** working as a hotel cleaner.

Case Studies

Time for tea?

1. 394,778 tonnes. (Halfway between the 3rd and 4th values of 439,857 and 349,699 or add these two numbers and divide by 2.)
2. 847,008.2 tonnes. (5,082,049 divided by 6.)

Is automation taking over?

1. Advantages include: it is quicker, cheaper, easier and safer; there is more consistency and higher quality.

   Disadvantages include: it is expensive to develop and buy the equipment, it is only worthwhile when making large quantities, workers lose jobs.
2. The jobs most likely to be replaced are where a similar product is made or a similar service is provided. In recent years, online banking and self-service tills in shops have reduced the number of people working in supermarkets and banks. A machine can probably be developed to carry out the work. The jobs least likely to be replaced are where every activity is different, for example services involving people. A machine would find it difficult to cover all the possible situations. For example, with people living longer in many countries, more carers are required to look after people.

1.2 – Progress Questions, Case Study

Progress Questions

1. Economic resources are also known as inputs or factors of production.
2. Land = **ii.** a field used to grow sorghum, **v.** an oilfield, **vii.** fish in the sea, **x.** clean air; Labour = **iii.** a bicycle-shop assistant, **iv.** a coal miner; Capital = **i.** a car factory, **viii.** a sweet-packing machine, **ix.** a parcel-delivery van; Enterprise = **vi.** a person who owns a window-cleaning business.

Case Study

Fish stocks

1. 87.5%.
2. For fish to be a renewable resource, they must be replaced naturally to keep up the total number. If too many fish are caught, there may not be enough left to breed to replace them. The fish must not become too depleted or at some point, none will be left. They will have run out, like a non-renewable resource. The case study suggests that this has been happening with tuna and jack mackerel with their stocks falling by 87.5% and 63% in the years covered. However, the recovery in stocks of large tuna between 2010 and 2016 shows that it may be possible to reverse the depletion.
3. Solutions include: more international agreements, including more countries; limits on how many of certain types of fish can be caught; rules on how fish can be caught and how large nets can be, so only larger fish are caught; better enforcement or higher fines, if laws are broken; increased awareness of the problem so consumers may stop buying certain fish or expect certain quality standards to have been met – for example, the blue fish tick in Australia and New Zealand.

1.3 – Progress Questions

Progress Questions

1. The basis economic problem is that scarce resources are not enough to satisfy our wants.
2. Choice is necessary because resources have alternative uses and/or people do not have enough money to satisfy all their wants (and whatever people have, they will always want more).
3. **i.** food; **ii.** the visit to the museum.

1.4 – Progress Questions, Case Study

Progress Questions

1. **i.** 4 Swifts (10 − 6); **ii.** 6 Swifts (6 − 0).
2. **i.** 10 cakes (30 − 20); **ii.** 34 buns (76 − 42); **iii.** 76 buns (76 − 0); **iv.** 10 cakes (50 − 40).
3. **i.** 60 buns (60 − 0); **ii.** 2 buns (constant opportunity cost of 1 cake to 2 buns); **iii.** 20 cakes (40 − 20); **iv.** 0.5 cakes (constant opportunity cost of 1 cake to 2 buns or 0.5 cakes to 1 bun).

Case Study

Bravo Bicycles

1. Any combination listed in the table is correct; for example, 13 Cheetahs and 24 Swifts. (To be productively efficient, it must be any combination of the two types of bicycle that is on the PPB.)
2. Bravo Bicycles may produce 10 Cheetahs and 20 Swifts because there is not enough demand for all the resources to be fully used.
3. Bravo Bicycles does not have a straight-line PPB. The PPB is concave. The opportunity cost increases as the output of one type of bicycle rises.
4. The firm may have moved to a smaller workshop or be operating with fewer workers, perhaps due to a lack of demand.

1.5 – Progress Questions, Exam-style Questions

Progress Questions

Positive = 1 and 4; Normative = 2, 3 and 5.

Exam-style Questions

1. D. When 1 bar of milk chocolate is produced, 9 bars of plain can also be made. When output of milk rises to 2 bars, plain output falls to 5 bars; 4 bars of plain have been forgone.
2. B. Capital is a human-made factor of production.
3. Value judgement is a view about what is right or wrong, good or bad, in a moral sense.
4. **i.** 8%. The median is 7.9%, halfway between the two middle values of 6.9% and 8.9%; **ii.** 9.6%. $\frac{57.4}{6} = 9.566$.
5. It is always useful to define relevant terms such as production possibility diagram, PPB and (increasing) opportunity cost. This can be done at the start, or when the terms are first used. You should draw a diagram like Figure 1.4.2, with the PPB bulging out (concave) to the origin. Ideally, you should label three different combinations of the two goods. You can then quote figures to show that increasingly more of one good is given up as the other is increased. This could be linked with the idea that some resources may be better suited to the production of one good than the other. An example would help to reinforce this point.

2.1 – Progress Questions, Case Study

Progress Questions

1. A movement along is caused by a change in the price of that good. A shift is caused by a change in any other factor affecting demand except a change in the price of that good.
2. Goods in joint demand.
3. Left. An increase in income reduces demand for inferior goods.

Case Study

Changes in China's automotive market
1 Substitute goods or goods in competitive demand.
2 Diagram involves shifting the demand curve to the left, as in Figure 2.1.4.

2.2 – Progress Questions, Case Study

Progress Questions

1 Negative. Price and quantity demanded change in opposite directions. For example, if price falls, quantity demanded rises.
2 Fall. The percentage rise in price is less than the percentage fall in quantity demanded.
3 +15%. −3 = % Δ in QD/−5, so % Δ in QD = −3 × −5.
4 Normal good. For example, a 10% rise in income may have caused a 3% rise in demand for the product.
5 Joint demand (another term for complementary goods). For example, a 20% rise in the price of one good may have caused a 6% fall in demand for the other.
6 High YED. YED is a measure of the responsiveness of quantity demanded to a change in income. Emerging economies will generally have rising incomes. The higher the value of YED, the more demand for the product will increase for a given percentage increase in income. This should increase the total revenue, and hopefully profit, of the firm.

Case Study

The price of postcards
1 −10/+20 = −0.5.
2 (120 LKR × 900) − (100 LKR × 1,000) = 8000 LKR increase (per week).
3 Inelastic. The value of PED is between -1 and zero and as price rose, so did total revenue.

2.3 – Progress Questions, Case Study

Progress Questions

1 It is usually assumed that firms try to maximise profit. Higher prices will encourage firms to supply more because they will receive more revenue from sales. Profit is total revenue minus total cost. If the extra revenue from sales is greater than the extra cost of producing more units, the firms will make more profit. So, as price rises, so does quantity supplied.
2 Increase. A subsidy is a payment from the government. This will reduce firms' costs and enable them to supply more.

Case Study

Problems hit Madagascar's vanilla crop
1 A shift of the supply curve to the left. There will be less supply available at each price.
2 Diagram involves shifting the supply curve to the left, as in Figure 2.3.4. Vanilla is a raw material for food products. Higher costs will mean that the firms will offer their food at a higher price.

2.4 – Progress Questions, Case Study

Progress Questions

1 Elastic. A value of PES greater than 1 shows elastic supply
2 An increase of 4.5%. If it is perfectly inelastic, supply stays the same when price changes. The revenue will therefore change by the same percentage as price.
3 −20%. 0.3 = −6/% Δ in P, so % Δ in P = 6/−0.3.

Case Study

Gepetto's toys
1 Increase production and price if he can. At a higher price, he will receive more income for the same quantity, making more profit. If he can increase production as well, his revenue will rise even more. As long as the cost of producing the extra toys is not higher than the extra revenue he receives from selling them, his profit will increase further.
2 How easily and quickly Gepetto can increase his supply of wooden toys. Relevant factors include:

- Spare capacity: Would his part-time worker be willing to work for more than 3 days a week? Would Gepetto be willing to work longer hours? Is there enough space in his workshop?
- State of the economy: Could Gepetto find another skilled worker or how long would they take to train? This may depend on whether he thinks the demand and prices will keep rising. Can he easily obtain more wood and other materials? Has the cost of the wood also increased?
- Availability of stock: Has Gepetto any toys in stock? If so, he could sell these at the higher price.
- Nature of the product: How long do the toys take to make? Can he easily increase the number he has for sale?
- Time: The longer the time period, the more changes can be made. For example, Gepetto could consider buying more machinery to speed up the production process or even move to a larger workshop.

2.5 – Progress Questions, Case Studies

Progress Questions

1 i. no change in price but the quantity sold increases.
   ii. no change in quantity sold but price increases.
   iii. both price and quantity sold increase.
2 Price. The demand for oil is likely to be inelastic, at least in the short run. If in doubt, draw an inelastic demand curve (D_i in Figure 2.5.8) and check what happens as supply shifts to the left. The percentage increase in price is greater than the percentage fall in quantity sold.
3 Rise. This is because demand will rise/shift to the right, as in Figure 2.5.4.
4 Fall. The increase in costs because of the higher wages are more than offset by the higher productivity, so costs (of labour) will fall. This will increase supply/shift supply to the right.

Case Studies

The market for strawberries
1 Diagram should have P(€) on the vertical axis and Q(kg) on the horizontal. D is a straight line sloping down to the right, from 12kg at €1 to 2kg at €6. Supply is a straight line sloping up to the right, from 2kg at €1 to 12kg at €6.
2 €3.50 and 7kg.
3 Excess supply of 6kg. Supply is 10kg at €6 but demand is only 4kg. They would be left with unsold strawberries at the end of the day if the price stays at €6. They should reduce their price which will lead to an extension of demand.
4 There is excess demand of 6kg. Demand is 10kg and their supply is 4kg. They will soon run out of strawberries and should increase their price.

Tulip mania
1 i. 12; ii. 1,100%; iii. 8.3%.
2 Example: the house price bubble in the US in the early 21st century. In the first few years of the 21st century, house prices in the US started to rise rapidly. A number of factors contributed to this. Most houses are bought using a mortgage/loan against the property. In 2001, interest rates fell to 1%, to help the US economy recover after the dotcom bubble. This made it cheaper to borrow. Many people, including those on low incomes bought houses (sometimes called the sub-prime market), often at a low starting interest rate. This increased demand for houses and raised their price. This rise in house prices encouraged even more people to buy houses. Those who had borrowed money could afford to pay their mortgage if interest rates stayed low and they still had jobs. Once the introductory rate of interest rose to its normal rate, an increasing number of people were unable to pay the interest on their loans and had to sell their homes. House prices had risen faster than incomes and had become overvalued. Demand fell and supply increased. House sales fell 13% in the year to March 2007 and the sub-prime lending market collapsed.

2.6 – Progress Questions, Case Study

Progress Questions

1 Diagram involves a shift of supply to the right, as in Figure 2.5.6: "An increase in supply". This will reduce the price of bus travel and increase the quantity sold.
2 Bus travel and cars are substitutes, so this is likely to lead to a fall in demand and a fall in the price of cars. As a result, the quantity sold of cars is likely to fall.

Case Study

The Kenyan flower industry

1 **i.** gift cards and flowers. These items may be packed together as part of the bouquet.

ii. two types of flower, for example lilies and roses. These are alternative flowers for bouquets.

iii. the workers, the land used for growing the flowers, the packaging shed or any factor of production involved in producing the flowers.

2 1:5. There are roughly 100,000:500,000 in total.

3 200. For 100,000 working on flower farms, there are 500,000 in the flower industry in total. For every worker on flower farms, there are 4 more in the flower industry.

2.7 – Progress Questions, Case Study, Exam-style Questions

Progress Questions

1 Rationing, signalling and incentive.

2 Advantages include: automatic allocation of resources and consumer sovereignty. Disadvantages include some goods and services are not produced and some people cannot afford basic necessities. See Table 2.7.1 for other acceptable answers.

Case Study

Magnificent Margaret

The new shape of birthday card was more popular than expected. At the original price, there was excess demand. The shop, with Margaret's agreement, then raised the price. This **signalled** to buyers that something in the market had changed. The higher price acted as a **rationing** device, since some buyers were unable and/or unwilling to pay the higher price. The higher price would have brought both Margaret and the shop owner more money/profit and provided an **incentive** to sell more.

Exam-style Questions

1 D. An increase in demand for pineapples will shift demand to the right, resulting in an extension of supply.

2 D. A fall in the quantity demanded for rice will increase demand for pasta/shift demand to the right, raising the equilibrium price and quantity sold.

3 B. If price rises and total revenue rises by a different percentage, demand must be inelastic but not perfectly inelastic.

4 Demand and supply, which determine the price and quantity sold of products in a market economy.

5 1.2. (18/15)

6 **i.** Washo and Cleano are substitute goods/in competitive demand. They are alternative products. For example, if the price of Washo increases and Cleano's price stays the same, fewer people will buy Washo. There will be a decrease in demand for Washo. The price of Cleano is now relatively cheaper and so more people will buy Cleano instead. There will be an increase in demand for Cleano and sales of Cleano will increase. One or more diagrams could be drawn to support the written explanation. For example, a demand curve for Washo showing a contraction of demand if price rises and/or a demand and supply diagram for Cleano, showing an increase in demand increasing sales.

ii. Some of the points that might be made include:

- Price of Washo and sales of Cleano peaked in same year – $6/kg and 2.4m kg in 2019
- Sales of Cleano lowest in both 2015 and 2018. In 2015, price of Washo also at its lowest, at $4/kg, but price was higher than this, at $4.75, in 2018
- In three of the four time periods, price of Washo and sales of Cleano moved in same direction. For example, 2015 to 2016, price of Washo rose from $4 to $4.50/kg and sales of Cleano rose from 2 to 2.3m kg. However, from 2016 to 2017, the price of Washo rose from $4.50 to $5 but sales of Cleano fell from 2.3 to 2.2m kg
- Overall, changes in price of Washo seem to have some effect on sales of Cleano but not the only factor
- For example, when price of Washo increased in 2017 but sales of Cleano dropped, this may have been due to successful advertising campaign for Washo
- Although Washo and Cleano are the two main brands of washing powder, another brand may be becoming more popular, so when price of Washo increases, more people switch to that brand instead of Cleano

7 Copper is a raw material used to make pipes. Copper is in derived demand for copper pipes. If the price of copper falls, this will reduce the cost of making copper pipes. This will increase the supply of copper pipes/shift the supply curve to the right. (Draw a diagram showing a shift of S to the right, as in Figure 2.5.6.) There will be excess supply at the old equilibrium price of p_1. Price will tend to fall. This will cause a contraction of supply as sellers are likely to make less profit and there will be an extension of demand as buyers are more able and willing to buy copper pipes at a lower price. The market will reach a new equilibrium of p_2 where q_2 is sold. (Labels should match the diagram.) As a result of the fall in the price of copper, there will be a fall in the price of copper pipes and an increase in the quantity sold.

8 Wool is in composite demand. It has a number of different uses, including to make woollen coats and woollen carpets. If there is an increase in popularity of woollen coats, this will increase their demand and raise their price. (A diagram showing the increase in demand for woollen coats could be drawn at this point and/or left until discussing the effects on the demand for wool.) This higher price will act as an incentive for producers to make more woollen coats available for sale. In order to produce more coats, they will need more wool, so there will also be an increase in demand for wool. (A diagram showing the effects of an increase in demand for wool, as in Figure 2.5.4, could be drawn and analysed at this point.) This will raise the price of wool. The higher price of wool will increase the cost of making woollen carpets, decreasing supply/shifting the supply curve to the left. (It could be helpful to draw and analyse another diagram here, showing the effects of a decrease in supply, as in Figure 2.5.7.). This will raise the price of woollen carpets and fewer will be sold.

3.1 – Progress Questions, Case Studies

Progress Questions

1 The natural environment provides inputs for the productive process, such as raw materials and food. It sustains economic activity. The environment can also be damaged by productive activity, for example through pollution.

2 Production is the total output, regardless of inputs. Productivity is where the amount produced is related to the inputs – how much is produced by a unit of a factor of production.

Case Studies

Palm oil – good or bad?

1 5. (10 times as much oil is obtained from palm trees than sunflowers but with only half the area used, there is only 5 times as much in total)

2 Advantages include:
- palm oil has many uses (+ examples)
- palm oil is more productive than other crops (+ evidence)
- there is a growing population and increased demand.

Disadvantages include:
- loss of habitat for animals
- increased danger of fires (+ other problems of this)
- having less forest to help with clean air.

3 Oil from soybeans and palm oil are substitute goods, so if there is a greater demand for palm oil, there will be less demand for soybeans. The diagram involves shift of demand to the left/a decrease in demand, as in Figure 2.5.5. As a result, there will be a fall in both the equilibrium market price and quantity sold of soybeans.

4 Your answer needs to weigh up pros and cons of palm oil, perhaps expanding advantages and disadvantages listed in answer to 2 and what the effects depend on. Other considerations include who gains and who loses. For example, there are growers and countries relying on palm oil for their income. Are there any health concerns for palm oil as well as other oils? If action is needed, what could be done and how likely is this to be successful? For example, there could be limits on the amount of land that can be used for growing trees for palm oil. How well will limits be enforced and what are the penalties for breaking the law? You need to reach a conclusion, supported by evidence.

The amazing growth of maize

1 Reasons include: better equipment; more productive varieties of maize; the use of more and/or better fertiliser; the use of pesticides; more irrigation; improved farming techniques/knowledge.

2 185%.

3 390,000,000 tonnes.

3.2 – Progress Questions, Case Study

Progress Questions

1   Specialisation is where different firms, regions, countries or factors of production concentrate on the production of different goods or services. It is a general term and when it involves the concentration of the factor of production labour on specific tasks, it is given the term division of labour.

2   Advantages of specialisation include:
   * being able to take advantage of natural resources and other strengths
   * gaining a larger market
   * receiving higher income
   * creating more jobs
   * more efficient use of resources.

   Disadvantages of specialisation include:
   * resources may run out
   * prices may fall
   * the country is more vulnerable to changes in demand.

3   Advantages of division of labour (which could be for the workers, the firms or consumers) include:
   * production is quicker
   * average cost is lower
   * consumers benefit from firms' reduced prices.

   Disadvantages of division of labour include:
   * workers becoming bored
   * workers having few skills to offer in other jobs
   * interdependence.

4   A medium of exchange, or money, is necessary; also, a good transport and communication system.

Case Study

Division of labour – how far to go?

1   Advantages include: jobs are less boring, there is more variety of work and more job satisfaction, so there is lower absenteeism and labour turnover; workers gain more skills; workers can cover for each other if necessary.

2   Disadvantages include: more training time is needed; team members might not work well together; what if some team members work harder than others?

3   Your answer needs to weigh up advantages and disadvantages of working in teams, perhaps expanding advantages and disadvantages listed in answers to 1 and 2 and what the effects depend on. You might mention the cost of different methods. Other considerations include the nature of the activity. Do some activities lend themselves more to teamwork? What is the best size for a team and what does this depend on? For evidence, you might use the comment that about 80% of the world's work is done by teams – this suggests that on balance, teamwork may be better than having people working individually.

3.3 – Progress Questions, Case Studies

Progress Questions

1   In the short run, at least one factor of production is fixed in supply. In the long run, all factors of production are variable.

2   i. rent, interest on loans or any other cost that does not change with output; ii. raw materials, packaging costs, electricity or any other cost that increases with output.

3   $10,000. Fixed costs of 20 × $500, with no variable costs.

4   FC + VC or AC × Q or (AFC + AVC) × Q

5   i. $22,000; ii. $220.

Case Studies

Sven's TT bats (part one)

1

Output (units)	FC (€)	AFC (€)	VC (€)	AVC (€)
0	1,000		0	
100	1,000	10	2,500	25
200	1,000	5	4,000	20
300	1,000	3.33	5,250	17.5
400	1,000	2.50	6,000	15
500	1,000	2	8,000	16

2   i. AFC will start at €10 for 100 units and then fall, steeply at first and then less steeply; and AVC will start at €25 for 100 units and then fall, rising slightly at the end. ii. FC will be a horizontal line at €1,000; and VC will start at 0 for 0 units and then increase, with a falling gradient, then more steeply again at the end.

Sven's TT bats (part two)

Output (units)	TC (€)	AC (€)
0	1,000	
100	3,500	35
200	5,000	25
300	6,250	20.83
400	7,000	17.5
500	9,000	18

3.4 – Progress Questions, Case Study

Progress Questions

1   Internal economies of scale are a fall in long-run average costs due to the growth of the firm. External economies of scale are a fall in long-run average costs of the firm due to the growth of the industry.

2   i. greater use of large pieces of equipment; more division of labour. ii. lower advertising costs per unit; bulk buying.

3   Examples of external economies are: training courses provided by local colleges; having related firms nearby; the benefits of joint research.

4   Growth may increase a firm's average costs because it is more difficult to coordinate the activities of different departments; communication is more time-consuming; workers' morale may be low.

Case Study

Silicon Valley

1   The case study is mainly discussing external economies and diseconomies of scale.

2   The area has: local universities and training colleges to supply skilled workers; suppliers nearby; networking opportunities with other firms; research facilities.

3   There are: shortages of key workers – so firms need to offer high pay; high house prices – another reason why pay may need to be high; high costs to buy or rent office and factory space.

3.5 – Progress Questions, Case Study, Exam-style Questions

Progress Questions

1   (TR – TC) ÷ Q or AR – AC.

2   The average revenue (AR) curve is the same as the demand curve.

3   There will be a loss of $50. (TR – TC = $200 – $250)

Case Study

Sven's TT bats (part three)

1

Quantity	AC (€)	AR (€)	TC (€)	TR (€)	Profit (€)
100	5.50	6	550	600	50
200	5	5.75	1,000	1,150	150
300	4.80	5.50	1,440	1,650	210
400	4.75	5.25	1,900	2,100	200

2   €5.50 and 300.

Exam-style Questions

1   C. In the short run, as extra units of variable factors of production are added, AVC may fall and then rise. Initially the cost of fixed factors is more spread but then there will be increasing pressure on them if more units of the variable factor are employed. In the long run, there could be economies or diseconomies of scale. This is true in either time period.

2   B. Something like money is needed for workers to be paid for their labour and to obtain the full range of goods and services that they need or want.

3   Division of labour is when a worker performs one task or a narrow range of tasks.

4   **i.** $12 $\left(\frac{\$600}{50}\right)$. **ii.** $5 (profit = TR – TC, so TC = $1100, this makes AC $11 and with AFC = $6, AVC is the remaining $5).

5   One way to start would be with definitions of long run and average costs. Since the question is about the long run, it will involve the effects of economies and diseconomies of scale. You should define or explain these with examples of different types or reasons, perhaps applied to specific businesses. A diagram of a U-shaped LRAC (for example, Figure 3.4.3) would help to illustrate this, including reference to the LRAC for different output levels.

6   Indicative content is given below. You should also try to include relevant references to data from the case study to support points.
   • what is meant by an expanding industry, perhaps with reference to Silicon Valley and IT and innovation
   • the benefits of a localised industry in terms of external economies of scale and specific examples
   • other advantages of a successful expanding industry in terms of jobs, sales both at home and abroad, incomes, tax revenue from incomes and firms' profits
   • disadvantages in terms of external diseconomies of scale, including specific examples (you could refer to a U-shaped LRAC curve)
   • whether economies of scale are likely to outweigh diseconomies if localised; how much localisation would help – this may depend on nature of industry
   • what government could do to help to establish an expanding industry in a growing area, for example spend money on infrastructure and other ways of attracting firms to the area
   • which industries it should support
   • the cost and opportunity cost of this money – whether is it worth it and other priorities
   • whether the money spent by government might be returned in the form of higher tax revenue if successful
   • whether government needs to spend this money – or an expanding industry would establish without intervention
   • an overall assessment of whether or not a government should intervene.

4.1 – Progress Questions, Case Study

Progress Questions

1   The three main characteristics are number of firms, degree of product differentiation and ease of entry into the market.

2   The four types of market structure are perfect competition, monopolistic competition, oligopoly and monopoly.

3   It will decrease the cross elasticity of demand for a product. If there is more product differentiation, the products are less likely to be good substitutes. A fall in the price of one, for example, is likely to reduce demand for the other by less than before.

Case Study

The smartphone market

1   Oligopoly best describes the smartphone market. A small number of firms is controlling the supply of the good or service; there are a few firms with significant market shares. (Alternatively, it could be argued that the characteristics of the other three types of market structure do not apply as well.)

2   Smartphone companies may differentiate through: a phone's number of features and/or quality of features; the length of contract and/or whether the phone is bought; image created through advertising; product design and styling.

3   Specialist equipment and staff may be difficult or expensive to obtain; money will be needed for research and development of new features; a firm will need to advertise to become known against established brands.

4.2 – Progress Questions, Case Study

Progress Questions

1   Increasing its market share may increase a firm's power in the market. This may enable it to make more profit in the long run.

2   Examples of firms' objectives are: maximising profits; survival; growth; job satisfaction; social objectives, for example giving profits to charity.

3   The main objective of firms is often assumed to be profit maximisation.

Case Study

Ecosia

1   44.

2   The project may provide jobs planting trees; food will be available from fruit or nut trees planted; there will be better soils improving crop yields; more income will be generated.

3   The extent to which Ecosia's use of profits for tree planting will encourage people to use its search engine will depend on people's values. To what extent do people think tree planting is important? Do they know that Ecosia does this? Are there any differences in using Ecosia rather than other search engines? For example, is Ecosia's search engine easy to install and use?

4   Objectives may include: covering costs in order to survive; growth; increasing market share; further differentiating and promoting the search engine to achieve these objectives; innovation or improvements in Ecosia to attract more customers.

4.3 – Progress Questions, Case Study

Progress Questions

1   There is perfect knowledge, so there is no need to advertise.

2   If there are low barriers to entry, it is easy for other firms to come into the market. If there is good market information, firms that are considering entering the market will know about the price being charged and what profits can be made. If firms are making high profits, other firms will become aware of this and be able to enter the market to take advantage of the situation. This will increase supply, lower prices and reduce profits. Firms will not be able to maintain high profits.

3   This means that demand is inelastic and will fall by 5%, which is less than the rise in price. If the firm increases its price by 10%, total revenue will rise, which suggests that profits are likely to rise.

Case Study

Central de Abasto – the largest market in the world

It has large numbers of buyers and sellers, with each being a very small percentage of the total market, so unlikely that any buyer or seller can influence price. Largely homogeneous goods are offered, with many suppliers selling identical products, for example potatoes of the same type, size and quality. There may be nothing to stop sellers entering or leaving the market but there is no information about how much it costs to have a stall there. It is likely that most buyers and sellers will be well informed, for example about the price of particular products. Overall, it mainly seems to have the characteristics of a perfectly competitive market.

4.4 – Progress Questions, Case Studies

Progress Questions

1   A pure monopoly is when there is only one firm in the market. Monopoly power is the ability of a firm to influence price and output. A pure monopoly will have monopoly power but a firm does not need to be a pure monopoly to have some monopoly power.

2   **i., iv.** and **v.** = decrease; **ii.** and **iii.** = increase.

3   A monopolist is limited by the market demand. If it chooses a particular price, the market will set the quantity that will be sold at this price. If it chooses the quantity it wishes to sell, it will have to accept what the market will pay for this quantity.

4   Advantages include: economies of scale, lower prices and more invention and innovation. Disadvantages include: higher prices, inefficiency and a misallocation of resources.

5   The firm may benefit from lower costs, greater sales and higher profits if the research and development is successful. It may also make it more difficult for new firms to enter the market. Consumers may benefit from a wider range and/or better products and maybe lower prices. Owners and shareholders may benefit from higher profits and dividends.

Case Studies

Flights to Shetland

1   Loganair has a pure monopoly if the market is considered to be flights to Shetland, since no other firm offers this service. If the market is considered to be travel to Shetland, the answer is no, since people can travel by ferry.

2 There is only one firm flying to Shetland but there is competition/two firms offering flights from Barcelona to Madrid. If Loganair increases its prices, most people will still continue to fly with this firm. If one of the firms offering flights between Barcelona and Madrid increases its prices, people may switch to the other firm. There may also be alternative ways of going from Barcelona to Madrid, such as by train or car, whereas a long trip on a ferry is the only alternative way to go to Shetland.

The market for gasoline in Japan

1 **i.** 57.7%; **ii.** 83.3%.

2 **i.** 71.9%; **ii.** 83.3%.

3 The initial concentration ratios, both for three and five firms, are high, and the market will be more concentrated after a merger between two of the four largest firms, which increases the three-firm concentration ratio to 71.9%. The number of firms and their market shares suggest that they will have some monopoly power. There are also likely to be barriers to entry into this market, such as economies of scale, making it difficult for new firms to enter. However, the products are similar or identical unless firms can differentiate their products through advertising. The limited product differentiation will reduce the firms' monopoly power, but if the firms work together, this could give them more power over the market.

4.5 – Progress Questions, Case Study, Exam-style Questions

Progress Questions

1 Reasons include: to increase sales; to increase market share; to survive; to maximise profits; to increase monopoly power.

2 Two main ways are price competition and non-price competition. Price competition involves lowering price to attract more buyers and increase market share, perhaps by driving another firm out of the market. Non-price competition involves other methods other than changes in price to outdo rival firms. These include improving products, reducing costs, improving quality and making products appear different to increase brand loyalty.

Case Study

Cola wars

"Price wars" is indicating price competition. There are various examples of non-price competition in the case study: advertising, including where and how the product is promoted (on television and in a film); who the firm uses in adverts ("well-known athletes"); Coke's distinctive packaging ("contour-shaped bottle"); innovation, such as use of cans and a diet version; slogans ("It's the Real Thing"); colour and style of logos.

Exam-style Questions

1 C. This will make the products in the market less of a substitute for each other, giving the firm more power to set price.

2 C. This is one of the characteristics (see 4.3 "Competitive markets" for a list).

3 When there is only one firm in the market.

4 58%. Adding Firm E, Firm D and Firm B = 27 + 16 + 15 (the shares of the three largest firms).

5 Your answer could start by defining competitive markets and monopoly power. You should draw a diagram like Figure 4.4.4. State clearly that in a competitive market, the price is likely to be lower and the quantity sold higher than when a firm has monopoly power. This can be explained in relation to the characteristics of a competitive market – many buyers and sellers, good market information and low barriers to entry. For example, firms in competitive markets have little power to set price or quantity. Price is set by market demand and supply. If one firm increases price, consumers are likely to switch to others selling similar products. If firms make high profits and there are few barriers to entry, other firms are likely to enter the market. This keeps prices lower in competitive markets and more will be sold at a lower price. Refer fully to the diagram in the course of your answer. If a firm has monopoly power, it can limit output to force up price.

6 A good starting point would be to explain what is meant by "a market becoming less competitive". You may add an example of how this could have happened. Effects to be analysed could include effects on price, quantity sold, profits, efficiency, allocation of resources, economies of scale and innovation. A diagram such as Figure 4.4.4 or 4.4.5 could help to support your analysis. The effects could be on consumers and/or firms, including those that now have more (or less) monopoly power or those that might want to enter the market.

5.1 – Progress Questions, Case Study

Progress Questions

1 Another word for unfair is "inequitable".

2 Resources could be allocated inefficiently.

3 The term used for side-effect is "externalities".

Case Study

The importance of education

1

Year	Total	Index (2011=100)
2003	67,295	100
2007	70,130	104.2
2011	65,986	98.1
2015	75,134	111.6
2019	80,263	119.3

2 **i.** 19.3%; **ii.** 1.9%.

3 A country may benefit because: the population is likely to have a higher literacy rate and likely to be more numerate and IT-literate with more transferable skills; less training will be needed; there will higher labour productivity, higher incomes and less poverty; people will have improved health; the country will earn more income and government will receive more tax revenue.

5.2 – Progress Questions, Case Study

Progress Questions

1 Public goods are non-rival in consumption and non-excludable. Consumption of a product by one person does not reduce the amount available to others and non-payers cannot be prevented from using the product. Private goods are rival in consumption and excludable. Consumption by one person reduces the amount available to others and non-payers can be prevented from using the product.

2 Examples include: street lighting; lighthouses; flood defences; the police service; national defence.

3 Examples include: chocolate bars; a chair; bus travel; a car; anything else that does not have the characteristics of a public good.

4 The free-rider problem is where people can consume as much as they like of a good, without having to pay for it.

Case Study

Flood defences in the Maldives

1 Flood defences are non-excludable. They cannot protect some people and not others. They are also non-rival in consumption. Consumption by one person does not reduce the amount of protection available to others.

2 There is a demand for the product and it is important for public safety. However, it is impossible for a firm to charge individuals if non-payers cannot be excluded from the benefits and the amount "consumed" cannot be measured. It is a missing market. Therefore, the government should become involved.

5.3 – Progress Questions, Case Study

Progress Questions

1 Private costs = **iii.** price paid and **iv.** wages; private benefits = **i.** pleasure from eating and **v.** revenue of seller; external costs = **ii.** dropped wrapper; external benefits = **vi.** lower welfare payments.

2 $25,000 ($20,000 + $5,000)

3 $2 ($22 – $20)

4 Examples include: a symbol; a brand name; a painting; sculpture; a film; a geographical location, such as Champagne.

5 Examples include: laws protecting the area or assigning rights to the developer, such as patents, perhaps for a set period of time; local or international cooperation to allow reasonable use.

Case Study

A new capital for Egypt

Examples include:

i. cost of building – airport, housing, roads, infrastructure, business and administrative areas; loss in value of homes; there may be higher taxes to pay for developments or worsening of other public sector services

ii. waste; air pollution from traffic; water pollution; health problems.

iii. more job opportunities – construction and tourism; higher incomes; cheaper houses; better health for individuals.

iv. less-crowded conditions for those living in Cairo; less congestion; less pollution; less strain on health care; all could benefit from more money being available if more tourists and businesses are attracted to the area (spillover effects).

5.4 – Progress Questions, Case Study

Progress Questions

1 Merit and demerit goods are products that society or government judges desirable or undesirable. This depends on views of what is good or bad, right or wrong (value judgements). This could vary between countries in terms of what is thought to be important, according to moral or political judgements.

2 Demerit goods are likely to have externalities in consumption.

3 Demand based on the social benefits is higher for a merit good.

4 The socially optimum quantity for a demerit good is lower than the free market quantity.

5 People may not know the full or long-term effects of actions they take now in terms of, for example, whether they should be vaccinated against an infectious disease. They may not know the likelihood of catching it and its full effects. The vaccine (health care) may therefore be underconsumed and underprovided.

Case Study

Education in Argentina and Chile

1 Reasons include: value judgements – the Argentinian government may feel it is more important to spend money on, for example, university education than other priorities; despite lower income per head, tax revenue to fund education may be higher in Argentina; use of vouchers in Chile is perhaps a way to offer more choice; tradition may be a factor.

2 This may be because of the importance of primary and secondary education to literacy, numeracy and other key skills, which everyone needs for their own benefit but which also benefits firms and society as a whole (there are considerable positive externalities). There may be greater private benefits from university education in the form of higher future incomes, so individuals benefiting should contribute.

5.5 – Progress Questions, Case Studies

Progress Questions

1 A person applying for a bank loan knows more about his or her financial situation and ability to make the interest payments than the person who has to agree to the loan. Similarly, the person applying for the job knows more about his or her ability to be a good, reliable worker than the person considering the application. In both cases, the applicant may also provide inaccurate or misleading information.

2 Monopoly power may lead to inequity and/or inefficiency. For example, forcing prices above those that would occur in a competitive market is unfair, particularly to those on low incomes. Also, insufficient quantity is being provided at a higher price, leading to a misallocation of resources, with possibly higher costs than necessary as well. This is inefficient.

3 The firm may use its profits to invest in research and development. This could result in better quality and/or cheaper products being available in future. The firm may be able to take advantage of economies of scale. This will reduce long-run average costs and enable the firm to charge lower prices. The firm may be run by the state, which may make it sell at the price and quantity that would occur in a competitive market.

Case Studies

The market for health insurance in Australia

1 There is imperfect information or information failure. There is too much choice (40,000 variations) on a difficult area for potential consumers to understand and compare. They will not be able to

weigh up all the costs and benefits of alternatives to make a rational decision and buy the "best" policy for their needs and circumstances, to maximise their utility. Some may simply buy health insurance because others have it, not considering whether it is right for them.

2 Health care is likely to be underprovided by the market, since individuals only consider the private benefits, ignoring the external benefits. Also, they may only consider the short-term benefits, undervaluing the long-term benefits. Demand will be too low to achieve the socially optimum output of health care. Subsidies lower the cost and enable more to be supplied. With an increased supply, price is likely to fall, causing an extension of demand (as in Figure 2.5.6). This will raise the equilibrium quantity consumed and provided, moving the market to, or closer to, the socially optimum output.

The price of cocoa

1 $707.97 ($2659.94 − 1951.97)

2 28.3%.

3 $2334 $\left(\frac{11668}{5}\right)$

4 The prices are unstable, with a 28.3% rise between January and March, and a difference of over $700 between the highest and lowest figures. The prices are unpredictable and the price changes may result in confusing signals. This may lead producers to overproduce or underproduce, or to overinvest or underinvest. This could result in an inefficient allocation of resources and therefore market failure.

5.6 – Progress Questions

Progress Questions

1 Income = **i.** pension, **ii.** salary and **v.** profits; wealth = **iii.** land, **iv.** painting, **vi.** car and **vii.** ring.

2 A statement about whether something is equitable will be normative.

3 Wealth often generates income, so a person with more wealth will have a greater ability to earn income than someone with less wealth. This higher income will also enable the person to accumulate more wealth to produce even higher income in future. For example, savings earn interest, ownership of shares results in dividends and property can earn rent.

4 Views about equity (fairness) will vary from person to person and involve value judgements. People will differ in their opinions about whether a particular level of inequality is inequitable or not. Inequality, as opposed to total equality, is unlikely to be inequitable since inequality provides incentives and acts as a reward, for example, to those who work more. If everyone has the same income and wealth, why should anyone work at all? Therefore, inequality of income and wealth is not "always" inequitable.

5.7 – Progress Questions, Case Studies

Progress Questions

1 Governments should intervene in markets to correct market failure (or to correct an inefficient or inequitable allocation of resources).

2 The three main government interventions are public expenditure, taxation and regulations.

3 Free-market (non-interventionist) economists believe that markets generally work well and that there is little need for intervention by governments except, for example, to provide public goods. Interventionist economists believe that markets are not necessarily competitive and that market failure is common. They believe there should be much more intervention by governments to increase welfare. Economists' views can also be affected by moral judgements.

4 When there are negative externalities in consumption, the government is more likely to intervene using tax, to reduce consumption.

5 If demand is elastic, will there be a greater percentage change in quantity sold.

6 There will be no change in either price or quantity sold, since a minimum price must be set above the current equilibrium to have any effect.

7 Inelastic demand for a product makes it more likely that intervention using a buffer stock scheme will be needed, because a change in supply will have a larger proportionate effect on price.

8 Problems include:
   - deciding who should pay what at the start
   - ongoing costs of storage, etc

- the product may be perishable
- where to set intervention prices
- it may encourage overproduction
- the price may be undercut by non-members.

9 Advantages of a pollution permits scheme include that it: internalises the externality; operates with a limited role for the government; can raise money for the government; is flexible; being tradable, provides an incentive to pollute less. Disadvantages include that: it is difficult to know how many permits to issue or at what price; the scheme needs to be monitored; penalties must be enforced; the scheme does not directly compensate those affected; and some areas will not experience a fall in pollution.

10 Air moves; if someone had property rights to air and the air was polluted, it would be difficult to prove who had caused the pollution; it is difficult to decide how high above the ground or above someone's property the rights to air should extend.

11 Advantages include: regulation is simple; easy to understand; and does not directly change the price to disadvantage those on low incomes. Disadvantages include that: it needs to be monitored; penalties must be enforced; it may add to the costs of firms, increasing prices; and measures may be considered paternalistic by some people, making them less likely to obey the law.

12 Factors include the following.
- How widespread is the campaign?
- Does it reach the target market?
- Does the message have popular support?
- How might "success" be measured?

Case Studies

Flu vaccinations in Ireland

1 They may be most likely to catch the flu or the consequences of them catching flu could be more serious. For example, for older people or those with long-term health conditions, the illness could turn into something worse, such as pneumonia. Health care workers are in even greater demand in the winter months and if they catch flu, this could leave hospitals short-staffed.

2 It could be difficult and undesirable to force people to have injections. If free flu jabs were offered to everyone, this would be much more expensive and have a greater opportunity cost than limiting jabs to selected groups. If only 10% of people are likely to catch flu, the vaccination would be a waste of resources for many people and others could afford to pay for it if they wished, since the cost of €20 is not unreasonable for most people.

3 Options include:
- advertising to make people more aware of its benefits, to reduce possible information failure
- subsidising vaccinations so the cost for those who have to pay is less than €20 and/or make it available free to people in lower-income groups
- setting a maximum price for the vaccination.

Pollution permit schemes – European Union, California and China

1 The extent to which emissions fall, particularly in relation to targets for particular dates is a key indicator. The impact on the industries or economies of the regions or countries affected is also important. What has happened to employment, incomes and investment, etc.? This may be of particular significance, for example if California is trying to reduce emissions but other US states are not.

2 Points include:
- gaining the support of different countries and industries
- setting the "right" price and quantity of permits, plus how much this will change over time
- what is done with money obtained by governments through selling or auctioning permits
- having sufficient penalties for breaking the rules and making sure these are enforced.

Universal basic income experiment – Kenya

1 If everyone is given the same amount of money, this will be a larger increase in income to those on lower incomes, lessening the relative gap between rich and poor. Also, helps to provide money to set up or invest in a business or to spend on training, which could increase the future income of those on low incomes who could not afford to do this otherwise.

2 Problems include:
- the financial cost and opportunity cost
- giving money to many who do not need it
- possibly reducing the incentive of some people to work.

5.8 – Progress Questions, Case Study, Exam-style Questions

Progress Questions

1 If demand is inelastic, the percentage change in quantity demanded will be less than the percentage change in price. When the price rises due to the tax, the total amount spent on these demerit goods will rise and it will also make up a larger percentage of people's incomes, leaving less money to be spent on other goods and services. This could particularly disadvantage those on low incomes.

2 This would lower the cost to US farmers of producing corn for ethanol, encouraging more farmers to grow corn to make ethanol. This may reduce the quantity of corn available for other uses, resulting in higher food prices.

Case Study

Government failure
Possible causes include the following.
- Conflicting objectives – environmental problems, low productivity, high food prices. Which is the biggest priority? Also, what is the cost of buffer stock scheme together with potential loss of revenue from income tax cut?
- Inadequate information – the information is out of date. There were poor harvests in 2015 but it took three years to complete report and another two years has now passed. Does the government have all the information it needs?
- Administrative costs – the report cost $30 million. Was it worth it? What is the opportunity cost of this money? If a buffer stock scheme is set up, this will be very expensive to run and administer.
- Corruption – there is pressure both from rich landowners and small farmers to take action to increase their incomes. The Prime Minister, as an owner of a large area of farmland, could be acting out of self-interest.
- Inappropriate policy – the problem applied to wheat and potatoes in 2015. Has it happened since? Why introduce a buffer stock scheme for all agricultural products? This would be too expensive and prices could be undercut by other countries.
- Regulatory capture – there is potential for the regulatory body to act more in interests of farmers than other economic agents.
- Short-termism – the government is trying to take action (both in terms of the buffer stock scheme and an income tax cut) before next year's election, to win votes.
- Buffer stock scheme – all the other problems of this type of intervention could be discussed as potential causes of market failure.

Exam-style Questions

1 B. This is effectively defining government failure.

2 C. With two demand curves, the externalities must be in consumption. With demand being higher when taking account of the social benefits, the externalities are positive.

3 A. Private goods are rival in consumption.

4 When a public good has some characteristics of a private good, either being excludable or rival in consumption.

5 $30 million. (Private benefit + External benefit) – (Private cost + External cost) = (70 + 80) – (100 + 20).

6 **i.** Average income is the flow of money received by a typical individual over a period of time whereas average wealth is the individual's stock of assets at a point in time. Those on high incomes do not need to spend all their money. The higher the income, the easier it is to save and to buy assets. Those with higher incomes are likely to have more money in banks and be able to afford to buy a house and other property. This will add to their wealth. Similarly, if the average income is low, people may be spending most, if not all, of their income. They may have no opportunity to accumulate wealth and may have to reduce any they have to buy what they need. Therefore, if average income rises, average wealth would be expected to rise and vice versa.

ii. Some of the points that might be made include the following.
- Average income and average wealth were both highest in 2019 at $2,120 and $7,000.
- Income was lowest in 2013 at $1,980 but wealth was lowest in 2011 at $6,000.
- In three of the four time periods (and for the period as a whole), income and wealth moved in the same direction. For example, from 2015 to 2017, income rose from $2,010 to $2,060 and wealth rose from $6,300 to $6,500. However, from 2011 to 2013, income fell from $2,000 to $1,980 but wealth rose from $6,000 to $6,100

- Overall, average income seems to have some effect on average wealth but it is not the only factor.
- There may have been, for example, a rise in house prices between 2011 and 2013 when average income fell but average wealth rose.
- Data is only provided for every other year. Could there be a time lag?
- The changes, especially for income, are relatively small. For example, there is a fall of only 1% between 2011 and 2013, followed by a rise back to 0.5% above the 2011 level by 2015. Is this likely to make much difference to wealth?
- No information on prices or whether average income takes account of this (in real terms).

7 You could start by defining minimum price. You should draw a diagram like Figure 5.7.7. If set above equilibrium, a minimum price will raise the price of rice, causing an extension of supply and contraction of demand. Reasons for these movements along can be explained, together with the excess supply. Explain that the quantity sold of rice will fall to the new demand, unless bought by the government or agency setting the minimum price. In this case, quantity sold will increase to the new quantity supplied at the minimum price. Refer fully to the diagram in the course of the answer.

8 A good starting point would be to explain what is meant by a "demerit good", giving an example. An explanation of other relevant concepts such as negative externalities in consumption would help and the fact that the overconsumption of a demerit good is partly linked to information failure. Individuals may not know about the harmful longer-term effects of their consumption. Improving information (perhaps including some examples of how this could be done) can help consumers to weigh up the costs and benefits of their consumption of demerit goods. A diagram such as Figure 5.4.3 would help to support the analysis. The effects analysed could be on demand, price and quantity sold, all of which should decrease with improved information.

9 Indicative content is given below; you should also try to include relevant references to data from the case study to support your points:
- education as a merit good likely to be underconsumed if left to the market and so an example of possible market failure
- examples of the private benefits of education
- positive externalities, plus examples, which may result from a well-educated population
- why education may be underconsumed, including information failure
- evidence from the case study – income per head, literacy rates, what happens if people have to pay
- would everything be free, including materials?
- practicality and significance of 21 – would people have to start paying to continue their course after their 21st birthday?
- free primary or secondary education, rather than university education
- financial cost and opportunity cost – is it worth it and other priorities?
- it would involve paying for the rich as well as the poor
- might money spent be returned in the form of higher tax revenue if successful?
- value judgements – may vary from country to country
- equity and efficiency
- possibility of government failure
- an overall assessment of whether or not a government should intervene or not to provide free education up to the age of 21.

6.1 – Progress Questions, Case Study

Progress Questions

1 An objective of economic policy is what the government is trying to achieve; an aim of the government.

2 The four main objectives of macroeconomic policy are: economic growth; stable prices (or low inflation); low unemployment; stable balance of payments.

3 Macroeconomics studies the behaviour of the economy as a whole. Microeconomics studies the behaviour of individuals, firms and particular markets (such as the market for rice).

4 A policy instrument is a tool that the government can use to achieve its objectives, for example fiscal, monetary and supply-side policies.

5 Economic growth is the rate at which the total output of the economy is increasing. Negative economic growth is when the total output of the economy is falling.

6 Inflation is the rate of change in the price level **or** the rate at which the average price of all goods and services is increasing.

7 A balance of payments deficit is when the value of imports is greater than the value of exports.

8 The opportunity cost of achieving an improvement in a policy objective. For example, the opportunity cost of reducing unemployment might be a higher rate of inflation.

9 Policy objectives are compatible when achieving an improvement in one policy objective is accompanied by an improvement in a different policy objective.

10 If total spending (aggregate demand) increases, this will encourage firms to produce more and therefore employ more people, reducing unemployment.

11 It may mean more raw materials and energy are needed for production of goods and services, which may damage the natural environment. As people consume more products it may lead to more waste, which may be hard to deal with.

Case Study

Economic growth and inflation in Malaysia, 2014–2018

1 The bar chart should have the same title as the table. The horizontal axis should show the year. The vertical axis should be labelled (%). The bars for the growth rate should be shaded differently from the bars for inflation, or they should be in a different colour. Check that each bar is drawn accurately.

2 Governments usually want to have high rate of growth and low inflation. In each year, when the growth rate increases, the rate of inflation also increases. When the growth rate falls, inflation falls. For example, between 2016 and 2017, the growth rate rises from 4.22% to 5.90% but this is accompanied by a rise in inflation, from 2.08% to 3.80%. The trade-off for a 1.68 percentage point increase in the growth rate is a 1.72 percentage point increase in the rate of inflation.

6.2 – Progress Questions, Case Study, Exam-style Questions

Progress Questions

1 GDP measures the monetary value of the total output of an economy over a given period of time, for example one year.

2 Nominal GDP increases faster than real GDP when the price level is rising; that is, when there is inflation.

3 The distribution of income has become more unequal.

4 The two main methods of measuring unemployment are: the ILO labour force survey method **and** the number of people claiming unemployment benefits.

5 Production is the total output produced in a given time period. Productivity measures output per unit of input per time period, for example output per person per hour.

6 18 baskets per person per day.

7 The base year is the starting point for an index. The value of the index in the base year is always set at 100.

8 Weights are used to reflect the relative importance of the different items in an index. For example, if the weight attached to an item in a price index is small, a change in the price of the item will not have much effect on the overall value of the price index.

9 The CPI measures changes in the price level. It shows changes in the weighted average price of a selection of goods and services. It is a measure of inflation.

10 Real value = money value × (base year price index ÷ current year price index)

11 Index of consumer spending in 2020 = (380 ÷ 240) × 100 = 158.3.

12 58.3%

Case Study

Unemployment and the labour force

1 (18 + 2 + 1) million = 21 million people

2 $\frac{1}{21} \times 100 = 4.76\%$

Changing patterns of expenditure in China affect the CPI

1 The organisation might conduct a large survey of household expenditure and choose those items on which households spend most of their money.

2 As people's incomes have increased, the proportion of income a typical household spends on transport and communication has increased. Transport and communication has a high, positive income elasticity of demand.

3 If a larger weight is given to those products that have the most rapidly increasing prices, the overall value of the index will increase more quickly, the rate of inflation will be higher. The opposite will be true if a larger weight is given to those products whose prices are rising more slowly.

4 The value of the index will be 100 in 2015 rather than in 2010. If prices have risen between 2010 and 2015, the index in 2010 will now be less than 100.

Exam-style Questions

1 D. Economic growth is one of the four main macroeconomic policy objectives.

2 C. The unemployment rate is calculated as a percentage of those who are working plus those who are unemployed. It is unemployment as a percentage of all those people who are working and looking for work.

3 B. A weight is used so that an index takes into account the relative importance of the different items in the index. In a price index, the weight depends on the percentage of total expenditure on the item.

4 **i.** The starting point for the index when its value is set at 100.
ii. The percentage increase in the price level.

5 **i.** $(97 - 92) \div 92 \times 100 = 5 \div 92 \times 100 = 5.434 = 5.4\%$ to one decimal place
ii. $915 \times 100 \div 109 = 839.449 = \$839$ billion to the nearest \$ billion.

7.1 – Progress Questions, Case Studies, Exam-style Questions

Progress Questions

1 National income measures the monetary value of all the goods and services that are produced by an economy in a given period of time. It is also equal to total expenditure and the sum of all the income earned by the factors of production.

2 The expenditure method calculates national income by adding together consumption, investment, government expenditure and exports, and the subtracting imports $(C + I + G + X - M)$.

3 Investment is the production of capital goods. Capital goods, such as machinery, are used to help produce other goods and service.

4 Depreciation is the fall in the value of an asset that happens over a period of time. For example, a piece of machinery will wear out with use. It will also become out of date.

5 The three injections into the circular flow of income are investment, government spending and exports.

6 The three withdrawals from the circular flow of income are saving, taxation and imports.

7 Firms will experience a fall in stocks and will increase production to meet the demand for their products. This increase in output means national income has risen. More output means more income for the factors of production producing that output.

8 The level of national output that will create enough jobs for everyone who is willing and able to work at current market wage rates.

Case Studies

Farina's Footwear

1 The contribution to national income in 2019 was the value added, which equalled $10.5 million.

2 $\$(46,000 - 1,000) \div 9 = \$5,000$

3 Wear and tear meant the machine was breaking down more often. Changes in technology meant the machine was not as efficient as newer machines and had become obsolete.

Indonesia's economy survives the world financial crisis

1 In some economies, the world financial crisis led to reductions in consumption, investment and government spending. This meant aggregate demand fell. A fall in aggregate demand causes firms to cut production. As a result, national output (or national income) falls.

2 In 2008, net exports = $\$(139.3 - 116)$ billion = $23.3 billion. In 2009 net exports = $\$(115.6 - 86.6)$ billion = $29 billion. Therefore, net exports rose by $5.7 billion.

3 The fall in exports will have reduced the demand for the products supplied by firms exporting goods and services. However, the increase in net exports will have helped to increase aggregate demand and national income. What happened to the other components of aggregate demand will also have to be considered.

7.2 – Progress Questions, Case Study

Progress Questions

1 Vertical axis: "Price level"; horizontal axis: "Real national income" **or** "Real GDP".

2 A change in the price level will cause a movement along the AD curve.

3 A shift of the AD curve to the left could be caused by anything that leads to a reduction in aggregate demand other than a rise in the price level. For example, an increase in income tax, causing a fall in consumer spending, would shift the AD curve to the left.

4 A shift of the SRAS curve to the left could be caused by an increase in costs of production, for example an increase in raw material prices.

5 The normal capacity level of output of an economy is the maximum amount that an economy can continue to produce in the long run. If it attempts to produce more than this level of output for very long, there will be excess demand and inflation is likely to increase rapidly.

6 More machinery increases the supply of capital allowing more goods and services to be produced. It is likely to increase labour productivity. New machinery might also incorporate new technology and be more productive than older machines.

7 A shift of the LRAS curve to the right could be caused by an increase in the supply of any factor of production, such as more women joining the labour force; also, anything that increases productivity, such as the development of new technologies.

8 The equilibrium level of national income is when the level of national income is stable and is not changing from one period to the next.

9 The conditions are: aggregate demand = aggregate supply = national output, injections = withdrawals, $(I + G + X) = (S + T + M)$, no involuntary change in stocks (inventory).

10 An increase in government spending shifts the AD curve to the right, the diagram is the same as Figure 7.2.9.

11 A negative demand-side shock is an event that causes a sudden or unexpected fall in aggregate demand. The AD curve shifts to the left.

12 An increase in exports shifts the AD curve to the right, leading to an increase in output. If the economy has plenty of spare capacity, real national income will increase but there will not be much, if any, effect on the price level, and hence inflation.

13 This is an AD/AS diagram that shows the SRAS curve shifting to the left. The diagram is the same as Figure 7.2.10.

14 If productivity improves, costs per unit of output will fall. At any given price level, firms' profits will increase, leading to a rightward shift in the SRAS curve.

Case Study

Falling commodity prices will help to keep inflation low

1 The AD/AS diagram should show a rightward shift in the SRAS curve. It should also show a fall in the equilibrium price level and a rise in real national income. The diagram should be the same as Figure 7.2.12.

2 If commodity prices fall, this will reduce the amount of money producing countries earn from exporting these products. A fall in the value of exports reduces the value of an injection into the circular flow of income, shifting the AD curve to the left.

7.3 – Progress Questions, Case Studies

Progress Questions

1 The main components of aggregate demand are: consumption, investment, government spending, exports minus imports: $(C + I + G + X - M)$.

2 Consumer spending will fall by €225 million. (-€300 million ×0.75)

3 One reason why firms invest is so they can produce enough products to satisfy demand. If there is spare capacity, they will be able to increase production to satisfy an increase in demand without investing in new capital. Other things being equal, if there is plenty of spare capacity in the economy investment will be lower than if firms are working at full capacity.

4 If a country's exchange rate increases, the foreign currency price of exports will rise. This will reduce the demand for exports and the volume, or quantity, sold.

5 If the world economy is growing fast, this will increase the demand for exports. If the domestic economy is growing more slowly, spending on imports will probably rise more slowly than exports. As a result, net exports $(X - M)$ will probably increase.

6 The savings ratio is household savings as a percentage of household disposable income.

7   Real interest rates will have fallen from 3% to 1% and so the real reward from saving will have fallen, reducing the incentive to save. However, some households may fail to take into account inflation, and consider the nominal rate of interest, when deciding how much to save.

8   Savings are a withdrawal from the circular flow of income. Savings are the part of household disposable income that is not spent. Investment is an injection into the circular flow and is spending on capital goods.

9   It is likely to be greater than 1 because the ratio between capital and output is greater than 1. For example, to produce an annual output of $10,000 takes much more than $10,000 worth of capital.

10 $300 million × 2.5 = $750 million

11 If national income and aggregate demand increase, this can be met by using some of the spare capacity. If there is spare capacity, there is no need to invest in new capacity when demand increases.

Case Studies

A slowdown in the growth of household consumption is forecast

1   Steady growth in household disposable income and lower interest rates will tend to increase consumption. Lower interest rates make it cheaper to borrow and less rewarding to save.

2   Rising unemployment and high levels of existing debt may make people cautious when deciding how much to spend. They may decide to save more as a precaution against the risk of losing their job and not want to take on more debt. This may mean consumption only grows slowly.

How will a growing economy affect the budget balance and net exports?

1   In 2020, national income is expected to rise by $800 billion × 0.05 = $40 billion. Tax revenue is expected to increase by $40 billion × 0.3 = $12 billion. Therefore the budget balance is expected to be $(400 – 372) billion = $28 billion. Since government spending is greater than tax revenue, this is a budget deficit.

2   The increase in imports is expected to be $40 billion × 0.25 = $10 billion. Net exports, X – M, is expected to be $(135 – 160) billion = −$25 billion.

7.4 – Progress Questions, Case Study

Progress Questions

1   Real GDP is the main indicator of economic activity but employment and unemployment are also indicators.

2   If aggregate demand falls, firms will reduce output and are likely to reduce the number of people they employ. Production, consumption and the exchange of goods and services will fall.

3   The change in national income is -$12 billion times the multiplier. The multiplier is 2. Therefore, national income will fall by $24 billion.

Case Study

What will happen to the economy?

1   The change in injections = $(40 + 25 – 5) billion = $60 billion. The multiplier is [1 ÷ (0.1 + 0.4 + 0.3)] = 1.25. Therefore the change in national income is $60 billion × 1.25 = $75 billion. National income is expected to rise to $1,275 billion.

2   The MPC is [1– (0.1 + 0.4 + 0.3)] = 0.2. Therefore consumption is expected to increase by $75 billion × 0.2 = $15 billion.

7.5 – Progress Questions

Progress Questions

1   The effect of a fall in price level is shown by a movement along the SRAS curve. It leads to a contraction in aggregate supply.

2   An increase in indirect taxes would shift the SRAS curve to the left because an increase in an indirect tax is the same as an increase in firms' costs of production.

3   An increase in labour productivity would shift the SRAS curve to the right because it reduces firms' unit labour costs, making production more profitable at any given price level. Firms will be willing to produce more at any given price level.

7.6 – Progress Questions, Case Study, Exam-style Questions

Progress Questions

1   The capital stock is the value of capital that exists at a point in time. Capital is the human-made factor of production and includes machinery, buildings, roads and other physical infrastructure. Investment is a flow of new capital produced over a period of time, for example one year. Some investment replaces capital that has depreciated but it also increases the capital stock.

2   A fall in the replacement ratio means a fall in the income people receive when they are out of work compared to what they would receive if they were working. This will act as an incentive: more people will want to work. This should increase the size of the working population.

3   If an economy produces beyond its normal capacity level of output for too long, the economy is likely to experience serious inflationary problems. There will be shortages of factors of production, leading to rising factor prices and increased production costs. Excess demand for goods and services will allow firms to increase prices. Rising inflation means that the economy cannot continue to produce beyond its normal capacity level of output.

Case Study

The female participation rate in different countries

1   The female participation rate has fallen most in India, from 30.0% to 23.4%.

2   It has risen most in Peru, from 43.5% to 70.2%.

3   It has been most stable in Vietnam, the lowest rate over the period was 71.7% in 2005 and the highest rate was 72.7% in 1991.

4   The female participation rate in Australia has increased from 52.0% to 59.6%. This suggests that more females have joined the labour force, assuming that the female population of working age has not fallen. Other things being equal, an increase in the labour force will increase the productive capacity of the economy and shift the LRAS curve to the right.

Exam-style Questions

1   C. Investment is an expenditure that increases the circular flow of income in an economy.

2   C. The MPM measures how spending on imports changes as income changes.

3   D. The multiplier is 1 ÷ (1 – MPC) = 2.5. The net change in injections is −$20 million and so national income will fall by 2.5 × $20 million = $50 million.

4   Aggregate demand is total planned spending on domestic output and is equal to C + I + G + X – M.

5   Change in imports = ΔY × MPM = $8 billion × 0.24 = $1.92 billion. Therefore, imports in 2020 = $25 billion + $1.92 billion = $26.92 billion, which is $26.9 billion to one decimal place.

6   **i.** An increase in national income is likely to lead to a rise in investment. When national income is increasing, aggregate demand is also increasing. To meet the increase in aggregate demand, firms may need to invest to increase their productive capacity. This is most likely to happen when the economy is close to full capacity. Since the marginal capital–output ratio is greater than 1, the accelerator theory suggests that the amount of investment will be larger than the increase in national income. An increase in national income will also increase confidence and firms' profits. Higher profits and increased confidence are likely to lead to an increase investment. A fall in national income will reduce confidence and the need to increase capacity. When national income is falling, investment is also likely to fall.

ii. Between 2016 and 2018 national income is rising and this is accompanied by an increase in investment. Over this period, national income increases from $530 billion to $605 billion and investment increases from $84 billion to $122 billion. This supports the view that a rise in national income leads to a rise in investment. Between 2018 and 2019, national income falls by $5 billion and investment falls by $35 billion. Again, this shows a direct (positive) relationship between changes in national income and investment. However, when national income increases by $12 billion between 2019 and 2020, investment falls by $4 billion. The increase in national income is quite small, and the increase in investment in previous years may have already created enough capacity to meet demand. Also, there are other factors, such as interest rates, that affect investment. Overall, the data supports the view that changes in national income affect investment.

7   Exports are an injection into the circular flow of income. An increase in exports will increase aggregate demand, represented by a rightward shift in the AD curve. This will lead to an increase in the equilibrium level of national income. (Draw a diagram showing a shift in the

AD curve to the right, as in Figure 7.2.9, and use the diagram to support the explanation.) The increase in exports will increase the incomes paid to the factors of production producing the exports. This increase in income will lead to a further increase in aggregate demand as consumption increases. This is the start of the multiplier process. The extent of the increase in equilibrium national income will depend on the marginal propensity to consume (MPC). The larger the MPC the larger the multiplier effect of the increase in exports. (Figure 7.4.2 could be used to illustrate the multiplier effect and a numerical example could also be used to support the explanation of the multiplier effect). The larger the multiplier, the larger the effect of an increase in exports on the equilibrium level of national income.

8   The normal capacity level of output is the amount an economy can continue to produce in the long run without experiencing significant inflationary pressures. An improvement in technology can affect the production process, leading to improvements in efficiency and productivity. For example, the development of robots and artificial intelligence (AI), have improved labour productivity in factories by reducing the number of workers needed to produce a given level of output. Workers who have lost their jobs in manufacturing can be employed elsewhere in the economy. Developments such as these increase the total value of goods and services that the economy is capable of producing, shifting the LRAS curve to the right. (Figure 7.2.7 could be used to illustrate the effect on the normal capacity level of output of an economy). However, some workers may find it difficult to adjust to these changes. If labour is occupationally and/or geographically immobile, the number of people employed may fall.

Improvements in technology also lead to new products becoming available. To produce these products, firms will have to invest. They may build new factories and buy new machinery. This investment will also increase the productive capacity of the economy. Overall, improvements in technology are likely to increase the normal capacity level of output because they lead to improvements in productivity and more investment, increasing the size of the capital stock.

8.1 – Progress Questions, Case Studies

Progress Questions

1   Short-run economic growth is the rate of increase in the total output of an economy, usual in one year. Long-run growth is the annual increase in the productive capacity of an economy averaged over a number of years.

2   Short-run rate of economic growth = (the change in real GDP ÷ original real GDP) × 100 = ($15 billion ÷ $600 billion) × 100 = 2.5%

3   If aggregate demand increases, firms will increase output to meet the increase in demand. If the growth of aggregate demand is increasing, it is likely that national output will increase at a faster rate and therefore the rate of economic growth will increase. If aggregate demand falls, output is likely to fall and short-run growth will be negative.

4   The fluctuations in economic activity around an economy's long-run trend rate of economic growth.

5   Boom – recession (downturn) – depression (slump) – recovery.

6   The main indicator of the economic cycle is real GDP (real national output).

7   The fluctuations in real GDP usually come before the changes in unemployment. For example, in a recession, after a fall in aggregate demand, firms will cut production to prevent stocks (inventory) increasing. Only when they are sure that the fall in aggregate demand is not temporary will they start to reduce the number of people they employ.

8   An output gap is the difference between the economy's equilibrium level of national income and its normal capacity level of national income. Output gap = $(Y_e - Y_N)$

9   When an economy is in recession, the equilibrium level of national income is less than the economy's normal capacity level of national income, therefore $(Y_e - Y_N)$ will be negative.

Case Studies

Exports support the growth of China's economy

1   A rise in exports increases aggregate demand. To meet the rise in aggregate demand, firms will employ more workers so they can produce more goods and services. The increase in output leads to an increase in real GDP and therefore contributes to short-run economic growth, the percentage increase in national output.

2   When aggregate demand is rising, firms will invest to increase productive capacity. There is likely to be an accelerator effect. Investment will also increase labour productivity. Multinational

companies have set up in China and exported products around the world. Investment by multinational companies also increases productive capacity and contributes to long-run growth.

3   Net exports is (X – M). Exports are an injection into the circular flow of income and imports are a withdrawal. AD = C + I + G + (X – M). If X > M, there is a net injection into the circular flow, which increases aggregate demand. If M > X, there is a net withdrawal, which reduces aggregate demand. If initially X > M but the difference between X and M gets smaller, this will reduce the net injection and reduce aggregate demand.

The 1973 oil crisis

1   A recession is a phase of the economic cycle when national output is falling and unemployment is rising. A technical recession is when real GDP falls for two or more successive quarters.

2   The demand for oil was price inelastic. Therefore, an increase in the world market price of oil meant that oil-consuming countries were spending a lot more on importing oil. The increase in spending on imports was a withdrawal from the circular flow of income, this reduced aggregate demand as net exports fell. The fall in aggregate demand led to lower output and a rise in unemployment. The increase in the price of oil increased firms' costs of production. For example, energy and transport costs increased. The increase in costs meant many firms increased prices, adding to inflationary pressures. The increase in the price of oil was a supply-side shock for the oil-consuming countries.

3   Unemployment is a lagging indicator. In the recovery phase of the economic cycle, aggregate demand rises and firms increase production. At the start of the recovery, many firms will have spare capacity without increasing the number of workers they employ. As aggregate demand continues to rise and firms become more confident that this will continue, they will start to employ more workers to enable them to meet the increase in aggregate demand.

The global financial crisis 2007–08

1   Two possible reasons are: Reason 1: a financial crisis will affect confidence and expectations about the economy. Households are likely to save more to protect themselves from a fall in income. Firms will reduce investment because they expect aggregate demand to fall. Reason 2: interest rates are likely to increase and banks will reduce their lending. As a result, consumption and investment will fall.

2   The multiplier effect means that an initial fall in spending will lead to a larger fall in national income. The initial fall in aggregate demand will lead to a fall in output and income, the fall in income will lead to a further reduction in consumption and aggregate demand. The multiplier effect means that the initial fall in aggregate demand is magnified. The impact of the fall in aggregate demand on the economy is increased.

3   The increase in aggregate demand in China led to an increase in national output, income and employment in China. As incomes and output increased, Chinese households bought more foreign goods and Chinese firms bought more raw materials and components from abroad. This increased the exports of other countries, increasing aggregate demand. The increase in exports and the multiplier effect led to an increase in national output and income. The rise in exports and increase in AD helped other countries recover from the recession caused by the global financial crisis.

8.2 – Progress Questions, Case Study

Progress Questions

1   Underemployment is when people are working but are working fewer hours than they would like to work, or they are in a job that is not making good use of their skills and abilities.

2   The main cause of cyclical unemployment is a reduction in aggregate demand, which leads to lower output and employment.

3   Any three of the following: technological change; a change in the pattern of demand; foreign competition; exhaustion of a natural resource or immobility of labour.

4   If labour is occupationally immobile and workers lose their job in a declining industry, they may remain unemployed because they do not have the skills needed to work in the growing industries. If labour is geographically immobile and workers lose their job in a declining region of the country, they may remain unemployed because they are unwilling or unable to move to a region where there are job vacancies.

5   Frictional unemployment is short-term unemployment when people are between jobs.

6   Unemployment is when someone is out of work and looking for work. Someone who is underemployed is working but would like to work more hours or is in a job that is not using the person's skills.

7 The replacement ratio is the ratio between the money that people would receive when not working compared to the money they earn when working.

8 A fall in the replacement ratio increases the incentive to find a job because the difference between the money people receive when they are out of work, and the money they earn when in work, increases.

9 An improvement in competitiveness should increase employment. An improvement in competitiveness should lead to an increase in firms' sales in their home and overseas markets. Increased sales means more output and more jobs.

Case Study

Unemployment is Spain is falling

1 The unemployment rate is the number of people unemployed as a percentage of the labour force.

2 In 2019, employment was just under 20 million and the number of people unemployed was just over 3.2 million. Therefore the labour force was about 23.2 million people.

3 An increase in exports will increase aggregate demand, leading to an increase in output. More jobs will be created in the export industries and the multiplier effect will lead to more jobs in other parts of the economy.

4 Some people are in a part-time job because they cannot find a full-time job. This indicates that some people are working fewer hours than they would like to work. However, some people choose part-time work and are not underemployed.

5 Changes in pattern of employment occur when the proportion of the working population in different types of work changes. Since 2013, the growth in employment in Spain has been in the service sector and the number of people employed in agriculture and manufacturing has fallen. Therefore, the percentage of the labour force employed in the service sector has increased and the percentages employed in agriculture and manufacturing have fallen. There has been a change in the pattern of employment from agriculture and manufacturing to the service sector.

8.3 – Progress Questions, Case Study

Progress Questions

1 Disinflation is when the rate of inflation is falling. The price level is still rising but more slowly than before. For example, inflation falls from 6% to 4%.

2 Deflationary policies are policies that reduce aggregate demand.

3 Demand-pull inflation is caused by a sustained increase in aggregate demand and usually occurs when the economy is close to its normal capacity level of output. Cost-push inflation is caused by a significant increase in firms' production costs, for example rising commodity prices. Cost-push inflation can occur when the economy has plenty of spare capacity.

4 If money wages increase, unless productivity increases, firms' costs of production will increase. Firms will increase prices to restore their profits. Workers will want another increase in their money wage to prevent their real wage falling. As a result, costs and prices will continue to increase. However, unless aggregate demand increases, unemployment is likely to increase and the increase in costs and prices is likely to stop.

5 If the global economy is growing rapidly, exports will increase; this will increase aggregate demand and demand-pull inflationary pressures. Oil, food and other commodity prices are also likely to increase fast; this will increase cost-push inflationary pressures.

6 If the exchange rate appreciates, the foreign currency price of exports will increase and the domestic currency price of imports will fall. Reason 1: domestic products will be less competitive, reducing aggregate demand and demand-pull inflationary pressures. Reason 2: the fall in the price of imports will help to reduce cost-push inflationary pressures.

Case Study

Inflation in India, 2000–2018

1 Between 2000 and 2005, inflation was stable at around 4%. Between 2006 and 2010, it steadily increased each year, peaking at 12% in 2010. Inflation remained high between 2010 and 2013 but then fell between 2013 and 2017 from 10.9% to 2.5%. Inflation rose in 2018 to 4.9%, which was slightly higher than at the start of the period in 2000.

2 The rate of inflation fell in the following periods: 2000 to 2001, 2002 to 2003, 2010 to 2011, 2013 to 2017.

3 121 ÷ 19 years = 6.37% = 6.4% to one decimal place.

4 The rate of inflation fluctuates but within a fairly limited range. The highest annual rate of inflation is 12% and the lowest is 2.5%. India has not experienced hyperinflation, but between 2007 and 2014 the rate of inflation was probably too high to conclude that India had creeping inflation over the whole period.

8.4 – Progress Questions, Case Study

Progress Questions

1 The balance of payments is a record of all of a country's financial transactions with the rest of the world during a given period of time.

2 The four main sections of the current account of the balance of payments are: trade in goods; trade in services; primary income; secondary income.

3 A deficit on the balance of trade in goods and services is when the total value of exports of goods and services is less than the total value of imports of goods and services.

4 Primary income is income received in return for investment and labour services whereas secondary income is a transfer from the residents of one country to another, no good or service is provided.

5 If a country has a higher rate of inflation than other countries, other things being equal, its exports will become relatively more expensive and imports will become relatively cheaper. The demand for its exports will fall and the demand for imports will increase. Fewer exports and more imports is likely to lead to a deterioration in its balance of payments on current account.

6 Spending on imports will increase by $30 billion × 0.27 = $8.1 billion and so the current account of its balance of payments will deteriorate by $8.1 billion.

7 Overseas investment will increase the stock of foreign assets owned. Foreign assets earn income, which appears as a credit item under primary income. For example, shares earn dividends, foreign government bonds earn interest and businesses abroad earn profits. The more foreign assets owned, the greater the income earned. However, the more assets foreign residents own in the domestic economy, the more income paid abroad.

Case Study

The US current account balance in the 3rd quarter of 2019

1 The US balance of trade in goods = $413.8 billion – $633.4 billion = a deficit of $219.6 billion

2 The US balance of trade in services = $212.0 – $149.8 billion = a surplus of $62.2 billion

3 The US current account balance was = $(-219.6 + 62.2 + 68.7 – 35.4) billion = a deficit of $124.1 billion

4 The current account balance improved by $1.1 billion. The current account deficit fell from $125.2 billion in the 2nd quarter to $124.1 billion in the 3rd quarter.

8.5 – Progress Questions, Case Study, Exam-style Questions

Progress Questions

1 A non-renewable resource is a finite natural material that has a limited supply. It can be recycled but its supply cannot be increased. A renewable resource is a natural material that can be replaced by natural processes. Iron is a non-renewable resource and rice is a renewable resource.

2 Two examples of how economic activity and growth can damage the environment are: creating pollution when using coal to generate electricity; generating plastic waste that gets into rivers and the sea.

3 When a non-renewable resource starts to run out, its price will increase. The increase in price will: encourage firms to look for new supplies, encourage users of the material to reduce the amount they use, make recycling more profitable and encourage firms to develop substitutes.

4 Some people will benefit from a large increase in their income while others will not benefit at all. Some people may become structurally unemployed and find it difficult to find work in expanding industries.

5 Economic growth means that more goods and services are produced. More workers are needed to produce the extra output.

6 Economic growth means that many industries grow but some will decline. People who lose their job in the declining industries may not be occupationally and geographically mobile and may find it difficult to find work in the industries that are growing.

7 Economic growth means incomes, profits and spending are increasing. This means the government will raise more money from direct and indirect taxes. As people's incomes increase, the government will not have to spend as much money on welfare benefits.

8 Demand-deficient unemployment will fall and inflation is likely to increase. However, inflation may not increase until the economy is close to full capacity and the negative output gap is small.

9 When an economy does not have an output gap, there is not any cyclical (demand-deficient) unemployment. However, even when the economy is producing at its normal capacity level of output, structural, frictional and voluntary unemployment will still exist. These types of unemployment are caused by supply-side problems and not insufficient aggregate demand.

10 A depreciation in the exchange rate reduces the foreign currency price of exports and increases the domestic currency price of imports. Domestic goods become more competitive. The demand for exports should increase and the demand for imports should fall. As a result, it is likely that the balance of payments will improve. The increase in net exports will increase aggregate demand and lead to an increase in short-run economic growth. Provided the improvement in competitiveness is not eliminated by a rise in inflation, investment in the economy may increase, leading to long-run economic growth.

Case Study

The Hungarian economy: selected economic indicators, 2016–18

1 The percentage change in real GDP, economic growth, increased from 2.2% to 5.1% while, over the same period, the current account of the balance of payments deteriorated. In 2016, the surplus was $5,845 million, but in 2018 there was a deficit of $678 million.

2 Between 2016 and 2018, the output gap in Hungary changed from a negative output gap to a positive output gap. In 2016, the Hungarian economy had a negative output gap of 1.7% of GDP. In 2017, negative output gap had fallen to 0.2% of GDP and in 2018 Hungary had a positive output gap of 1.2% of GDP.

3 Between 2016 and 2018, there is an inverse relationship between unemployment and inflation in Hungary. Between 2016 and 2018, the unemployment rate fell from 5.1% of the labour force to 3.7%. Over the same period, CPI inflation increased from 0.4% to 2.8%.

4 Supply-side reforms should improve the productivity and efficiency of the Hungarian economy. This will increase its productive capacity and help to keep costs under control. An increase in productive capacity will allow GDP to grow to meet any increase in aggregate demand, making demand-pull inflation less likely. An improvement in productivity will also help to reduce the rate at which costs increase, and control cost-push inflationary pressures.

Exam-style Questions

1 B. With rising incomes, there is likely to be more tax revenue and less spending on welfare benefits.

2 D. With a minimum wage above equilibrium, the demand for labour will fall while more people will be willing to work, resulting in an excess supply of labour and hence an increase in unemployment.

3 B. The other options relate to cyclical, seasonal and frictional respectively.

4 Deflation is when the price level is falling.

5 i. $130 billion (150 + 70 – 90)
   ii. $120 billion (200 = ? + 80 – 70 + 100 – 30)

6 i. The Gini coefficient is a measure of inequality with 0 representing perfect equality and 1 perfect inequality. The percentage change in real GDP is a measure of economic growth. When an economy is growing, incomes are rising and, on average, people are better off. This does not necessarily mean that everyone is better off. As the economy grows, more people have the opportunity to earn a higher income and there may be more tax revenue available for governments to increase the incomes of those on welfare benefits. However, some people may not benefit and the distribution of income may become more unequal. For example, structural unemployment and labour immobility may cause some people to remain unemployed for a long while.

   ii. The following are some points that might be made.
   - Inequality of income, as measured by the Gini coefficient fell throughout the period, from 0.403 to 0.365, and economic growth was positive throughout the period. Economic growth in this economy is consistent with a fall in inequality.
   - However, economic growth, as measured by the annual percentage change in real GDP, fluctuated and the highest rates of economic growth were not always linked to the biggest reduction in inequality. For example, in 2012, economic growth was 7.2% whereas the fall in the Gini coefficient between 2010 and 2012 was only 0.001.

- When the rate of economic growth was lowest in 2014 at 1.0%, the fall in inequality was highest, the Gini coefficient fell from 0.393 to 0.370. However, the economy had grown by 7.2% in 2012 and the rate of growth in 2013 is not known.
- While positive economic growth is consistent with a fall in inequality, the data do not fully support the view that the highest rates of economic growth lead to the largest reductions in inequality in this economy.
- There may have been other factors affecting the inequality of income such as government policy.
- Data is only provided for every other year. Could there be a time lag or might the intervening years show even more fluctuation in economic growth perhaps?

7 It is best to start by defining negative output gap. A diagram like Figure 8.1.7 should be drawn to show this output gap. Government spending is a component of aggregate demand and if government spending rises, aggregate demand will also increase, which should be shown as a rightwards shift in the AD curve on the diagram. Higher aggregate demand will increase the demand for labour and raise incomes, leading to multiplier effects, increasing aggregate demand by more than the initial rise in government spending. A third AD curve could be drawn to show the impact of these multiplier effects, further reducing the negative output gap. Either way, the equilibrium national income is now closer to the normal capacity level of output, reducing the negative output gap. Refer fully to the diagram in the course of the answer.

8 Indicative content is shown below, plus try to include references to data to support points when appropriate:
- oil as a key primary product, including its use as a fuel and raw material
- examples of oil-consuming and oil-producing countries
- higher oil prices as an example of a supply-side shock
- example of OPEC raising prices in 1973 by restricting the supply of oil
- impact on inflation through effects on costs of firms
- cost-push inflationary process
- impact of higher inflation on competitiveness plus what this depends on, such as changes in the exchange rate
- effect on real GDP and potential for recession, as in the case study for the UK between 1973 to 1975
- effects on unemployment, plus evidence from the UK from 1975 to 1977
- potential effects on tax revenue, government spending and the budget balance
- impact on balance of payments of the increase in the price of imported oil
- significance of price elasticity of demand for oil
- AD/AS analysis
- relevance of extent and duration of the increase in oil prices plus what else is happening in that country and the world generally
- depends on the current state of the oil-consuming country's economy and its other characteristics
- depends on any action taken by government
- why some oil-consuming countries will be more affected than others
- an overall assessment of the likely effects and whether, on balance, they are likely to be good or bad.

9.1 – Progress Questions, Case Studies

Progress Questions

1 The main objective of monetary policy is to maintain the value of the currency through price stability. In practice, this usually means keeping inflation low.

2 If there is deflation, monetary policy should be used to increase aggregate demand and try to stop prices falling. This means the central bank should use an expansionary monetary policy. It should reduce interest rates, encourage an increase in the supply of money and credit and allow the exchange rate to depreciate.

3 If the central bank wishes to reduce the growth in the supply of credit, it should increase its discount rate. This should lead to an increase in other interest rates. An increase in interest rates makes borrowing more expensive and should reduce the demand for loans and the supply of credit.

4 Reasons why a fall in interest rates will increase aggregate demand include: it is less rewarding to save; it is cheaper to borrow; mortgage

repayments fall; it is more profitable for firms to borrow and invest; it tends to reduce the exchange rate; asset prices will rise, causing a positive wealth effect.

5 A cut in interest rates will increase aggregate demand and add to demand-pull inflationary pressures.

6 An increase in interest rates will reduce aggregate demand. Firms will cut production to avoid an unplanned increase in inventory. If aggregate demand and output remain low, firms are likely to reduce the number of workers they employ. The initial fall in aggregate demand may also result in a negative multiplier effect, leading to a further reduction in economic activity.

7 The original price of the car in China would be ¥166,667 (25,000 ÷ 0.15) and the new price would be ¥125,000 (25,000 ÷ 0.20). The rise in the exchange rate has reduced the domestic currency price of imports.

8 An appreciation in the exchange rate makes exports less competitive abroad and imports more competitive in the domestic market. As a result, net exports and aggregate demand will fall. The fall in aggregate demand will lead to a fall in output and employment.

9 Aggregate demand will increase, adding to demand-pull inflationary pressures. The price of imports will rise adding to cost-push inflationary pressures.

Case Studies

The Bank of Zambia increases the Statutory Reserve Ratio
1 An increase in the SRR means that banks are likely to reduce lending and interest rates on loans are likely to increase. As a result, aggregate demand will fall and this will reduce demand-pull inflationary pressures.

2 If banks are forced to restrict lending, existing firms may have to reduce investment. People who want to set up a new business may not be able to borrow the money they need to get the business started. Restrictions on lending and higher interest rates will also affect consumer spending. This will make it more difficult for firms to sell their goods and services and profits are likely to fall.

Monetary policy in Canada
1 Changes in the official interest rate will have a knock-on effect on other interest rates in the economy. For example, an increase in the official interest rate is likely to increase the interest rates on saving, mortgages and other loans. A higher interest rate on savings will encourage more people to save, since they will receive a greater return on their money. A higher rate on mortgages and other loans will make them less attractive since borrowers will have to repay more money each month because the interest on their loans has increased.

2 Factors include the following.
- Predictions for future inflation rates – if inflation is expected to increase, it may be better to raise interest rates now, due to time lags.
- If unemployment is low, it suggests that there is little spare capacity and wages might be expected to rise. An increase in interest rates will help to reduce inflationary pressures.
- If consumer spending is increasing quickly, an increase in interest rates may be needed to reduce demand-pull inflationary pressures.
- If wages are increasing quickly, a rise in interest rates may be needed to reduce demand-pull and cost-push inflationary pressures.
- If the exchange rate is falling, an increase in interest rates may be needed to support the currency and prevent import prices rising.
- If the amount of money and credit is growing fast, an increase in interest rates may be needed to reduce borrowing and the growth in aggregate demand.

3 A flexible or floating exchange rate involves the price of the currency being determined by its supply and demand rather than by government or central bank intervention. Economic activity is concerned with the production, distribution and consumption of goods and services. Canada is an open economy that exports and imports a high proportion of its output. A fall in exports will reduce aggregate demand and economic activity. It may also lead to inflation falling below the target of 2%. A fall in exports will reduce the demand for the Canadian dollar and the exchange rate will fall. This will increase aggregate demand and help to stimulate economic activity. It will also help to prevent inflation falling below the target. A rise in exports will increase aggregate demand and economic activity but may also lead to inflation rising above the 2% target. A rise in exports will increase the demand for the Canadian dollar and the exchange rate will appreciate. This will reduce aggregate demand and help to prevent inflation rising above the target. A flexible exchange rate helps to offset changes in aggregate demand that result from changes in the demand for exports and imports.

9.2 – Progress Questions, Case Studies

Progress Questions

1 A large increase in taxes on tobacco is likely to reduce the demand for tobacco products. Therefore the amount of resources allocated to producing tobacco products will fall. This affects the pattern of production or economic activity and is a microeconomic effect. Higher taxes on tobacco will also increase government tax revenue, particularly since the demand for tobacco products tends to be inelastic. An increase in tax revenue is a withdrawal from the circular flow of income and will reduce aggregate demand, which is a macroeconomic effect.

2 A budget surplus is when T > G. This is a net withdrawal from the circular flow of income and will reduce aggregate demand, leading to a fall in employment and national income.

3 When an economy is in a depression and suffering from deflation, people lack confidence and are likely to save rather than spend any increase in income. Although cutting taxes may lead to some increase in spending, it may not have much effect. An increase in government spending, for example on infrastructure, will increase aggregate demand and have a positive multiplier effect. This will help to increase economic activity and may help to restore confidence as output and employment increase.

4 If the government spends more on education, it is likely to build more schools and colleges. This will increase economic activity in the construction industry. The government is also likely to employ more teachers. The increase in demand for teachers may mean that teachers' wages have to be increased and people may move from other jobs into the education sector. Schools may spend more money on textbooks and other products used in the education sector, leading to more resources being devoted to producing such products. The increase in demand for education services is likely to lead to more resources being devoted to this sector of the economy and fewer resources to other parts of the economy. The pattern of economic activity will change.

5 The main reason for levying taxes is to pay for government spending.

6 A sales tax is an indirect tax. It is an indirect tax because the business that has to pay the tax to the government can pass on at least some of the tax by increasing the price it charges to its customers.

7 A proportional tax takes the same percentage of everyone's income and therefore it leaves the distribution of income unchanged.

8 Taxable pay = $20,000 – $8,000 = $12,000. Income tax payable is 15% of $12,000 = $1,800.

9 A budget deficit is when G > T and is the amount the government has to borrow in a financial year. The budget deficit is the accumulated total of past government borrowing, it is the total amount the government owes at a point in time.

10 At the end of the year the national debt will equal $(254 – 17) billion = $237 billion.

11 A recovery in the economy will lead to an improvement in the government's budget balance, for example, the budget deficit will fall. This is because, in a recovery, tax revenues will increase and spending on welfare will fall.

Case Studies

Income tax in South Africa
1 The person would not have to pay any income tax because the first R79,000 of any income earned is tax free.

2 Taxable income = R300,000 – R79,000 = R221,000. The first R195,850 of taxable income is taxed at 18% = R35,253. The other R221,000 – 195,850 = R25,150 of taxable income is taxed at 26% = R6,539. Therefore the total income tax payable is R35,253 + R6,539 = R41,792.

3 The amount the person has left to spend after paying income tax is R300,000 – R41,792 = R258,208.

4 (R41,792 ÷ R300,000) × 100 = 13.93%

Changes to taxation in Singapore
1 i. Direct taxes are taxes on income and wealth and indirect taxes are taxes on spending; ii. Progressive taxes are those where, as income rises, so does the percentage paid in tax and regressive taxes are those where, as income rises, the percentage paid in tax falls.

2 Effects include the following.
- Indirect taxes may be regressive, disadvantaging those on lower incomes but it depends on rates, the range of goods upon which they are levied and any offsetting measures.
- Higher indirect taxes are likely to raise prices, which may cause workers to seek higher incomes and some people to buy less.

- Impact of higher indirect taxes on international competitiveness depends on whether the indirect taxes are also placed on imports (which they are in Singapore) and exports (which they are not).
- Lower corporate taxes may encourage investment, since higher profits after tax provide both an incentive and a source of funds but depends on the extent of the cut in corporate tax rates and also corporate tax rates in other countries.
- Lower income taxes may increase incentives to work, reduce voluntary unemployment and increase the size of the labour force.

A Greek tragedy

1   The recession meant that aggregate demand fell and unemployment increased. This led to a fall in revenue from indirect taxes and from direct taxes on household incomes and company profits. Government spending on welfare, such as unemployment benefit, increased. The fall in taxation and rise in government spending increased the cyclical part of the budget deficit.

2   The recession led to an increase in the already large budget deficit. It was 15.7% of GDP in 2009. The large budget deficit led to a large increase in the national debt. Also, in a recession GDP falls. The large increase in the national debt and fall in GDP resulted in the national debt as a percentage of GDP increasing rapidly.

3   In the short run, the cut in government spending and increase in taxation would have reduced aggregate demand. The reduction in aggregate demand would have made the recession worse and led to a further increase in unemployment. However, in the long run, if the Greek government had continued to run a large budget deficit, the problems for the Greek economy would probably have been even more serious.

9.3 – Progress Questions, Case Study, Exam-style Questions

Progress Questions

1   Supply-side improvements shift the LRAS to the right. They result in an increase in productive capacity, may reduce unemployment and increase the underlying rate of economic growth. Supply-side policies are measures taken by the government that should lead to supply-side improvements in the economy.

2   Investment in human capital is spending on education and training to improve the knowledge, skills and abilities of people.

3   Investment in human capital should increase labour productivity, which will increase the productive capacity and underlying rate of economic growth. It should also improve the occupational mobility of labour and reduce structural unemployment. A highly trained and skilled labour force is likely to be more flexible, adaptable and innovative.

4   A cut in income tax rates may encourage more people to work, increasing the number of people in the labour force. People may be willing to work more hours.

5   A cut in tax on company profits may encourage more people to set up a business. Investment may increase as it is more profitable and the firm has more money available to finance the investment; and/or it might encourage more inward investment from abroad.

6   If the tax cuts lead to an increase in economic activity, more people will be working and spending and firms will make more profits. This could lead to more revenue from direct and indirect taxes, despite the lower tax rates.

7   There are lots of ways. Here are four examples.
- More spending on education and training may increase labour productivity.
- More investment in infrastructure may lead to a more efficient transport system.
- Subsidies for spending on research and development may lead to technological change that improves efficiency and creates better products.
- Spending on housing may improve the geographical mobility of labour, reducing structural unemployment.

8   Fewer regulations will reduce business costs and may allow firms to enter new markets. It might also allow competition to develop, leading to further improvements in efficiency.

Case Study

Norway – a success story
1   Examples include:
- education, particularly the focus on STEM subjects, which may benefit the economy and lead to more innovation

- grants and tax incentives for research and development to encourage new developments in technology
- cuts in corporate tax, to provide more incentive for existing firms to invest and to encourage new investment from abroad
- subsidised childcare and the "40% policy" to encourage women to stay in the labour force and aim for more influential jobs.

2   Norway is rich in natural resources, particularly compared to the size of its population. North Sea oil and gas have provided large sums of tax revenue as well as jobs and incomes. This will have encouraged inward investment and had multiplier effects. The Oil Fund and income from it can help to finance supply-side improvements. Norway has been active in diversifying the economy, for example 98% of its energy now comes from renewable sources (making the most of its natural resources, such as hydroelectric power). Not being part of the EU may have given the government more flexibility, although as a member of the European Economic Area, it has free trade with other EU countries.

Exam-style Questions

1   D. This will increase the availability of funds for lending and may also help to reduce interest rates. It will lead to an increase in aggregate demand.

2   B. The higher the income, the higher the percentage paid in tax.

3   B. This will act as an incentive for firms to invest and will also leave more funds available for investment.

4   The accumulated total of past government borrowing. It is the total amount of money that the government owes at a point in time.

5   $(2,000,000 \div 110) = \$18,182$

6   Supply-side policies could be defined and supported by examples. Similarly, the potential output of an economy and its illustration by a vertical LRAS curve could be explained. Factors that determine the position of the LRAS can be analysed in general terms. Analysing how one or more specific examples of supply-side policies, such as changes to tax and welfare payments increasing incentives to work and/or government spending on training increasing productivity, can increase the potential output of an economy would also help. The analysis can be supported by a diagram showing a shift of the LRAS curve to the right (as in Figure 7.2.7 in the chapter) or the PPB shifting to the right (as in Figure 8.1.2).

7   Indicative content is given below, plus try to include diagrams and relevant references to data to support points:
- changes in interest rates as an instrument of monetary policy
- definition of inflation and what is meant by "low and stable", perhaps with reference to Canadian target
- causes of inflation
- why the target may be low, rather than zero, due to risk of deflation
- the importance of stable inflation for predictability and expectations
- how changes in the official interest rate affect other interest rates on both saving and borrowing plus analysis of the effects of this
- evaluation of what the effects of changes in interest rates depend on
- monetary policy as a demand-side policy and how interest rates affect aggregate demand
- how interest rates affect demand-pull inflation
- how interest rates may affect cost-push inflation
- potential short-term conflicts with other policy objectives
- low and stable inflation as a necessary but not sufficient condition for a strong economy
- the need for supporting policies such as other instruments of monetary policy ("a flexible exchange rate") and supply-side policies
- AD/AS analysis
- ability to deal with internal and external shocks
- time lags and the need to be forward looking
- the significance of frequency, extent and timing of interest rate changes
- an overall assessment of the effectiveness of changes in interest rates in keeping inflation low and stable.

Index

Page numbers in **bold** indicate key terms boxes.